A Handbook
on the European
Economic Community

PRAEGER SPECIAL STUDIES IN
INTERNATIONAL ECONOMICS

A Handbook on the European Economic Community

Edited by

GORDON L. WEIL

Director of Research and Studies
The European Community Information Service

Published in Cooperation with

THE EUROPEAN COMMUNITY INFORMATION SERVICE
Washington, D.C.
by

FREDERICK A. PRAEGER, Publishers
New York • Washington • London

FREDERICK A. PRAEGER, *Publishers*
111 Fourth Avenue, New York 3, N.Y., U.S.A.
77-79 Charlotte Street, London W.1, England

Published in the United States of America in 1965
by Frederick A. Praeger, Inc., Publishers

© 1965 by Frederick A. Praeger, Inc.

Library of Congress Catalog Card Number: 64-25594

Printed in the United States of America

THE PURPOSE of the Praeger Special Studies is to make specialized research monographs in international economics and politics available to the academic, business, and government communities. For further information, write to the Special Projects Division, Frederick A. Praeger, Publishers, 111 Fourth Avenue, New York, N.Y. 10003.

FOREWORD

The European Economic Community is coming of age, bringing with it the unity of Europe. Six nations, Belgium, France, the Federal Republic of Germany, Italy, Luxembourg, and the Netherlands, are engaged in the complex and difficult task of shaping the new Europe. They have carried out internal tariff disarmament in advance of the timetable laid down by the Rome Treaty and are ahead of schedule in establishing a single external tariff toward non-member countries.

The EEC is to be not only a customs union but a full economic union. Full economic unification requires common policies for agriculture, social affairs, transport and energy, a common trade policy, common rules ensuring fair competition, freedom of movement for workers, goods, and services, and the harmonization of fiscal, monetary and financial policies. Now in the second of three-stages of its transition period, the Community is beginning to develop and apply these policies and practices. By January 1, 1970, the end of the transition period, these common policies and rules will be fully in force. Between now and then, it will be important that the difficulties and complexities standing in the way of economic union not be under-estimated. Vested interests, narrow national reactions, and outmoded economic safeguards are a heritage of the past that are obstacles to be surmounted along the way.

Politically and economically, the EEC is a vital factor on the world scene. The Community has close association with 17 African countries and Madagascar which aids in their economic development. Association agreements provide for a customs and economic union with Greece, and economic aid and trade facilities for Turkey. The Community's first bilateral commercial agreements with Iran and Israel set the pattern for future relations with many other countries. Through tariff concessions, the EEC endeavors to help the export trade of developing countries. Finally, in the framework of the General Agreement on Tariffs and Trade (GATT), the EEC has become a major participant in multilateral negotiations for trade liberalization. In the "Kennedy Round" of GATT, the Community, as the world's biggest trading unit, has a leading role in proposing methods for reducing barriers to trade handling the difficult

vii

agricultural trade problem, and aiding the exports of developing countries.

Since its beginning in 1958, the EEC's activities have increased in scope and scale. Its institutions have faced a great variety of problems and challenges, both internal and external, which were unforeseen in 1957 when the Rome Treaty was signed. They have shouldered new responsibilities of global consequence.

The experience gained in creating a customs union and an economic union has been followed by specialists and the general public, both inside and outside the Community. EEC documents are basic for those working in the Community and those outside who follow its development closely. This handbook complements the Community's publication program, by making available a variety of detailed information on EEC activities in readily-usable form.

The economic union being created by the EEC is a step towards, and an essential part of, a politically united Europe. Robert Schuman said in 1950 that these developments should be regarded as "the first concrete foundations of the European Federation which is indispensable to the preservation of peace...." The documents in this handbook chronicle the movement toward that objective.

Professor Walter Hallstein
President of Commission of the
European Economic Community

CONTENTS

INTRODUCTION

The Handbook on the European Economic Community is designed to meet the need for a concise compilation of the basic EEC documents.

The selection of documents was based upon the experience of the Washington Office of the European Community Information Service in providing information to lawyers, businessmen, government officials, teachers, students, farm and labor groups, and many others. Excerpts of documents have been included rather than full texts in order to broaden the scope of the Handbook. Documents have been included relating to every major aspect of the EEC. Brief introductory notes for each chapter include comments on matters not covered in the documents.

For many, the Handbook will be the starting point for more extensive research on the Community. All references have been left as cited in the original documents to facilitate the use of the Handbook in conjunction with the original unexcerpted documents. An extensive bibliography of EEC documents and publications is included, arranged by subject. All items listed in the bibliography are available from the European Community and may be ordered through the European Community Information Service, 808 Farragut Building, Washington, D.C. 20006. The Community offices in Washington and New York (2207 Commerce Building, 155 East 44th Street) are prepared to provide more detailed information on any of the subjects dealt with in the Handbook.

The European Community would welcome comments on the selection of documents, the method of excerpting and other comments which would improve later editions of the Handbook.

Two observations should be made on the limits of the Handbook. It deals exclusively with the activities and policies of the European Economic Community. Thus, it does not cover, except incidentally, the evolution of Community programs as they were debated in the institutions of the EEC. Nor does this volume cover the activities of the European Coal and Steel Community and the European Atomic Energy Community. Because of space limitations, it was decided to concentrate on the Common

Market.   The second limitation is that the <u>Handbook</u> covers events and decisions in the history of the EEC through the spring of 1964, i.e. through the seventh general report of the Community.

The editor would like to acknowledge the encouragement and assistance given him by Leonard B. Tennyson, Director of the Washington office of the European Community Information Service, Mrs. Alma Dauman of that office and Mrs. Glenda Rosenthal and Miss Cheryl Stern of the New York office who prepared the typescript.

G. L. W.

CHAPTER 1

BACKGROUND OF THE EUROPEAN ECONOMIC COMMUNITY

The European Economic Community, created in 1958, provides the broad foundation for a united Europe. The development began centuries ago; the first practical steps were taken in the years following the Second World War.

In 1946, Winston Churchill called upon European states to create "a kind of United States of Europe." This initiative was followed in 1947 by the Marshall Plan which asked the European nations to draw up a joint program for the reconstruction of the devastated continent. That same year, the Benelux customs union between the Netherlands and the Belgium-Luxembourg Economic Union, the first concrete step toward economic unity, entered into force.

The Organization for European Economic Cooperation (OEEC) was established in 1948 as a result of the Marshall Plan. It had two objectives: reconstruction of Europe with American aid and liberalization of trade among the European countries.

During the same year, the Congress of Europe at The Hague took steps toward the creation of the Council of Europe. The Council became a forum for discussing means for creating a politically unified Europe, but was unable to take any concrete steps in this direction.

Convinced that co-operation and discussion, though necessary, were not sufficient, French Foreign Minister Robert Schuman proposed, in 1950, the European Coal and Steel Community, designed to merge the coal, iron, and steel industries of those European countries willing to accept control by a supranational High Authority. Under the concept of supranationality, states would accept and execute decisions made by a group of officials completely independent of national control.

1

The ECSC began functioning in 1952.

Shortly after the Paris Treaty establishing the ECSC was signed, a draft treaty for a European Defense Community was prepared. The EDC was designed to solve the problem of a German contribution to European defense, but it was rejected by the French parliament.

The European unity movement took a new direction after the defeat of the EDC. The "relance europeenne" in the economic sphere was the natural outcome of the success, in a limited sector, of ECSC activities. The Six members of the ECSC -- Belgium, France, the Federal Republic of Germany, Italy, Luxembourg and the Netherlands -- agreed at Messina, Italy in 1955 to create a full economic union and to unite their effort in the field of the peaceful uses of atomic energy. A committee headed by Belgian Foreign Minister Paul-Henri Spaak drew up a preliminary report on the Common Market and Euratom.

Negotiations were carried on in the last half of 1956 on the treaties for the new communities: the European Economic Community and the European Atomic Energy Community. On March 25, 1957 the treaties were signed in Rome and ratified by the national parliaments by the end of that year. The votes in the parliaments on the EEC treaty were:

		for	against	abstentions
Belgium	Chamber of Representatives	174	4	2
	Senate	134	2	2
France	National Assembly	341	235	-
	Council of the Republic	231	69	-
F.R. Germany	Bundestag	Voted by a large majority on show of hands		
	Bundesrat	Voted by a large majority on show of hands		
Italy	Chamber of Deputies	311	144	54
	Senate	Voted by a large majority on show of hands		
Luxembourg	Chamber of Deputies	46	3	-
Netherlands	Lower House	144	12	-
	Upper House	46	5	-

The EEC Treaty entered into effect on January 1, 1958, and the institutions of the Community were immediately set up in Brussels. The Treaty provided for a transition period of 12 to 15 years before the Economic Community would be fully developed. On January 14, 1962, the Council of Ministers voted unanimously that the EEC should advance from the first stage of the transition period to the second. The EEC is to move into the third and final stage on January 1, 1966. The transitional period will end on December 31, 1969, twelve years after the EEC Treaty went into effect. Many of the objectives, which according to the Treaty, must be accomplished by 1970 will actually be achieved three to six years earlier. In its Action Program for the second stage of the transitional period The EEC Commission has indicated the ways in which this acceleration will take place.

The fusion of the EEC Commission with the Commission of the European Atomic Energy Community and the High Authority of the European Coal and Steel Community will be a milestone in the history of the EEC. This fusion, planned for 1965, would require changes in the Rome Treaty and would be the first step toward the total fusion of the three Communities.

1.1 THE MARSHALL PLAN

Speech by Secretary of State George C. Marshall at Harvard
University on June 5, 1947. (excerpts)

In considering the requirements for the rehabilitation of
Europe, the physical loss of life, the visible destruction of
cities, factories, mines and railroads was correctly estimated,
but it has become obvious during recent months that this visible
destruction was probably less serious than the dislocation of the
entire fabric of European economy. For the past ten years conditions have been highly abnormal.

The feverish preparation for war and the more feverish
maintenance of the war effort engulfed all aspects of national
economies. Machinery has fallen into disrepair or is entirely
obsolete. Under the arbitrary and destructive Nazi rule,
virtually every possible enterprise was geared into the German
war machine. Long-standing commercial ties, private institutions, banks, insurance companies and shipping companies disappeared, through loss of capital, absorption through nationalization or by simple destruction.

In many countries, confidence in the local currency has
been severely shaken. The breakdown of the business structure
of Europe during the war was complete. Recovery has been
seriously retarded by the fact that two years after the close of
hostilities a peace settlement with Germany and Austria has not
been agreed upon. But even given a more prompt solution of
these difficult problems, the rehabilitation of the economic
structure of Europe quite evidently will require a much longer
time and greater effort than had been foreseen.

There is a phase of this matter which is both interesting
and serious. The farmer has always produced the foodstuffs to
exchange with the city dweller for the other necessities of life.
This division of labor is the basis of modern civilization. At
the present time it is threatened with breakdown. The town and
city industries are not producing adequate goods to exchange with
the food-producing farmer. Raw materials and fuel are in short
supply. Machinery is lacking or worn out.

The farmer or the peasant cannot find the goods for sale
which he desires to purchase. So the sale of his farm produce
for money which he cannot use, seems to him an unprofitable
transaction. He, therefore, has withdrawn many fields from

4

crop cultivation and is using them for grazing. He feeds more grain to stock and finds for himself and his family an ample supply of food, however short he may be on clothing and the other ordinary gadgets of civilization. Meanwhile, people in the cities are short of food and fuel. So the governments are forced to use their foreign money and credits to procure these necessities abroad. This process exhausts funds which are urgently needed for reconstruction. Thus a very serious situation is rapidly developing which bodes no good for the world. The modern system of the division of labor upon which the exchange of products is based is in danger of breaking down.

The truth of the matter is that Europe's requirements for the next three or four years of foreign food and other essential products--principally from America--are so much greater than her present ability to pay that she must have substantial additional help, or face economic, social and political deterioration of a very grave character.

The remedy lies in breaking the vicious circle and resorting the confidence of the European people in the economic future of their own countries and of Europe as a whole. The manufacturer and the farmer throughout wide areas must be able and willing to exchange their products for currencies, the continuing value of which is not open to question.

Aside from the demoralizing effect on the world at large and the possibilities of disturbances arising as a result of the desperation of the people concerned, the consequences to the economy of the United States should be apparent to all. It is logical that the United States should be doing whatever it is able to do to assist in the return of normal economic health in the world, without which there can be no political stability and no assured peace.

Our policy is directed not against any country or doctrine but against hunger, poverty, desperation and chaos. Its purpose should be the revival of a working economy in the world so as to permit the emergence of political and social conditions in which free institutions can exist. Such assistance, I am convinced, must not be on a piecemeal basis as various crises develop. Any assistance that this Government may render in the future should provide a cure rather than a mere palliative.

Any government that is willing to assist in the task of recovery will find full cooperation, I am sure, on the part of the

United States Government. Any government which maneuvers to block the recovery of other countries cannot expect help from us. Furthermore, governments, political parties or groups which seek to perpetuate human misery in order to profit therefrom politically or otherwise will encounter the opposition of the United States.

It is already evident that, before the United States Government can proceed much further in its efforts to alleviate the situation and help start the European world on its way to recovery, there must be some agreement among the countries of Europe as to the requirements of the situation and the part those countries themselves will take in order to give proper effect to whatever action might be undertaken by this Government. It would be neither fitting nor efficacious for this Government to undertake to draw up unilaterally a program designed to place Europe on its feet economically. This is the business of the Europeans. The initiative, I think, must come from Europe. The role of this country should consist of friendly aid in the drafting of a European program and of later support of such a program so far as it may be practical for us to do so. The program should be a joint one, agreed to by a number, if not all European nations.

An essential part of any successful action on the part of the United States is an understanding on the part of the people of America of the character of the problem and the remedies to be applied. Political passion and prejudice should have no part. With foresight, and a willingness on the part of our people to face up to the vast responsibility which history has clearly placed upon our country, the difficulties I have outlined can and will be overcome.

1.2 CONVENTION FOR EUROPEAN ECONOMIC COOPERATION

Signed at Paris on April 16, 1948. (excerpts)

The Governments of Austria, Belgium, Denmark, France, Greece, Ireland, Iceland, Italy, Luxembourg, Norway, the Netherlands, Portugal, the United Kingdom, Sweden, Switzerland and Turkey, and the Commanders-in-Chief of the French, United Kingdom and United States Zones of Occupation of Germany:

CONSIDERING that a strong and prosperous European economy is essential for the attainment of the purposes of the United

Nations, the preservation of individual liberty and the increase of general well-being, and that it will contribute to the maintenance of peace;

RECOGNIZING that their economic systems are interrelated and that the prosperity of each of them depends on the prosperity of all;

BELIEVING that only by close and lasting co-operation between the Contracting Parties can the prosperity of Europe be restored and maintained, and the ravages of war made good;

RESOLVED to implement the principles and to achieve the aims set forth in the General Report of the Committee of European Economic Co-operation, particularly the speedy establishment of sound economic conditions enabling the Contracting Parties as soon as possible to achieve and maintain a satisfactory level of economic activity without extraordinary outside assistance, and to make their full contribution to world economic stability;

DETERMINED to combine their economic strength to these ends, to join together to make the fullest collective use of their individual capacities and potentialities, to increase their production, develop and modernise their industrial and agricultural equipment, expand their commerce, reduce progressively barriers to trade among themselves, promote full employment and restore or maintain the stability of their economies and general confidence in their national currencies;

TAKING NOTE of the generous resolve of the American people expressed in the action taken to furnish the assistance without which the aims set forth above cannot be fully achieved;

RESOLVED to create the conditions and establish the institutions nessary for the success of European economic co-operation and for the effective use of American aid, and to conclude a Convention to this end;

HAVE ACCORDINGLY APPOINTED the undersigned Plenipotentiaries who, having presented their full powers, found in good and due form, have agreed on the following provisions:

Article 1

The Contracting Parties agree to work in close co-operation in their economic relations with one another.

As their immediate task, they will undertake the elaboration and execution of a joint recovery programme. The object of this programme will be to achieve as soon as possible and maintain a satisfactory level of economic activity without extraordinary outside assistance, and to this end the programme will take special account of the need of the Contracting Parties to develop their exports to non-participating countries to the maximum extent possible.

Accordingly the Contracting Parties pledge themselves to carry out, by their efforts of self help and in a spirit of mutual aid, the following General Obligations, and hereby set up an Organization for European Economic Co-operation, hereinafter referred to as the Organization.

PART I

General Obligations

Article 2

The Contracting Parties will, both individually and collectively, promote with vigour the development of production, through efficient use of the resources at their command, whether in their metropolitan or overseas territories and by the progressive modernization of equipment and techniques, in such manner as may best assist the accomplishment of the joint recovery programme.

Article 3

The Contracting Parties will, within the framework of the Organization and as often and to such extent as may be necessary, draw up general programmes for the production and exchange of commodities and services. In so doing they will take into consideration their several estimates or programmes and general world economic conditions.

Each Contracting Party will use its best endeavours to secure the fulfilment of such general programmes.

Article 4

The Contracting Parties will develop, in mutual co-operation, the maximum possible interchange of goods and services. To this end they will continue the efforts already initiated to achieve as soon as possible a multilateral system of payments among themselves, and will co-operate in relaxing restrictions on trade and payments between one another, with the object of abolishing as soon as possible those restrictions which at present hamper such trade and payments.

Article 5

The Contracting Parties agree to strengthen their economic links by all methods which they may determine will further the objectives of the present Convention. They will continue the study of Customs Unions or analogous arrangements such as free trade areas, the formation of which might constitute one of the methods of achieving these objectives. Those Contracting Parties which have already agreed in principle to the creation of Customs Unions will further the establishment of such Unions as rapidly as conditions permit.

Article 6

The Contracting Parties will co-operate with one another and with other like-minded countries in reducing tariff and other barriers to the expansion of trade, with a view to achieving a sound and balanced multilateral trading system such as will accord with the principles of the Havana Charter.

Article 7

Each Contracting Party will, having due regard to the need for a high and stable level of trade and employment and for avoiding or countering the dangers of inflation, take such steps as lie within its power to achieve or maintain the stability of its currency and of its internal financial position, sound rates of exchange and, generally, confidence in its monetary system.

Article 8

The Contracting Parties will make the fullest and most effective use of their available manpower.

They will endeavour to provide full employment for their

own people and they may have recourse to manpower available in the territory of any other Contracting Party. In the latter case they will, in mutual agreement, take the necessary measures to facilitate the movement of workers and to ensure their establishment in conditions satisfactory from the economic and social point of view.

Generally, the Contracting Parties will co-operate in the progressive reduction of obstacles to the free movement of persons.

1.3 BENELUX CUSTOMS CONVENTION

Signed at London on September 5, 1944. (excerpts)

The Government of Her Majesty the Queen of the Netherlands on the one hand;

The Governments of His Majesty the King of the Belgians and of Her Royal Highness the Grand Duchess of Luxembourg on the other hand,

Desiring at the moment of liberation of the Territories of the Netherlands and the Economic Union of Belgium and Luxembourg, to create the most favourable conditions for the ultimate formation of an Economic Union and for the restoration of economic activity, have decided to further these ends by establishing a system of common duties and to this end have agreed to the following articles:

Article 1

The Netherlands and the Economic Union of Belgium and Luxembourg shall impose identical customs duties on the importation of goods, according to the appended tariff which forms an integral part of this agreement.

Apart from the duties provided for in this tariff, they shall be entitled to levy excise duties--including import duties equivalent to excise--as well as any other dues, according to the system in force in their respective Territories; they shall reserve their right to modify the rates.

Article 2

No customs duty shall be levied on goods entering the Netherlands from the Economic Union of Belgium and Luxembourg and reciprocally on goods entering the Economic Union of Belgium and Luxembourg from the Netherlands.

The Netherlands and the Economic Union of Belgium and Luxembourg shall be entitled to levy entry duties--including import duties equivalent to excise--as well as any other taxes, according to the system in force in their respective territories; they reserve the right to modify the rates.

1.4 THE SCHUMAN PLAN

Declaration by the French Minister of Foreign Affairs at Paris on May 9, 1950. (excerpts)

World peace cannot be safeguarded without constructive efforts equal to the dangers which threaten it.

The contribution which an organized and living Europe can bring to civilization is indispensable to the maintenance of peaceful relations. In taking upon herself for more than twenty years the role of champion of a united Europe, France has always had as her essential aim the service of peace. A united Europe was not achieved, and we had war.

Europe will not be made all at once, or according to a single, general plan. It will be built through concrete achievements, which first create a de facto solidarity. The gathering of the nations of Europe requires the elimination of the age-old conflict between France and Germany.

The first concern in any action undertaken must be these two countries.

With this aim in view, the French Government proposes to take action immediately on one limited but decisive point. The French Government proposes to place Franco-German production of coal and steel under a common High Authority, within the framework of an organization open to the participation of the other countries of Europe.

The pooling of coal and steel production will immediately provide for the setting-up of common bases for economic development as a first step in the federation of Europe, and will change the destinies of those regions which have long been devoted to manufacturing the armaments of war of which they themselves have been the most constant victims.

The solidarity in production thus established will make it plain that war between France and Germany becomes not merely unthinkable but materially impossible. The setting-up of this powerful production unit, open to all countries willing to take part, and eventually capable of providing all the member countries with the basic elements of industrial production on the same terms, will lay the real foundations for their economic unification.

This production will be offered to the world as a whole without distinction or exception, with the aim of contributing to the raising of living standards and the promotion of peaceful achievements.

Europe, with new means at her disposal, will be able to pursue the realization of one of her essential tasks, the development of the African continent.

In this way there will be realized, simply and speedily, that fusion of interests which is indispensable to the establishment of an economic community; and will be the leaven from which may grow a wider and deeper community between countries long divided by bloody conflicts.

By pooling basic production and by setting up a new High Authority, whose decisions will be binding on France, Germany and other member countries, these proposals will build the first concrete foundations of the European Federation which is indispensable to the preservation of peace.

1.5 TREATY ESTABLISHING THE EUROPEAN COAL AND STEEL COMMUNITY

Signed At Paris on April 18, 1951. (excerpts)

THE PRESIDENT OF THE GERMAN FEDERAL REPUBLIC, HIS ROYAL HIGHNESS THE PRINCE ROYAL OF BELGIUM, THE PRESIDENT OF THE FRENCH REPUBLIC, THE PRESIDENT OF THE ITALIAN REPUBLIC, HER ROYAL HIGHNESS THE GRAND DUCHESS OF LUXEMBOURG, HER MAJESTY THE QUEEN OF THE NETHERLANDS,

CONSIDERING that world peace may be safeguarded only by creative efforts as great as the dangers menacing it;

CONVINCED that the contribution which an organized and vital European can bring to civilization is indispensable to the maintenance of peaceful relations;

CONSCIOUS of the fact that Europe can be built only by concrete actions creating a real solidarity and by the establishment of common bases for economic development;

DESIROUS of assisting through the expansion of their basic production in raising the standard of living and in furthering the works of peace;

RESOLVED to substitute for historic rivalries a fusion of their essential interests; to establish, by creating an economic community, the foundation of a broad and independent community among peoples long divided by bloody conflicts; and to lay the bases of institutions capable of giving direction to their future common destiny;

HAVE DECIDED to create a European Coal and Steel Community.

Article 1

By this Treaty the High Contracting Parties establish among themselves a EUROPEAN COAL AND STEEL COMMUNITY, based on a common market, common objectives, and common institutions.

Article 2

The mission of the European Coal and Steel Community is to contribute to the expansion of the economy, the development of employment and the improvement of the standard of living in the participating countries through the creation, in harmony with the general economy of the member States, of a common market as defined in Article 4.

The Community must progressively establish conditions which will in themselves assure the most rational distribution of production at the highest possible level of productivity, while safeguarding the continuity of employment and avoiding the creation of fundamental and persistent disturbances in the economies of the Member States.

Article 3

Within the framework of their respective powers and responsibilities and in the common interest, the institutions of

13

the Community shall:

(a)   ensure that the common market is regularly supplied, while taking into account the needs of third countries;

(b)   assure to all consumers in comparable positions within the common market equal access to the sources of production;

(c)   seek the establishment of the lowest possible prices without involving any corresponding rise either in the prices charged by the same enterprises in other transactions or in the price-level as a whole in another period, while at the same time permitting necessary amortization and providing the possibility of normal returns on invested capital;

(d)   ensure that conditions are maintained which will encourage enterprises to expand and improve their ability to produce and to promote a policy of rational development of natural resources, while avoiding undue exhaustion of such resources;

(e)   promote the improvement of the living and working conditions of the labour force in each of the industries under its jurisdiction so as to harmonize those conditions in an upward direction;

(f)   foster the development of international trade and ensure that equitable limits are observed in prices charged in foreign markets;

(g)   promote the regular expansion and the modernization of production as well as the improvement of quality, under conditions which preclude any protection against competing industries except where justified by illegitimate action on the part of such industries or in their favour.

Article 4

The following are recognized to be incompatible with the common market for coal and steel, and are, therefore, abolished and prohibited within the Community in the manner set forth in this Treaty:

14

(a)   import and export duties, or taxes with an equivalent effect, and quantitative restrictions on the movement of coal and steel;

(b)   measures or practices discriminating among producers, among buyers or among consumers, especially as concerns prices, delivery terms and transport rates, as well as measures or practices which hamper the buyer in the free choice of his supplier;

(c)   subsidies or state assistance, or special charges imposed by the state, in any form whatsoever;

(d)   restrictive practices tending towards the division or the exploitation of the market.

Article 5

The Community shall accomplish its mission, under the conditions provided for in this Treaty, with limited intervention.

To this end, the Community shall:

-    assist the interested parties to take action by collecting information, organizing consultations and defining general objectives;

-    place financial means at the disposal of enterprises for their investments and participate in the expenses of readaptation;

-    assure the establishment, the maintenance and the observance of normal conditions of competition, and take direct action with respect to production and the operation of the market only when circumstances make it absolutely necessary;

-    publish the reasons for its action and take the necessary measures to ensure observance of the rules set forth in this Treaty.

The institutions of the Community shall carry out these activities with as little administrative machinery as possible and in close co-operation with the interested parties.

Article 6

The Community shall be a legal person.

In its international relationships, the Community shall enjoy the legal capacity necessary to exercise it functions and to achieve its purposes.

In each of the member States, the Community shall enjoy the most extensive legal capacity pertaining to legal persons in that country. Specifically, it may acquire and transfer real and personal property, and may sue and be sued in its own name.

The Community shall be represented by its institutions, each one of them acting within the framework of its own powers and responsibilities.

Article 8

The High Authority shall be responsible for assuring the achievement of the purposes stated in this Treaty within the terms thereof.

Article 9

The High Authority shall be composed of nine members designated for six years and chosen for their general competence.

A member shall be eligible for reappointment. The number of members of the High Authority may be reduced by unanimous decision of the Council.

Only nationals of the member States may be members of the High Authority.

The High Authority shall not include more than two members of the same nationality.

The members of the High Authority shall exercise their functions in complete independence, in the general interest of the Community. In the fulfilment of their duties, they shall neither solicit nor accept instructions from any government or from any organization. They will abstain from all conduct incompatible with the supranational character of their functions.

Each member State undertakes to respect this supranational character and not to seek to influence the members of the High Authority in the execution of their duties.

The members of the High Authority shall not exercise any business or professional activities, paid or unpaid, nor acquire or hold, directly or indirectly, any interest in any business related to coal and steel during their term of office or for a period of three years thereafter.

Article 10

The governments of the member States shall appoint eight members of the High Authority by agreement among themselves. These eight members shall elect a ninth member, who will be deemed elected if he receives at least five votes.

Article 13

The High Authority shall act by vote of a majority of its members.

Its quorum shall be fixed by its rules of procedure. However, this quorum must be greater than one-half of its members.

Article 14

In the execution of the tasks entrusted to it by this Treaty and in accordance with the provisions thereof, the High Authority shall take decisions, formulate recommendations and issue opinions.

Decisions shall be binding in every respect.

Recommendations shall be binding with respect to the objectives which they specify but shall leave to those to whom they are directed the choice of appropriate means for attaining these objectives.

Opinions shall not be binding.

When the High Authority is empowered to take a decision, it may limit itself to formulating a recommendation.

Article 20

The Assembly, consisting of representatives of the peoples of the member States of the Community, shall exercise the supervisory powers which are granted to it by this Treaty.

Article 26

The Council shall exercise its functions in the cases and in the manner laid down by this Treaty, in particular with a view to harmonizing the action of the High Authority and that of the governments which are responsible for the general economic policy of their countries.

To this end, the Council and the High Authority shall exchange information and consult together.

The Council may request the High Authority to examine any proposals and measures which it may deem necessary or appropriate for the realization of the common objectives.

Article 27

The Council shall consist of representatives of the member States. Each State shall appoint thereto one of the members of its government.

The Presidency of the Council shall be exercised for a term of three months by each member of the Council in rotation in the alphabetical order of the member States.

Article 31

The function of the Court is to ensure the rule of law in the interpretation and application of the present Treaty and of the regulations for its execution.

Article 33

The Court shall have jurisdiction over appeals by a member State or by the Council for the annulment of decisions and recommendations of the High Authority on the grounds of lack of legal competence, major violations of procedure, violation of the Treaty or of any rule of law relating to its application, or abuse of power. However, the Court may not review the High Authority's evaluation of the situation, based on economic facts and circumstances, which led to such decisions or recommendations, except where the High Authority is alleged to have abused its powers or to have clearly misinterpreted the provisions of the Treaty or of a rule of law relating to its application.

The enterprises, or the associations referred to in Article 48, shall have the right of appeal on the same grounds against individual decisions and recommendations affecting them, or against general decisions and recommendations which they deem to involve an abuse of power affecting them.

The appeals provided for in the first two paragraphs of the present article must be lodged within one month from the date of notification or publication, as the case may be, of the decision or recommendation.

Article 49

The High Authority is empowered to procure the funds necessary to the accomplishment of its mission:

-        by imposing levies on the production of coal and steel;

-        by borrowing.

It may also receive grants.

Article 97

This Treaty is concluded for a period of fifty years from the date of its entry into force.

Article 98

Any European State may request to accede to this Treaty. It shall address its request to the Council, which shall act by unanimous vote after obtaining the opinion of the High Authority. Also by an unanimous vote the Council shall fix the terms of accession , which shall become effective on the day the instrument of accession is received by the government acting as depository of the Treaty.

1.6 REPORT OF THE INTERGOVERNMENTAL COMMITTEE ON EUROPEAN INTEGRATION (SPAAK COMMITTEE)

Basic Working Document of the Brussels Convention to Draft
the European Economic Community Treaty
Convened on June 26, 1956. (excerpts)

TITLE I

THE FUSION OF MARKETS

CHAPTER 1 - THE CUSTOMS UNION

I.   Elimination of customs duties within the common market.

1. The starting point for the reduction is the average duty
levied during the years 1953, 54 and 55 or the scheduled duty if it
is lower. The first reduction will be applied across the board on
all commodities. The following reductions will be applied to the
average for groups of commodities.

2. Commodities are grouped according to the duties levied
on them by intervals of 5 points for duties up to 10% and above 50%,
and by intervals of 2 1/2 points for duties between 10% and 50%.
Any two of these groups can be linked together at the choice of
the Governments.

3. The average reduction applied to the groups thus established by uniting two intervals is calculated by weighting the
percentage of reduction on each tariff position by the value of
corresponding imports from other Community countries during the
three last years for which statistical information is available.

4. During the first stage reductions take place initially
at the end of the first year, and thereafter at 18 month intervals;
during the second stage, they again take place at 18 month intervals and at the end of the eighth year. There remains 40%
to be eliminated before the end of the transitional period.

5. Modifications in the system envisaged will require
unanimous approval of the Council of Ministers if it is a question of reducing the time periods.

In other cases and on the proposal of the European Commission a majority of 2/3 of the Council will suffice. However,
the delays can be extended only for three years so that the
transitional period will end after a maximum of 15 years.

6. After the fifteenth year certain temporary derogations

can still be proposed if they are recognized as necessary to prevent fundamental and persistent troubles in the economies of the member States. These derogations would come into play only within the limits fixed in the Treaty and with the agreement of the common institutions.

II.   Establishment of a Common External Tariff.

A.   The system for the establishment of a common external tariff will be the following:

1. The starting point for the calculation of the tariff is based either on the average of the duties levied during the years 1953-1954 and 1955 or on the scheduled duty rate if it is lower.

2. The tariff positions, classified in three categories according to a nomenclature already agreed upon, will be brought down to certain maximum levels which will differ for raw materials, semi-finished products and finished products.

3. The level of the external tariff will be established on the basis of an arithmetic average of the duties levied on each product, after the high tariffs have been brought below the maximum envisaged for each category.

4. In order to achieve the level thus defined the following schedule will be applied:

a)   On items where the present unadjusted duties are not more than 15% above or below or more than three points away from their arithmetic average this average will be applied when the first decrease of 10% is made on customs duties within the common market.

b)   On other items at the end of the first stage of four years each country, in its relations with third countries, will reduce by 30% the difference between its own duties and the level of the corresponding duties of the common tariff. A second reduction of 30% of the difference will be made at the end of the second stage of four years.

c)   The application of the common tariff itself will take place at latest at the time when customs duties are completely eliminated within the common market.

d)   Advance actions will have to be taken in harmonizing the

21

national tariffs with the common (external) tariff whenever the reduction of internal duties threatens to bring about tranship- ments, because of the difference from the external duties.

e)   If the mechanisms proposed above do not permit a satis- factory formula to be determined in certain cases, a solution will have to be sought through negotiations among the member States, and facilitated by proposals of the European Commission.

The European Commission will be able to grant a country the benefit of a safeguard clause for a limited period and for tariff positions not exceeding 5% of its imports from third countries. If this(safeguard) should not be granted, the inter- ested State would be able to have recourse either to the Council of Ministers or the Court.

B.   Negotiations with Third Countries.

It is the common tariff defined above which will be applied towards third countries, except for concessions obtained from them by negotiations.

The European Commission will make proposals and con- duct tariff negotiations with third countries under a mandate approved unanimously by the Council.

However, beginning with the ninth year a qualified majority will be sufficient to modify duties which do not differ by more than 30% or 5 points from the common basic tariff.

Negotiations for the establishment of associations between the Community and third countries will take place as soon as possible after the Treaty comes into effect on the basis of pro- posals of the European Commission approved unanimously by the Council of Ministers.

CHAPTER 2 - QUOTAS

Section 1 - Import Controls

After the first lowering of customs duties, the new mechan- ism proposed for the Community will be as follows:

1.   All bilateral quotas open to one partner on imports from others will be added together in order to establish global quotas, by commodity, open to all producers

22

of the Community.

2.   These global quotas will be increased each year
on the order of 20% above the preceding year. As
a result of being progressively increased, they
should become inoperative, not later than a year
before the time that the customs duties themselves
are to be eliminated.

3.   The starting point for an increase of the very
small or non-existing quotas will be, at the choice
of each interested State, either 1% of the national
production in question or imports corresponding to
the average of the Community for the products in
question.

4.   When the quota takes the form of a purchasing monopoly (governmental or business), the proposed
system will be replaced by proposals of the European
Commission concerning the adaptation of the existing
organizations which will have either to disappear, be
adapted to the common market or, where necessary,
be replaced by a common organization in such a way
as to eliminate progressively the discriminations
among the different suppliers of the common market.
This procedure will be applied equally to fiscal monopolies.

Section 2 - Export Controls

In relations with third countries and within the framework authorized by GATT, export controls for the duration of the transitional
period will remain under the responsibility of each of the States to
the extent that there is, in practice, a certain autonomy in the
commercial policy of the member States. At the end of the last
stage, export restrictions will be subject to the common commercial
policy of the Community vis-a-vis third countries.

CHAPTER 3 - SERVICES

The Treaty itself will specify the principles and rules of
procedure binding the member States:

a)   during the first two stages (8 years) the European Commission
will make proposals for the modification of existing national
regulations concerning services and the elaboration of a

23

common regulation. The proposals of the Commission should:

1.   in the first instance deal with services directly connected with the costs of production and facilitating the free circulation of goods;

2.   see to it that national regulations, as long as they are maintained, are applied without discrimination on the basis of residence and nationality;

3.   determine to what extent the national regulations correspond or not to the requirements of public order.

The proposals of the Commission will be submitted to a vote by the Assembly. In order to put them into effect a unanimous approval of the Council will be required up to the end of the second stage, and thereafter a qualified majority.

b)   At the end of the transitional period, the rules proposed by the European Commission should be uniform. Only certain national rules can be maintained which, on the proposal of the Commission, are adopted by a qualified majority of the Council of Ministers.

Transport Services

On proposals of the European Commission put forward during the transitional period and to be put into effect on the same conditions as those indicated for services in general, discriminations on the basis of nationality should be eliminated in such a way that at the end of the last stage, all the nationals of member States will be assured the right to furnish and accept freely transportation services over the territory of the member States as a whole.

CHAPTER 4 - AGRICULTURE

A.   Establishment of the Common Market for Agriculture.

b)   Definitive Arrangements

Products for which a common organization of the market would be justified will be chosen during the transition period. The common organization of the market for these products will be prepared by the establishment of a provisional balance sheet on resources and markets, which will include the stabilizing mechanisms

24

that will eventually be necessary.

For products which are not under a common organization the market within the Community will be free. Protection with respect to third countries will be assured by customs duties in preference to quotas which would be seasonal rather than permanent.

In the exceptional case in which a national economy is both so limited and so little diversified that it cannot get rid of fundamental and persistent troubles affecting the agricultural sector, special solutions would have to be applied in order to complement, if necessary, the stabilizing mechanisms envisaged above.

B.   The Common Market for Agriculture and Third Countries.

The common market for agriculture cannot be an entity protected against the outside world, while aligning its prices on marginal internal production. However, it will be protected against abnormal competition from third countries that employ dumping prices. This is why certain arrangements should be applied to permit producers of the Community who up to now used low-priced raw materials to continue to export at competitive prices to third countries.

C.   Institutional Organization.

The European Commission within a period of two years should make proposals for a common policy and organization of the agricultural market. Furthermore, it should be the body to make the examination which is envisaged of existing national regulations.

The proposals of the Commission will be submitted to a vote in the Assembly and should during the first stage, be adopted by a unanimous vote of the Council of Ministers. From the second stage onward a qualified majority of the Council of Ministers will suffice.

TITLE II

RULES AND COMMON ACTIONS

CHAPTER 1 - RULES CONCERNING COMPETITION

Section I   Standards Applicable to Enterprises.

At the end of the transitional period anti-dumping legislation of member countries of the common market in their relation with third countries should be uniform.

b) Action against monopolies within the common market will be developed in conformity with the basic rules contained in the treaty. It will be limited to practices affecting interstate commerce which take the form of cartel organizations (ententes) and monopolies using discriminatory practices, dividing markets, limiting production and controlling the market for a particular product. On the basis of principles in the treaty the European Commission will establish the general executive regulations which will be submitted to a vote by the Assembly and which can be appealed before the Court.

c) The States, the enterprises and the Committee itself will be able to make complaints against infractions of the general rules. The European Commission will try to present, within a fixed period, a compromise solution with the assistance of a Consultative Committee on cartels and discriminations which should be created. In case a compromise solution fails the Commission or the States could bring the matter before the Court.

Section 2   Rules Concerning Financial Assistance Granted by the States.

1. Financial assistance, no matter in what form it is granted, is incompatible with the common market if it distorts competition and the distribution of economic activities by favoring certain enterprises or certain types of production.

CHAPTER 2 - CORRECTION OF DISTORTIONS AND HARMONIZATION OF NATIONAL LEGISLATION

Section 1   Distortions

The procedure will be the following:

- proposals of the Commission will be adopted only after unanimous approval by the Council of Ministers during the first four years; after that by a qualified majority until the end of the 12th year, and finally by a simple majority after that period;

- governments will be obliged only to use their good offices towards their "social partners" or recommend appropriate

legislation when the correction of distortions depends either
on working conditions freely negotiated or on legislative
measures;

- if the proposals of the Commission are rejected, it has the
right, until the end of the transitional period, to grant the
benefit of a safeguard clause to industries which are harmed
(protecting them in their national markets and aiding their
sales in the rest of the common market and in third countries).

Section 2   Harmonization of Legislation

When the elimination of a distortion calls for the harmonization of legal regulations in the different countries, the European
Commission will propose the necessary decisions which will be
taken only by a unanimous vote of member States during the first
stage, and by a qualified majority thereafter. If agreement cannot
be reached, and if there is a distortion effect, the Commission
will have to grant to the interested State the benefit of a safeguard
clause.

CHAPTER 3 TRANSPORT RATES AND POLICY

Section 1   Transport Rates

Discriminations which, for the same routes and for the same
merchandise, result in different prices and conditions according
to the country of origin or destination of products will be eliminated
at the end of the first stage.

Section 2   Transport Policy

In order to prepare a common policy for transport a "transport account of each nation" will be established by a group of transport and national revenue experts in order to bring into relief the
expenditures directly borne by the transporter and also the charges
borne by the Community.

CHAPTER 4 BALANCE OF PAYMENTS

I.   The Problem of Payments Equilibrium and Mutual Assistance.

The obligations undertaken in the framework of the International Monetary Fund, the GATT, and the OEEC bind the Six
States that are members of them.

The Six States, in order to assure equilibrium in the balance of payments:

1) will establish a closer cooperation among their central banks,

2) will give the European Commission the right to grant safeguard clauses and to propose mutual assistance in order to avoid the possibility that, in spite of the rules of the IMF, devaluations might take place with the sole aim of extracting competitive advantages; and in order to prevent the maintenance or the re-establishment of restrictions and blocks in the way of the common expansion.

b. The Final Period

A State in difficulty will be able to re-establish quotas vis-a-vis third countries only in conformity with its international obligations and after consultation with the European Commission. The Commission will present the alternatives to the other member States: either to take the necessary measures to prevent the restrictions from being applied against them, or to grant credits, to the extent that the common commercial policy does not suffice to resolve these problems.

Within the common market there is reason to think that the evolution of the general system of payments will enable these difficulties to be surmounted. The granting of credits, proposed by the European Commission and decided by a simple majority of the Council, will permit the definitive renunciation of the safeguard clauses.

II Unification of Commercial Policy.

Besides the establishment of a common external tariff, the States must employ a commercial policy which will be that of the Community as a whole when the common market has been firmly established. Within this framework the European Commission, acting in liaison with the Council of Ministers, will play a role notably in matters concerning anti-dumping measures, protective quotas, encouragement of exports, and short-term (governmental) interventions, which must also be on a common basis.

28

TITLE III

DEVELOPMENT AND FULL UTILIZATION
OF EUROPEAN RESOURCES

CHAPTER 1   THE INVESTMENT FUND

Section 1   Objective

Acting in cooperation with the other international financial institutions, the fund will have the objective of participating in the financing of:

1. Projects of a European character and interest whose magnitude and nature do not lend themselves to the financing available in each State separately.

2. Less favored regions and notably regional development plans for agriculture;

3. Reconversion of enterprises by opening up credit possibilities for them which psychological factors in the market might jeopardize. This is why it is necessary to have a division endowed with certain resources within the organization of the fund itself.

CHAPTER 2   READAPTATION

1. In cases of:

   - total shut-down of an enterprise,

   - partial shut-down through definite abandonment of certain manufacturing,

   - reduction of employment affecting at least 10% of the working force and at least ten employed persons,

   The Fund will participate in covering:

   - resettlement payments if workers change their residence,

   - expenses for re-training of workers if they change their jobs.

29

CHAPTER 3 FREE MOVEMENT OF LABOR

The European Commission will propose to the States measures for the progressive elimination of all discriminatory regulations (legal, administrative, or administrative practices) which, on the basis of nationality, reserve more favorable treatment for nationals than that accorded foreigners with regard to access to an independent profession or the practice of that profession.

This principle will also apply to regulations concerning entry and residence without prejudice to provisions governing public order and safety.

CHAPTER 4 FREE MOVEMENT OF CAPITAL

3. As soon as possible, the European Commission will make proposals to establish the free circulation of capital. These proposals will be submitted to a vote of the Assembly and their adoption will require during the first four-year period the agreement of each State on matters of concern to it, and thereafter a qualified majority of the Council.

4. The European Commission can authorize safeguard clauses which can take the form either of suspension of liberalization decisions already taken or the postponement of measures to be taken. Nevertheless, even after the end of the transitional period safeguard clauses can be introduced in order to prevent speculative movements of capital.

1.7 TREATY ESTABLISHING
THE EUROPEAN ECONOMIC COMMUNITY

Signed at Rome on March 25, 1957. (excerpts)

HIS MAJESTY THE KING OF THE BELGIANS, THE PRESIDENT OF THE FEDERAL REPUBLIC OF GERMANY, THE PRESIDENT OF THE FRENCH REPUBLIC, THE PRESIDENT OF THE ITALIAN REPUBLIC, HER ROYAL HIGHNESS THE GRAND DUCHESS OF LUXEMBOURG, HER MAJESTY THE QUEEN OF THE NETHERLANDS,

DETERMINED to establish the foundations of an ever closer union among the European peoples,

DECIDED to ensure the economic and social progress of their countries by common action in eliminating the barriers which divide Europe,

DIRECTING their efforts to the essential purpose of constantly improving the living and working conditions of their peoples,

RECOGNISING that the removal of existing obstacles calls for concerted action in order to guarantee a steady expansion, a balanced trade and fair competition,

ANXIOUS to strengthen the unity of their economies and to ensure their harmonious development by reducing the differences existing between the various regions and by mitigating the backwardness of the less favoured,

DESIROUS of contributing by means of a common commercial policy to the progressive abolition of restrictions on international trade,

INTENDING to confirm the solidarity which binds Europe and overseas countries, and desiring to ensure the development of their prosperity in accordance with the principles of the Charter of the United Nations,

RESOLVED to strengthen the safeguards of peace and liberty by establishing this combination of resources and calling upon the other peoples of Europe who share their ideal to join in their efforts,

HAVE DECIDED to create a European Economic Community.

PART ONE

Principles

Article 1

By the present Treaty the HIGH CONTRACTING PARTIES establish among themselves a EUROPEAN ECONOMIC COM - MUNITY.

Article 2

It shall be the aim of the Community, by establishing a Common Market and progressively approximating the economic policies of Member States, to promote throughout the Community

31

a harmonious development of economic activities, a continuous and balanced expansion, an increased stability, an accelerated raising of the standard of living and closer relations between its Member States.

Article 3

For the purposes set out in the preceding Article, the activities of the Community shall include, under the conditions and with the timing provided for in this Treaty:

(a)   The elimination, as between Member States, of customs duties and of quantitative restrictions in regard to the importation and exportation of goods, as well as of all other measures with equivalent effect;

(b)   The establishment of a common customs tariff and a common commercial policy towards third countries;

(c)   The abolition, as between Member States, of the obstacles to the free movement of persons, services and capital;

(d)   The inauguration of a common agricultural policy;

(e)   The inauguration of a common transport policy;

(f)   The establishment of a system ensuring that competition shall not be distorted in the Common Market;

(g)   The application of procedures which shall make it possible to co-ordinate the economic policies of Member States and to remedy disequilibria in their balances of payments;

(h)   The approximation of their respective municipal law to the extent necessary for the functioning of the Common Market;

(i)   The creation of a European Social Fund in order to improve the possibilities of employment for workers and to contribute to the raising of their standard of living;

(j)   The establishment of a European Investment Bank intended to facilitate the economic expansion of the Community through the creation of new resources; and

(k)   The association of overseas countries and territories

32

with the Community with a view to increasing trade and to pursuing jointly their effort towards economic and social development.

Article 4

1.   The achievement of the tasks entrusted to the Community shall be ensured by:

> an ASSEMBLY,
> a COUNCIL,
> a COMMISSION,
> a COURT OF JUSTICE.

Each of these institutions shall act within the limits of the powers conferred upon it by this Treaty.

2.   The Council and the Commission shall be assisted by an Economic and Social Committee acting in a consultative capacity.

Article 5

Member States shall take all general or particular measures which are appropriate for ensuring the carrying out of the obligations arising out of this Treaty or resulting from the acts of the institutions of the Community. They shall facilitate the achievement of the Community's aims.

They shall abstain from any measures likely to jeopardise the attainment of the objectives of this Treaty.

Article 6

1.   Member States, acting in close collaboration with the institutions of the Community, shall co-ordinate their respective economic policies to the extent that is necessary to attain the objectives of this Treaty.

2.   The institutions of the Community shall take care not to prejudice the internal and external financial stability of Member States.

Article 7

Within the field of application of this Treaty and without prejudice to the special provisions mentioned therein, any discrimination on the grounds of nationality shall hereby be prohibited.

The Council may, acting by means of a qualified majority vote on a proposal of the Commission and after the Assembly has been consulted, lay down rules in regard to the prohibition of any such discrimination.

Article 8

1.   The Common Market shall be progressively established in the course of a transitional period of twelve years.

The transitional period shall be divided into three stages of four years each; the length of each stage may be modified in accordance with the provisions set out below.

2.   To each stage there shall be allotted a group of actions which shall be undertaken and pursued concurrently.

3.   Transition from the first to the second stage shall be conditional upon a confirmatory statement to the effect that the essence of the objectives specifically laid down in this Treaty for the first stage has been in fact achieved and that, subject to the exceptions and procedures provided for in this Treaty, the obligations have been observed.

This statement shall be made at the end of the fourth year by the Council acting by means of a unanimous vote a report of the Commission. The invocation by a Member State of the non-fulfilment of its own obligations shall not, however, be an obstacle to a unanimous vote. Failing a unanimous vote, the first stage shall automatically be extended for a period of one year.

5.   The second and third stages may not be extended or curtailed except pursuant to a decision of the Council acting by means of a unanimous vote on a proposal of the Commission.

6.   The provisions of the preceding paragraphs shall not have the effect of extending the transitional period beyond a total duration of fifteen years after the date of the entry into force of this Treaty.

7.   Subject to the exceptions or deviations provided for in this Treaty, the expiry of the transitional period shall constitute the final date for the entry into force of all the rules laid down and for the completion of all measures required for the establishment of the

Common Market.

PART TWO

Bases of the Community

TITLE I

Free Movement of Goods

Article 9

1.   The Community shall be based upon a customs union
covering the exchange of all goods and comprising both the
prohibition, as between Member States, of customs duties on
importation and exportation and all charges with equivalent
effect and the adoption of a common customs tariff in their
relations with third countries.

CHAPTER 1

THE CUSTOMS UNION

Section 1: THE ELIMINATION OF
CUSTOMS DUTIES AS BETWEEN MEMBER STATES

Article 13

1.   Customs duties on importation in force between Member States
shall be progressively abolished by them in the course of the transitional period under the conditions laid down in Articles 14 and 15.

2.   Charges in force between Member States having an effect
equivalent to customs duties on importation shall be progressively
abolished by them in the course of the transitional period.

Section 2: ESTABLISHMENT OF THE
COMMON CUSTOMS TARIFF

Article 18

Member States hereby declare their willingness to contribute to the development of international commerce and the
reduction of barriers to trade by entering into reciprocal and
mutually advantageous arrangements directed to the reduction

oms duties below the general level which they could

as a result of the establishment of a customs union

between themselves.

Article 19

1.   Under the conditions and within the limits laid down
below, the duties under the common customs tariff shall be
at the level of the arithmetical average of the duties applied
in the four customs territories covered by the Community.

2.   The duties taken into account for calculating this average
shall be those applied by Member States on 1 January 1957.

CHAPTER 2

THE ELIMINATION OF
QUANTITATIVE RESTRICTIONS
AS BETWEEN MEMBER STATES

TITLE II

Agriculture

Article 39

1.   The common agricultural policy shall have as its objectives:

(a)   to increase agricultural productivity by developing
technical progress and by ensuring the rational development
of agricultural production and the optimum utilisation of
the factors of production, particularly labour;

(b)   to ensure thereby a fair standard of living for the
agricultural population, particularly by the increasing
of the individual earnings of persons engaged in agriculture;

(c)   to stabilise markets;

(d)   to guarantee regular supplies; and

(e)   to ensure reasonable prices in supplies to consumers.

2.   In working out the common agricultural policy and the
special methods which it may involve, due account shall be taken of:

(a)   the particular character of agricultural activities, arising from the social structure of agriculture and from structural and natural disparities between the various agricultural regions;

(b)   the need to make the appropriate adjustments gradually; and

(c)   the fact that in Member States agriculture constitutes a sector which is closely linked with the economy as a whole.

TITLE III

The Free Movement of Persons, Services and Capital

CHAPTER 1

WORKERS

Article 48

1.   The free movement of workers shall be ensured within the Community not later than at the date of the expiry of the transitional period.

CHAPTER 2

THE RIGHT OF ESTABLISHMENT

Article 52

Within the framework of the provisions set out below, restrictions on the freedom of establishment of nationals of a Member State in the territory of another Member State shall be progressively abolished in the course of the transitional period. Such progressive abolition shall also extend to restrictions on the setting up of agencies, branches or subsidiaries by nationals of any Member State established in the territory of any Member State.

Freedom of establishment shall include the right to engage in and carry on non-wage-earning activities, and also to set up and manage enterprises and, in particular, companies.

CHAPTER 3

SERVICES

Article 59

Within the framework of the provisions set out below, restrictions on the free supply of services within the Community shall be progressively abolished in the course of the transitional period in respect of nationals of Member States who are established in a State of the Community other than that of the person to whom the services are supplied.

The Council, acting by means of a unanimous vote on a proposal of the Commission, may extend the benefit of the provisions of this Chapter to cover services supplied by nationals of any third country who are established within the Community.

CHAPTER 4

CAPITAL

Article 67

1.   Member States shall, in the course of the transitional period and to the extent necessary for the proper functioning of the Common Market, progressively abolish as between themselves restrictions on the movement of capital belonging to persons resident in Member States and also any discriminatory treatment based on the nationality or place of residence of the parties or on the place in which such capital is invested.

TITLE IV

Transport

Article 74

The objectives of this Treaty shall, with regard to the subject covered by this Title, be pursued by the Member States within the framework of a common transport policy.

Article 75

1.   With a view to implementing Article 74 and taking due account of the special aspects of transport, the Council, acting

on a proposal of the Commission and after the Economic and
Social Committee and the Assembly have been consulted,
shall, until the end of the second stage by means of a unanimous
vote and subsequently by means of a qualified majority vote,
lay down:

(a)   common rules applicable to international transport
effected from or to the territory of a Member State or
crossing the territory of one or more Member States;

(b)   conditions for the admission of non-resident carriers
to national transport services within a Member States; and

(c)   any other appropriate provisions.

PART THREE

Policy of the Community

TITLE I

Common Rules

CHAPTER 1

RULES GOVERNING COMPETITION

Section 1: RULES APPLYING TO ENTERPRISES

Article 85

1.   The following shall be deemed to be incompatible with the
Common Market and shall hereby be prohibited: any agreement
between enterprises, any decisions by associations of enterprises
and any concerted practices which are likely to affect trade between the Member States and which have as their object or result
the prevention, restriction or distortion of competition within
the Common Market, in particular those consisting in:

(a)   the direct or indirect fixing of purchase or selling
prices or of any other trading conditions;

(b)   the limitation or control of production, markets,
technical development or investment;

(c)   market-sharing or the sharing of sources of supply;

(d)   the application to parties to transactions of unequal terms in respect of equivalent supplies, thereby placing them at a competitive disadvantage; or

(e)   the subjecting of the conclusion of a contract to the acceptance by a party of additional supplies which, either by their nature or according to commercial usage, have no connection with the subject of such contract.

Section 2: DUMPING PRACTICES

Article 91

1.   If, in the course of the transitional period, the Commission, at the request of a Member State or of any other interested party, finds that dumping practices exist within the Common Market, it shall issue recommendations to the originator or originators of such practices with a view to bringing them to an end.

Where such dumping practices continue, the Commission shall authorise the Member State injured to take protective measures of which the Commission shall determine the conditions and particulars.

Section 3: AIDS GRANTED BY STATES

Article 92

1.   Except where otherwise provided for in this Treaty, any aid, granted by a Member State or granted by means of State resources, in any manner whatsoever, which distorts or threatens to distort competition by favouring certain enterprises or certain productions shall, to the extent to which it adversely affects trade between Member States, be deemed to be incompatible with the Common Market.

CHAPTER 2

FISCAL PROVISIONS

Article 95

A Member State shall not impose, directly or indirectly on the products of other Member States any internal charges of any kind in excess of those applied directly or indirectly to like domestic products.

Furthermore, a Member State shall not impose on the products of other Member States any internal charges of such a nature as to afford indirect protection to other productions.

CHAPTER 3

APPROXIMATION OF LAWS

Article 100

The Council, acting by means of a unanimous vote on a proposal of the Commission, shall issue directives for the approximation of such legislative and administrative provisions of the Member States as have a direct incidence on the establishment or functioning of the Common Market.

TITLE II

Economic Policy

CHAPTER 1

POLICY RELATING TO ECONOMIC TRENDS

Article 103

1.   Member States shall consider their policy relating to economic trends as a matter of common interest. They shall consult with each other and with the Commission on measures to be taken in response to current circumstances.

2.   Without prejudice to any other procedure provided for in this Treaty, the Council may, by means of a unanimous vote on a proposal of the Commission, decide on measures appropriate to the situation.

3.   The Council, acting by means of a qualified majority vote on a proposal of the Commission, shall, where necessary, issue any requisite directives concerning the particulars of application of the measures decided upon under the terms of paragraph 2.

4.   The procedures provided for in this Article shall apply also in the event of difficulties arising in connection with the supply of certain products.

CHAPTER 2

BALANCE OF PAYMENTS

Article 104

Each Member State shall pursue the economic policy necessary to ensure the equilibrium of its overall balance of payments and to maintain confidence in its currency, while ensuring a high level of employment and the stability of the level of prices.

Article 105

1.   In order to facilitate the attainment of the objectives stated in Article 104, Member States shall co-ordinate economic policies. They shall for this purpose institute a collaboration between the competent services of their administrative departments and between their central banks.

The Commission shall submit to the Council recommendations for the bringing into effect of such collaboration.

2.   In order to promote the co-ordination of the policies of Member States in monetary matters to the full extent necessary for the functioning of the Common Market, a Monetary Committee with consultative status shall hereby be established with the following tasks:

-    to keep under review the monetary and financial situation of Member States and of the Community and also the general payments system of Member States and to report regularly thereon to the Council and to the Commission; and

-    to formulate opinions, at the request of the Council or to the Commission or on its own initiative, for submission to the said institutions.

The Member States and the Commission shall each appoint two members of the Monetary Committee.

CHAPTER 3

COMMERCIAL POLICY

Article 110

By establishing a customs union between themselves the Member States intend to contribute, in conformity with the common interest, to the harmonious development of world trade, the progressive abolition of restrictions on international exchanges and the lowering of customs barriers.

The common commercial policy shall take into account the favourable incidence which the abolition of customs duties as between Member States may have on the increase of the competitive strength of the enterprises in those States.

TITLE III

Social Policy

CHAPTER 1

SOCIAL PROVISIONS

Article 117

Member States hereby agree upon the necessity to promote improvement of the living and working conditions of labour so as to permit the equalization of such conditions in an upward direction.

They consider that such a development will result not only from the functioning of the Common Market which will favour the harmonization of social systems, but also from the procedures provided for under this Treaty and from the approximation of legislative and administrative provisions.

CHAPTER 2

THE EUROPEAN SOCIAL FUND

Article 123

In order to improve opportunities of employment of workers in the Common Market and thus contribute to raising the standard of living, a European Social Fund shall hereby be established in accordance with the provision set out below; it shall have the task of promoting within the Community employment facilities and the geographical and occupational mobility of workers.

TITLE IV

The European Investment Bank

Article 130

The task of the European Investment Bank shall be to contribute, by calling on the capital markets and its own resources, to the balanced and smooth development of the Common Market in the interest of the Community. For this purpose, the Bank shall by granting loans and guarantees on a non-profit-making basis facilitate the financing of the following projects in all sectors of the economy:

(a) projects for developing less developed regions,

(b) projects for modernising or converting enterprises or for creating new activities which are called for by the progressive establishment of the Common Market where such projects by their size or nature cannot be entirely financed by the various means available in each of the Member States; and

(c) projects of common interest to several Member States which by their size or nature cannot be entirely financed by the various means available in each of the Member States.

PART FOUR

The Association of Overseas Countries and Territories

Article 131

The Member States hereby agree to bring into association with the Community the non-European countries and territories which have special relations with Belgium, France, Italy and the Netherlands. These countries and territories, hereinafter referred to as "the countries and territories", are listed in Annex IV to this Treaty.

The purpose of this association shall be to promote the economic and social development of the countries and territories and to establish close economic relations between them and the Community as a whole.

TITLE II

Financial Provisions

Article 200

1.　The revenues of the budget shall comprise, apart from any other revenues, the financial contributions of Member States fixed according to the following scale:

Belgium	7.9
Germany	28
France	28
Italy	28
Luxembourg	0.2
Netherlands	7.9

PART SIX

General and Final Provisions

Article 210

The Community shall have legal personality.

Article 237

Any European State may apply to become a member of the Community. It shall address its application to the Council which after obtaining the opinion of the Commission, shall act by means of a unanimous vote.

The conditions of admission and the amendments to this Treaty necessitated thereby shall be the subject of an agreement between the Member States and the applicant States. Such agreement shall be submitted to all the contracting States for ratification in accordance with their respective constitutional rules.

Article 238

The Community may conclude with a third country, a union of States or an international organization agreements creating an association embodying reciprocal rights and obligations, joint actions and special procedures.

Such agreements shall be concluded by the Council acting

by means of a unanimous vote and after consulting the Assembly.

Where such agreements involve amendments to this Treaty, such amendments shall be subject to prior adoption in accordance with the procedure laid down in Article 236.

Article 240

This Treaty shall be concluded for an unlimited period.

1.8 THE SECOND STAGE*

1. On 14 January 1962 the Council unanimously found that the essence of the objectives laid down in the Treaty of Rome for the first stage had in fact been achieved. Under Article 8(3) of the Treaty this finding made it possible to embark upon the second stage of the transitional period as from 1 January 1962.

On 6 December 1961 the European Commission had submitted to the Council the report called for in Article 8(3). This report reviewed the progress made in all the fields covered by the Treaty, progress sufficient to satisfy the strict conditions laid down for such a move; it also stressed the strides made in the other sectors and pointed to the speed-up in particular as an expression of the Member States' desire to press on towards the customs union and economic union.

At its session of 29 and 30 December 1961 the Commission restated its opinion, pointing out to the Council that the balanced development of the common market would be seriously undermined if the first decisions on the execution of the common agricultural policy were not taken at the same time.

As early as 24 November 1961 the European Parliament had expressed its support of transition to the second stage, but urged that the Council should simultaneously take the most important of the decisions which were still pending, particularly in the agricultural sphere. A resolution to this effect had been adopted at the joint meeting of the Community Institutions on 20 and 21 November 1961.

The decision to move on to the next stage was therefore closely linked with the group of decisions taken by the Council during its 60th session from 18 December onwards, dealing in the main with competition policy (first regulation on cartels), social policy (adoption of a time-table for the introduction of equal pay for men and women workers as provided for in Article 119) and the common agricultural policy (adoption of a first set of regulations, decisions and resolutions).

2.   The authors of the Treaty of Rome looked upon the Community as a development that was irreversible. Nevertheless it was agreed that once only, namely at the end of the first four-year stage, the forward march of the Community could be halted if " the essence of the objectives specifically laid down in the Treaty for the first stage" had not been achieved and if "the obligations had not been observed".

This decision authorizing the move into the second stage must therefore be considered in all its significance: not only does it set the seal of approval on the favourable balance sheet for the first period and confirm the resolve of the Member States to continue the implementation of the Treaty and the strengthening of the Community , but it also opens the way to a new stage of development.

The various chapters of this report give a detailed account of the achievements that made the move into the second stage possible. It will suffice at this point simply to recall their salient features.

Considerable progress has been made in the sphere of the free movement of goods, thanks to the customs and quota measures: on 1 January 1962 customs duties were lowered by 40% for industrial products and, as regards agricultural products, by 35% for non-liberalized and 30% for liberalized products. Quantitative restrictions have been totally abolished except for agricultural products and goods produced by state monopolies. Finally, the first approximation of national tariffs towards the common customs tariff was effected on 1 January 1961, i.e. one year ahead before the time-limit set by the Treaty. The duties of the common tariff had, with very few exceptions, already been fixed.

The first measures have been taken for progressively freeing the movement of workers, capital and services and giving effect to the right of establishment and in matters of trade, transport and competition decisions have been taken which pave the way for the common policies.

Finally, and this is the decisive p oint, substantial progress has been made with the common agricultural policy. The decisions setting up common market organizations for certain products and the establishment of a levy system set the seal of success on what has without doubt been the most arduous task of all, namely to create conditions for a common market in agriculture, traditionnally the least liberalized sector of all. This success has made a deep impression on public opinion and strengthened confidence in the future Europe.

The association of the overseas countries and territories with the Community has become a reality, thanks to the first measures taken in regard to trade and thanks to the operations of the Development Fund.

In its relations with the outside world, the Community has already begun to take its rightful place as the economic unit which it will soon be. Its growth and influence have had effects not only in Europe, with the association of Greece and other countries' applications for membership and association, but throughout the free world where the Community's example is such that it is inspiring endeavours to put economic relations between countries on a new basis.

Hence the impetus that has carried the Community forward in these four years and the rigid application of the formal provisions of the Treaty go to show that the move by the EEC into the second state signifies more than simply that the requirements set out in Article 8(3) have been met. The Community has not only avoided a possible delay and the difficulties it might have encountered if the decisions on the move had been postponed for a year, but its development has fulfilled, and more than fulfilled, the hopes of those who negotiated the Treaty: above and beyond its economic effects, it is having more general consequences of a political nature.

3.   The second stage, from 1 January 1962 onwards, is also for four years. This and the third stage can only be prolonged by an unanimous vote of all the Member States. On the other hand, its duration can be reduced by a decision of the Council, again acting by unanimous vote and on a proposal of the Commission. Consequently the Council's decision on 14 January 1962 launched the Community on a process of integration which, as was pointed out at the joint meeting of the Community Institutions by M. Erhard, President in office of the Council, will progress automatically. Thus is it now possible to count on the transition period ending at latest by 1 January 1970. The second stage, in which tariff disarmament will continue, will still be a preparatory phase in some fields(commercial policy, transport policy, etc.) but in other sectors it will see the application of decisions taken in the first stage (agricultural policy, competition policy, right of establish-

ment, freedom to supply services) and the gradual harmonization of economic, social, fiscal, financial and budgetary policies.

The transition to the second stage had to be made before various developments could occur in quite a number of fields; it will also create in other sectors favourable conditions for development which do not under the terms of the Treaty have to be completed within the coming four-year period. These include:

Customs disarmament. Further global tariff reductions of 10% will come into force, according to the Treaty, by the following dates: 1 July 1963, 31 December 1964 and 31 December 1965. The Council must also decide on 15 May 1962 on the details of an additional reduction due to take place on 1 July 1962 under the speed-up decisions (1).

Alignment on the common external tariff. The Member States will carry out a second 30% approximation of the national tariffs towards the common external tariff on 31 December 1965. The gap between the national tariffs and the CET will then be reduced by 60%, subject to any speed-up measures to be decided by the Council on 15 May (2).

Right of establishment and freedom to supply services. The general programme will be applied according to the time-table: before the end of 1963 for almost all branches of industry, for the wholesale trade and reinsurance; before the end of 1965 for the food industry, retail trade, certain branches of agriculture, certain liberal professions, certain branches of insurance, and pharmacy.

The monopolies mentioned in Article 37. The move into the second stage will make it possible to adjust these progressively at the rate already adopted in the first stage. At the beginning of 1962 the Commission made a second series of recommendations on this adjustment.

Competition. Regulation No. 17 (on cartels and dominant positions) settles the detailed arrangements required for implementing Articles 85 and 86 in all the member countries. In addition Member States may not, from the beginning of the second stage, impose on the products of other Member States any internal charges in excess of those applied to like domestic products (Article 95). Finally the work on the harmonization of turnover taxes and other forms of indirect taxation (Article 99) will reach the decision stage.

Social problems. Regulations will be prepared in the second

stage to secure the completely free movement of workers in the Community; a European Clearing Office for the co-ordination of vacancies and applications for employment will be established in Brussels. Furthermore, wages for men and women will be gradually brought into line in accordance with the time-table drawn up by the Council.

Transport. A common policy will be adopted in this field. Rates and conditions involving any element of support or protection must be abolished as from the beginning of the second stage (Article 80(1)).

Agriculture. The regulations, decisions and resolutions made by the Council on 14 January 1962 will be put into effect; in addition regulations covering several other products and a policy on agricultural structure will be worked out(3).

4. Institutional developments. The transition to the second stage involves the substitution of the qualified majority vote for the unanimous vote in the Council when certain decisions are to be taken. This applies to six clearly defined sectors.

When there is difficulty over ensuring the progressive removal of quantitative restrictions on imports, as required by Article 33(8), any decision by the Council to raise the percentages fixed will be taken by qualified majority vote. In view of the progress made already, this will only arise in connection with certain agricultural products.

The Council will also be acting by qualified majority vote when it issues the directives needed to implement the general programme for the suppression of restrictions on freedom of establishment (Article 54 (2)) and freedom to supply services (Article 63 (2)).

The same will apply to the mutual recognition of diplomas, certificates and other qualifications (Article 57 (1)) and the co-ordination of national legislation (Article 57 (2)) concerning the engagement in an exercise of non-wage-earning activities. Unanimity is however still required on matters which are subject to legislative provisions in a Member State and on measures concerning the granting of credit, the protection of savings and the exercise of certain professions (banking, medicine, pharmacy). Finally, voting by qualified majority will apply to the directives by which the Council seeks to eliminate distortions of competition caused by legislative or adminstrative provisions (Article 101).

Finally, it should be noted that after the expiry of the fourth year the Council may amend, by qualified majority vote, the statute of service for officials and the conditions of employment for other employees (Article 212).

In all these cases the Council acts on a proposal of the Commission. In addition the States are to delegate to the Council power to fix the duties in the common customs tariff for those List G products on which no agreement was reached before the end of the first stage; these include petroleum oils and certain derivatives, petroleum gases, certain gaseous hydrocarbons and petroleum jelly.

It is true that the unanimity rule will remain for a number of important questions. But the extension of the qualified majority vote is itself a further move towards integration. This is carried a step further by the institutional procedures whic the Council has laid down for the common agricultural policy, where the qualified majority vote is often to be used in the second stage or powers are to be delegated to the Commission.

Thus both in the application of the Treaty's provisions and in the institutional procedures in the various sectors, the move from the first to the second stage will carry the Community forward into a phase where advances will be made which will take it beyond the stage of a customs and economic union.

---

(1) See sec. 8.

(2) See sec. 8.

(3) See Chapters II and III for more detailed information on these programmes as a whole.

*Fifth General Report on the Activities of the Community, pp. 21-27.

1.9 THE ACTION PROGRAMME*

1.   In accordance with the procedure agreed on by the Parliament and Council the officers of the European Parliament, in a letter to the Council on 1 October, proposed as a topic for discussion at the annual joint meeting of the Parliament, the Council and the Executives the tasks of the Community during the second stage, which began on 1 January 1962, of the transition period laid down in the Treaty of Rome for the attainment of its objectives.

In preparation for this discussion, to which the Council agreed on 25 October, the President of the European Parliament asked the Executives and more particularly the EEC Commission to inform him of their plans and prospects with regard to the tasks to be accomplished by the Community during the second stage.

In reply the Commission prepared an Action Programme for the second stage, which was submitted to the Parliament on 26 October and also to the Council. It subsequently served as a basis for discussion at the joint meeting on 20 and 21 November.

The Commission drew up the Action Programme in considerable detail, feeling that its publication would be of interest not only to the Parliament but also to the Council, the Governments and the general public in the Community countries.

It was thought important to keep the Council and member governments informed of what the Treaty implied for the Commission, and no less important for the European Parliament (like the national parliaments and the public in the member countries) to be able to view in a general context the measures on which it was called on from time to time to decide. The Action Programme is of assistance to the Parliament in keeping its watching brief over the Commission's activities.

It is also useful for the rest of the world, and especially countries seeking membership of or association with the Common Market, to be well informed of the Community's aims.

2.   In the introduction to the document the Commission states that the economic integration of Europe is in essence a political phenomenon and that together with the ECSC and the EAEC the Community forms a political union embracing the economic and social spheres.

This political aspect of the Community came to the fore at the beginning of the second stage. The first stage was marked by substantial progress towards a customs union which, however, can only be fully effective if it is followed by the economic union also provided for in the Treaty. Here the stress will no longer be, as in the customs union, on negative measures - the abolition of restrictive rules and regulations - but on constructive action. What now remains to be achieved is the gradual merging of national economic policies into a common short-term and long-term policy. Without this there can be no common market, no economic area where conditions are those of a domestic market.

Besides this first reason for the opening up of markets
to be followed by common policies in a wide range of sectors,
there is another. Integration of the economic and social aspects
of national policies is effected by the Treaty of Rome as a means
of achieving political unity in Europe; for what is being brought
together, what is here being welded into a community is the
policies of the individual States. What is being built up is a union
of Member States in the eminently political sphere of economics
or more precisely of the influence exercised by the State on
economic affairs, i.e. economic policy. It is a union which
affects an essential part of the internal policies of Member States
and part of their external policy, namely, trade policy. With the
Community political integration has already begun in one essential
field.

3. The eleven chapters of the Action Programme outline what
steps must be taken if the Community's objectives are to be achieved;
they present an overall view of the anticipated development of the
Community.

As regards the internal market, the Commission stresses
its twofold task: the pace at which the customs union is developing
must be kept up, and the Community must give increased attention
to indirect obstacles to the free movement of goods, which are
becoming all the more conspicuous as further progress is made
in the abolition of customs duties and quotas properly so called.

In order to attain the first objective the Commission announces
that the directives it proposes for tariff disarmament during the
third stage will aim at eliminating all internal customs duties by
1 January 1967.

As to the objective, the Commission sets out a detailed programme for dealing with various obstacles to trade such as charges
equivalent in effect to customs duties and measures equivalent in
effect to quotas.

The Commission also stresses how important it is to harmonize legislation governing professions and trades if freedom of
establishment and freedom to supply services are to be achieved.

Chapter II emphasizes the essential function of competition
in the Common Market, describing it as an important tool in the
building of the Common Market, with an essential role to play in the

53

control of the economic process on the many new Community markets, and as a guarantee of economic freedom for all those concerned in those markets. The Commission considers that the constructive competitive policy described in detail in Chapter II of the Action Programme is one of the most important and effective instruments for realizing the aims of the Treaty.

The chapters on energy and transport mainly reproduce earlier proposals published by the Commission in other documents (Memorandum of the Inter-Executive Working Party on Energy, Action Programme for a Common Transport Policy). The chapter on agricultural policy restates, in the light of intervening Council decisions, the general ideas put forward by the Commission in a previous memorandum.

The chapter on social policy particularly stresses that the Community must have its own social policy, co-ordinated of course with the other elements of Community policy but not subordinate to them. Besides applying and amplifying Community Regulations the Commission will be mainly concerned with implementing a policy on vocational training and employment and with harmonizing social systems.

The chapter on economic policy announces that by the middle of 1963 the Commission is to submit to the Council proposals for "Community planning". The first step will be to make a comparative study of the long-term plans, programmes, projections or forecasts of Member States with the aim of dove-tailing the national policies and the various Community measures and of laying the technical and political foundations for a consolidated plan covering, it is suggested, the 1964-68 period.

As regards structural policy, the memorandum provides for research into industrial sectors faced with special problems; three working parties are to be set up to study regional policy problems.

Monetary policy is of special importance in bringing about an economic union, a condition for which is that exchange rates must be stabilized within very narrow limits. To strengthen co-operation on monetary policy in the Common Market the Commission proposes the formation of a Council of Governors of Central Banks and advocates that Member States adopt a common attitude on world monetary problems.

In the chapter on external relations the Commission emphasizes that the Community is keenly aware of its duties towards non-member countries in Europe and in the world at large, and that it desires to follow a policy of co-operation and progress for all. This policy finds specific expression in the following fields: the widening of the Community, partnership with the United States and the shaping of the Community's trade policy along liberal lines.

The Commission's programme for aid to developing countries, dealt with in Chapter X, comprises the improvement of the association system considered as a comprehensive effort covering a vast area of the developing world and, with due regard at all times to the special situation of the associated countries, consideration for the interests of developing countries not linked with the Community and implementation of solutions appropriate in their case.

In the chapter on administration and finance the Commission draws attention to the staff shortage, which has become more acute as a result of the additional work involved in the implementation of the common agricultural policy and policy in regard to competition.

4.   The Action Programme has been widely circulated among the Community institutions and in non-member as well as member countries and has aroused keen interest everywhere.

5.   Since the interruption of the negotiations for the entry of the United Kingdom, the European Parliament has formally stated on two occasions the importance it attaches to the implementation of the Action Programme. In a resolution of 19 February it explicitly urged that a start should be made as soon as possible on implementing the Action Programme, so that the harmonization and gradual integration of member countries' economic policies in all sectors might soon become a reality. In another resolution on 29 March 1963 the Parliament said that the establishment of a customs union and an economic union must be pursued along the lines laid down in the programme, which it termed as "essential instrument for a European order".

---

*Sixth General Report on the Activities of the Community, pp. 21-26.

1.10   1964 INITIATIVE

Communication by the Commission to the Council and the
Member Governments

1.   The success of the European Communities is already an
established fact, their influence is worldwide, and they have become
the hub of the efforts being made to unite Europe politically.
These Communities are called "economic because they combine
the economic and social policies which, if the Communities did not
exist, would be handled by the political organs of the individual
Member States, but they are already part and parcel of, and not
simply a preparatory stage for, "political union". Progress on
the road to economic integration increases the "inclination" towards
complete political union, and it provides increasingly cogent reasons
for establishing such union. If these Communities should fail,
the political Community would also be lost for our generation. On
the other hand, as long as the Communities maintain their dynamism
undiminished, there will still be a real chance for complete European
Federation.

2.   The Commission, whilst not wishing to dramatize the present
psychological malaise, is certainly inclined to take it seriously.
The Commission believes that it can be transformed into a driving
force for further European progress. The policy of European
integration has overcome greater setbacks than this.

3.   Political union comprises in fact two elements:

    -    The extension of the process of European unification
    beyond the pooling of economic and social policies to cover
    defence, foreign policy (over and above the part already covered
    by the economic policies merged under the European Economic
    Community) and cultural policy. The Commission has insisted
    on the need for this extension to take place soon. It has urged
    moreover that what has been achieved so far (the institutional
    shape and structure of the Communities) should be left intact.
    It holds in addition that any new elements which are created
    also comprise genuine and independent representation of the
    Community interest.

    -    Improvement of the constitution of the European Com-
    munities (merger of the Community executives, merger of
    of the Communities themselves, and strengthening of the role
    of the European Parliament). One decisive motive for the
    efforts made under this last heading is the conviction that
    the sharing of democratic responsibilities laid down in the
    Treaty become all the more unsatisfactory the deeper the
    Community's activity permeates matters hitherto the preserve
    of national legislatures and the further the budget resources at
    the disposal of the Community increase, particularly as a re-

sult of the establishment of special funds. Within the framework of Treaty law the Commission will in future continue to follow up with the same determination as in the past any possibilities of improvement open to it and to support any similar initiative taken by the Parliament.

4.   The Commission therefore warns against making the further advance of economic integration dependent on the fulfilment of certain demands. Apart from the legal situation, which does not allow of any such conditions, a policy of this kind is dangerous, since its effect on what is immediately necessary - the completion of the Communities - is negative and delaying. It can all to easily become a convenient pretext for putting off necessary decisions.

5.   Apart from the need to keep the longer-term aim always in view, the immediate task of the European Economic Community is to maintain its own vitality and dynamism. The Commission is therefore proposing a number of measures for which the time seems ripe and which it considers would constitute a particularly impressive demonstration of the continuing elan of the Community. This set of proposals is not a package deal, on the contrary, the Commission is of the opinion that each individual suggestion must be examined separately.

6.   In addition to these new proposals there are others which the Commission has already made and on which no action has yet been taken, in particular its demand for the fixing of a common cereals price, these have lost none of their urgency. The fact that the Council has made no decision on this means that there is no common agricultural policy, with serious consequences for the progress of integration and for the clarification of the Community's external relations in the Kennedy Round.

I.   Customs Union

The Commission considers that the time has now come to fix the date for completing the customs union and that this should be January 1, 1967.

The Commission proposes that on January 1, 1965, the member States should again reduce total customs charges by 15%, in conformity with Article 14(4) of the Treaty. On this date customs duties should be reduced for each product by at least 10% in relation to the basic duty. However the reduction may be limited to 5% in certain special cases.

On January 1, 1966, the Member States would again reduce total customs charges by 15%. Customs duties would again be reduced for each product by at least 10% in relation to the basic duty. On January 1, 1967, any remaining customs duties on industrial products would be abolished.

As regards agricultural products - those which carry customs duties or "fixed components" - the speed-up provides for the abolition of these duties by January 1, 1968.

The Commission will also submit in due course, if possible before January 1, 1966, and without prejudice to any other action which it considers appropriate, proposals concerning definition of origin, the application of anti-dumping and compensatory duties, rules for the definition of customs value, the elaboration of common arrangements for processing traffic, the unification of national provisions concerning free entry on economic grounds, bonded warehouses and free ports the working out of a procedure for operating Community tariff quotas and of rules for the uniform application of the common customs tariff.

The aim is free movement of goods between the Member States beginning 1967. For a large proportion of agricultural products it is the introduction - which in any case can no longer be deferred of the common cereals price which will permit this free movement, whereas in the industrial sector it will be the elimination of the remaining intra-Community duties. These two operations, which can be planned and executed independently of each other, consequently converge towards the same objective, which is to favour the rapid completion of the customs union after the beginning of the third stage of the transitional period thanks to freedom of trade in goods between the Member States.

As to complete establishment of the common customs tariff with effect from January 1, 1966, it would give not only the European economy but also our partners in non-member countries every certainty as to the shape of the European Customs Union which will confront them. This would in particular be a great advantage for the Kennedy negotiations.

As it had already pointed out in its action programme of October 1962, the Commission considers that the elimination of customs duties should carry with it the abolition of indirect obstacles to the free movement of goods, in particular all controls at internal frontiers.

58

Not only do these controls prevent the establishment of a true Common Market, but they also tend to obscure from the citizens of Europe the political significance of the undertaking embarked on by the Six Member States. As long as travellers have to pass through customs controls at frontier crossing points between the Member States and lorries have to queue for customs clearance, the citizens of the Community will continue to feel that there has been no decisive change.

Without waiting for solutions which will make possible the simultaneous abolition of all the obstacles referred to, the Commission will propose, after study in conjunction with national customs departments, measures to facilitate frontier crossing to the maximum.

The Commission:

(a)   Proposes that the Council adopt a resolution abolishing by January 1, 1970, at the latest all frontier controls on trade in goods between Member States,

(b)   Will simplify to the maximum degree and as rapidly as possible, in pursuance of Article 10 of the Treaty, the formalities imposed on trade by easing to the fullest extent possible the system introduced six years ago in the field of intra-Community   trade,

(c)   Will propose to the Council at an early date a new series of measures which must be taken to attain the objective set out in (a) above,

(d)   Requests the Council to introduce, in advance of the complete establishment of the customs union, measures of commercial policy which will make it possible to dispense with procedure under Article 115,

(e)   Recalls the directive which it submitted to the Council on the harmonization of turnover taxes and stresses the importance of its adoption.

II.   Monetary Policy.

The Commission considers that the aims set out in its action programme of October 1962 have become even more pressing and that they should be examined in the light of experience. The interpenetration of markets which has meanwhile come about between the Member States makes progress in the field of monetary policy increasingly urgent.

The aim of the Community is not merely to expand trade between the Member States, it implies merging the six markets in a single internal market and the establishment of an economic union. It therefore appears indispensable to adapt the monetary policy of the six to the degree of integration already attained in other fields.

The Commission will submit without delay to the Council proposals for the progressive introduction of a monetary union. The monetary committee will be consulted in advance on these proposals.

III. Social Policy.

In the social field the Commission places the emphasis on two lines of action. As indicated in the action programme of October 1962, the Commission has concluded from the experience of the first years "That the Fund should not merely be an organization for refunding Member States' expenditure on retraining schemes, but that it should also be in a position to encourage the various countries to initiate schemes and carry out experiments in this field, in this way the Fund could fully achieve its purpose".

The second line of action is of a more general nature. The Commission wishes to call the attention of Member States to the need to intensify the close collaboration provided for by Article 118 with a view to levelling living and working conditions in a upward direction. The general balance sought by the Treaty makes it indispensable that substantial progress should be made in this field on the lines of the programmes of work submitted by the Commission to the six governments. Such levelling upwards would, moreover, facilitate the attainment of economic union inasmuch as differences between national systems create disparities which affect the terms of competition or set up obstacles to trade.

CHAPTER 2

INSTITUTIONS OF THE EUROPEAN ECONOMIC COMMUNITY

The Rome Treaty has provided the Community with a quasi-federal structure: to formulate, administer, and supervise common rules and policies of the EEC. An executive, independent of governments and private interests and subject to parliamentary and judicial control, acts in close cooperation with a Council of Ministers which represents the six member governments.

The principal organs of the EEC are:

> the European Parliament
> the Council of Ministers
> the Commission
> the Court of Justice.

Other EEC agencies created by the Rome Treaty are:

> the Economic and Social Committee
> the European Investment Bank
> the Monetary Committee
> the Transport Committee
> the European Social Fund
> the Overseas Development Fund
> the Foreign Trade Committee (Article III).

The EEC, in coordination with the European Coal and Steel Community and Euratom, supervises and utilizes three joint services:

> the Legal Service of the European Executives
> the Press and Information Service of the European
>   Communities
> the Statistical Office of the European Communities.

Consultative committees, usually composed of representatives of member governments and the Commission and often including representatives of specialized interests in the member countries, have been created. Such committees exist for almost all sectors of Community activity including: economic policy, social security for migrant workers, free movement of workers, vocational training, insurance, ententes, parity and technical assistance. Marketing committees have been created for each of the commodities under the EEC common agricultural policy.

THE INSTITUTIONS OF THE EUROPEAN COMMUNITIES

Consultation and joint action
Parliamentary control
Judicial control

Coal and Steel Community
HIGH AUTHORITY

Economic Community
COMMISSION

Euratom
COMMISSION

Consultative Committee

European Investment Bank
Monetary Committee
European Social Fund
Development Fund

Economic and Social Committee

Commercial Agency
Scientific and Technical Committee
Joint Nuclear Research Centre

COURT OF JUSTICE

COUNCILS OF MINISTERS

ASSEMBLY

2.1 THE EUROPEAN PARLIAMENT

Provisions in the EEC Treaty

Article 137

The Assembly, which shall be composed of representatives of the peoples of the States united within the Community, shall exercise the powers of deliberation and of control which are conferred upon it by this Treaty.

Article 138

1. The Assembly shall be composed of delegates whom the Parliaments shall be called upon to appoint from among their members in accordance with the procedure laid down by each Member State.

2. The number of these delegates shall be fixed as follows:

Belgium	14
Germany	36
France	36
Italy	36
Luxembourg	6
Netherlands	14

3. The Assembly shall draw up proposals for election by direct universal suffrage in accordance with a uniform procedure in all Member States.

The Council, acting by means of a unanimous vote, shall determine the provisions which it shall recommend to Member States for adoption in accordance with their respective constitutional rules.

Article 139

The Assembly shall hold an annual session. It shall meet as of right on the third Tuesday in October.

The Assembly may meet in extraordinary session at the request of a majority of its members or at the request of the Council or of the Commission.

Article 140

The Assembly shall appoint its President and its officers from among its members.

Members of the Commission may attend all meetings and shall, at their request, be heard on behalf of the Commission.

The Commission shall reply orally or in writing to questions put to it by the Assembly or its members.

The Council shall be heard by the Assembly under the conditions which the Council shall lay down in its rules of procedure.

Article 141

Except where otherwise provided for in this Treaty, the Assembly shall act by means of an absolute majority of the votes cast.

The quorum shall be laid down in the rules of procedure.

Article 142

The Assembly shall adopt its rules of procedure by a vote of the majority of its members.

The records of the Assembly shall be published in accordance with the provisions of its rules of procedure.

Article 143

The Assembly shall discuss in public meeting the annual general report submitted to it by the Commission.

Article 144

If a motion of censure concerning the activities of the Commission is introduced in the Assembly, a vote may be taken thereon only after a period of not less than three days following its introduction, and such vote shall be by open ballot.

If the motion of censure is adopted by a two-thirds majority of the votes cast, representing a majority of the members of the Assembly, the members of the Commission shall resign their office in a body. They shall continue to carry out current business until their replacement in accordance with the provisions of Article 158 has taken place.

Structure

President: Jean DUVIEUSART (Belgian Christian Socialist)

Executive Committee: the President and 8 Vice-Presidents

Political groups: Christian Democratic   64

Socialist   35

Liberals and associates   26

Others   15

Committees of the Parliament: Political, Foreign Trade, Agriculture, Social, Internal Market, Economic and Financial, Cooperation with Developing Countries, Transport, Energy, Research and Culture, Health Protection, Budgets and Administration, Legal.

General Secretariat:

H.R. NORD   Secretary General

General Directorates for: General Affairs, Parliamentary Committees and Studies, Parliamentary Documentation and Information, Administration.

Address: 19, rue Beaumont, Luxembourg, Grand-Duche

Tel: 219-21.

Parliament sits at Maison de l'Europe, Strasbourg, France.

2.2 THE COUNCIL OF MINISTERS

Provisions in the EEC Treaty

Article 145

With a view to ensuring the achievement of the objectives laid down in this Treaty, and under the conditions provided for therein, the Council shall:

- ensure the co-ordination of the general economic policies of the Member States; and

- dispose of a power of decision.

Article 146

The Council shall be composed of representatives of the Member States. Each Government shall delegate to it one of its members.

The office of President shall be exercised for a term of six months by each member of the Council in rotation according to the alphabetical order of the Member States.

Article 147

Meetings of the Council shall be called by the President acting on his own initiative or at the request of a member or of the Commission.

Article 148

1. Except where otherwise provided for in this Treaty, the conclusions of the Council shall be reached by a majority vote of its members.

2. Where conclusions of the Council require a qualified majority, the votes of its members shall be weighted as follows:

Belgium	2
Germany	4
France	4
Italy	4
Luxembourg	1
Netherlands	2

Majorities shall be required for the adoption of any conclusions as follows:

- twelve votes in cases where this Treaty requires a previous proposal of the Commission, or

- twelve votes including a favourable vote by at least four
  members in all other cases.

3.   Abstentions by members either present or represented
shall not prevent the adoption of Council conclusions requiring
unanimity.

Article 149

When, pursuant to this Treaty, the Council acts on a proposal of the Commission, it shall, where the amendment of
such proposal is involved, act only by means of a unanimous
vote.

As long as the Council has not so acted, the Commission
may amend its original proposal, particularly in cases where
the Assembly has been consulted on the proposal concerned.

Article 150

In case of a vote, any member of the Council may act
as proxy for not more than one other member.

Article 151

The Council shall adopt its rules of procedure.

These rules of procedure may provide for the establishment of a committee composed of representatives of Member
States. The Council shall determine the task and competence of
that committee.

Article 152

The Council may request the Commission to undertake any
studies which the Council considers desirable for the achievement
of the common objectives, and to submit to it any appropriate proposals.

Article 153

The Council shall, after obtaining the opinion of the Commission, lay down the status of the Committees provided for in this Treaty.

Article 154

The Council, acting by means of a qualified majority vote, shall fix the salaries, allowances and pensions of the President and members of the Commission, and of the President, judges, advocates-general and registrar of the Court of Justice. The Council shall also fix, by means of the same majority, any allowances to be granted in lieu of remuneration.

Structure

President: Federal Republic of Germany (July 1964-December 1964)

Members: Belgium, France, Italy, Luxembourg, Netherlands.

Permanent Representatives of the member states:

Belgium   Ambassador Joseph VAN DER MEULEN

    62 rue Belliard, Brussels Tel: 13.45.70

F.R. Germany Ambassador Gunther HARKORT

    64-66 rue Royale, Brussels Tel: 13.45.00

France   Ambassador Jean-Marc BOEGNER

    42 boulevard du Regent, Brussels Tel:13.64.45

Italy   Ambassador Antonio VENTURINI

    62 rue Belliard, Brussels Tel: 13.40.70

Luxembourg Ambassador Albert BORSCHETTE

    75 avenue de Cortenberg, Brussels Tel: 35.20.60

Netherlands Ambassador D.P. SPIERENBURG

    62 rue Belliard, Brussels Tel: 13.44.80

General Secretariat:

Christian CALMES   Secretary General

Divisions: A.   Administration, budget, general services, translation.

B.   Institutional, political, economic, financial, agricultural and social questions, documentation.

C.   Common market in steel, general industrial common market, transport.

D.   Traditional forms of energy, nuclear energy.

E.   Commercial and tariff policy, OECD countries, overseas states and territories.

Addresses:

2 rue Ravenstein, Brussels Tel: 13.40.20

3-5 rue Auguste-Lumiere, Luxembourg Tel: 2.18.21

2.3 THE COMMISSION

Provisions in the EEC Treaty

Article 155

With a view to ensuring the functioning and development of the Common Market, the Commission shall:

ensure the application of the provisions of this Treaty and of the provisions enacted by the institutions of the Community in pursuance thereof;

formulate recommendations or opinions in matters which are the subject of this Treaty, where the latter expressly

70

so provides or where the Commission considers it
necessary;

- under the conditions laid down in this Treaty dispose of a
power of decision of its own and participate in the preparation of acts of the Council and of the Assembly; and

- exercise the competence conferred on it by the Council
for the implementation of the rules laid down by the latter.

Article 156

The Commission shall annually, not later than one month
before the opening of the Assembly session, publish a general
report on the activities of the Community.

Article 157

1.   The Commission shall be composed of nine members
chosen for their general competence and of indisputable independence.

The number of members of the Commission may be
amended by a unanimous vote of the Council.

Only nationals of Member States may be members of the
Commission.

The Commission may not include more than two members
having the nationality of the same State.

2.   The members of the Commission shall perform their
duties in the general interest of the Community with complete
independence.

In the performance of their duties, they shall not seek or
accept instructions from any Government or other body. They
shall refrain from any action incompatible with the character of
their duties. Each Member State undertakes to respect this
character and not to seek to influence the members of the Commission in the performance of their duties.

The members of the Commission may not, during their
terms of office, engage in any other paid or unpaid professional
activity. When entering upon their duties, they shall give a
solemn undertaking that, both during and after their term of

71

office, they will respect the obligations resulting therefrom and in particular the duty of exercising honesty and discretion as regards the acceptance, after their terms of office, of certain functions or advantages. Should these obligations not be respected, the Court of Justice, on the application of the Council or of the Commission, may according to circumstances rule that the member concerned either be removed from office in accordance with the provisions of Article 160 or forfeit his right to a pension or other advantages in lieu thereof.

Article 158

The members of the Commission shall be appointed by the Governments of Member States acting in common agreement.

Their term of office shall be for a period of four years. It shall be renewable.

Article 159

Apart from retirements in regular rotation and the case of death the duties of a member of the Commission shall be terminated in individual cases by voluntary resignation or by removal from office.

Vacancies thus caused shall be filled for the remainder of the term of office. The Council, acting by means of a unanimous vote, may decide that such vacancies need not be filled.

Except in the case of removal from office referred to in Article 160, a member of the Commission shall remain in office until provision has been made for his replacement.

Article 160

If any member of the Commission no longer fulfils the conditions required for the performance of his duties or if he commits a serious offence, the Court of Justice, acting on a petition of the Council or of the Commission, may declare him removed from office.

In such case the Council, acting by means of a unanimous vote, may provisionally suspend the member from his duties and make provision for his replacement pending the ruling of the Court of Justice.

The Court of Justice may, on a petition of the Council or of the Commission, provisionally suspend such member from his duties.

Article 161

The President and the two Vice-Presidents of the Commission shall be appointed from among its members for a term of two years in accordance with the same procedure as that laid down for the appointment of members of the Commission. Their term of office shall be renewable.

Except in the case of an entire renewal of the Commission, such appointments shall be made after the Commission has been consulted.

In the event of resignation or death, the President and the Vice-Presidents shall be replaced for the remainder of their terms of office in accordance with the procedure laid down in the first paragraph of this Article.

Article 162

The Council and the Commission shall consult each other and shall settle by mutual agreement the particulars of their collaboration.

The Commission shall adopt its rules of procedure with a view to ensuring its own functioning and that of its services in accordance with the provisions of this Treaty. It shall be responsible for the publication of its rules of procedure.

Article 163

The conclusions of the Commission shall be reached by a majority of the number of members provided for in Article 157.

A meeting of the Commission shall only be valid if the number of members laid down in its rules of procedure are present.

Article 189

For the achievement of their aims and under the conditions provided for in this Treaty, the Council and the Commission shall adopt regulations and directives, make decisions and formulate recommendations or opinions.

Regulations shall have a general application. They shall be binding in every respect and directly applicable in each Member State.

Directives shall bind any Member State to which they are addressed, as to the result to be achieved, while leaving to domestic agencies a competence as to form and means.

Decisions shall be binding in every respect for the addressees named therein.

Recommendations and opinions shall have no binding force.

Article 190

The regulations, directives and decisions of the Council and of the Commission shall be supported by reasons and shall refer to any proposals or opinions which are to be obtained pursuant to this Treaty.

Article 191

The regulations shall be published in the Official Gazette of the Community. They shall enter into force on the date fixed in them or, failing this, on the twentieth day following their publication.

Directives and decisions shall be notified to their addressees and shall take effect upon such notification.

Article 192

Decisions of the Council or of the Commission which contain a pecuniary obligation on persons other than States shall be enforceable.

Forced execution shall be governed by the rules of civil procedure in force in the State in whose territory it takes place. The writ of execution shall be served, without other formality than the verification of the authenticity of the written act, by the domestic authority which the Government of each Member State shall designate for this purpose and of which it shall give notice to the Commission and to the Court of Justice.

After completion of these formalities at the request of the party concerned, the latter may, in accordance with municipal law, proceed with such forced execution by applying directly to the authority which is competent.

Forced execution may only be suspended pursuant to a decision of the Court of Justice. Supervision as to the regularity of the measures of execution shall, however, be within the competence of the domestic courts or tribunals.

Structure

		Responsibilities
President	Walter HALLSTEIN	General, Administration
Vice-President	Sicco MANSHOLT	Agriculture
Vice-President	Robert MARJOLIN	Economic and Financial Affairs
Vice-President	Lionello LEVI SANDRI	Social Affairs
Member	Jean REY	External Affairs
Member	Hans von der GROEBEN	Competition
Member	Lambert SCHAUS	Transport
Member	Henri ROCHEREAU	Development of Overseas Areas
Member	Guido COLONNA DI PALIANO	Internal Market

Executive Secretariat of the Commission: Emile NOEL
Executive Secretary

External Relations General Directorate: Axel HERBST
General Director

Directorates for: General affairs; multilateral trade policy; Relations with European countries; Relations with Developing countries; General commercial policy; Special projects and negotiations.

GATT Liaison Office(Geneva); OECD Liaison Office (Paris)

Special Commission Representative GATT Negotiations: Theordorus HIJZEN.

75

Economic and Financial Affairs General Directorate: Franco
BOBBA General Director

Directorates for: National economies and economic situa-

tion; Monetary problems; Structure and Economic Develop-

ment.

Internal Market General Directorate: Pierre MILLET General
Director

Directorates for: Movement of goods; Customs problems;

Right of establishment and services; Industry, handicrafts

and commerce.

Competition General Directorate: Pieter VERLOREN van
THEMAAT General Director

Directorates for: Ententes, monopolies, dumping; Approxi-

mation of legislation; Fiscal problems; States aids and dis-

crimination by states.

Social Problems General Directorate: Jose D. NEIRINCK
General Director

Directorates for: Social policy; Manpower; Social fund

and occupational training; Social security and social

services.

Agriculture General Directorate: Louis Georges RABOT
General Director

Directorates for: General affairs; Organization of markets

in crop products; Organization of markets in livestock pro-

ducts; Organization of markets in specialized crops,

fisheries and forestry; Agricultural structure; Agricultural economy and legislation.

Transport General Directorate: Bruno MINOLETTI General
Director

Directorates for: General affairs; Development and mod-

ernization; Transport rates.

Overseas Development General Directorate: Heinrich HENDUS
General Director

Directorates for: General Affairs; Research and develop-

ment programmes; Financial and technical directorate of

the Development Fund; Trade.

Administration General Directorate: Bernard M. SMULDERS
General Director

Directorates for: Personnel; Budget and Finance; Internal

matters.

Official Spokesman: Beniamino OLIVI

Address(provisional): 23-27 avenue de la Joyeuse Entree,
Brussels Tel: 35.00.40

2.4 THE COURT OF JUSTICE

Provisions in the EEC Treaty

Article 164

The Court of Justice shall ensure observance of laws and
justice in the interpretation and application of this Treaty.

Article 165

The Court of Justice shall be composed of seven judges.

The Court of Justice shall sit in plenary session. It may,
however set up chambers, each composed of three or five judges,

in order either to conduct certain enquiries or to judge certain categories of cases in accordance with provisions to be laid down in rules for this purpose.

The Court of Justice shall, however, always sit in plenary session in order to hear cases submitted to it by a Member State or by one of the institutions of the Community or to deal with preliminary questions submitted to it pursuant to Article 177.

Should the Court of Justice so request, the Council may, by means of a unanimous vote, increase the number of judges and make the requisite amendments to the second and third paragraphs of this Article and to Article 167, second paragraph.

Article 166

The Court of Justice shall be assisted by two advocates-general.

The duty of the advocate-general shall be to present publicly, with complete impartiality and independence, reasoned conclusions on cases submitted to the Court of Justice with a view to assisting the latter in the performance of its duties as laid down in Article 164.

Should the Court of Justice so request, the Council may, by means of a unanimous vote, increase the number of advocates-general and make the requisite amendments to Article 167, third paragraph.

Article 167

The judges and the advocates-general shall be chosen from among persons of indisputable independence who fulfil the conditions required for the holding of the highest judicial office in their respective countries or who are jurists of recognised competence; they shall be appointed for a term of six years by the Governments of Member States acting in common agreement.

A partial renewal of the Court of Justice shall take place every three years. It shall affect three and four judges alternately. The three judges whose terms of office are to expire at the end of the first period of three years shall be chosen by lot.

A partial renewal of the advocates-general shall take place every three years. The advocate-general whose term of office is to expire at the end of the first period of three years shall be chosen by lot.

The retiring judges and advocates-general shall be elibible for reappointment.

The judges shall appoint from among their members the President of the Court of Justice for a term of three years. Such term shall be renewable.

Article 168

The Court of Justice shall appoint its registrar and determine his status.

Article 169

If the Commission considers that a Member State has failed to fulfil any of its obligations under this Treaty, it shall give a reasoned opinion on the matter after requiring such State to submit its comments.

If such State does not comply with the terms of such opinion within the period laid down by the Commission, the latter may refer the matter to the Court of Justice.

Article 170

Any Member State which considers that another Member State has failed to fulfil any of its obligations under this Treaty may refer the matter to the Court of Justice.

Before a Member State institutes, against another Member State, proceedings relating to an alleged infringement of the obligations under this Treaty, it shall refer the matter to the Commission.

The Commission shall give a reasoned opinion after the States concerned have been required to submit their comments in written and oral pleadings.

If the Commission, within a period of three months after the dates of reference of the matter to it, has not given an opinion, reference to the Court of Justice shall not thereby be prevented.

Article 171

If the Court of Justice finds that a Member State has failed to fulfil any of its obligations under this Treaty, such State shall take the measures required for the implementation of the judgement of the Court.

Article 172

The regulations laid down by the Council pursuant to the provisions of this Treaty may confer on the Court of Justice full jurisdiction in respect of penalties provided for in such regulations.

Article 173

The Court of Justice shall review the lawfulness of acts other than recommendations or opinions of the Council and the Commission. For this purpose, it shall be competent to give judgement on appeals by a Member State, the Council or the Commission on grounds of incompetence, of errors of substantial form, of infringement of this Treaty or of any legal provision relating to its application, or of abuse of power.

Any natural or legal person may, under the same conditions, appeal against a decision addressed to him or against a decision which, although in the form of a regulation or a decision addressed to another person, is of direct and specific concern to him.

The appeals provided for in this Article shall be lodged within a period of two months dating, as the case may be, either from the publication of the act concerned or from its notification to the appellant or, failing that, from the day on which the latter had knowledge of that act.

Article 174

If the appeal is well founded, the Court of Justice shall declare the act concerned to be null and void.

In the case of regulations, however, the Court of Justice shall, if it considers it necessary, indicate those effects of the regulation annulled which shall be deemed to remain in force.

Article 175

In the event of the Council or the Commission in violation of this Treaty failing to act, the Member States and the other institutions of the Community may refer the matter to the Court of Justice with a view to establishing such violation.

Such appeal shall only be admissible if the institution concerned has previously been invited to act. If, at the expiry of a period of two months after such invitation that institution has not stated its attitude, the appeal may be lodged within a further period of two months.

Any natural or legal person may submit to the Court of Justice, under the conditions laid down in the preceding paragraphs, a complaint to the effect that one of the institutions of the Community has failed to address to him an act other than a recommendation or an opinion.

Article 176

An institution originating an act subsequently declared null and void or an institution whose failure to act has been declared contrary to the provisions of this Treaty shall take the measures required for the implementation of the judgement of the Court of Justice.

This obligation shall not affect any obligation arising from the application of Article 215, second paragraph.

Article 177

The Court of Justice shall be competent to make a preliminary decision concerning:

(a) the interpretation of this Treaty;

(b) the validity and interpretation of acts of the institutions of the Community; and

(c) the interpretation of the statutes of any bodies set up by an act of the Council, where such statutes so provide.

Where any such question is raised before a court or tribunal of one of the Member States, such court or tribunal may, if it considers that its judgement depends on a preliminary de-

cision on this question, request the Court of Justice to give
a ruling thereon.

Where any such question is raised in a case pending before a domestic court or tribunal from whose decisions no
appeal lies under municipal law, such court or tribunal shall
refer the matter to the Court of Justice.

Article 178

The Court of Justice shall be competent to hear cases
relating to compensation for damage as provided for in Article
215, second paragraph.

Article 179

The Court of Justice shall be competent to decide in any
case between the Community and its employees, within the
limits and under the conditions laid down by the relevant statute
of service or conditions of employment.

Article 180

The Court of Justice shall be competent, within the limits
laid down below, to hear cases concerning:

(a)   the fulfilment by Member States of the obligations
      arising under the Statute of the European Investment
      Bank. The Board of Directors of the Bank shall, in
      this respect, dispose of the powers conferred upon
      the Commission by Article 169;

(b)   the conclusions of the Board of Governors of the
      Bank. Any Member State, the Commission or the
      Board of Directors of the Bank may lodge an appeal
      in this matter under the conditions laid down in
      Article 173; and

(c)   the conclusions of the Board of Directors of the
      Bank. Appeals against such conclusions may be
      lodged, under the conditions laid down in Article 173,
      provided that they may only be lodged by a Member
      State or by the Commission, and only on the grounds
      of an infringement of formal procedures laid down
      in Article 21, paragraph 2 and paragraphs 5 to 7 in-
      clusive of the Statute of the Bank.

Article 181

The Court of Justice shall be competent to make a decision pursuant to any arbitration clause contained in a contract concluded, under public or private law, by or on behalf of the Community.

Article 182

The Court of Justice shall be competent to decide in any dispute between Member States in connection with the object in this Treaty, where such dispute is submitted to it under the terms of a compromise.

Article 183

Subject to the powers conferred on the Court of Justice by this Treaty, cases to which the Community is a party shall not for that reason alone be excluded from the competence of domestic courts or tribunals.

Article 184

Where a regulation of the Council or of the Commission is the subject of a dispute in legal proceedings, any of the parties concerned may, notwithstanding the expiry of the period laid down in Article 173, first paragraph, in order to allege before the Court of Justice that the regulation concerned is inapplicable.

Article 185

Appeals submitted to the Court of Justice shall not have any staying effect. The Court of Justice may, however, if it considers that circumstances so require, order the suspension of the execution of the act appealed against.

Article 186

The Court of Justice may, in any cases referred to it, make any necessary interim order.

Article 187

The judgements of the Court of Justice shall be enforceable under the conditions laid down in Article 192.

Article 188

The Statute of the Court of Justice shall be laid down in a separate Protocol.

The Court of Justice shall adopt its rules of procedure. They shall be submitted to the Council for unanimous approval.

Structure

President:	Andreas M. DONNER

First Chamber

President:	Alberto TRABUCCHI
Judges:	Louis DELVAUX
	Walter STRAUSS
Advocate-General:	Maurice LAGRANGE

Second Chamber

President:	Charles Leon HAMMES
Judges:	Rino ROSSI
	Robert LECOURT
Advocate-General:	Karl ROEMER
Registrar:	Albert VAN HOUTTE

Address: 12 rue de la Cote-d'Eich, Luxembourg   Tel: 2.15.21

2.5 THE ECONOMIC AND SOCIAL COMMITTEE

Provisions in the EEC Treaty

Article 193

There shall hereby be established an Economic and Social Committee with consultative status.

The Committee shall be composed of representatives of

the various categories of economic and social life, in particular, representatives of producers, agriculturists, transport operators, workers, merchants, artisans, the liberal professions and of the general interest.

Article 194

The number of members of the Committee shall be fixed as follows:

Belgium	12
Germany	24
France	24
Italy	24
Luxembourg	5
Netherlands	12

The members of the Committee shall be appointed for a term of four years by the Council acting by means of a unanimous vote. This term shall be renewable.

The members of the Committee shall be appointed in their personal capacity and shall not be bound by any mandatory instructions.

Article 195

1.   With a view to the appointment of the members of the Committee, each Member State shall send to the Council a list containing twice as many candidates as there are seats allotted to its nationals.

The Committee shall be composed in such a manner as to secure adequate representation of the different categories of economic and social life.

2.   The Council shall consult the Commission. It may obtain the opinion of European organisations representing the various economic and social sectors concerned in the activities of the Community.

Article 196

The Committee shall appoint from among its members its chairman and officers for a term of two years.

It shall adopt its rules of procedure and shall submit
them for approval to the Council which shall act by means
of a unanimous vote.

The Committee shall be convened by its chairman at the
request of the Council or of the Commission.

Article 197

The Committee shall include specialized sections for the
main fields covered by this Treaty.

It shall contain, in particular, an agricultural section and
and a transport section, which are the subject of special provisions included in the Titles relating to agriculture and transport.

These specialized sections shall operate within the framework of the general competence of the Committee. They may
not be consulted independently of the Committee.

Sub-committees may also be established within the Committee in order to prepare, in specific matters or fields,
draft opinions to be submitted to the Committee for consideration.

The rules of procedure shall determine the particulars
of the composition of, and the rules of competence concerning
the specialized sections and sub-committees.

Article 198

The Committee shall be consulted by the Council or by
the Commission in the cases provided for in this Treaty. The
Committee may be consulted by these institutions in all cases
in which they deem it appropriate.

The Council or the Commission shall, if it considers it
necessary, lay down for the submission by the Committee of its
opinion a time-limit which may not be less than ten days after
the communication has been addressed to the chairman for this
purpose. If, on the expiry of such time-limit, an opinion has
not been submitted, the Council or the Commission may
proceed without it.

The opinion of the Committee and that of the specialized
section, together with a record of the deliberations, shall be

transmitted to the Council and to the Commission.

President: Piero GIUSTINIANI

Special sections for: agriculture, economic questions, transport, social questions,non-salaried activities and services, overseas states, and territories, nuclear labor and health problems and instruction, nuclear economic problems.

Secretary General: Jacques GENTON

Address: 3 Bd. de l'Empereur, Brussels Tel: 12.39.20

2.6 THE EUROPEAN INVESTMENT BANK

Provisions in the EEC Treaty

Article 129

A European Investment Bank having legal personality shall hereby be established.

The members of the European Investment Bank shall be the Member States.

The Statute of the European Investment Bank shall form the subject of a Protocol annexed to the Treaty.

Article 130

The task of the European Investment Bank shall be to contribute, by calling on the capital markets and its own resources, to the balanced and smooth development of the Common Market in the interest of the Community. For this purpose, the Bank shall by granting loans and guarantees on a non-profit-making basis facilitate the financing of the following projects in all sectors of the economy:

(a)   projects for developing less developed regions,

(b)   projects for modernising or converting enterprises or for creating new activities which are called for by the progressive establishment of the Common Market where such projects by their size or nature cannot be entirely financed by the various means available in each of the Member States; and

(c)   projects of common interest to several Member States which by their size or nature cannot be entirely financed by the various means available in each of the Member States.

President: Paride FORMENTINI

Address (provisional): 11 Mont des Arts, Brussels   Tel: 13.40.00

2.7 MONETARY COMMITTEE

Provisions in the EEC Treaty

Article 105(2)

2.   In order to promote the co-ordination of the policies of Member States in monetary matters to the full extent necessary for the functioning of the Common Market, a Monetary Committee with consultative status shall hereby be established with the following tasks:

-    to keep under review the monetary and financial situation of Member States and of the Community and also the general payments system of Member States and to report regularly thereon to the Council and to the Commission; and

-    to formulate opinions, at the request of the Council or of the Commission or on its own initiative, for submission to the said institutions.

The Member States and the Commission shall each appoint two members of the Monetary Committee.

Article 107

1.   Each Member State shall treat its policy with regard to exchange rates as a matter of common interest.

2.   If a Member State alters its exchange rate in a manner which is incompatible with the objectives laid down in Article 104 and which seriously distorts the conditions of competition, the Commission may, after consulting the Monetary Committee, authorize other Member States to take for a strictly limited period the necessary measures, of which it shall determine the conditions and particulars, in order to deal with the consequences of such alteration.

Article 108

1.   Where a Member State is in difficulties or seriously threatened with difficulties as regards its balance of payments as a result either of overall disequilibrium of the balance of payments or of the kinds of currency at its disposal and where such difficulties are likely, in particular, to prejudice the functioning of the Common Market or the progressive establishment of the common commercial policy, the Commission shall without delay examine the situation of such State and the action which, in making use of all the means at its disposal, that State has taken or may take in conformity with the provisions of Article 104.   The Commission shall indicate the measures which it recommends to the State concerned to adopt.

If the action taken by a Member State and the measures suggested by the Commission do not prove sufficient to overcome the difficulties encountered or threatening, the Commission shall after consulting the Monetary Committee, recommend to the Council the granting of mutual assistance and the appropriate methods therefor.

The Commission shall keep the Council regularly informed of the situation and of its development.

Article 109

1.   Where a sudden crisis in the balance of payments occurs and if a decision, within the meaning of Article 108, paragraph 2, is not immediately taken, the Member State concerned may provisionally take the necessary measures of safeguard.   Such measures shall cause the least possible disturbance in the

functioning of the Common Market and shall not exceed the minimum strictly necessary to remedy the sudden difficulties which have arisen.

2.   The Commission and the other Member States shall be informed of such measures of safeguard not later than at the time of their entry into force. The Commission may recommend to the Council mutual assistance under the terms of Article 108.

3.   On the basis of an opinion of the Commission and after consulting the Monetary Committee, the Council, acting by means of a qualified majority vote, may decide that the State concerned shall amend, suspend or abolish the measures of safeguard referred to above.

Article 73

1.   In the event of movements of capital leading to disturbances in the functioning of the capital market in any Member State, the Commission shall, after consulting the Monetary Committee, authorize such State to take, in regard to such movements of capital, protective measures of which the Commission shall determine the conditions and particulars.

The Council, acting by means of a qualified majority vote, may revoke this authorization and may modify such conditions and particulars.

2.   The Member State which is in difficulty may, however, on the ground of their secret or urgent character, itself take the above-mentioned measures if they should become necessary. The Commission and the other Member States shall be informed of such measures not later than at the date of their entry into force. In this case, the Commission may, after consulting the Monetary Committee, decide that the State concerned shall modify or abolish such measures.

Secretary: R. de KERGORLAY

Address: 80 rue d'Arlon, Brussels 4 Tel: 13.67.51

2.8 TRANSPORT COMMITTEE

Provisions in the EEC Treaty

Article 83

A Committee with consultative status, composed of experts appointed by the Governments of Member States, shall be established and attached to the Commission. The latter shall, whenever it deems it desirable, consult this Committee on transport questions, without prejudice to the competence of the transport section of the Economic and Social Committee.

2.9 EUROPEAN SOCIAL FUND

(part of Commission General Directorate for Social Affairs)

Provisions in the EEC Treaty

Article 123

In order to improve opportunities of employment of workers in the Common Market and thus contribute to raising the standard of living, a European Social Fund shall hereby be established in accordance with the provision set out below; it shall have the task of promoting within the Community employment facilities and the geographical and occupational mobility of workers.

Article 124

The administration of the Fund shall be incumbent on the Commission.

The Commission shall be assisted in this task by a Committee presided over by a member of the Commission and composed of representatives of Governments, trade unions and employers associations.

Article 125

1.   At the request of a Member State, the Fund shall, within the framework of the rules provided for in Article 127, cover 50 per cent of expenses incurred after the entry into force of this Treaty by that State or by a body under public law for the purpose of:

(a) ensuring productive re-employment of workers by means of:

-        occupational re-training,

-        resettlement allowances; and

(b)   granting aids for the benefit of workers whose employment is temporarily reduced or wholly or partly suspended as a result of the conversion of their enterprise to other productions, in order that they may maintain the same wage-level pending their full re-employment.

2.   The assistance granted by the Fund towards the cost of occupational re-training shall be conditional upon the impossibility of employing the unemployed workers otherwise than in a new occupation and upon their having been in productive employment for a period of at least six months in the occupation for which they have been re-trained.

The assistance granted in respect of resettlement allowances shall be conditional upon the unemployed workers having been obliged to change their residence within the Community and upon their having been in productive employment for a period of at least six months in their new place of residence.

The assistance given for the benefit of workers in cases where an enterprise is converted shall be subject to the following conditions:

(a)   that the workers concerned have again been fully employed in that enterprise for a period of at least six months;

(b)   that the Government concerned has previously submitted a plan, drawn up by such enterprise, for its conversion and for the financing thereof; and

(c)   that the Commission has given its prior approval to such conversion plan.

Article 126

At the expiry of the transitional period, the Council, on the basis of an opinion of the Commission and after the Economic and Social Committee and the Assembly have consulted, may:

(a)   acting by means of a qualified majority vote, rule that all or part of the assistance referred to in Article 125 shall no longer be granted; or

(b)   acting by means of a unanimous vote, determine
the new tasks which may be entrusted to the Fund within the
framework of its mandate as defined in Article 123.

Article 127

On a proposal of the Commission and after the Economic
and Social Committee and the Assembly have been consulted, the
Council, acting by means of a qualified majority vote, shall lay down
the provisions necessary for the implementation of Articles 124 to
126 inclusive; in particular, it shall fix details concerning the
conditions under which the assistance of the Fund shall be granted
in accordance with the terms of Article 125 and also concerning
the categories of enterprises whose workers shall benefit from
the aids provided for in Article 125, paragraph 1 (b).

Article 128

The Council shall, on a proposal of the Commission and after
the Economic and Social Committee has been consulted, establish
general principles for the implementation of a common policy of
occupational training capable of contributing to the harmonious development both of national economies and of the Common Market.

2.10 OVERSEAS DEVELOPMENT FUND

(part of Commission General Directorate for Overseas Development)

Provisions in the EEC Treaty

Implementing Convention Relating to the Association with the
Community of the Overseas Countries and Territories

THE HIGH CONTRACTING PARTIES,

DESIROUS of establishing the Implementing Convention
provided for in Article 136 of this Treaty,

HAVE AGREED upon the following provisions which shall
be annexed to this Treaty:

Article 1

The Member States shall, under the conditions determined

93

below and by means of efforts complementary to those made by the responsible authorities of the countries and territories listed in Annex IV to this Treaty, participate in any measure suitable for the promotion of social and economic development of those countries and territories.

For this purpose, a Development Fund for the overseas countries and territories shall hereby be set up, into which the Member States shall, during a period of five years, pay the annual contributions provided for in Annex A to this Convention.

The Fund shall be administered by the Commission.

Article 2

The responsible authorities of the countries and territories shall, in agreement with the local authorities or with the representatives of the populations of the countries and territories concerned, submit to the Commission any social or economic projects for which financing by the Community is requested.

Article 3

The Commission shall annually draw up general programmes in which the funds available in accordance with Annex B to this Convention shall be allocated to the different categories of projects.

Such general programmes shall contain projects for financing:

(a) certain social institutions, in particular, hospitals, teaching or technical research establishments and institutions for vocational training and for the promotion of professional activities among the populations; and

(b) economic investments of general interest directly connected with the implementation of a programme including productive and specific development projects.

Article 4

At the beginning of each financial year, the Council, acting by means of a qualified majority vote after consulting the Commission, shall determine the amounts to be devoted to the financing of:

(a) the social institutions referred to in Article 3(a); and

(b) the economic investments of general interest referred to in Article 3(b).

The Council shall, in taking its decision, aim at a distribution of the amounts available on a rational geographical basis.

Article 5

1. The Commission shall determine the distribution of the amounts available in accordance with Article 4 (a) between the various requests received for the financing of social institutions.

2. The Commission shall draw up proposals for financing those economic investment projects which it approves in accordance with Article 4(b).

It shall communicate these proposals to the Council.

If, within a period of one month, no Member State requests that such proposals be considered by the Council, they shall be regarded as approved.

If such proposals are considered by the Council, the latter shall act by means of a qualified majority vote within a period of two months.

3. Any amounts not allocated during any one year shall be carried forward to the following years.

4. The amounts allocated shall be made available to the authorities responsible for carrying out the work concerned. The Commission shall ensure that such amounts are utilised in accordance with the purposes decided upon and expended to the best economic advantage.

Article 6

The Council, acting by means of a qualified majority vote on a proposal of the Commission, shall, within a period of six months after the entry into force of this Treaty, lay down the particulars as to calls for and transfers of financial contributions, budgeting and the administration of the resources of the Development Fund.

The qualified majority referred to in Article 4, 5 and 6 shall be 67 votes. The Member States shall have the following number of votes:

Belgium	11
Germany	33
France	33
Italy	11
Luxembourg	1
Netherlands	11

Article 8

The right of establishment shall, in each of the countries or territories, be extended progressively to nationals and companies of Member States other than the State having special relations with the country or territory concerned. Particulars of such extension shall be determined, in the course of the first year of application of this Convention, by the Council, acting by means of a qualified majority vote on a proposal of the Commission, in such a manner that any discrimination progressively disappears in the course of the transitional period.

2.11 FOREIGN TRADE COMMITTEE (ARTICLE 111)

(secretariat in Commission General Directorate for Internal Market)

Provisions in the EEC Treaty

Article 111

2. The Commission shall submit to the Council recommendations with a view to tariff negotiations with the third countries concerning the common customs tariff.

The Council shall authorize the Commission to open such negotiations.

The Commission shall conduct these negotiations in consultation with a special Committee appointed by the Council to assist the Commission in this task and within the framework of such directives as the Council may issue to it.

2.12 LEGAL SERVICE OF THE EUROPEAN EXECUTIVES

General Director for EEC Affairs: Michel GAUDET

Address: 51-53 rue Belliard, Brussels 4 Tel: 13.40.90

2.13 PRESS AND INFORMATION SERVICE OF THE EUROPEAN COMMUNITIES

Director: Jacques-Rene RABIER

Sections for: general affairs, labor information, agricultural information, overseas development information, university information, fairs and expositions, publications, radio-television-films.

Addresses:

244 rue de la Loi, Brussels 4 Tel: 35.00.40

18 rue Aldringer, Luxembourg Tel: Luxembourg(066) 292.41

Offices:

Paris
61 rue des Belles-Feuilles   Tel: KLEber 53-26
Paris 16

Bonn
Zitelmannstrasse 11   Tel: 26.041/42/43
Bonn

Rome
via Poli, 29   Tel: 670.696
Rome   Tel: 681.348
                                          Tel: 688.182

The Hague
Mauritskade 39   Tel: 18.48.15
The Hague

Geneva
72 rue de Lausanne   Tel: 31.87.30
Geneva

London
Chesham Street 23   Tel: BELgravia 49-04
London, S.W. 1

New York
2207 Commerce Building   Tel: MU 2-0458
155 East 44th Street
New York, N.Y. 10017

Washington
Farragut Building 808   Tel: 296-5131
900-17th Street
Washington 6, D.C.

2.14 STATISTICAL OFFICE OF THE EUROPEAN COMMUNITIES

General Director: Rolf WAGENFUHR

Directorates for: general statistics; statistics for energy;

associated overseas states; multicopied statistics; foreign

trade and transport; industrial and craft statistics; social

statistics; agricultural statistics.

Addresses:

188 A, avenue de Tervueren, Brussels 15 Tel: 71.00.90

Hotel Star, Luxembourg Tel: Luxembourg(066) 408.41

51-53 rue Belliard, Brussels 4 Tel: 13.40.90

CHAPTER **3**

EXTERNAL RELATIONS

The European Economic Community, one of the largest economic units in the world, has developed an extensive "foreign policy." The External Relations General Directorate is responsible for the execution of this policy under the guidance of the Commission and along lines laid down by the Council.

The Community's common external tariff is the basic factor in the Community's trade relations with non-member countries. The six EEC members are pledged to harmonize their tariffs on the basis of the arithmetical average of the four national tariff systems (Benelux, France, Germany, Italy) which existed before 1958. The method of adjustment is described in Chapter 6. Under the Common External Tariff some traditionally high European tariffs are being lowered. Lower tariffs are expected to be increased by a lesser amount since the Community has already made some reductions in the Dillon Round of tariff negotiations in the framework of the General Agreement on Tariffs and Trade and expects to make even greater reductions in the Kennedy Round.

Over sixty countries have established diplomatic relations with the EEC. Missions have been established in Brussels permitting continuous contact between high ranking economic and political officials of the major nations of the world and the staff of the Community. Conversations on matters of mutual interest can be scheduled with ease; in 1963 the Latin American representatives held a series of discussions with Commission officials on proposed Community policy in their region.

The following countries have established diplomatic relations with the EEC:

Associated states- Burundi,   Cameroon, Central African

Republic, Chad, Congo (Brazzaville), Congo (Leopoldville), Dahomey, Gabon, Ivory Coast, Madagascar, Mali, Mauritania, Niger, Rwanda, Senegal, Somalia, Togo, Upper Volta;

Other states- Algeria, Argentina, Australia, Austria, Brazil, Canada, Ceylon, Chile, Colombia, Costa Rica, Denmark, the Dominican Republic, Ecuador, El Salvador, Greece, Guatemala, Haiti, Iceland, India, Iran, Ireland, Israel, Jamaica, Japan, Lebanon, Mexico, Morocco, New Zealand, Nigeria, Norway, Pakistan, Peru, Portugal, Spain, Sweden, Switzerland, Thailand, Trinidad and Tobago, Tunisia, Turkey, South Africa, South Korea, the United Kingdom, the United States, Uruguay, Venezuela.

The EEC reached several important agreements through its bilateral contacts. It has concluded trade agreements with Iran and Israel (see documents). In agreement with the United Kingdom it has suspended customs duties on tea, mate and tropical woods in order to facilitate Indian exports of these products. It has also suspended or reduced duties on other important Indian exports: ginger, curry, capiscum pigments and cashew nuts.

The EEC has expanded its relations with other multilateral organizations. The closest possible relations are maintained with the European Coal and Steel Community and Euratom, especially on such common matters as institutional arrangements and energy policy. Article 230 of the Rome Treaty requires that the EEC should "establish suitable cooperation with the Council of Europe." In practice, the General Report is forwarded to the Council of Europe and is debated in the Consultative Assembly. Joint meetings between the European Parliament and the Consultative Assembly are scheduled each year. Article 231 calls for "close collaboration" with the Organization for European Economic Cooperation. When the OEEC was transformed into the Organization for Economic Cooperation and Development, a new agreement was reached by both organizations permitting Community representatives to take part in OECD deliberations. A permanent EEC representative to the OECD has been stationed at OECD headquarters. As a major donor of foreign aid, the EEC is an active participant in the work of the OECD Development Assistance Group.

The principal EEC activity in the United Nations has been its participation in the U.N. Conference on Trade and Development held in Geneva March - June 1964. Speaking on behalf of the Community, both the President of the Council and the Commission representative explained the EEC's policies and made constructive contributions to the discussions.

The multilateral arrangement with which the EEC has been most concerned is, of course, the General Agreement on Tariffs and Trade (GATT). In establishing its common external tariff, the EEC had to obtain the consent of the GATT parties and, in some cases, to offer compensations when tariffs were increased. These adjustments were completed in the Dillon Round of negotiations which ended in 1962. The net result of the adoption of the common external tariff was a greater trade liberalization throughout GATT. The aim of the Kennedy Round of negotiations, which began in 1964, is an even greater trade liberalization through lower tariffs and non-tariff barriers, fewer restrictions on agricultural trade and special arrangements for the developing countries.

3.1 COMMON COMMERCIAL POLICY

The Common Commercial Policy*

93.　The capital importance of co-ordinating the trade
policies of the Member States, in particular with respect
to low-wage or State-trading countries, rapidly became
apparent. With a view to implementing Article 111 of the
Treaty on the co-ordination of the trade relations of the
Member States with non-member countries, the Commission as early as 1959 undertook a number of studies on
the contractual obligations of the Member States.

　　　On 20 July 1960 a first Council decision, made on a
Commission recommendation, stipulated that in trade
agreements with non-member countries Member States
must arrange for the insertion of an EEC clause whereby
any amendments to such agreements made necessary by
obligations under the Treaty of Rome may be negotiated
without delay.

　　　On 25 July 1961 the Council took two decisions proposed by the Commission: the first concerned a procedure
for consultation on the negotiation of agreements relating
to trade between Member States and non-member countries
and changes in liberalization arrangements vis-a-vis these
countries, and the second concerned uniformity in the duration of trade agreements with non-member countries.

　　　The first decision introduces a systematic procedure
for reciprocal information on any negotiations for trade
agreements undertaken by the Member States and for consultations on all the terms of such agreements; the second
decision restricts the duration of trade agreements to the
transition period under the Treaty and fixes at one year the
maximum duration for agreements which include neither an
EEC clause nor a clause providing that the agreement may
be denounced any year. These two decisions provide solid
foundations for an approximation of the trade policies of the
Member States and a transition towards the common trade
policy.

94.　Independently of the Council's formal decisions, other
steps are being taken towards this same end. Thus the
Member States have become more and more accustomed to
consulting among themselves and with the Commission and

to having a single spokesman in international bodies on these matters, showing that it is their intention to propound a uniform Community policy.

One of the most striking examples was the attitude adopted by the Member States and the Commission at the international conference on trade in cotton textiles held in Geneva, at the instance of the United States Government and in the framework of GATT, from 17 to 21 July 1961. The parties to this conference decided to conclude a short-term agreement and to prepare a long-term agreement on opening the markets of certain industrialized countries to imports of low-price cotton goods, while avoiding any disruption of markets in the importing countries.

To sum up in a few words the Commission's course of action in keeping national trade policies under review, in making proposals for approximating those policies and in the decisions taken, it may be said that the aim of the Treaty -- that the commercial policy of the Community shall contribute to "the harmonious development of world trade, the progressive abolition of restrictions on international exchanges"--has been unremittingly pursued.

But the Community's commercial policy must also pay due heed to the economic situation of the various non-member countries. This means a differentiation of attitude towards industrialized countries and developing countries, countries in and outside GATT and in particular the State-trading countries, whose trade presents special problems because of its strict bilateralism and the fact that it is designed to serve the aims of national planning.

Finally, on a special plane, future trade co-operation with the developing countries poses specific problems which have engaged the attention of the Commission, particularly from the angle of finding possible ways of increasing the consumption of basic products in Community countries so as to stabilize the incomes of the developing countries and to ensure a better division of labor throughout the world.

Under the Treaty the Community must apply a common commercial policy vis-a-vis non-member countries at the latest by the end of the transition period. The Commission has always considered that this common policy was indispensable for an effective merging of markets within the Community. The common commercial policy is also a corollary to this merging of markets. The extensive work already accomplished with a view to better co-ordination of the national policies is therefore only a stage towards the more far-reaching integration which will give the Community its definitive image in the eyes of the outside world.

95.   The need for a common policy that will take account of special conditions in the various non-member countries or groups of non-member countries and of their relations with Member States has led the Community:

i)   To set up its own information system, with the assistance of Member States' diplomatic posts outside the Community working in conjunction;

ii)   Thanks to the information thus obtained, to form an idea of the relative importance of the problems raised by each of these non-member countries or groups of non-member countries (experts of the Member States and of the Commission will meet at regular intervals for this purpose);

iii)   To make a systematic study of the 250 or so economic agreements between Member States to non-member countries.

Arrangements have been made for a regular exchange of information between the Community's institutions and the Governments in the six capitals so as to pursue this study in the light of the constant development of individual situations.

————————

* The First Stage of the Common Market: Report on the Execution of the Treaty (January 1958 - January 1962) pp. 105-108.

Action Programme for a Common Commercial Policy*

263. On the initiative of the Commission, the Council has, in recent years, taken decisions designed to introduce a common commercial policy which, according to Article 111 of the Treaty, must be applied by the end of the transition period. In 1960, there was the insertion of an "EEC clause" in trade agreements between Member States and non-member countries (1); then, in 1961, the establishment of a procedure for consultation on the trade negotiations of

Member States (2) and standardization of the term of trade agreements with non-member countries (2). Both these measures were taken on the basis of proposals in the first memorandum on commercial policy drawn up by the Commission.

On 25 September 1962 (3) the Council approved a second memorandum which the Commission had submitted to it on 24 March 1962. This new document contains an initial action programme for a common commercial policy, whose objective is to enable the Member States to harmonize their national commercial policies gradually, taking into account the actual problems arising for different products and various geographical areas. In this process due regard must be paid to the objectives of the Treaty itself, i.e. the harmonious development of world trade, the abolition of restrictions and lowering of customs barriers.

The Commission attaches considerable importance to a balanced implementation of this policy. There must in the first place be a balance between the introduction of the common external tariff and the application of other commercial policy measures if serious disturbances are to be avoided. This balance must above all be applied to the development of imports and exports. Likewise, the degree of Community organization already achieved for a large number of agricultural products in the context of the common· agricultural policy means that a common commercial policy has been created for these products. Corresponding progress must be achieved for manufactured products since the Community, which is the world's biggest importer of agricultural products, is also one of its principal exporters of manufactured goods.

The action programme lays down more specifically that the Member States should bring into line their import and export policies. Alignment of import policy must in particular relate to the list of products liberalized in respect of those countries which are members of GATT or other countries having similar economies, to quota policy in trade with countries not belonging to GATT, and to defensive trade measures. Standardization of export arrangements implies harmonization, to the necessary extent, of arrangements for aid to exports to non-member countries, standardization of measures for liberalization of exports and harmonization of efforts directed towards expanding trade in markets outside the Community.

Within the framework of this programme, and with the collaboration of the Member States, the Commission has already made a good start on harmonizing the lists of liberalized products and on adjustments to quota policy, as will be seen below.

---

* Sixth General Report on the Activities of the Community, pp. 238-239.
(1) See Fourth General Report, Chap. IV, sec. 192.
(2) See official gazette of the European Communities, No. 71, 9 October 1961.
(3) See official gazette of the European Communities, No. 90, 5 October 1962.

3.2 IMPORT LIBERALIZATION

Liberalization Measures*

92. It is significant that the liberalization measures vis-a-vis non-member countries taken since 1959 and more particularly in 1960 and 1961 by the Member States, expecially France, and which in a way were the natural corollary to the Community's effort in the tariff field, have had the important side effect of eliminating many divergencies between the national trade policies while strengthening the liberal character of the Community's courses of commercial policy. These measures have smoothed the path for applying Article 111(5) of the Treaty, which provides for bringing into alignment at the highest possible level the Member States' lists of liberalized products in trade with third countries. At the same time they have made it possible to eliminate in substantial measure the discrimination which existed against the dollar area. As regards industrial products, there are only 37 tariff headings in Germany and 9 in Italy for which differences remain. For agricultural products there are differences in only 3 headings in Germany, 1 in France and 9 in Italy. In addition, new liberalization measures have been introduced vis-a-vis other GATT countries and countries not belonging to GATT. This trend is in keeping with the spirit of the decision which the Council took on 12 May 1960 as part of the decision to speed up the implementation of the Treaty of Rome, which provided

for the abolition of quantitative restrictions in the industrial sector of the Common Market by 31 December 1961 and the elimination as soon as possible of restrictions still existing in respect of all the GATT countries. In future more systematic means of bringing about uniformity of liberalization lists in the Member States will be sought through the consultation procedure agreed to by the Council on 25 July 1961 on a proposal from the Commission.

Development of the Liberalization Policy Towards Non-Member Countries*

201.   With effect from May 1961 the Member States again widened the range of liberalized imports from non-member countries. They made a noteworthy effort with regard to the freeing of products from the dollar area, and have almost entirely liberalized imports of industrial products from the countries of what is now OECD. The almost total elimination of discrimination between European and dollar area products is one result of this liberalization policy.

Further advances in liberalization have also been made with regard to other countries, whether members of GATT or not. The quests for solutions to the problem of imports from low-cost countries has been actively pursued both on the plane of bilateral relations between Member States and non-member countries and at Community level. Italy has further liberalized imports from Japan, and France has taken similar action vis-a-vis several of these countries.

This trend is in keeping with the spirit of the Council's decision of 10 May 1960 which provides for the early elimination of the remaining restrictions in respect of GATT countries.

---

*Fifth General Report on the Activities of the Community, pp. 231-232.

Developments in Import Liberalization Policy*

264.   The Member States have considerably increased the number of products whose importation from non-member countries has been liberalized. The efforts already made to liberalize products originating in the dollar area have been continued and the six countries have almost completely liberalized imports of manufactures from the present OECD countries.

Further progress has also been made in relation to
other countries, whether or not members of GATT, and especially Japan. France and Italy in particular have adopted
measures extending their liberalization of imports from
these countries in order to get as close as possible to the
ex-OEEC liberalization (last instalments: Italy, 1 October
1962; France, 4 December 1962).

This process will moreover be continued, in pursuance of the above-mentioned commercial policy provisions
of the action programme, particularly those calling for the
greatest possible standardization of the lists of liberalized
products, in respect of countries belonging to GATT, or
non-member countries which regulate their foreign trade
on the principles of GATT. Before 1 July 1963 the Commission is to address to the Member States recommendations on the standardization of lists of liberalized products
in respect of the ex-OEEC countries and the dollar area.

In accordance with the action programme, the Member States' national quotas and national liberalization lists
in respect of the State-trading countries of the Eastern
bloc are to be replaced by Community procedures.

265. The Cotton Textiles Agreement. In 1962 the Member
States and the Commission took part in the work of the Cotton Textiles Committee which led to the conclusion of a
long-term (5-year) agreement in this field (1). This agreement, which came into force on 1 October 1962, superceded
a provisional agreement which expired on 30 September
1962.

In accordance with the decision taken by the Council
on 24 September 1962, the Member States of the Community
made a declaration on signing the agreement that "should
the obligations flowing from the Treaty establishing the
European Economic Community and relating to the progressive introduction of a common commercial policy make this
necessary, negotiations will be opened as quickly as possible for the purpose of making appropriate modifications to
the present agreement".

---

* Sixth General Report on the Activities of the Commission,
pp. 239-240.
(1) See Fifth General Report, sec. 200.

3.3 PROTECTIVE MEASURES*

96.   In the transition period the Treaty has provided for
measures to alleviate any grave difficulties which might
arise in a Member State, since the cumulative effect of internal tariff and quota disarmament measures, of freedom
for products from non-member States to be moved from
State to State when accompanied by free circulation certificates, and of any divergences between national trade policies which persist in other fields may well be to place certain States in situations where protective measures are
called for.   In such cases the Treaty has provided for recourse to co-operation among the Member States by methods recommended by the Commission; failing this, the Commission may authorize the Member State affected to take
protective measures.   In urgent cases the Treaty provides
that the Member State may itself take protective measures,
but may later be required by the Commission to amend or
withdraw them.

In 1959 and early in 1960, certain Member States
(Germany, France and Italy) made use of the emergency
procedure and excluded from free circulation about 70 products, chiefly from low-wage or State-trading countries.
The Commission recognized that the Governments had
sound reasons for taking such measures, but urged the
Member States in future to follow the normal procedure under Article 115, which provides for prior approval by the
Commission, and not to take emergency action without
showing good cause.

Although one other product (roasted coffee) was the
subject of further protective action by France in 1961, new
liberalization measures introduced since 1959 have reduced
by about 20 the number of products from non-member countries still excluded from Community treatment.

----

* The First Stage of the Common Market: Report on the Execution of the Treaty (January 1958 - January 1962) pp. 108-
109.

3.4 BILATERAL CONTRACTUAL ENGAGEMENTS*

202. As early as 1960, the work undertaken in conjunction

with the Governments of the Member States to lay down the
bases for co-ordination of bilateral relations had issued in
the formulation of an EEC clause (1) for inclusion in any bilateral agreements entered into by Member States. On a
proposal from the Commission the Council on 9 October
1961 took two further decisions important for the future of
bilateral contractual relations.

The first of these decisions established a consultation
procedure for negotiating agreements concerning trade relations of Member States with non-member countries and
for modifying the system of liberalization with regard to the
same countries. In this way a systematic procedure for reciprocal information on all negotiations for commercial
agreements entered upon by Member States and prior consultations on all provisions of such agreements were officially introduced. These consultations take place at the request of a Member State or of the European Commission; in
exceptional cases, where consultations would not be possible, it is provided that an observer from the Commission
may be invited to the negotiations between a Member State
and a non-member country.

The second decision is concerned with standardizing
the duration of trade agreements with non-member countries. It limits the duration of such agreements to the
transition period of the Treaty and fixes a maximum life of
one year for agreements which include neither EEC clause
nor a clause providing for denunciation from year to year.
The Council will be able to authorize exceptions on a proposal from the Commission, but in such cases any quota
lists appended to the agreements would be subject to annual
review. It is also planned to synchronize the expiry dates
of these agreements. The Council's decision also provides
that the Commission shall examine with the Member States,
as soon as possible and in any case by 1 January 1966, all
existing agreements on commercial relations in order to
see that they do not obstruct the inauguration of the common
commercial policy.

The European Commission has been engaged upon an
inventory of commercial agreements and so far has recorded nearly 300 conventions, treaties or agreements of various kinds. This inventory has greatly facilitated joint
study and discussion of the problems facing certain Member States or the Community as a whole. This work has

been done at meetings of government experts in "geographical groups", which have been taking place regularly since
early in 1961.

---

* The First Stage of the Common Market: Report on the Execution of the Treaty (January 1958 - January 1962), pp. 232-
233.
(1) See Fourth General Report, Chap. IV, sec. 192.

3.5 EXPORT POLICY

Export Policy*

Uniform Systems for Exports to Third Countries
203. Article 113 of the Treaty provides that export policy
shall be uniform after the end of the transition period and
Article 111 says that during the transition period the Member States shall co-ordinate their commercial relations
with non-member countries.

The abolition of export restrictions between the Member States provided for in Articles 16 and 34 of the Treaty
by the end of the first stage implies that within the limits of
existing international commitments a uniform attitude should
by now be adopted with regard to non-member countries. If
the abolition of these restrictions within EEC were not accompanied by the introduction of a uniform export system
vis-a-vis non-member countries, the Member States might
have difficulty in obtaining supplies of certain products,
owing to deflection of trade.   Aided by experts from the
member countries the European Commission studied t h e
situation in 1961 and listed a number of products in respect
of which common commercial policy measures vis-a-vis
non-member countries were deemed necessary.   The Commission which on 4 August 1959 had already made a recommendation concerning the export to non-member countries
of certain categories of raw hides, addressed to the Member States, on 20 December 1961, four recommendations in
pursuance of Article 115(1) on the export system to be adopted vis-a-vis non-member countries for the following
products: raw hides (widening of the above-mentioned recommendation to include other categories of hides); certain
types of wood; uncut diamonds; hemp seed; non-ferrous metal scrap.

With the adoption of these measures the export policy of the Member States towards non-member countries is already to a great extent uniform.

Aids for Exports to Non-member Countries

204. In co-operation with the Member States the Commission has continued to list and analyze existing aids with a view to taking the measure of the divergencies between them with respect to both systems of credits and export credit insurance and to aids of a non-financial character (1), all this with a view to possible proposals under Article 112. Furthermore, some progress has been made in the Council towards the solution of problems involved in financial export aids for the developing countries (2).

---

* Fifth General Report on the Activities of the Community, pp. 233-234.
(1) See Chapter II, sec. 57.
(2) See Chapter IV, sec. 180.

Standardization of Export Arrangements*

266. The Member States have acted on the recommendations addressed to them by the Commission early in 1962, on arrangements for exports to non-member countries of raw hides, uncut diamonds, certain types of wood, hemp seed, and non-ferrous metal scrap (1).

The application to these products of measures under the common commercial policy appeared to be desirable in order to prevent the Member States experiencing difficulties (deflection of trade) following the implementation of the provisions of Article 34 of the Treaty relating to the abolition of quantitative restrictions on exports between the Member States.

The Member States and the Commission are to take stock of the situation in this sector before the end of 1963.

---

* Sixth General Report on the Activities of the Community, pp. 240-241.
(1) See Fifth General Report, sec. 203.

Export Aids*

267. As the systems of aids for exports to non-member countries become better known, the necessity of harmonizing the credit-insurance and export-credit schemes operated by the Member States becomes more apparent; differences between these schemes may distort competition between undertakings.

The Commission has turned its attention to certain situations such as drawback of customs and excise duties in Italy on exports of certain products of the engineering industry (Act 103) and certain textile fibres; though the rates applying to intra-Community trade have been appreciably lowered, they remain unchanged in trade with non-member countries (see sec. 49). The same is true of shipbuilding, particularly in the Federal Republic of Germany, where credit measures have been introduced for the sole benefit of exports (see sec. 48). Generally speaking, and particularly since the beginning of the year, the Commission has been considering to what extent aids which are likely in certain circumstances to be abolished in respect of intra-Community exports (medium-term credit facilities, market-research insurance, commercial risk insurance, exchange guarantees, etc.) can be retained and harmonized in respect of exports to non-member countries.

The "Co-ordinating Group for Credit-Insurance, Guarantees and Financial Credits" set up under the aegis of the Council, which made its first report on 14 May 1962, has, in addition to its activities in connection with aid to developing countries, undertaken a twofold task (see sec. 232):

i)   Establishment of procedure for consultation between the Member States on the granting of guarantees and credits in excess of the "Bern Union" standards;

ii)   Harmonization of the terms and conditions of credit insurance with a view to the gradual introduction of a uniform system.

The consultation arrangements proposed by the Co-ordinating Group and approved by the Council came into force at the end of May. The Member States will consult each other whenever one of them -- or an official body in that State -- is considering granting guarantees for export credits or financial credits linked with the supply of home-produced goods and having a duration exceeding five years.

113

has also been made for the exchange of informa-
rning credits granted directly by the Member
dit ceilings and outline agreements. The object
nsultations is to prevent unregulated competition
markets of non-member countries, and to permit the
co-ordination of the Member States' policies vis-a-vis the
developing countries in the field of credits linked with the
purchase of capital goods. The consultation procedure has
functioned satisfactorily and has enabled useful discussions
to be held on many topics. On several occasions the examination of specific cases has led to the adoption of a common attitude.

The work on harmonization of the terms and conditions
of credit insurance has been continued and has given rise to
some important decisions. Thus a convention regulating the
liabilities of credit-insurance organizations in respect of
joint guarantees has been signed, while reciprocal agreements have been reached for covering sub-contracts originating in another country of the Community. But the main
result has been the Co-ordinating Group's adoption in principle of a uniform system of premiums, the ways and means
of which are still under study. The agreements reached on
these points are important milestones in the elaboration of
a model credit-insurance system to which the Member
States will gradually approximate their own credit-insurance systems.

As a result of the introduction of common measures
concerning export refunds on most of the products in which
the market is subject to Community regulations, the Community's common export policy is much more advanced in
the agricultural sector. However, for agricultural products which do not fall under Community regulations the
position is undecided. The general list of State aids in this
sector now in preparation (see sec. 143) will make it possible here also to establish a Community policy.

---

* Sixth General Report on the Activities of the Community,
pp. 241-242.

3.6 AGRICULTURE AND TRADE

Effects of the Common Agricultural Policy
on Community Trade*

268. Since the decisions of 14 January 1962 the Member States can no longer apply the conventional machinery of commercial policy -- customs duties and quotas -- in trade with non-member countries in the products falling under the common organization of markets. As is well known, this machinery has been replaced by a variable levy in principle covering the gap between world prices and the prices fixed for the internal market. Thus, the internal price becomes a factor regulating not only the internal market but also the Community's international agricultural trade.

It would obviously be premature to say what repercussions this new system will have on Member States' trade with non-member countries. The liberalization measures and the abolition of customs duties to which the Member States have agreed are in fact moves towards freer international trade, but the levy system is of too recent date for its effects on that trade to be assessed. In any case, the Commission has always maintained that in this field it will have due regard for the interests of importing or exporting non-member countries, particularly in fixing the prices of the products in question.

In the context of this general policy the Commission has given some thought to the question of how far the liberalization which has taken place should be extended to State-trading countries, and to the possible consequences of such extension. The price manipulation which these countries are able to practise might cause imbalances in their trade with Member States which could not be compensated by the safeguard measures for which provision is made in the regulations. Furthermore the strictly bilateral conditions and the reciprocal granting of quotas which are a feature of trade relations with these countries conflict with the multilateral orientation of the Community's agricultural policy in respect of non-member countries. Consequently the Council, on a proposal of the Commission, authorized the Member States to avail themselves provisionally of the option provided in the agricultural regulations, of waiving the principle of liberalization in respect of the Eastern bloc countries. The arrangement approved by the Council on 24 January 1963 permits the removal of all quantitative restrictions on imports of the products in question from these countries, but this removal is accompanied by a system of control and suspension in the event of disturbance of the market.

As the problems of trade in agricultural products are world problems it would be advisable to seek co-ordination of world markets for these commodities in order to obtain, on the one hand, a fair distribution of rights and obligations and, on the other hand, a better organization of world trade. The Community has already explained its views in this field in connection with the work of GATT; it has urged that limits be set to market interventions, since they distort both import prices and export prices, and has advocated concerted action to aid famine-stricken countries. In the negotiations with Great Britain, it proposed the negotiation of world agreements to promote the stabilization and expansion of trade in agricultural products (see sec. 248).

---

* Sixth General Report on the Activities of the Community, pp. 243-244. See also Chapter 9.

Vice-President Mansholt Visits the United States*

9.   From 4 to 10 April 1963 Vice-President Mansholt was in the United States, where he met President Kennedy and other members of the Administration, and gave a number of lectures. These contacts provided an opportunity to discuss the problems which would have to be faced by the common agricultural policy in connection with the negotiations to be held in GATT as a consequence of the Trade Expansion Act.

In a speech delivered at the National Press Club, Dr Mansholt took issue with French President Charles de Gaulle's concept of Europe, according to which the renaissance of Europe was possible only under the leadership of one nation.

Speaking of the recent Franco-German treaty, Dr. Mansholt said: "We are all glad to see friendship between these two great nations, and we welcome a bilateral treaty that would underline it. But the actual treaty in its present form creates a serious problem. It requires the government of both nations to consult with each other in all matters concerning Common Market affairs and to strive for prior agreement; this treaty obligation quite naturally disturbs the other four members. Looking ahead to 1 January 1966, these two major nations will have the voting strength to block every Community decision in the Common Market's Council of Ministers. Their prior consultation

116

will deny the essential quality of our Community - which is the mutual confidence and equality of all members. ''

Dr Mansholt answered US charges that Community agricultural policy is ''protectionist and inward-looking''. ''You have technology and chemistry to blame for rising European self-sufficiency in agriculture'', he declared, ''not the Common Market''.

Speaking of US complaints regarding Community levies on poultry, Dr Mansholt called attention to the EEC Commission's recent action in recommending a ''moderate'' reduction of the levy, while at the same time describing the small European poultry farmer's difficult position.

Dr Mansholt expressed the hope that, in the trade expansion negotiations, the full range of agricultural barriers to trade could be considered. These would include the Community's price level on wheat and sluice-gate price on poultry, as well as the United States' marketing, production and subsidy policies.

---

*Bulletin of the EEC, June 1963, pp. 18-19.

3.7 TARIFF NEGOTIATIONS

The Community and GATT

The EEC offered in the GATT negotiations proposed in 1958 by Mr. Dillon, then United States Under-Secretary of State, an across-the-board reduction of 20%, subject to reciprocity, in the duties on industrial products shown in the common customs tariff.

If the United States Congress agrees to the President's request for wider tariff-negotiating powers from 1 July 1962 onwards, including the right to offer across-the-board reductions, the breach in tariff walls opened by the Community's offer will rapidly widen(1). Before embarking on the multilateral negotiations proper at the Tariff Conference which opened in Geneva on 1 September 1960, the Commission went through a first phase of negotiations for the replacement, under Article XXIV (6) of GATT, of the former tariff concessions of the Member States by new concessions in the

common tariff. On the conclusion of these negotiations the
Commission reported to the Council, which confirmed on behalf of the Community the agreements signed with seventeen
Contracting Parties. The Commission then fixed the implementing details of the tariff concessions granted to the member
countries under these agreements.

The second phase of the Conference, consisting of multilateral negotiations for new tariff concessions on a reciprocal
basis, opened on 29 May 1961. In view of its offer of a 20%
across-the-board reduction in the common tariff, made in
accordance with the Council's acceleration decision of 12 May
1960, the Commission invited the countries taking part to put
forward offers of substantial concessions which would make
it possible to balance concessions on both sides.

An important stage in the tariff negotiations was completed by the agreement in principle reached in Brussels on
16 January 1962 between the United States and the Commission,
negotiating on behalf of the Community. The agreement covers
both re-negotiations under Article XXIV (6) and concessions to
be exchanged in the multilateral negotiations.

---

(1) See Chapter III.

*The First Stage of the Common Market: Report on the Execu-
tion of the Treaty (January 1958 - January 1962) pp. 102-103.

The Community's Tariff Negotiations*

Re-negotiations Under Article XXIV (6) of GATT
205. The Fourth General Report has described the first stage
of the Tariff Conference organized in the framework of the
General Agreement on Tariffs and Trade (GATT), which
opened in September 1960 and at which the Commission represented the Community and conducted negotiations in conformity
with Article 111 of the Treaty.

In the first stage the Community re-negotiated, under
Article XXIV (6) of the General Agreement, the tariff concessions previously granted by the Member States which
could no longer be maintained by reason of the gradual approximation of national duties towards the common tariff. These re-
negotiations ended in May 1961. The Commission reported to

113

the Council, which in July 1961 approved the agreements reached with 17 countries. The agreements subsequently reached with other countries were submitted to the Council, which formally concluded them.

Under all these agreements the Community grants concessions to offset the withdrawal of those previously accorded by the Member States under their national tariffs. The Community's concessions have taken the form either of a binding of duties under the common customs tariff(i.e. an undertaking not to increase them) or, in the case of 200 tariff headings, of reducing the common tariff duties. In relation to the value of Community imports from GATT countries in 1958 the proportion of binding and reduced duties resulting from the re-negotiations is about 80%, which is not surprising when we consider the often higher percentages of binding in the tariffs of several Member States. By transposing into the common tariff the former concessions of the Member States at a no less favourable level for non-member countries, the Community has fully honoured its obligations under Article XXIV(6) of the General Agreement.

Dillon Negotiations

206. The second stage of the Conference consisted of a series of multilateral negotiations for the exchange of new tariff concessions following the proposal made by Mr. Dillon, then United States Under-Secretary of State, in 1958.

These negotiations opened on 29 May 1961.

The European Commission began by offering an across-the-board reduction of the common customs tariff in the way suggested in the acceleration decision of the Council of Ministers on 12 May 1960. The Community's trading partners, particularly the industrial countries which would substantially benefit from this offer were invited to reciprocate so that there would be a balance of concessions on both sides and the reduction would be definitely bound.

The offer of an across-the-board reduction applied to all the headings of the common customs tariff in respect of which the first approximation of national duties on 1 January 1961 had been effected on the basis of a 20% tariff reduction. It was nevertheless specified that the other headings of the common tariff would not be systematically excluded from the negotiations; the possibility of negotiating on them would have to be determined case by case.

The EEC-USA Agreement

207. By reason of the predominant trading position of the two partners, the negotiations between the Community and the United States represented the corner-stone of the negotiations as a whole. On 7 March 1962 they resulted in the conclusion of a tariff agreement of considerable economic and political importance.

The tariff concessions granted by the Community in the re-negotiations under Article XXIV (6) of the General Agreement during the first stage of the Conference cover approximately the same value of imports as the concessions previously granted by the Member States in their national tariffs. Calculated on the basis of the Community's imports from the United States in 1958 they affect about 1, 500 million dollars' worth of trade.

In the second stage of the negotiations, the Community and the United States made further tariff concessions on a basis of reciprocity and mutual advantage. These covered about 1, 600 million dollars' worth of trade in both directions.

The Community's concessions consist mainly in a reduction of the duties of the common tariff for items of which the United States is the chief supplier. With the exception of certain categories of products excluded from the across-the-board offer, in almost all cases these reductions are in the neighbourhood of the 20% initially offered by the Community. Moreover, in the case of the United States, the Community withdrew its initial offer for certain chemical products as the US delegation was not able, in view of the limits imposed by the tariff laws of the United States, to grant sufficient concessions to ensure reciprocity. Concessions were made to the United States on about 560 tariff lines of the common customs tariff.

Conversely, although it was not possible to negotiate them on the basis of a linear reduction, but product by product, according to the selective method, the tariff reductions granted by the United States to the Community are also generally of the order of 20%, in some cases more, and concern about 575 lines of the US tariff. It should be noted, however, that the reductions granted by the United States are less varied than those granted by EEC and that, generally speaking, the duties under the common tariff are free from any extreme positions such as still exist in the US tariff.

On the other hand, although agricultural products count for little in the agreement reached, the accompanying protocols provide for agreements on wheat and certain coarse grains and for the re-opening of conversations in the near future with a view to finding ways and means to develop trade on a mutually advantageous basis, particularly after the establishment of the common agricultural policy. The products concerned in these arrangements are particularly wheat, certain coarse grains and poultry(1).

On the political plane the agreement reached certainly marks an important stage in world trade relations. Not only does it confirm the official recognition of the Community's customs tariff but the spirit in which it is conceived is evidence of the common desire of the two great partners to contribute to the expansion of trade through a liberal tariff policy consonant with the responsibilities which their dominating economic and commercial position entails.

The successful conclusion of the negotiations between the Community and the United States is an important part of the general tariff negotiations. The benefit of the concessions made will be extended to all trade partners to whom the most-favoured-nation clause applies. Already it justifies favourable forecasts on the final outcome of the negotiations between the Community and other Contracting Parties.

---

(1) A similar agreement on wheat only is envisaged with Canada.

*Fifth General Report on the Activities of the Community, pp. 234-238.

The Community's Tariff Negotiations*

269. At the time of publication of the previous General Report, the fifth tariff conference held at GATT was drawing to a close. Although this Conference, at which the Community was represented by the Commission was officially concluded on 16 July 1962, some of the Community's negotiations continued until the following November.

The Community's "re-negotiations" under Article XXIV (6) of GATT were described in the last General Report. We need only add that the total number of agreements concluded during these negotiations finally rose to twenty-two, Denmark and Norway having decided towards the end of the Conference to accept the Community's proposals. In addition, a special arrangement was concluded with Brazil under which the Community has bound certain concessions which it had offered during the "re-negotiations"; for her part Brazil decided to maintain the concessions enjoyed by the Member States.

The only concessions by the Member States the withdrawal of which has still to be compensated by concessions in the common tariff relate to manufactured tobacco products and petroleum products, headings for which the duties under the common external tariff were not yet known.

The multilateral negotiations ("Dillon round") had as their object new concessions on a reciprocal basis. A first important agreement was reached on 7 March 1962 between the Community and the United States; this agreement, the cornerstone of the whole structure of tariff agreements resulting from the Conference, has already been described in the Fifth General Report (see sec. 206).

This was closely followed by the conclusion of an agreement with the United Kingdom. The special interest of this agreement lies in the fact that the United Kingdom is the only country which agreed to negotiate on the basis of "across-the-board" reductions proposed by the Community. The agreement reached on this basis provided for a 20% reduction in the respective customs tariffs for a wide range of manufactured products, representing a considerable proportion of the Community's trade with the United Kingdom.

With the above-mentioned exception of the United Kingdom, the Community's trading partners kept to the selective method, this consisting of presenting offers and requests for concessions on selected products one at a time. Under these conditions, and in view of the fact that the Community's across-the-board offer also contained a selective element, the negotiations were in general conducted products by product, in order to reach a bilateral balance of concessions with each partner. Nevertheless, the Community did not demand full reciprocity from the developing countries.

In the end the tariff negotiations did not effect as large a reduction in the common external tariff as was contained in the

offer of a 20% across-the-board cut made by the Community
at the beginning of the Conference. Broadly speaking, the
reductions granted by the Community may be said to represent less than half of the original across-the-board offer.

In a resolution passed on 26 June at the close of a debate
on relations between the Community and GATT, the European
Parliament expressed the hope that negotiations would shortly
be opened for more sweeping reductions in the obstacles to
international trade and drew the Council's attention to the
necessity of strengthening the Commission's hand in the context of a common commercial policy.

In the field of tariff agreements it should also be noted
that, in accordance with a decision by the Council of 4 December 1961, the Commission entered into negotiations under
various provisions of GATT with a number of countries wishing
to withdraw or to modify concessions granted in their customs
tariffs and of interest to the Community. In particular the
Commission has entered into negotiations for compensation
with the Government of the United States under Article XXVIII
of the General Agreement on the reform of the American tariff
nomenclature, since in many cases this affects the tariff concessions granted by the United States. These negotiations are
proceeding.

---

*Sixth General Report on the Activities of the Community,
pp. 244-246.

Declaration of the GATT Trade Negotiations Committee
Meeting at Ministerial Level - Geneva, May 6, 1964*

NOTE: The following is the text of the declaration
agreed to unanimously by the Trade Negotiations Committee
(TNC) of the General Agreement on Tariffs and Trade(GATT),
at its meeting at Ministerial level, May 4-6, in Geneva,
Switzerland. The TNC is responsible for conducting the
Sixth Round of GATT trade negotiations, widely known as the
"Kennedy Round." Membership in the TNC is open to every
country of the GATT participating in the Kennedy Round and
presently includes over 40 nations. The Ministers had met
in Geneva May 16-21, 1963, and at that time had agreed that
the TNC should work during the following year to formulate
negotiating rules for the Kennedy Round. The May 4-6, 1964

Ministerial meeting was for the purpose of receiving the reports of the several TNC subcommittees concerning progress made in the past twelve months. The Declaration takes account of these reports and also records the decisions made by the Ministers at the meeting.

A.   Tariffs

1.   The Trade Negotiations Committee in opening the trade negotiations, notes that:

> (i)   The rate of 50 per cent has been agreed as a working hypothesis for the determination of the general rate of linear reduction provided for in paragraph 4 of the Resolution of 21 May 1963;

> (ii)   the ultimate agreement on tariff reductions in accordance with the application of this hypothesis is linked with the solution of other problems arising in the negotiations, for example, tariff disparities, agricultural problems, exceptions and non-tariff problems, and, in general, with the achievement of reciprocity;

> (iii) it is the intention of the participants to co-operate to solve these problems.

2.   The Trade Negotiations Committee decides that exceptions lists will be tabled on the basis of the hypothesis of a 50 per cent linear reduction.

It is recognized that nothing in the negotiating rules would preclude any participant from making a larger reduction in, or completely eliminating, duties on particular products.

3.   The Trade Negotiations Committee notes the progress made towards solving the problems relating to the question of disparities.

4.   The Trade Negotiations Committee recalls that it was agreed, on 21 May 1963, that there should be a bare minimum of exceptions which should be subject to confrontation and justification.

It decides that the method to be followed for such confrontation and justification shall be elaborated as rapidly as
possible and that the study of that method shall be undertaken
immediately. The method shall take account of the need to
safeguard the confidential nature of the negotiations.

It decides also that exceptions lists shall be tabled on
10 September 1964, such exceptions to be necessitated only
by reasons of overriding national interest(1).

B.   Agriculture

The Committee, while reaffirming that the trade negotiations shall provide for acceptable conditions of access to world
markets for agricultural products in furtherance of a significant
development and expansion of world trade in such products, notes
that it has not yet been possible to formulate agreed rules to
govern, and methods to be employed in, the negotiations. In
view of the importance of this subject to the success of the
negotiations, the necessary rules and procedures shall be
established at an early date.

The Committee notes that negotiations have been initiated
with a view to the formulation of general arrangements on
certain products. The negotiations have so far related to
cereals and meat, and preparations have been made for the
early initiation of such negotiations on dairy products.

C.   Non-tariff barriers

The Committee recalls that the trade negotiations must
relate not only to tariffs but also to non-tariff barriers.

It notes that many participants have already indicated
the measures on which they wish to negotiate, and that others
will shortly do so. In view of the importance for the full success of the negotiations of solving these problems, the Trade
Negotiations Committee shall, at an early date, draw up the
necessary procedures.

D.   Participation of less-developed countries

The Committee reaffirms that in the trade negotiations
every effort shall be made to reduce barriers to exports of less-
developed countries and agrees that this consideration should be
borne particularly in mind in the approach to the question of

exceptions.

The Committee notes with satisfaction that all participants are prepared to consider the possibility of taking such
steps as are open to them to make cuts deeper than 50 per cent
in, or to eliminate completely, duties on products of special
interest to less-developed countries.

The Committee also notes with satisfaction the intention
to entrust to a special body the task of examining and calling
attention to any problems arising in the negotiations which are
of special interest to the less-developed countries and of acting
as a focal point for bringing together all issues of interest to these
countries.

The Committee agreed that it would pursue further the
question of trade in tropical products with a view to working
out arrangements and procedures for their treatment in the
negotiations.

The Committee recalls the decision of the Ministers that
developed countries cannot expect to receive reciprocity from
the less-developed countries. It agrees that the contribution
of the less-developed countries to the overall objective of
trade liberalization should be considered in the light of the
development and trade needs of these countries(2).

E.   The problem of countries with a low average level of
      tariffs or a special economic or trade structure such
      that equal linear tariff reductions may not provide an
      adequate balance of advantages

      (a)   Countries with a very low average level of tariffs

             The Committee notes that the countries concerned
             reserve the right to submit proposals in this con-
             nection at a later date.

      (b)   Countries with a special economic or trade structure

1.   The Committee agrees that Canada falls in the category of
countries with a special economic or trade structure such that
equal linear tariff reductions may not provide an adequate balance
of advantages.

2.   The Committee further agrees that Australia, New Zea-

126

land and South Africa are countries which have a very large dependence on exports of agricultural and other primary products and therefore, by virtue of the understanding reached at the Ministerial Meeting in May 1963, also fall in the category of countries referred to in 1 above.

3.   The Committee reaffirms that the objective in the case of all these countries should be the negotiation of a balance of advantages based on trade concessions by them of equivalent value.

4.   The Committee notes that appropriate procedures in pursuance of this objective have been agreed.

5.   The Committee notes with satisfaction that Greece and Portugal have indicated their intention to participate actively in the negotiations and will be submitting proposals at a later date on the basis for their participation.

F.   Participation of Poland in the trade negotiations

The Committee notes that there has been under consideration for some time the question of ways and means of Poland's participation in the Kennedy Round.   This consideration has taken place on the basis of the Polish proposals listed and explained in TN.64/NTB/15.   The interest of Poland in participating actively in the trade negotiations is warmly welcomed and there is general agreement that it should be feasible to work out a practical arrangement.   The Committee recommends that these discussions should be actively pursued to an early conclusion.

---

(1) These exceptions are distinct from any modification of its offers which, as agreed by the Ministers at their meeting in May 1963, it shall be open to each country to make in the course of the negotiations, where this is necessary to obtain an overall balance of advantages between it and the other participants.

(2) Argentina and Brazil accepted this paragraph on the understanding that the phrase "development and trade needs" covers the requirements of the current financial situation .

*Note by U.S. Government, GSA-WASH DC 64-15657

3.8 RELATIONS WITH NON-MEMBER STATES

Relations With The United States*

During the period covered by the present report, however, a number of disputes have arisen in trade relations between the Community and the United States. For example, the decision taken by the President of the United States on 19 March 1962 to increase the customs duties on window glass and carpets, which came into effect on 17 June 1962, provoked a lively reaction in the industrial circles affected in certain Member States (Belgium, France and the Federal Republic) and in the European Parliament. On 26 June 1962 the Parliament passed a resolution in which it approved the countermeasures taken by the Community on 18 June 1962, affecting certain American exports, such as polyethylene and polystyrene.

---

*Sixth General Report on the Activities of the Community, pp. 247-248.

Negotiations with the United States on the Poultry Problem*

17.   The panel set up by the GATT Council on 28 October 1963 at the request of the European Economic Community and the United States, to give an advisory opinion in the dispute concerning poultry (1), ended its work on 19 November 1963.

In its report, published 21 November 1963, the panel recognized that the matter before it fell to be dealt with in the context of the Article XXIV(6) negotiations. This was relevant both to the question of the reference period on the basis of which, as of 1 September 1960, the value of the United States poultry exports to the Federal Republic of Germany should be determined, and to the manner in which this determination was to be made.

In its choice of a reference period the panel was guided by the practice normally followed by contracting parties in tariff negotiations, namely to lay particular emphasis on the period for which the latest data were available. As, in its view, the latest data which could reasonably have been expected to be available on 1 September 1960 would run up to 30 June 1960, the panel decided to take as reference period the year 1 July 1959 to 30 June 1960.

The panel then considered what corrections to the figures for the reference period might be necessary to enable it to take account of the discriminatory quantitative restrictions existing in the Federal Republic of Germany during that period. It was the panel's view that, in the absence of quantitative restrictions, United States exports would have had a larger share of the existing German market.

Having taken account of these factors, and basing itself entirely on information which could have been known on 1 September 1960, the panel came to the conclusion that a figure of $26 million would reasonably represent the value to be ascribed, as of 1 September 1960, in the context of the unbindings concerning this product, to United States exports of poultry to the Federal Republic of Germany. It will be remembered that the United States had put forward the figure of $46 million, whereas the EEC Commission's estimate was from $16 to 19 million.

The United States and the European Economic Community accepted the opinion of the panel. The Community's approval was given by the Council at its session of 2 and 3 December 1963.

Following the opinion of the GATT panel, on 4 December the United States Government decided to suspend the tariff concessions on brandy, trucks, dextrin and potato starch. Higher tariffs on these articles will go into effect on 7 January 1964. This step has been brought to the notice of the concessions upset by restrictions imposed on poultry imports by the European Economic Community.

Mr. Christian A. Herter, Special Representative of the President of the United States, stressed that the new tariffs would be charged on imports of these products no matter where they came from, although the former tariff concessions applicable to them had been negotiated with the Member States of the EEC, which accounted for 94% of the United States' imports of these goods. The value of imports coming from the Community affected by the higher American tariffs was equivalent to the $26 million estimated by the GATT panel.

Mr. Herter emphasized that the tariff concessions had been suspended, not withdrawn; they could therefore be reinstated whenever an agreement was made with the European Economic Community to restore reasonable access for United States poultry.

(1) See Bulletin 12-63, Chap. IV, sec. 10. Ed. note: U.S. had
asked for lower poultry protection because of increased EEC
levies under the Common Agricultural Policy. In the absence of a settlement satisfactory to both sides, a GATT
panel was asked to determine the amount of trade involved
and consequently the amount of concessions that the U.S.
might withdraw.

*Bulletin of the EEC, January 1964, pp. 25-26.

Relations with Latin America*

4.   The Commission has for several months been considering
the question of the Community's relations with the countries of
Latin America. With the aim of strengthening Community relations with this part of the American continent, the Commission
submitted a paper to the Council in January 1963 announcing its
intention of opening a Community liaison bureau in these countries
and of organizing series of lectures on technical subjects. Moreover, in the commercial field, the Commission considered that
measures to reduce or bind CET duties on items of interest to
South America might be envisaged in the forthcoming round of
multilateral negotiations. In the financial field, it urged that a
study be made of ways and means by which European finance
could contribute to development.

In this paper the Commission also proposed the setting up
of a contact group in Brussels to hold regular technical discussions
with representatives of the Latin-American countries.

Conscious of the importance of the harmonious development of these relations, the Council agreed to the Commission's
proposal for the establishment of a contact group. It decided
that the Community should invite the heads of Latin-American
missions to attend meetings for the purpose of mutual information on economic and commercial relations.

_____

*Bulletin of the EEC, July 1963, p. 21.

Trade Agreement Between the European Economic Community
and Iran*

The tariff content of the agreement

130

The agreement mainly provides for temporary reductions of the common external tariff and a tariff quota, which is also non-discriminatory, all of which concern exports of particular importance to Iran. The measures provided for are as follows:

1. Carpets, carpeting and rugs knotted (58.01 A). The duty under the common external tariff remains at 32%; the maximum charge per sq. metre, which is at present $5, is temporarily reduced to $4.50;

2. Dried grapes (08.04 B). The present 8% duty is temporarily reduced to 7.2%;

3. Dried apricots (08.04 B). The present 8% duty is temporarily reduced to 7%;

4. Caviar (16.04 A). The present 30% duty is temporarily reduced to 24% for a tariff sub-heading referring to sturgeon's eggs.

The Community will also open an annual quota for dried grapes equal to 15% of the imports of this product from all non-member and non-associated countries. This is a non-discriminatory quota for which the duty under the CET will be temporarily reduced to 2%. It will be for the Member States to approximate their national tariffs to this 2% rate in conformity with Article 23 of the Treaty of Rome.

For carpets the two 30% alignments towards the common external tariff will be applied by the member countries as soon as the agreement comes into force. For agricultural products only one alignment applies.

Establishment of a Joint Committee

As soon as the agreement comes into force a Joint Committee of representatives of the Community and of the Iranian Government will be set up. This Committee will watch over the implementation of the agreement, observe the trend of trade between the Community and Iran and make any appropriate suggestions to the competent authorities for improving this trade.

The Joint Committee will meet once a year, the two delegations providing the chairman alternately.

Duration of the agreement

The agreement has been concluded for three years. It may be extended for a period of one year renewable by common consent.

_____

*Doc. 1P (63) 167.

Trade Agreement Between the European Economic Community and Israel*

Content of the agreement

The agreement provides for temporary reductions of the Community's common external tariff and immediate alignment on the present or reduced rates of the CET to be applied to certain products by Member States whose customs duties are at present in excess of these rates. It also provides for liberalization of several products by Member States.

The temporary reductions of the common external tariff concern 21 agricultural and industrial products and range from 40 to 10% of the present rates. Among the products affected are the following:

(i) Grapefruit (08.02 D) - 7.2% (present rate 12%)

(ii) Grapefruit juice (20.07 B II) - 17.1% (present rate 19%)

(iii) Avocado pears (08.01) - 8% (present rate 12%)

(iv) Stockings of man-made fibres (ex 60.03) - 17.6% (present rate 22%)

(v) Bathing costumes (3 tariff sub-headings) - 16%(20%) and 16.8%(21%)

(vi) Outer garments of man-made fibres (two sub-headings) - 16%(20%)

(vii) Window glass for hothouses (ex 70.05) - 8%(10%).

The list also includes reductions of about 20% for some chemical and aluminium products.

132

For all the products in question those member countries which at present have a higher customs duty than the rate of the common external tariff thus reduced will apply the lower rate as soon as the agreement comes into force.

Moreover, alignment on the present CET rates will be effected by those member countries whose customs duties are at present above this level for seven headings or sub-headings, such as oranges, natural citrus fruit juice, certain types of processed vegetables, and asbestos thread.

These speedier alignments on the CET increase the economic importance of the reductions proposed.

For seven tariff headings or sub-headings partial or total liberalization measures for imports will be applied by certain Community States. For France this concerns natural citrus juice and lobes of grapefruit; for Italy it concerns certain bromides and potassium sulphate.

The agreement contains a declaration of intention by Israel concerning Community exports to that country.

A Protocol provides that if the Community should conclude with one or more third countries which are large producers of oranges any agreement likely to affect materially the outlets for these products in Community markets, the question will be examined by the Joint Committee to be set up.

The Joint Committee of representatives of the Community and of Israel will supervise the application of the agreement and follow the trends in trade between the Community and Israel.

The agreement is signed for three years and is renewable.

The two heads of delegations also exchanged letters containing a declaration of intention according to which the Community, in the course of the Kennedy negotiations, will give every consideration to the question of Israeli exports.

---

*Doc. 1P (64) 84.

274. The relations between the Community and the Eastern bloc countries continue to lack any formal basis. While continuing their violent attacks on the Community, to which the Commission has suitably replied, the Eastern bloc countries have shown a growing interest in the Community, and their reactions to its development seem to reflect a certain fundamental change of attitude.

By decision of 24 January 1963 the Council also laid down procedure relating to agricultural imports from the Eastern bloc countries (see sec. 268).

275. Yugoslavia: In September 1962, the Yugoslav Government approached the Community with a view to technical discussions on trade between that country and the Community.

The Council decided during its session of 3 and 5 December 1962 to inform the Government of Yugoslavia that, in principle, the Community was in favour of exploratory talks between Yugoslav and Commission experts. The date would be settled later having regard to the Commission's timetable.

---

*Sixth General Report on the Activities of the Community, pp. 250-252.

Possible Tariff Concessions to the USSR*

3. At its session of 23-24 September 1963 the Council took a final decision on the question of tariff concessions to the Soviet Union. It approved a memorandum which will be handed to the Soviet Government by the diplomatic representatives in Moscow of the country in the chair at the Council.

The memorandum states that the EEC Council and Commission reject as lacking any legal basis the applications made by the USSR to certain Member States for Community customs treatment. The Community would nevertheless be prepared to take tariff measures to promote imports of certain products for which the USSR is its main supplier if the Soviet Government is prepared to consider the present applications as finally disposed of.

The products in question are vodka, caviar and tinned crab.

_____

*Bulletin of the EEC, November 1963, p. 12.

3.9 APPLICATION FOR MEMBERSHIP OR ASSOCIATION

From Proposals for a Free Trade Area to Applications for Membership by Great Britain and Other States*

71.   From the moment the Treaty came into force the Community had to face difficult problems raised by the negotiations which had been on foot for several months to create a free trade area embracing the Community countries and the other Member States of OEEC.

The latter States were reluctant to surrender any aspect of sovereignty, to harmonize their economic policies and to accept the common external tariff, but they wished to share in the work of the Community and enjoy the advantages of tariff disarmament and the liberalization of trade in industrial products.

Negotiations on the Free Trade Area

72.   In these negotiations, where good will on both sides was undeniable but the difficulties very real, the Community was constantly on its guard to preserve its integrity. Its institutions had a duty to avoid solutions that might have robbed the Community of its effectiveness and entailed the risk of its disruption. Furthermore, the Community had to bear in mind the interests of the non-European states of the free world.

There is no need to review here the various stages of these negotiations. In December 1958 the other parties expressed dissatisfaction with the Community's proposals. These were, first, to apply unilaterally to the Contracting Parties of GATT the initial reduction, required by the Treaty as between the Member States of the Community, of 10% in customs duties on industrial products wherever these duties were higher than the future common external tariff; and, secondly, to increase by 20% - subject to reciprocity - the quotas for industrial products from the other OEEC countries. These proposals were

put forward with the object of keeping the door open, without
prejudice to final solutions, while offering another token of
the Community's good will. But the other side were not prepared to accept an arrangement, even if provisional, which introduced an initial discrimination in trade by denying them
the benefit of the Treaty provisions bringing nil or negligible
quotas up to 3% of national output and making of them a global
quota open to all Member States. Despite lack of agreement,
the Community later applied unilaterally to all outside countries the tariff reduction offered on 3 December 1958.

The negotiations for a multilateral association of the
other Member States of OEEC with the Community ended with
an adjournment sine die and were not resumed in 1959.

Apart from the reasons given above, the breaking-off
of negotiations resulted mainly from a misunderstanding of
the nature of the Europe that was being built and of the aims
of the Six. The Community Member States, true to the spirit
of the Treaty of Rome, held that liberalization of trade would
only be feasible and lasting if it were based on firm and precise commitments, not only as to tariffs and trade but in all
matters fundamentally affecting national economies, and hence
indirectly trade. Furthermore, the Six considered that the
European preference system to be set up could only be really
justified in the eyes of the outside world by the economic union
and political rapprochement of European peoples that should
be its final outcome.

On these points there were major differences of opinion,
but the negotiations also laboured under the great difficulty presented on the technical plane by the formula of a free-trade
area championed by the United Kingdom, largely with an eye
to maintaining the system of Commonwealth preference.
Lastly, the diversity of the economic structures of the seventeen European members of OEEC made it difficult to find
common solutions.

74. The Commission recommended a pragmatic approach
to the European problem in order to break through the deadlock caused by the failure of the negotiations in OEEC. This
pragmatic approach called for the immediate adoption of a
set of practical measures which should encourage intra-European trade but which, by their inclusion in the GATT framework, should also have a liberalizing and non-discriminatory
effect on world trade.

75.   The policy outlined by the Commission in its two memor-
anda was approved by the Member States in November 1959.

Basing itself on this policy, the Community endeavoured,
in the Dillon negotiations, to promote a general cut in tariffs on
a basis of reciprocity, particularly in Europe, and proposed
that machinery should be set up for consultation between the
other European countries and itself which would make it possible
to pinpoint and resolve any special difficulties.

The Contact Procedure

76.   On this last point the Community proposed to set up a
"Contact Committee" to study the flow of trade between the
Community and other European countries, propose methods
of ironing out any special difficulties and hold consultations
with a view to broadening the scope of the proposed tariff
negotiations in GATT during 1960 and 1961.   The tasks that
the Community intended to entrust to the Contact Committee
were finally taken over by the Committee on Trade Problems -
made up of the Member States of OEEC, the USA, Canada and
the EEC Commission - set up after the intergovernmental confer-
ences in December 1959 and January 1960, and more particularly
by a study group drawn from that Committee.

This study group carried out two of the tasks that the
Community had had in mind for the Contact Committee: to
analyse intra-European trade flows and to draw up a programme, if only in outline, for the tariff negotiations in
GATT.

On the other hand, no special difficulties were referred
to the group.   However, this absence of complaints is not
surprising if it is borne in mind that exports from non-member
countries to the Community market have progressed very
favourably in recent years.

Development in the British Position and Applications for Membership

77.   In addition to the questions mentioned above, the Committee
on Trade Problems was asked to study the problems involved
in a long-term settlement of economic and commercial relations
in Europe.   In actual fact the most important developments in
this matter took place outside this Committee from the autumn
of 1960 onwards.   Although a member of the European Free Trade
Association since 20 November 1959, the British Government

had apparently realized that some form of association with the Community was the only way the United Kingdom could play an effective part in creating an economically integrated Europe and share on an equal footing in any political union that might emerge.

In the autumn of 1960 British experts began discussions with experts from the Six on the possibilities and chances of success of a plan for British membership of the Community.

The Commission welcomed the change in the British attitude. Though it had denied that the existence of the Community, with its liberal policy, represented any threat to the interests of the other European countries, it had never questioned that there was a great deal to be gained by extending the Common Market in Europe. It regarded its "pragmatic" policy as one fitted to meet the needs of the hour and not an ideal long-term solution.

While the British experts and those of the Six continued their discussions, the Commission made it clear that the idea of membership and the advantages that went with it presupposed that the applicant State fully accepted the principles and content of the Treaty of Rome; the entry of a new member should not jeopardize the aims of the Community, and consequently the Treaty should not be subjected to any changes other than those required by the actual expansion of the Community to take in a new member.

78. On 31 July 1961, Mr. Macmillan, the British Prime Minister, announced in the House of Commons that Her Majesty's Government intended to open negotiations with a view to signing the Treaty of Rome. In a letter dated 9 August to the President of the EEC Council, the Prime Minister informed the Community of the British Government's intentions; this letter states that "Her Majesty's Government have need to take account of the special Commonwealth relationship as well as of the essential interests of British agriculture and of the other Members of the European Free Trade Association". On 2 August the President of the EFTA Council of Ministers presented to the Community a statement in which all the Members of EFTA expressed their desire to achieve a single European market by way of membership of, or association with, the Community and reaffirmed their solidarity at a time when some of their number were about to open negotiations. In the summer of 1961 applications for membership of the Community were also submitted by the

138

Government of the Republic of Ireland and by the Danish Government.

79.   In accordance with the procedure laid down in Article 237 of the Treaty of Rome, the Council referred each of the applications to the Commission for its opinion. In its reply to the Council the Commission said that it would render its opinion only as the negotiations proceeded and in the light of their outcome.

The Opening of Negotiations with Great Britain and Denmark

80.   A ministerial meeting took place on 10 October 1961 between the Six and Great Britain, the Commission being represented, and this was followed on 26 October by a meeting of the ministers of the Six and Denmark. As the Community had requested, the British and Danish delegations put forward at these first meetings their views on the specific problems that would arise from accession to the Treaty of Rome and on means of cushioning their effects. The negotiations proper began on 9 and 10 November with Great Britain and on 30 November with Denmark. At these meetings, which were again at ministerial level, the Six and the Commission made known their initial reactions to the British and Danish applications. The day after the second ministerial meeting between the Six and Great Britain the senior officials entrusted with the next stage of negotiations started work on the basis of a programme prepared by the ministers. As for the negotiations with Denmark - and in particular their timing - agreement was reached with the Danish representatives that the Community's negotiations with the United Kingdom should have a certain priority, since any progress made in negotiations with the United Kingdom would greatly simplify those between the Community and Denmark.

The Commission feels it appropriate to express in this report the satisfaction felt by the Community's at the British Government's declaration, made in the first ministerial meeting, that the objectives set out in Articles 2 and 3 of the Treaty and the institutions provided for in Article 4 were accepted without reservation. The Commission also recognizes the importance of Great Britain's acceptance in principle of the common customs tariff. Finally, it has noted that the United Kingdom intends to join the European Atomic Energy Community and the European Coal and Steel Community when the current negotiations have been successfully concluded. The Commission has always contended that membership of all three Communities

is the only way for a European State to play a full part in
any one of them.

81.   The attitude of the Six and the Commission in negotiating
with Great Britain and other countries wishing to adhere to the
Treaty of Rome will be determined by their determination to
preserve the Community's integrity at all costs and in particular to maintain the balance established by the Treaty between the
several elements of the economic union and between one Member
State and another. The Community, aware that continued economic and political links between the Commonwealth countries are
of value to the free world, will therefore try to work out with
Great Britain solutions to the problems which will face certain
Commonwealth countries if Great Britain enters the Community,
so as to give these countries the time and the opportunity to
adapt their economies to the new situation. But the Community
could never agree to schemes that might, by means of protocols
or otherwise, introduce exceptions to the Treaty's rules which
would be permanent or on so large a scale as to make the
application of these rules an exception in itself. But thus setting
the limits within which negotiations may proceed, the Community
is making sure that its vital interests are respected.

---

*The First Stage of the Common Market: Report on the Execu-
 tion of the Treaty (January 1958 - January 1962), pp. 91-98.

The Negotiations for the Accession of the United Kingdom*

239.   The Fifth General Report contained an account of the
preparatory stage of the negotiations for Britain's entry into
the Community, which was devoted to exploring the problems
which would have to be solved during the negotiations proper.

        During the second stage, which ended in July 1962, the
Conference began discussing the problems raised by the leader
of the British delegation,particularly those relating to the Commonwealth. Mr. Heath reserved the right to raise other subjects
connected with various Articles of the Treaty and the implementing
texts adopted since its entry into force.

        The third stage of the negotiations began in the autumn of
1962 and ended in January 1963. It was devoted mainly to examining how British agriculture might be adapted to the common
agricultural policy.

During these sixteen months, therefore, the negotiations bore mainly on the major problems peculiar to Great Britain. They were conducted with a desire to find solutions in conformity with British interests, but also in conformity with the spirit of the Treaty and compatible with its continued smooth operation.

Ed. note: The principal matters discussed during the negotiations were: the general level of the common external tariff, British requests for zero duties in the industrial sector, Commonwealth problems and particularly Commonwealth agricultural exports, British agriculture and problems arising from membership in the European Free Trade Association. Progress had been made in all areas. The most important questions still pending when the negotiations were suspended concerned British and Commonwealth agriculture.

Denmark, Ireland and Norway applied for EEC membership in conjunction with the British application. All three states agreed that their negotiations with the EEC could not be concluded until after the British negotiations. Hence these negotiations were suspended in January 1963 when the British talks were interrupted.

See EEC Commission, Report to the European Parliament on the State of the Negotiations with the United Kingdom, March 1963.

_____

*Sixth General Report on the Activities of the Community, pp. 215-216.

Contacts Between the United Kingdom and the Community*

2.   At its session of 10-11 July 1963 the Council took a decision regarding contacts between the Community and the United Kingdom and asked its President to transmit to the British Government the following proposal:

"The Council proposes to the British Government that quarterly contacts be arranged within the framework of Western European Union in order to enable the seven member countries to discuss and take stock of the political and economic situation in Europe. It proposes to include every three months in the agenda of the ministerial meetings, besides political subjects, an item worded: 'Exchange of views on the European economic situation'. The discussions will normally take place at ministerial level.

When economic problems are under discussion, the EEC Commission will be invited by the Ministers of the Six to take part in the meeting."

In his comments to the press the President of the Council, M. Luns, said that under the heading "Exchange of views on the European economic situation", each of the WEU member countries could bring up for discussion any economic problem which concerned the Community or Great Britain.

M. Luns added that the Council was unanimous in considering that the discussions proposed within the framework of the WEU should aim at preventing, as far as possible, the Community and Great Britain from pursuing courses which might adversely affect their relations, leaving open the possibility of Great Britain's future entry into the Community, which in the meantime would go ahead with its development.

The British Government was immediately informed of the Community's proposal.

On 26 July the British Government made known its agreement to the proposal as a whole and in particular to the participation of the Commission in discussions on economic problems.

---

*Bulletin of the EEC, September - October 1963, pp. 34-35.

CHAPTER 4

ASSOCIATION WITH EUROPEAN STATES

Article 238 of the Rome Treaty provides: "The Community may conclude with a third country, a union of States or an international organization, agreements creating an association embodying reciprocal rights and obligations, joint actions and special procedures." Such association permits limited agreement on specific matters and has enabled two countries, Greece and Turkey, to join forces with the Community although they are as yet unable to accept all the obligations and implications of full EEC membership.

Both the Greek and Turkish Association agreements are expected to lead to full membership in the EEC, when the economies of the countries concerned are sufficiently developed. In the meantime, the Community is extending many of the benefits of membership to these countries on a non-reciprocal basis.

The Community is considering applications for association from Austria, Portugal, Sweden, Switzerland and Spain. All except Spain are members of the European Free Trade Association which was established in 1961. Since most of these applications were submitted when the United Kingdom, the principal member of EFTA, applied for membership in the EEC, final decision on these applications may depend upon the future of EFTA and its relations with the EEC.

The Austrian application is under active consideration by the EEC. Although a member of EFTA, Austria carries on more than half of its trade with the EEC countries, and is seeking a form of association with the EEC which will not jeopardize its neutral status. The question of whether Austria would be required to leave EFTA before becoming an EEC associate has not yet been settled.

EEC TRADE WITH ASSOCIATES AND PROSPECTIVE ASSOCIATES

IMPORTS (in million $)

	1958	1959	1960	1961	1962	1963
Greece	111	96	88	93	113	112
Turkey	95	153	141	153	189	179
Austria	441	452	536	579	623	652
Portugal	78	72	82	80	96	111
Spain	234	203	343	375	354	370
Sweden	699	732	881	1001	1055	1112
Switzerland	591	657	772	842	924	1014

EXPORTS (in million $)

	1958	1959	1960	1961	1962	1963
Greece	232	193	226	282	303	341
Turkey	152	205	225	201	183	197
Austria	599	657	817	919	961	1031
Portugal	187	186	236	262	219	240
Spain	255	231	254	365	503	640
Sweden	917	954	1110	1165	1197	1272
Switzerland	1046	1189	1465	1777	2015	2177

4.1 APPLICATIONS FOR ASSOCIATION*

82.   Whereas Article 237 of the Treaty enables European
countries to apply for membership of the Community, under
Article 238 the Community may conclude "with a non-member
country, a union of States or an international organization"
agreements creating an association embodying reciprocal
rights and obligations.

At the beginning of 1959 the Tunisian Government said
that it would be interested to know what possibility there was
of negotiating an association agreement under Article 238.
Exploratory discussions were held in a cordial atmosphere at
the beginning of June 1959, but there the matter rested.

83.   Greece and Turkey also applied for association under
Article 238 of the Treaty. The Greek application, which was
the first to be made (8 June 1959), met with a favourable
reception from the EEC Council in July 1959, as did that of
Turkey some months later. Whereas the negotiations with
Greece, in spite of difficulties due to the economic situation
both in Greece and in certain Member States, issued in an
agreement, the talks with Turkey were held up by various
circumstances.

_____

*The First Stage of the Common Market: Report on the Execu-
tion of the Treaty (January 1958 - January 1962), p. 98.

4.2 ASSOCIATION WITH GREECE*

Mutual Tariff Cuts

Customs duties between Greece and the Community will
be gradually abolished over a 12-year period beginning with the
entry into force of the Association Agreement, but:

- on the entry into force of the Agreement, the Community
countries will as an exception cut their tariffs on imports
from Greece to the level already reached in the cutting of the
Community's internal tariffs on the way to the full common
market;

- in order to protect her young industries, Greece may during
the first 12 years, and within prescribed limits, apply new

duties or increase existing ones, on condition that they are abolished or reduced to their previous level within 9 years and then gradually removed;

- while Greece will abolish her tariffs on imports from the Community according to the normal Rome Treaty timetable, for a number of items produced in Greece and representing about one-third of her imports from the Community, she may space out her tariff reductions over a 22-year period (see timetable).

The Common External Tariff

Greece will adopt the Community's common external tariff, in step with the mutual tariff cuts detailed above. For products subject to a twelve-year transition period, this will be achieved as follows: First move: common tariff to be applied in cases where previous Greek duty no more than 15% higher or lower than the common tariff, and in other cases the difference to be reduced by 30%. Second move: difference between remaining tariffs and common tariff reduced by a further 30%. Third move: common tariff to be fully applied. For products subject to a 22-year transition period, the process will be as follows: First move: Difference between Greek duties and common tariff reduced by 20%. Second move: common tariff to be applied in cases where Greek tariff now no more than 15% higher or lower than the common tariff, and in other cases this difference to be reduced by 30%. Third Move: difference again to be reduced by 30%. Fourth move: common tariff to be fully applied.

In a limited number of cases, however, Greece will be able to take special measures to avoid undue disturbance to her economy. For a number of products amounting to no more than 5% of her 1958 imports, she may postpone the lowering of her tariff vis-a-vis non-member countries until the end of the 22-year transition period; while for a number of products representing not more than 3% of her 1958 imports, she may thereafter apply duties higher than the common external tariff. She may also open duty-free or reduced duty tariff quotas up to a limit of 10% of her imports from non-member countries during the last year for which figures are available, and may also use tariff quotas to acquire US goods if this is necessary for the use of American aid. Finally, for tobacco, raisins, olives, rosin, and

oil of turpentine, the Community agrees not to alter the
common tariff beyond certain limits during the 12-year
transition period without the consent of Greece.

Eliminating Quota Restrictions

Quantitative restrictions on trade between Greece and
the Community will first be subject to a standstill, then
eliminated by the end of the transition period (see timetable).
The Community will extend to Greece, moreover, the
arrangements obtaining among the Member States, with some
exceptions for agriculture.

The Community countries will bind vis-a-vis Greece
the lists of products they have bound among themselves,
while Greece will bind 60% of its trade with the Community
when the Association Agreement comes into force, this
percentage rising to 75% during the next five years.

Should Greece reintroduce quantitative restrictions for
products which have been liberalised but not bound, she must
open global quotas for the Community equal to 75% of her
imports from it during the previous year.

Agriculture

Greek agricultural policy is to be harmonized with that
of the Community at the latest by the end of the 22-year transition period; a consultation procedure is to be established
to take into account, in the formation of the Community's
policy, legitimate Greek interests for such products as
tobacco.

For many Greek agricultural products, the Community
will extend to Greece the benefits already granted each other
by the Member States, even before Greek agricultural policy
is harmonized with that of the Community. The latter will,
however, be able to apply safeguard clauses restricting
imports of Greek citrus fruits, dessert grapes, peaches, wine,
etc., should these rise beyond an agreed level in the period
before harmonization has been carried out. At the same time,
the Community will lower its duties on Greek tobacco and
raisins in advance of the normal timetable, and will open
tariff quotas for Greek wine. The French and Italian state
tobacco monopolies also undertake to increase their purchases
from Greece.

In other cases, the removal of barriers to trade in agricultural products will be conditioned on the harmonization of agricultural policies. However, since the exceptions to this rule cover mainly Greek products, Greece will take more rapid unilateral disarmament measures for such Community agricultural products as meat, some dairy products, rice, oils, etc.

Free Movement of Persons, Services, and Capital

Workers: Free movement of workers is to be put into effect at the end of the 12-year transition period. The Agreement also provides for technical assistance programmes for labour, for vocational training, and for the exchange of young work-people.

Right of Establishment and Services: Greece and the Community are to fix timetables for the progressive freeing of the right of establishment and the right to supply services, the former as a necessary concomitant of the increased influx of private capital into Greece.

Capital: Restrictions on capital movements are to be eased by joint agreement, particularly with a view to stimulating investments in Greece.

Transport, Competition, Economic & Foreign Trade Policy

Transport: The Rome Treaty's provisions are to be extended to Greece.

Competition: Greece accepts the Community's competition rules, but will be granted special latitude as regards state aids intended to assist her economy, provided that these do not affect the conditions of trade to a degree detrimental to both parties. On anti-trust rules, dumping, fiscal policy, and the approximation of legislation, Greece and the Community are to fix within two years the terms and conditions for implementing the Rome Treaty's provisions.

Economic Policy: The general provisions of the Rome Treaty are to be applied through joint consultation procedures.

Foreign Trade Policy: Policy is to be co-ordinated during the 12-year transition period; thereafter, Greece and the Community are to work towards a policy based on uniform principles.

The two parties are to consult each other in the case of the association with the Community of non-member countries, in order to settle jointly the new relations between Greece and the future associate. In the case of new members joining the Community, any new rights or obligations for Greece are to be settled by an additional protocol to the Association Agreement.

Financial Aid

During the first five years of the Agreement, Greece may obtain loans from the Community up to a total of $125 million, in accordance with the rules of the European Investment Bank.

Institutions

The Agreement provides for a joint Council of Association composed of members of the Greek Government and members of the Community's Commission and Council of Ministers, each side to have one vote. Any disputes will be referred to the Council of Association, which may in turn submit them to an existing body such as the Community Court of Justice. In other cases, they will be submitted to arbitration: each side will appoint one arbiter, who will jointly name a third. During the first five years of the Agreement, the third arbiter will be the President of the Community Court of Justice.

---

*EEC Document P/9322, pp. 2-5.

Association with Greece*

On 5 April the EEC-Greece Council of Association held its second session with Ambassador Tranos, Permanent Representative of Greece with the Community, in the chair, and adopted decisions and recommendations drawn up by the Association Committee.

The first of these decisions, based on Article 71 of the Athens Agreement, is to set up a Parliamentary Association Committee composed of 14 members of the Greek Parliament and 14 members of the European Parliament. Article 2 of the decision states that "each year the Council of Association shall submit a report on its activities to the Parliamentary Association Committee to help the latter in its work". This decision therefore completes the institutional framework of the Association.

A second decision adopted by the Association Council under Article 70 of the Agreement authorized Greece, by way of exception and on account of weather conditions, to suspend until 15 April 1963 the duties in its customs tariff on potatoes under heading 07. 01 A.

The Council also addressed two recommendations to Greece requesting that country to apply to third countries the export arrangements accorded them by the Community for certain categories of raw hides and skins and for wood. These recommendations were necessary because, under Protocol 6, the Community States had extended to Greece the measures for the removal of customs duties and quantitative export restrictions which they apply between themselves under Articles 16 and 34 of the Rome Treaty.

---

*Bulletin of the EEC, June 1963, p. 15.

Association with Greece*

The fifth session of the EEC-Greece Association Council was held on 26 July, with Ambassador Tranos, the permanent representative of Greece to the Community, in the chair.

The Council fixed at 55% the proportion of the duties under the common external tariff which, in accordance with Article 8 of the Agreement, are to be taken into consideration in determining the rate of the levy applicable from 1 July 1963 to goods in processing traffic.

After consulting the Greek Government, the representatives of the Governments of the Member States meeting in the Council on 30 July, took two decisions concerning the Association.

The first of these speeds up progress towards customs union in the matter of dried grapes; it provides for a further 20% reduction of internal duties on 1 October 1963 (thus bringing basic duties down by 70%) and a second approximation of

150

the national tariffs to the common external tariff. Two
further 10% reductions will follow, one on 1 January 1965
and the other on 1 January 1966. This decision is in conformity with the aims of Protocol No. 17 to the Agreement.

The second decision introduces measures to promote
imports of Greek wines into the Community. The Member
States decided that a customs duty equal to the arithmetical
mean of that applicable to imports from other Member States
and of the duty applied to countries not associated with the
Community shall be applied:

1)   By France and Italy within the quota they are opening for
Greek wines;
11)   By the Federal Republic of Germany to wines from
Samos.

By these new measures the Community hopes to facilitate the sale in its markets of these products, which are
particularly important for Greek export trade, and thus to
make a further contribution to the attainment of the objectives
of the Association.

---

*Bulletin of the EEC, September - October 1963, p. 30.

4.3 ASSOCIATION WITH TURKEY*

Structure of the Agreement

The agreement provides for the progressive introduction
of a customs union between Turkey and the Community, with
the longterm prospect of the new associate joining as a full
member. However, in view of the situation of the Turkish
economy and its present problems, it did not seem feasible
to follow the example of the Agreement with Greece and
institute machinery for progressively establishing a customs
union, beginning at once. It was considered necessary to
start with a "preparatory" stage during which Turkey would
strengthen its economic situation with the aid of the Community, without making any specific concession to the Community
in return. Community aid during this stage will take the form
of financial assistance and commercial preferences for a few
of Turkey's most important exports. This preparatory period
will be followed by a "transition" stage during which the

customs union will be gradually built up; this will lead to the "final" period, which will be a definitive customs union.

The advance from the preparatory period to the transition period will not be automatic. It will be decided by procedure in the Association Council, which will consider the position for the first time after four years. This procedure requires that the Contracting Parties must examine whether, having due regard to Turkey's economic situation, it is possible to make the changeover and establish ways and means of gradually bringing the customs union into being. If by this procedure the desired result is not attained by the end of the ninth year, the Association Council will decide on subsequent arrangements for the preparatory stage, still within the framework of the Association, although the Council will not be obliged to extend the arrangement previously applied.

It should therefore be stressed that the preparatory stage is an integral part of the association arrangement, and that the general clauses, notably those concerning the entry into operation of common institutions, will be applicable as soon as the Agreement comes into force. But the provisions concerning the opening of the transition stage, and particularly those concerning the customs union, which are already part of the Agreement and which are set out under Title II, will be brought into force only from the changeover to the transition stage onwards.

The Content

1. The Preparatory Stage

During this stage, which is to last five years with possible extension to nine years, the Community will grant Turkey preferential tariff quotas for four items (representing roughly 40% of Turkish exports to the Community) and over the first five years will provide through the European Investment Bank financial aid worth the equivalent of $175 million.

Implementing procedure for this stage is established in a Provisional Protocol and a Financial Protocol which cover the following points:

a)   Tariff quotas

As soon as the Agreement enters into force the Member States will open the following annual tariff quotas for imports from Turkey:

	BLEU	FRG	France	Italy	Neth.	Total
			(in metric tons)			
Unmanufact-ured tobacco; tobacco refuse (24. 01)	1250	6600	2550	1500	600	12500
Dried grapes (put up in pack-ages containing not more than 15 kg) (ex 08. 04)	3250	9750	2800	7700	6500	30000
Dried figs (ex 08. 03)	840	5000	7000		160	13000
Fresh or dried nuts, shelled or not: hazelnuts (ex 08. 05)	540	14500	1250		710	17000

When national duties are finally aligned on the CET for all the products in question, the Community will open tariff quotas every year for a quantity of imports corresponding to the sum of the national quotas. From the second year following the entry into force of the Agreement onwards, the Association Council will be at liberty to increase the volume of tariff quotas. Further, at the end of the third year from the entry into force of the Agreement, the Association Council may take steps to encourage sales on the Community market of products other than those mentioned above. Lastly, as soon as the common agricultural policy applies to tobacco, hazel-nuts or dried figs, the Community will adopt, with due regard to its common policy arrangements, any measures necessary to preserve outlets for Turkish exports equivalent to those secured under the Protocol.

2. The Transition Stage

This stage may not exceed twelve years. Provided,
however, they do not protract unduly the completion of the
customs union, certain exceptions may be allowed by common
consent. During the transition stage, the Contracting
Parties will:

i)   Gradually institute a customs union between Turkey and
      the Community;

ii)   Bring into alignment the economic policies of Turkey
      and of the Community.

The Agreement covers the following fields:

a)   Customs union

The union will cover all commodity trade and will
involve a ban on all customs duties or equivalent charges,
quantitative restrictions and any other measure of equivalent effect between the Member States of the Community
and Turkey; Turkey will adopt the Community's common
external tariff (Article 10).

b)   Agriculture

It has been provided that the association arrangement
will extend to agriculture and to trade in agriculture products "on special terms and conditions duly related to the
Community's common agricultural policy" (Article 11).

c)   Other economic provisions

On the basis of the relevant Articles of the Rome
Treaty, the Contracting Parties have agreed to introduce
gradually the right for workers to move about freely between their territories (Article 12), and to eliminate restrictions on freedom of establishment (Article 13) and on
freedom to supply services (Article 14).

As regards transport(Article 15) ways and means of
extending Community measures to cover Turkey will be
worked out with due regard to the geographical situation of
the latter. The Agreement provides that the Treaty provisions on competition, taxation and the approximation of

legislation will apply to the association arrangements between Turkey and the Community (Article 16). Article 17 extends to Turkey the obligation already accepted by the Member States to pursue an economic policy which will ensure the equilibrium of their overall balance of payments and maintain confidence in their currency, whilst ensuring at the same time a balanced and steady expansion of the economy against a background of stable prices and to pursue appropriate cyclical, and particularly financial and monetary, policies to attain these objectives. The Contracting Parties are to consult with each other on ways and means of facilitating capital movements (Article 20). They will seek ways of attracting capital from EEC member countries for investment in pro- jects which are likely to assist the development of the Turkish economy. Countries will enjoy all tax and exchange privileges granted by Turkey to any other Member State or to any non- member country. The Contracting Parties have agreed to institute procedure for consultation whereby they may co- ordinate their commercial policies vis-a-vis non-member countries (Article 21).

3.   The Final Situation

This will be based on the customs union introduced during the preceding stage in pursuance of the Additional Protocol and it will also involve a growing co-ordination of the econ- omies of the Contracting Parties.

4.   Institutions

The Association Council (Article 6), which will be set up as soon as the Agreement enters into force, will comprise members of the six Governments, of the Council of Ministers and of the EEC Commission on the one hand, and members of the Turkish Government on the other. The Association Council will act by unanimous vote, each party having equal voting rights.

The Association Council will from time to time examine the results achieved through the association arrangement, and will take decisions regarding any concerted action not provided for in the Agreement which may appear necessary for the attainment of the association's objectives. Both parties are required to take appropriate measures to implement the decisions adopted.

Disputes

Any State party to the Agreement may refer to the
Association Council any dispute relating to its application
or interpretation. The Council may either settle the dispute by a decision or refer it to the Court of Justice of the
European Communities or any other existing tribunal.

*EEC Document P-35/63, pp. 1-9.

4.4 APPLICATIONS FOR ASSOCIATION FROM AUSTRIA, SWITZERLAND, SWEDEN AND SPAIN*

195. The Austrian Government (12 December 1961), the
Swedish Government (12 December 1961) and the Swiss
Government (15 December 1961) have asked for the opening
of negotiations on the basis of Article 238 of the Treaty of
Rome with a view to an agreement or arrangement with the
EEC. Among the general considerations in these applica-
tions one common factor stands out: the policy of neutrality
followed by these countries.

The Council has not so far taken any stand on the
substance of these applications; it sent letters of acknowl -
edgement to the three governments on 21 December 1961.

On 9 February 1962 the Spanish Government submitted
to the EEC an application for association which was acknowl-
edged by the Council on 6 March 1962.

*Fifth General Report on the Activities of the Community,
p. 227.

Requests for Association
by Austria, Sweden and Switzerland*

259. On 12 and 15 December 1961 Austria, Sweden and
Switzerland addressed to the President of the Council letters
in which they made known their desire to participate in an
enlarged European market. They wished to conclude an
agreement with the Community and expressed the hope that
a date might be fixed for the opening of negotiations such that

the solutions adopted for all the countries in the European Free Trade Association might come into force simultaneously (in accordance with the statement made on 31 July 1961 by the Council of Association).

Although couched in different terms, the Austrian, Swedish and Swiss approaches were all directed towards an agreement under Article 238 of the Treaty of Rome. The three Governments considered that on this basis formulas could be found which would safeguard their permanent neutrality - a common factor in their policy - but which would not affect the Community's integrity.

While taking into account in varying degree the economic objectives and the content of the Treaty of Rome, they drew attention to the exceptions which the policy of neutrality that they wished to maintain would mean for them. At a hearing of their representatives before the Council and the Commission on 28 July 1962 (for Austria and Sweden) and 24 September 1962 (for Switzerland), the three Governments expressed the following desiderata:

i)   A certain freedom of action in commercial policy, particularly the right to negotiate trade and tariff agreements with third countries; this would not prevent co-ordination of their commercial policy with that of the Community;

ii)   Means of ensuring certain vital supplies in time of war;

iii)   The right to abstain from taking measures inconsistent with the requirements of neutrality. This might extend to total or partial suspension of the association agreement and even to denunciation of the entire agreement in the event of serious international tension; this could be done by means of a provision which the neutral governments considered might be on the lines of Article 224 of the Treaty.

---

*Sixth General Report on the Activities of the Community, p. 236.

Portugal*

260. Following the example of the neutral countries and of Spain, which on 9 February 1962 had requested association

157

with the Community with a view to full membership in due course, Portugal also approached the Community. In a letter addressed to the President of the Council on 18 May 1962 Portugal requested the opening of negotiations to establish the terms for co-operation with the Community.

Acknowledgement of receipt of this letter was sent to the Portuguese Government on 29 June 1962. Acting on a decision taken on 5 December 1962, the Council invited the Portuguese Government to explain its desiderata at a hearing similar to that which had been arranged for the neutral countries. This hearing was fixed for 11 February but did not take place.

---

*Sixth General Report on the Activities of the Community, p. 237.

Cyprus*

261. As indicated in section 247 the Republic of Cyprus asked the Council if negotiations could be opened for association with the Community and the Council agreed to initiate the appropriate procedure.

---

*Sixth General Report on the Activities of the Community, p. 237.

CHAPTER 5

ECONOMIC AND FINANCIAL AFFAIRS

The Rome Treaty lays down the Community's economic development objectives. The EEC is to:

- bring about continuous and balanced expansion;

- rapidly increase the standard of living;

- foster a high level of employment;

- stabilize prices;

- maintain a favorable balance of payments.

Marked advances in all these sectors characterized the first five years of the EEC. The Community has grown faster than any other major economic area in the West. It has stimulated increases in the gross national products of its members and in production, consumer purchasing, employment, trade, and overall economic strength. By 1963, these increases had brought about fundamental changes in the European economy. The gold and currency reserves of the member states enhanced their importance in the world financial and monetary centers.

The Community passed into a new stage of economic development in 1963-64. The rapid growth of the Community economy created inflation in some areas where wages and prices rose as demand rose. This change in the Community's economic situation limited the degree to which the Treaty's objectives could be fulfilled. The member states, acting in cooperation with the EEC Commission, agreed to take measures to alleviate the situation. These measures encompassed monetary and financial consultations and medium-range economic planning or programming.

The EEC has pressed forward with regional economic

159

planning. The activities of the European Investment Bank have been important in fortifying the weaker economic regions.

The economic developments in the principal sectors mentioned in the Treaty are shown in the following charts. A more detailed view of the current situation is also provided in the documents.

Expansion of the GNP

1958 - 1963 Index of Volume
(1958 = 100)

	1958	1959	1960	1961	1962	1963
Belgium	100	102.4	107.2	112.2	117.0	121.5
France	100	102.7	110.5	115.5	123.1	128.4
Germany(F.R.)	100	106.9	116.2	122.5	127.6	131.7
Italy	100	107.3	114.6	124.1	132.0	138.3
Luxembourg	100	101.5	..	..	..	..
Netherlands	100	105.2	114.6	118.1	121.3	126.8
Community	100	105.1	113.3	119.4	125.7	130.7

Standard of living

Per capita increases in Private Consumption and GNP percentage increase 1958/1963 in 1958 prices

	Consumption	GNP
Belgium	17	17
France	21	20
Germany (F.R.)	23	24
Italy	36	35

Netherlands	20	19
Community	24	24
without Luxembourg		
U.S.	11	13

Employment

Number of Unemployed
(in thousands) at end of month

	1958	1961	1963
Belgium	116.4	89.1	59.1
France	93.0	112.1	96.6
Germany (F.R.)	769.1	180.9	185.6
Italy	1758.7	1406.8	1068.8
Luxembourg	.15	.12	.22
Netherlands	81.4	31.4	31.9

Price Stability

Index of Consumer Prices (1958 = 100)

	1958	1959	1960	1961	1962	1963
Belgium	100	101	102	103	104	106
France	100	106	110	114	119	125
Germany (F.R)	100	101	102	105	109	112
Italy	100	100	102	104	109	117
Luxembourg	100	100	101	101	102	105
Netherlands	100	102	103	105	108	113

161

Balance of Payments

Surpluses (+) and Deficits (−) 1958 − 1963

	1958	1959	1960	1961	1962	1963
Bel-Lux (in billion Belgian francs)	+ 18.7	+ 36	+ 55	+ 2.2	+ 4.1	− 5.0
France (in billion $)	− 221	+ 741	+ 634	+ 953	+ 829	+ 440
Germany F.R. (in billion D Marks)	+5980	+ 4112	+ 4603	+ 3046	− 2217	+ 998
Italy (in billion $)	+ 564	+ 755	+ 317	+ 508	+ 278	− 636
Netherlands (in billion Florins)	+1665	+ 1551	+ 1408	+ 889	+ 499	+ 413

5.1 ECONOMIC POLICY*

37.   By the terms of Article 103 of the Treaty, the Member
States consider that the policy by which they deal with economic
developments is a matter of common interest. They co-ordinate
their economic policies in close collaboration with the Community's institutions and consult with each other and with the Commission on the measures to be taken in the light of developments.

Since the Treaty came into force, the Commission has
drawn up periodic analyses of the economic situation and endeavoured, in collaboration with the national administrations, to
improve methods of analysis and forecasting by working the information available in Member States into the most harmonious
form possible, so that it should be easier to make comparisons
and to draw up tables covering the Community as a whole. A
panel of economic experts is attached to the Commission to
assist with this work.

Some of the findings of these studies are published periodically in the form of detailed quarterly surveys covering the
economic situation and the outlook, and of monthly graphs and
notes. In addition, a large number of special studies have been
published.

To ensure the co-ordination of policies in this field, two
consultative bodies have been constituted - the Monetary Committee and the Economic Policy Committee.

38.   The task of the Monetary Committee set up under Article
105 of the Treaty is to help Member States to co-ordinate their
policies in monetary and financial matters - two very important
aspects of general economic policy. The Committee carries out
periodical examinations of the situation in the member countries,
and reports its findings to the Council and the Commission. In
1958 the Commission requested the Committee's opinion on the
situation in France, and in 1960 on the consequences of the
restrictive monetary measures then being applied by the German
authorities. At each meeting of the Committee members report
on the most recent monetary and financial trends in their respective countries and the measures introduced or planned by the
authorities. In this way Member States are able to consult each
other their monetary and financial policies both as part of the
regular reviews of the situation in the various countries, and
whenever the monetary and financial policy of a country calls
for special attention.

39.   The Economic Policy Committee was proposed to the
Council in January 1960 as part of the Commission's action to
start the consultations on economic policy required by Article
103 of the Treaty; by its terms of reference the Committee
was to analyse the way in which the instruments of economic
policy were used and the economic effects they produced, and to
make any necessary proposals.   The Committee was set up
by the Council at its session of 9 March 1960 and held its first
meeting on 7 April of the same year.   The Committee consists
of three representatives from the Commission and three from
each Member State.   Its task is to advise the Commission on
the proposals it makes to the Council whenever the economic
and monetary situation requires it.   This task had proved very
necessary, for the economic climate created by the re-establishment of external convertibility for the European currencies and
by the measures of commercial liberalization which accompanied
this move has reinforced the interdependence of the economies of
the various countries in Europe, and particularly among the
Six.

40.   The economic policy pursued at Community level has
constantly reflected the desire to maintain a rapid rate of
economic expansion, which is all the more desirable as the
Community's surpluses on external account have continued to
be high.

        With this in mind, the Commission has repeatedly re-
commended that any measures which might prove necessary in
certain countries to combat the strains caused by the boom
should be such that they would have as little influence as possible on the economies of other countries.   At the same time,
the Commission has made quite clear its preference for action
which would increase supplies on the domestic market and
reduce existing strains by stepping up trade and intensifying
the mobility of labour.

41.   In this connection the Commission has insisted first and
foremost on the advisability of ensuring a better use of manpower
within the Community.   As soon as severe labour shortages
appeared in certain member countries, a working party was set
up to study the lack of balance on labour markets and to propose
remedies.   One result has been the setting up of a vocational
training programme for Italian workers.

42.   The commercial policy that the Commission considered
it should advocate also aimed at maintaining equilibrium in the

various Member States by increasing supply rather than by putting a brake on demand. Because of the persistence of a considerable overall surplus in the Community's external payments, the pursuit of a liberal policy towards the non-member countries not only contributed to an improvement in the economic situation throughout the world and in the balance-of-payments position of the various countries, but it eased the strains felt on domestic markets. The simultaneous existence of a surplus demand on some markets and of unused capacity on others made a more rapid expansion of trade between Member States desirable.

Various measures taken by the Community since the end of 1958 have in fact shown, sometimes in spectacular fashion, the Community's desire to apply a liberal commercial policy towards non-member countries both by eliminating quotas and by vigorous action to encourage the reductions of customs duties throughout the world.

The Commission has found it necessary to introduce important measures concerning trade between Community countries. The speed-up in the implementation of the Treaty of Rome was looked upon not only as an aim of general policy but also as an instrument of economic policy.

43.   It is not possible in this report to review, however briefly, the economic developments which have occurred in the Member States between 1958 and 1961. As is shown by the indications below, the trend has on the whole been very satisfactory. The results obtained in the course of the Community's first four years of existence doubtless reflect in large measure the dynamism displayed by economic circles in connection with the gradual advance being made towards the Common Market. But, as can be seen from what has been said above, the high rate of growth in conditions approaching equilibrium is in part due to the measures taken by Governments and to the action of the Commission.

Some economic indicators (combined Community figures)

	1961 index (1957=100)
Gross national product (volume)	121
Industrial production	132
Consumption per head (volume)	115
Gross fixed capital formation (volume) (1)	131
Intra-Community trade (value)	173

(1) Estimated.

*The First Stage of the Common Market: Report on the Execution
of the Treaty (January 1958 - January 1962) pp. 44-47.

5.2 STRUCTURAL POLICY AND REGIONAL POLICY*

44.   During the four years of the first stage the Commission,
in conformity with the Treaty, has tried to work out the long-
term aims that will have to be pursued if the economic development of the Community is to be harmonious not only in its overall
aspects but also from the regional angle.

With the help of independent experts, the Commission's
staff have studied two general hypotheses concerning the Community's economic expansion up to 1970, based on estimates of
the way in which the labour force and productivity may develop.

The forecasts of future expansion used in structural
policy cannot be based exclusively on global figures; they must
also give due weight to the analysis of inter-industrial flows,
which are at present being studied by the staff of the Commission.
Substantial progress has also been achieved in the examination
in ad hoc working parties of the particular problems affecting
various industries.

As for regional policy, the Commission has from the
beginning sought to define the regional problems arising within
the Community (under-development of the South of Italy and of
certain outlying areas of Europe, the decline of certain industrial areas, economic concentrations with an excessive industrial density, etc.).

With the aid of a working party of national experts an
attempt has been made to agree on the boundaries of regions.
The experts took as their basic social and economic regions
those used by Member States in applying their own policies.
These basic regions have been regrouped to create larger areas
which will make possible structural analysis on a Community
scale and will constitute the framework of the Community's regional policy. In addition, the Commission has also undertaken,
with assistance from experts, an analysis of the regional repercussions of the policies followed by Member States and has
systematically examined the regional implication of the common
policies elaborated by the EEC.

At the end of 1961 the Commission convened a conference on regional economies at which 300 representatives of the public, the universities, industry, agriculture, the trade unions, etc., in the six countries of the Community took part in a broad discussion on a score of reports on the experience recently gained in the Community on the development of the regions. This conference brought out the lessons to be drawn from the measures intended to promote a more harmonious development of the various regions and highlighted those aspects of regional problems which are of common interest.

The European Investment Bank gave particular attention to projects for developing underdeveloped regions and took an interest in the schemes of modernization and conversion made necessary by the gradual establishment of the Common Market, and also to certain projects which were of interest to several Member States. Since it was set up at the end of 1961, the Bank has approved 22 loans totalling 160.2 million units of account. The investments which the Bank has helped to finance in this way add up to more than 1,000 million units of account.

---

*The First Stage of the Common Market: Report on the Execution of the Treaty (January 1958 - January 1962) pp. 47-49.

Regional Policies*

105.   The economic expansion of the Community which according to the Rome Treaty should be not only continuous but balanced presupposes an active regional policy. In its Action Programme the Commission moreover emphasized that the mobilization of the great productive potential of the under-developed areas could make a special contribution to increasing the overall national product.

In this field the Commission's action is largely based on the lessons of the European Conference on regional economies which it organized at the end of 1961. The programme of work adopted after this Conference, by agreement with the competent national authorities, includes not only inquiries into the problems of certain regions but also studies which should make it possible to lay down the main lines of concerted action at Community level to reduce the leeway of the less-favoured regions of the Community.

The most important of the Community's regional inquiries deals with the establishment of a centre of industrial
development in a backward region of the Community. Taking
a fairly small area whose material and human resources
would allow of extensive industrial development, it is a matter of
studying how much investment will need to be concentrated
on the area to obtain the desired result.

On this basis the Commission, in full agreement with
the Italian authorities, has chosen a region of Southern Italy
which includes the most backward areas in the Community.
It is studying the installation between the cities of Tarento and
Bari of an industrial complex mainly devoted to steel production
and processing. This complex will embrace certain projects
already in train and create a coherent whole which can continue
to develop, after the initial action, through the simple play of
market forces.

This operation constitutes a pilot scheme for the study
of methods of industrialization. The experiment can be repeated
not only in other Community regions, but perhaps, with some
adaptation, in certain developing countries.

A second inquiry deals with the common problems of two
regions separated by a frontier. The experiments are of special
interest in a Community whose internal economic frontiers are
destined to disappear. The area chosen is at the Franco-Belgian
frontier and includes the southern part of the Belgian province
of Luxembourg and the north of Lorraine. The aim is to bring
out the existing or potential interdependence of the two frontier
zones considered as a single economic area. The studies so far
have shown that the solution of a number of problems such as
water supply, training of manpower, communications and
frontier-crossing conditions, and the promotion of investments
in the less developed areas, would be considerably facilitated
by increased co-operation between the authorities on the two
sides of the frontier, and the Commission intends to encourage
such co-operation.

106. The establishment of the Action and Liaison Committee
for the sulphur industry in Italy is another example of the Commission's localized action. This committee, set up in September
1962 by decision of representatives of the Governments of the
Member States, was instructed to study the real prospects of
the sulphur industry in Sicily in the context of the reorganization programme for this industry submitted by the Italian

Government. It will examine the existing and potential employment situation in the area and make suggestions on how to maintain employment at a satisfactory level, in particular by calling
on private initiative.

107.   The Commission does not intend to confine its endeavours
to inquiries on certain regions of the Community - inquiries which
can, moreover, serve as lessons for other regions. Like the
Economic and Financial Committee of the European Parliament,
the Commission thinks that an overall regional policy should be
worked out to avoid the occurrence of dispersion or duplication
of efforts instead of genuine co-operation.

With the view to defining this broader concept, which
obviously includes social aspects, the Commission has decided
by agreement with the national authorities to obtain the opinion
of personalities specially qualified in this field (as announced in
its Action Programme). To this end it has set up three small
working parties.

108.   The first working party is studying how development can
be speeded up in the peripheral regions of the Community which
are lagging behind in relation to the central areas. It is seeking
means of ensuring a balanced distribution of economic development - both in industry and agriculture - by land improvement
schemes planned in a Community context.

109.   The problems of industrial regions in which certain
long-established trades are declining are being examined by the
second working party. Here it is a matter of studying how
technological and economic changes and a new pattern of trade
have brought about the decline of regions which until recently
were in the vanguard of Europe's industrial advance, and of
looking for appropriate methods of countering this decline.

110.   The task of the third working party is to appraise the
effectiveness of the various forms of preferential treatment
granted to promote regional development. Comparison of aids
and the results achieved should make it possible to draw conclusions as to the most suitable means of resolving the Community's regional problems.

In the eyes of the Commission, the establishment of
these working parties goes some way towards meeting the
European Parliament's call for an advisory committee on regional economies. When these working parties, which are

still only in their early stages, have reached conclusions, it
will be possible to envisage their holding joint meetings in
which other authorities on regional matters could take part.

111.   Among the Community's further activities in this
field mention should be made of the work of the joint working
party on the conversion of mining areas, in which the EEC,
ECSC and the European Investment Bank are represented.
This working party has examined applications for finance
from industrial firms situated in declining coal-mining
areas (1).

_____

(1) See ECSC Eleventh General Report, sec. 102.

*Sixth General Report on the Activities of the Community,
pp. 120-122.

5.3 LONG-TERM DEVELOPMENT POLICY*

101.   The alignment of economic policies, which is recognized
as essential if the objective of balanced development assigned
to the Community by the Treaty is to be achieved, is first of all
needed in conjunctural policy. But it cannot be confined to short-
term measures, since these, if they are to be on the right lines,
must fit into the longer-term perspective. The long-term growth
policy of the governments and Community institutions must be
dovetailed into a Community programme if it is to be really coherent and effective.

The concept of programming which the Commission
sketched out in its Action Programme and proposed for implementation is well known in several Member States. It has been well
received by the European Parliament, the great majority of
whose members saw no incompatibility between this idea of a
programme and the concepts of a market economy and a competitive economy which are fundamental to the Treaty. On the
contrary, they pointed to the drawbacks which unco-ordinated
economic action by the Member States could have, particularly
if general business trends were to slacken.

In any case, it is necessary to assemble reliable information on the long-term economic trend in order to determine the
general conditions for expansion during the transition period and
to clarify both national growth policies and the common policies

introduced or planned in particular fields, of which the most important are agriculture, transport and energy.

102.   In recent years the Commission has been studying the potentialities of economic expansion and has sought ways and means of improving existing development policies. It has been assisted in these studies by a Working Party on structures and long-term economic development under the chairmanship of M. Uri.

103.   The first fruits of the Working Party's studies were set out in a report on development prospects in the Community between 1960 and 1970 published on 3 December 1962.   The working hypotheses chosen on the future trend of overall employment and on general productivity trends together determine the forecasts of the growth in the gross product for the period considered.   The increase in the Community's gross product between now and 1970 could be between 53 and 60%, according to the hypotheses adopted by the experts.

The purpose of the Working Party's present studies is to verify the expansion hypotheses adopted, particularly by breaking down the preceding estimates between certain main branches of activity.

To take one stage further these studies on structures and economic development in the Community, the Commission is also endeavouring to bring into line the methods of analysis used in the various Member States, particularly as regards surveys of inter-industry trade.

The object of this work done by the Commission with the help of independent experts is to enable the Community to consider its development in terms of a period of several years and thus lay the technical foundations for the long-term development policy proposed in the Action Programme for the second stage.

---

*Sixth General Report on the Activities of the Community, pp. 118-119.

5.4 CO-OPERATION IN MONETARY AND
FINANCIAL POLICY*

17.   On June 19, 1963 the Commission submitted to the
Council the recommendations on collaboration in monetary and
financial matters in the Common Market announced in the
Action Programme. These recommendations are based on
Article 105 (1) of the Treaty, which provides for collaboration
between the responsible Government departments and between
the Central Banks in co-ordinating the economic policies of
the Member States, and requires the Commission to submit
to the Council recommendations for bringing into effect such
collaboration.

In the past years fruitful collaboration has already
developed in the Monetary Committee and by informal meetings
of Ministers of Finance and of Governors of Central Banks.
This sufficed to meet requirements in the first stage, during
which, moreover, co-operation was greatly facilitated by the
prevailing boom conditions with favourable trends in the payments balances of all Member States.

But as economic union is gradually built up and the
economic frontiers between Member States disappear, the
monetary situation in each Member State will be still more
affected by developments in the other countries than is already
the case owing to currency convertibility. The monetary situation in the Common Market, which is in any case becoming more
uniform, can therefore only be purposefully directed and influenced if the responsible authorities in the Member States
collaborate closely and pursue monetary policies that are
mutually compatible.

To this end the Commission recommends, firt the establishment of a Committee of Governors of Central Banks, which
would hold consultations on the main lines of Central Bank policy,
exchange information on the more important measures under
this policy, and as far as possible examine such measures before they are introduced by the competent national authorities.

Collaboration in monetary policy would, however, be
incomplete if it covered only action taken by the Central Banks.
Budgets and the economic policy decisions they reflect have as
much importance for monetary developments as Central Bank
policy and are sometimes even more decisive.

Budget surpluses and deficits and the way the latter are financed decisively affect internal liquidity and the overall monetary situation. In its last annual report the Monetary Committee drew the logical conclusion from this that Central Bank policy and budget policy must be co-ordinated in each Member State and at Community level also.

The Commission has accordingly recommended to the Council that a Budget Policy Committee be set up, drawn from officials in Ministries of Finance responsible for these matters and including a representative of the Commission. This Committee would examine in the early stages of national budgeting the basic features of budget policy from the angle of their effects on the economic development of the Community as a whole. Its studies would also provide the groundwork for discussions in the Monetary and Economic Policy Committees of the specifically monetary and conjunctural aspects of the execution of the budget.

Finally, the Commission has recommended to the Council that there should be consultations before all major decisions by Member States on international monetary policy. Such decisions can be of great moment for the functioning of the Common Market itself. One needs only think of the problems which would arise in the common agricultural policy if a Member State altered its rate of exchange. The principle of prior consultations in the event of modifications in exchange rates between Member States should therefore be recognized and, in view of the complexity of the questions which this brings up, the Monetary Committee should be instructed to work out appropriate procedures for such consultations.

The Commission further recommends that there should be consultations in the Monetary Committee if a Member State contemplates calling on the International Monetary Fund to cover a deficit in its payments balance, if Member States contribute to large-scale international aid for third countries and, in a general way, before any decisions which affect the operation of the international monetary system. The discussion of international monetary questions is already an essential aspect of the Monetary Committee's work. As a member of an international monetary system the Member States are dependent on its proper functioning, for which they bear growing responsibility. Besides being of great importance for the ordering of international monetary relations in general, the way in which this system functions can also have considerable repercussions on the spread of deflationary or inflationary tendencies throughout the Common Market itself.

The Commission recommendations summarized above
are a natural further development and intensification of what
already exists today. If implemented they would clear the
ground for a homogeneous economic policy in the Common
Market, which is indispensable if it is to develop into an economic union.

_____

*Bulletin of the EEC, August 1963, pp. 22-24.

5. 5 THE COMMUNITY'S MEDIUM-TERM
ECONOMIC POLICY*

13. In its memorandum on the Action Programme for the
Community's second stage, the Commission expressed its
opinion that the Community should consider its future development in terms of a period of several years and announced that
it would make suitable proposals to the Council in 1963. A
memorandum and the draft for a decision on the Community's
medium-term economic policy have just been approved by the
Commission and laid before the Council.

These are intended to give effect to the aims of the
Treaty of Rome - particularly those embodied in Article 2,
which states that the Community shall promote throughout its
territory a harmonious development of economic activities, a
continuous and balanced expansion, an increase in stability and
an accelerated raising of the standard of living.

The measures (which were published in the supplement
to Bulletin 8-63) so far taken to co-ordinate Member States'
economic policies have been mainly of a short-term character -
economic budgets being the most important. But to ensure
lasting full employment and a balanced expansion together with
monetary stability, the Commission believes that plans must
be made to cover several years. Decisions taken by the public
authorities have consequences that extend well beyond a period
of one year, and there is a risk that decisions may be taken
by the authorities in the various countries and by those of the
European institutions without sufficient thought being given to
their longer-term incidence on the Community's economy. A
medium-term picture would facilitate co-ordination, would
ensure that the decisions of national authorities and European

institutions, each in its own sphere, are better concerted, and that they all pursue common aims.

A medium-term view of this sort would in no way restrict the freedom of the market, but would rather provide a framework for Government and Community action.

There is no question of setting up production and employment targets for the various sectors of economic activity in the EEC. In those sectors where the play of competition is sufficiently free, the normal operation of the market is the most effective instrument for distributing resources; it is not therefore a case of setting rigid bounds to economic activity, but only of co-ordinating Member States' economic policies so as to make them more effective. The medium-term picture would also make it possible for the proposed common policies for agriculture, transport, energy, vocational training and external trade to be fitted into one economic framework.

A medium-term picture is also needed in connection with public investment. European living conditions in 1970 will largely reflect the decisions on hospital equipment, school building, road networks and urban facilities taken some years earlier by the public authorities. The Commission sees no good reason why existing means of investigation should not be used to ensure that lack of foresight does not lead, a few years hence, to the emergence of a society geared to the satisfaction of personal needs while education, scientific and technical research, health and other social services and transport infrastructure are neglected - or, for that matter, of a society in which the excessive priority accorded to collective needs entails an impairment of personal liberty.

The Community must also have a picture of the situation some way ahead in order to promote the harmonious development of the regions of the EEC; the progress of scientific and technical research must also be kept in view.

The purpose of the Commission's proposals is to encourage the Member States to consider together, and jointly with the European institutions, the problems referred to and any decisions affecting the future. It is suggested that flexible and effective machinery should be set up to facilitate such joint consultation.

First of all, the progress made in national accounting

175

and economic analysis should be used to provide an overall picture of the main lines likely to be followed by economic developments, using all the information available. This task would be entrusted to a group of experts that the Commission intends to call together shortly to continue the work it has already begun.

The next step would be to call a meeting of those responsible for economic policy in the Member States, where a medium-term economic policy programme would be prepared which could serve the Member States and the European institutions as a background for major decisions whose effects extend over a number of years. This would be the task of the 'committee on medium-term economic policy' which has been suggested. Workers and employers would collaborate in drawing up the programme, chiefly through the Economic and Social Committee. It would be submitted to the European Parliament and adopted by the competent institutions of the Community.

In view of the amount of preparatory work involved, it is proposed that the programme should cover a period of five years beginning on 1 January 1966.

---

*Bulletin of the EEC, September/October 1963, pp. 40-42.

5.6 RECOMMENDATION 64/246 TO MEMBER STATES ON MEASURES FOR RESTORING INTERNAL AND EXTERNAL ECONOMIC BALANCE

The Council, in accordance with Article 103 of the EEC Treaty, and in consideration of the Assembly resolution of March 23, 1964 and the proposal of the Commission, recommends to the Member States the following measures to restore the internal and external economic balance of the Community.

1.   The Member States should pursue an economic and financial policy necessary to insure that the stability of prices and per unit product costs is restored or consolidated, at the latest, by the end of 1964. Economic and financial policy measures, prepared or decided in 1964, but scheduled to go into effect in 1965, should have the same objectives.

2.   For this reason the Governments of the Member States should, during the coming months, give priority to the objectives listed in Paragraph 1 above all other goals which they plan to attain in economic policy or other fields.

3.   The Member States consider the maintenance of a liberal import policy, in both intra-Community trade and trade with non-members, as essential to stabilizing, or maintaining the stability of, prices.

4.   A stricter policy on public spending should be the principal method of achieving rapid price and cost stability. The Council recommends that the Member States limit any public spending which has effect domestically. Aside from any changes in ways of financing the public debt, annual increase of this spending should not exceed 5%. As allowed by their constitutions, the Member States should see that in general regional and local authorities and State owned or controlled enterprises follow the same policy. If this is not possible, the Member State Governments should make every effort to get these authorities and concerns -- through negotiation -- to adopt such an outlook.

The Council also recommends that Member States take appropriate measures to apportion public spending so that it is not excessively concentrated in one period of the year or in specific regions.

5.   When the Member States either lack the legal or administrative power to limit the increase in public spending to 5%, or cannot induce their parliaments to make the necessary decisions quickly enough or, finally, consider it absolutely essential to increase spending, it is recommended that they supplement budgetary action by fiscal measures: temporarily raising taxes or introducing new taxes in order to influence the expansion of domestic monetary demand in a way identical to the effect which would have resulted from the strict application of the rule given in Paragraph 4. Additional revenue resulting from the gradual increase of certain taxes should be calculated on the basis of constant prices and an increase in domestic production not exceeding 5%. The above recommendation does not eliminate the possibility of certain changes in existing tax systems, provided that the total effect is not modified.

The Council recommends that the member governments reduce as far as practicable the deficit of public enterprises by raising corresponding rates subject to special measures in favor of the low income groups. The resultant revenue can be considered, under the terms of this paragraph, as an additional fiscal charge.

In introducing and raising taxes, as well as in raising public rates, the Member States should bear in mind the sliding scale clauses and indices in force in each Member State so as not to strengthen the upward movement of monetary income. In France and Italy, it would be desirable to spread the increase of taxes so that its main result is to slow the expansion of private consumption and to affect business investments as little as possible.

6. If, despite the application of the provisions of Paragraphs 4 and 5, a Treasury deficit still exists, the member governments should finance this deficit exclusively by long-term loans and not by banking credits, including central bank credits, short-term Treasury bonds or, directly or indirectly, credits in foreign currency. To the extent that the domestic financial market does not allow the Treasury the necessary funds, the governments should undertake without delay all measures likely to improve its operation. A higher degree of consolidation should characterize the management of the public debt.

7. The appropriate authorities of the Member States should continue the measures undertaken to introduce a restrictive credit policy, and if necessary strengthen it. This stipulation applies as well to provisions designed to limit consumer credit.

8. The member governments should inform the representatives of the main economic and social groups, especially workers and employers, of the needs and main principles of their stabilization policies. They should attempt during negotiations with these groups to follow an income policy for the remainder of 1964 and 1965 which will insure as far as possible that the increase in income in monetary terms per worker and the percentage increase of the GNP per worker are in line.

At the same time, they should intensify the policing of imperfectly competitive markets, and the action against the limitations on competition leading to price increases. To the extent that intervention in the areas of income and competition do not have the expected result, the provisions to restrict the aggregate growth of domestic demand should be strengthened.

9.   In all the member states where increased demand for buildings and construction exceeds the supply capacity (an increase in building prices noticeably higher than the rise in the general price level for other goods and services is a sure sign of such an excessive demand) and where the productive capacity of the industry cannot be expanded quickly, the Government should take special restraining measures; reduce government demand for construction, reduce government tax reliefs, subsidies and premiums, limit mortgage credits, temporarily ban luxury building. In the countries with a shortage of school buildings or hospitals, or of low-income housing, the construction of such buildings should neither be reduced nor made more difficult.

10.   To the extent that Member States do not finance their balance of payments deficits with their own foreign currency or gold reserves, they should act with the other Member States in the Community's Monetary Committee on ways of financing the deficit. In this regard, their close solidarity makes it advisable for the Member States to turn first to Community solutions and to the mutual help which the Member States can provide under terms to be fixed jointly. The Commission may recommend the introduction of mutual help.

11.   The Council recommends that the Italian Government undertake additional anti-inflationary measures designed to stabilize rapidly domestic costs and prices and to improve the competitive position and the balance of payments. It is particularly desirable that the financial policy objectives be achieved by the second half of 1964.

     In general, the Italian Government should pursue by taxation a policy directed at limiting the growth of domestic demand, continue its policy of restraining credit expansion and effect a balanced income policy.

12.   For France, Belgium, the Netherlands and Luxembourg continuation of the Commission's general policy for all the Member States, which is already in force, should insure the return to stability.

13.   The Governments of the Federal Republic of Germany should insure that the relative stability of prices and production costs in effect since 1963 is not jeopardized, and should pursue the policy already implemented according to the recommendation listed in Paragraphs 1-9.

Credit policy should not be made more restrictive under present conditions; nevertheless, the rate of advance of bank credit should not be appreciably accelerated.

The Government should pursue the current policy to neutralize the growth of liquidity resulting from the surplus balance of payments, and should attempt to re-export this liquidity. Taxes and other barriers to the export of capital, which result for the most part from the requirements on capital holding groups with regard to their investments, should be abolished as rapidly as possible.

In addition, steps should be taken to slow the increase in the surplus balance on current account. All necessary steps should be taken to encourage imports, and to avoid stimulating exports. The provisions for the anticipated reduction of customs duties states in Article 15 Paragraph 2 of the Treaty should be widely used. Similarly, where the German customs duties are higher than those of CET the difference should be reduced or eliminated. The German Government should take all appropriate steps to stimulate imports of farm products. Finally, German export of capital should be made less dependent on the export of goods and services, and government orders abroad should be increased.

14.   The Member Governments will inform the Commission within two months of the steps they have taken to put this recommendation into effect. The Commission, after consulting to the fullest extent possible with the Economic Policy Committee and the Monetary Committee will report to the Council, and will keep it regularly informed of the state of the situation and its developments. If necessary, the Commission will submit new proposals.

––––––––

5.7 HOW THE EUROPEAN INVESTMENT BANK FUNCTIONS*

The European Investment Bank is an independent body under public law, forming part of the European Economic Community. It is administered and controlled by nationals of each of the six countries (Belgium, France, Germany, Italy, Luxembourg and the Netherlands). Its object is to finance investment projects of interest to the Community.

Resources Capital: one thousand million units of account(1), of which 250 million units of account are paid up.

The Bank raises the funds needed for its intervention by way of loans floated on the capital markets.

Activities   The Bank operates in the Member States
and in the Associated States. The Board of Governors may
in exceptional cases decide to finance projects in other
countries.

The Bank may grant loans for the financing of projects to be executed by any public or private organization
or company in any sector of the economy.

In the European territories of the Member States,
a project is eligible only if:

a- it contributes to the improvement of an under-developed
   area, or

b- it is used to modernize or convert an enterprise, or

c- it represents a venture of common interest to several
   Member States.

Conditions of loans   Loans by the Bank may cover
only a part of the total cost of any project. In principle,
loans are paid in instalments in the currencies available at
the Bank at the time of the payment; they are repaid in
the same currencies. Irrespective of the currency of the
payment or of the Member State on whose territory the
relevant project is situated, the rates of interest are fixed
by the Bank in accordance with the conditions at which
it can obtain loans on the capital market(2).

The duration of loans varies with the normal duration of the technical amortization of each project. Contracts
may include provision for a period of grace.

The Bank requires the borrower to provide the
usual bankers' security or a state guarantee.

Loans

Country Breakdown of Loans Approved

(Member countries and associated countries)
at 31 December 1963

Country	Number of loans	Amount in million units of account	%
Member countries			
Belgium	1	4.8	1
Germany	3	32.4	9
France	10	58.0	16
Italy	47	236.1	66
Luxembourg	1	4.0	1
Total	62	335.3	93
Associated countries			
Greece	5	23.0	7
Grand Total	67	358.3	100

Sector Breakdown of Loans Approved

(Member countries and associated countries)
at 31 December 1963

Sector	Number of loans	Amount in million units of account	%
Agriculture	2	10.5	3
Energy	10	74.6	21
Transport	10	108.2	30
Industry	45	165.0	46
Grand Total	67	358.3	100

Borrowing
at 31 December 1963

Bond issues

4 1/2%, 1961, for seven years, in guilders (Fl. 20, 000, 000)	5, 524, 861. 88 u. a.
4 1/2%, 1961, for twenty years, in guilders (Fl. 50, 000, 000)	13, 812, 154. 70 u. a.
5%, 1962, for fifteen years, in Italian lire (Lit. 15, 000, 000, 000)	24, 000, 000. 00 u. a.
4 3/4%, 1962, for twenty years, in guilders (Fl. 30, 000, 000)	8, 287, 292. 82 u. a.
5%, 1963, for twenty years, in French francs (FF 60, 000, 000)	12, 152, 981. 73 u. a.
6%, 1963, for twenty-four years, in Belgian francs (Bfrs. 400, 000, 000)	8, 000, 000. 00 u. a.
5 1/2%, 1963, for seven years, in German marks (DM 60, 000, 000)	15, 000, 000. 00 u. a.

Other borrowing

Bank credit, 1961. for six years, in Swiss francs	1, 646, 534. 72 u. a.
Total	88, 423, 825. 85 u. a.

(1)   1 unit of account = 50 Belgian francs = 4 German marks = 4. 93706 French francs = 625 Italian lire = 50 Luxembourg francs = 3. 63 Dutch guilders = 1 US dollar = 4. 37282 Swiss francs.

(2)   On 31 March 1964, the current rate charged by the Bank was 5 7/8%.

*European Investment Bank 1958-1963, April 1964, p. 40.

5.8 THE OVERALL ECONOMIC SITUATION*

In 1963 economic activity in the Community again expanded quite considerably. True, the rise in real gross Community product at about 4% was somewhat smaller than 5% between 1961 and 1962 and the 5.3% between 1960 and 1961. This does not, however, mean that there has been any significant strengthening of the longer-term factors which tend to weaken economic growth in the Community. The slower expansion of production in 1963 can be ascribed more to chance factors, in particular the exceptionally unfavourable weather. The tendencies which made for slower economic growth were without doubt still present at the beginning of 1963 - and mainly affected the development of investment by enterprises - but they gave way to a more or less distinct recovery as the year went on.

Total demand in monetary terms rose none the less almost as much as between 1961 and 1962. Since, however, supply from domestic sources grew more slowly - the continuing labour shortages, which even became more acute in some areas, made it impossible to expand production more rapidly - this greater demand in monetary terms was in part reflected in higher prices and a considerable further deterioration in the Community's balance of current payments.

In 1963 external demand (from non-member countries) made a greater contribution than in 1962 to the expansion of total demand. For the full year, exports of goods were probably up about 4.5% in value and 4% by volume over 1962, after rising only about 1% (value and volume) between 1961 and 1962. If we look at the way exports developed in 1963, the change in trend - from the continued slackening in the pace of expansion that persisted into the early months of the year to the acceleration that marked the rest of the year - becomes clearly recognizable. The recovery is certainly to be attributed in the main to the direct and indirect impact of the business revival in leading non-member industrial countries.

Internal demand continued to expand briskly. If growth was somewhat slower than between 1962 and 1963, this was mainly due to slower expansion of gross fixed asset formation. Investment in building and construction did not attain the growth rate of the preceding year, despite efforts to recoup the relatively large production losses of the 1962/63 winter and despite a considerable increase in the numbers employed in this industry. In addition, the industrial propensity to invest was still relatively weak in the first half of the year, and this attitude affected in particular the demand for investment goods; though investment recovered somewhat in the second six months, its effect on the full year could not completely compensate for the earlier slowdown.

The expansion of consumer demand also weakened, albeit very slightly. This does not apply to current spending by the public authorities, but to consumer spending by households. Here again the slowdown was mainly confined to the Federal Republic of Germany, where the rise in wages lost momentum and the savings ratio increased. Although in Italy and France the opposite trend prevailed, there was on balance a slight slowdown for the Community as a whole. In volume the growth of private consumption between 1962 and 1963 was about 5%, compared with 6% from 1961 to 1962.

As already stated, supply from domestic sources rose somewhat more slowly than in the preceding year. Industrial production (as defined in the Index of the Statistical Office of the European Communities) was probably up 5%, after increasing by 6% between 1961 and 1962. The growth of agricultural output was decidely weaker than in the preceding year, whereas the lively expansion in the services sector continued.

Imports from non-member countries rose rather more rapidly than in 1962. Imports of goods were up about 10.5% by volume and in value, compared with 8% between 1961 and 1962.

The internal trade of the Community expanded even faster. The increase in merchandise trade between the member countries may be estimated at about 16% in value, as against 14% for 1962. Decisive for this development were not only the further steps taken to establish the common market and the lively expansion that despite everything was a feature of overall demand, but also the appreciable differences from one member country to another which developed during 1963 in the relation between expansion of internal demand and expansion of internal supply.

These differences are clearly reflected in the way price levels developed. For the Community as a whole the trend was again upward, with relative stability in the Federal Republic of Germany and also - in the first half of the year - in the Netherlands and Belgium, but a stronger upward price push in Italy and France. It is clear that expansion of the Community's internal trade was an essential factor in preventing prices in these two countries from rising even further. On the other hand, there can be no doubt that it also affected prices in those member countries where they are still comparatively stable.

Since imports increased more than exports, the Community's deficit on trade swelled further: in 1963 it probably amounted to about $2,800 million. This means that the deterioration since 1959 has been almost $4,000 million.

Although, mainly because of the trend in merchandise trade, there were practically no further surpluses on current account, the Community's overall balance of payments again showed a surplus in 1963, particularly as a result of greater imports of private capital. However, these trends grew distinctly weaker in the second half of the year.

With these estimates of results for the full year 1963 it may be useful to give a few figures about longer-term economic developments in the Community. Between 1958 (the first measures to set up EEC came into force at the beginning of that year) and 1963, the gross Community product grew by about 30% (USA 22%; United Kingdom 16%). The index of industrial production alone rose 41%. The general standard of living, in terms of real private consumption per head, has gone up about 23%, in the last five years, while the Community's internal trade has risen by approximately 130%. In trade with non-member countries, imports have advanced 51% and exports 35% (world trade, exclusive of intra-Community trade, rose by 31%).

In 1964 economic expansion will continue. Demand should grow at roughly the same pace as between 1962 and 1963 and the growth of supply from sources within the Community might speed up a little.

On the demand side a speed-up is expected mainly in external demand, i.e. in exports of goods and services from the Community to non-member countries. This is chiefly because of the expansive outlook for world business.

Within the Community the volume, and perhaps also the value, of investment can be expected to grow more rapidly. The livelier trend in the expansion of investment by enterprises observed in the second half of 1963 will probably continue. Despite certain limitations on the expansion of public activity in building and construction, normal weather in 1964 after the abnormal conditions of 1963 should of itself ensure that investment in building rises more rapidly than between 1962 and 1963 - an additional impetus will come from the continued briskness of demand.

The growth of private consumers' expenditure on the other hand will probably slow down somewhat. However, since the price rise might simultaneously flatten out a little, the real increase in consumption is unlikely to fall off significantly.

Assuming normal weather, the increase in production could be somewhat greater than between 1962 and 1963. All in all, the Commission's staff at present consider that an increase of about 4. 5% in the Community's real gross product between 1963 and 1964 is possible.

Imports from non-member countries will probably again rise appreciably, although their annual growth may be somewhat smaller than between 1962 and 1963. There could be some further deterioration in the balance of trade, and current payments may even show a moderate deficit in 1964.

The forecasts at present established in no way suggest that there will be a sufficient movement towards stable prices. Even if there is a fall in the rate at which prices rise in France and Italy (there will be more chance of this if stabilization policy is tightened up), in the Netherlands and Belgium stronger rises are probable. In the Federal Republic of Germany it is quite conceivable that upward pressures on prices will become more marked as 1964 advances.

For the Community in general it must be noted that inflationary pressure will be the main problem facing those responsible for economic policy: such pressure must be eliminated or prevented from reappearing. Unless budget policy and credit policy are used in most member countries to slow down the expansion of internal demand generally, there is no prospect of success in this direction. One merit of this policy of general restraint, which has in part been put into practice already, is that it is the most likely to ensure that the balance of external transactions does not deteriorate too far and too long; if this were to occur, the Community would eventually have great difficulty in fulfilling its obligations in connection with development aid. Should such a policy result in a somewhat smaller real economic growth than at present forecast, this would have to be accepted in the interest of equilibrium, the more so as establishment of this balance would in turn be a major factor in rendering economic growth possible over a longer period.

187

Trend of supply and utilization of goods and services(1)

	1961 (2)	1961 (3)	1962 (3)	1963 (3)(4)	1964 (3)(5)
	At current prices ($'000m.)	Changes in volume compared with the previous year in %			
Gross Community product	205.7	5.3	5.0	4	4.5
Private consumption	125.0	6.2	6.1	5	4.5
Public consumption	28.5	5.6	6.7	5	3.5
Gross fixed asset formation	46.2	9.5	6.3	4	5.5
Balance: Exports(6) minus imports(6)	+ 3.1	+ 2.6	+ 1.2	-0.1	- 0.6

(1) The aggregates for the Community are computed on the basis of the official exchange rates.

(2) In 1961 prices; average 1961 exchange rates.

(3) In prices of the preceding year; exchange rates of the preceding year.

(4) Estimates by the Commission's staff.

(5) Forecasts by the Commission's staff.

(6) Goods, services and factor income.

Balance of Trade
(in millions of dollars)

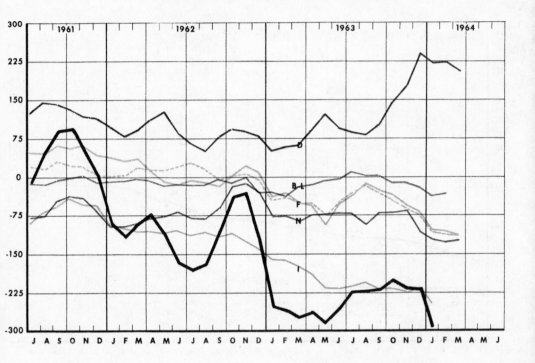

NOTES: Three-month moving average - Exports fob, imports
cif; excluding gold for monetary purposes. - Conversion at
official exchange rates. - France: broken line is for trade with
countries outside the franc area only; unbroken line is for overall trade. - The curves for France and the Community in 1961
have been modified to take into account a residual item in France's
imports for 1961 which figured in the French statistics for January
1962. The effects of the change in methods of compiling statistics
in Western Germany at the beginning of 1962 have also been
eliminated.

189

Industrial Production
1958 = 100

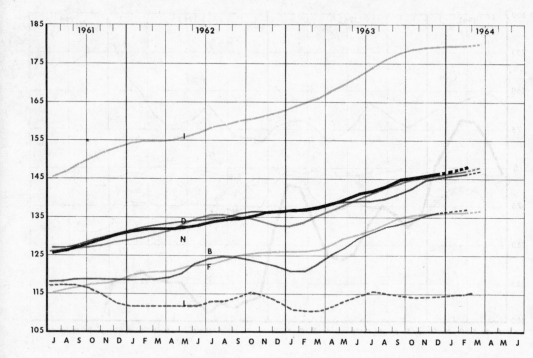

NOTES: The curves represent estimated trends, which have been established - with exception of the last two months - on the basis of indices, adjusted by the S O E C for seasonal variations. - Excluding construction, food, beverages and tobacco. - Netherlands: including food, beverages and tobacco.

---

*Economic Situation in the Community, December 1963 and Graphs and Notes on the Economic Situation in the Community, April, 1964.

CHAPTER 6

THE INTERNAL MARKET

The most fundamental part of the Community's work is
in the realm of the internal market created by the customs union
of the Six. The development of this market depends upon the
elimination of all barriers to trade among the member states.

To remove barriers to trade, tariffs, quotas and other
barriers having the same affect as tariffs, the member states
are harmonizing customs regulations and legislation (see
schedule for the removal of these barriers). Rules governing
the processing traffic are also in effect.

The creation of the customs union means the free movement
of goods (see chart and graph showing intra-Community trade). As
a corollary, the Rome Treaty provides for the free movement of
services, capital, and labor (see Chapter 8) and the right of establishment. These policies have resulted in increasing interpenetration of markets. The ultimate objective of these efforts is
the benefit for the consumer. The EEC has begun analysing the
effect of the new internal market on consumers.

Two areas not covered by the documents reproduced here,
but important in the development of the internal market, are
the policies on monopolies and on national safeguards.

Member states are required, under Article 37 of the Treaty,
progressively to adjust state monopolies which discriminate between "nationals of the member states in regard to conditions of
supply or marketing of goods". Such monopolies exist in France,
the German Federal Republic, and Italy. These countries have
made important reductions in their barriers to tobacco imports,
permitting increasingly larger imports of tobacco from other
countries. Salt, cigarette paper, lighters, flints, and quinine,
all of which have been under state control in Italy, and have been
brought under the scope of Article 37.

Safeguard measures may be used by member states which experience persistent economic difficulties in general or in a particular region. In the industrial sector measures for safeguarding certain industries, mainly in Italy and Germany, have been granted for limited periods by the Commission. Usually the grant has been conditioned by provisions for the reorganization of the industry or sector concerned.

Trade in certain processed agricultural products was possible during the first stage because of grants of authorization for safeguard measures, mainly to Germany. After January 1962 more general rules were established for agriculture. States notify the Commission and other member states of safeguard measures. The Commission decides, within four working days, whether the measures are to be upheld, amended or withdrawn. Member states can appeal the Commission decision to the Council which decides by a qualified majority. Two exceptions to the general rules apply: 1) for grain products, the Council can suspend the Commission decision for ten days before making its own decision and 2) no measures can be taken without advance approval of the Commission (for special grades of fruits and vegetables.) States may request prior authorization from the Commission. The final appeal in all cases is to the Court of Justice.

Cases Before the Court of the European Communities Relating to the Internal Market

Chapter 14, Document 14.1 cases: 7/61, 10/61, 2/62, 3/62, 26/62, 28-30/62, 24/62, 25/62, 34/62, 13/63, 27/62, 73-74/63.

Document 14.2 cases: 22/63, 90-91/63, 1/64.

COMMON MARKET TIMETABLE

Underlined entries show measures taken under the decisions of May 12, 1960, and May 15, 1962, to speed up the Common Market timetable

Date	Internal Tariff Cuts		Quota Enlargements	Alignment of National Tariffs on Common External Tariff Reduction of difference (up or down)
	Total	Minimum for each product	(total)	
Stage I				
1958				
1959 Jan. 1	By 10%	—	By 20%	
1960 Jan. 1		By 10%	By 20%	
1960 July 1	By 10%	By 10%	—	
1960 Dec. 31	By 10%	By 10%*		
1961 Jan. 1	By 10%	By 10%	By 20%	
Dec. 31	By 10%	By 10%	Abolition of quota restrictions on industrial goods**	By 30% (common tariff fully applied where difference amounted to 15% or less)

By end of Stage I: Total internal tariff cuts on each product amounted to 40%. Export duties had been abolished. This Stage ended on December 31, 1961.

*By 5% only for agricultural products.
**Special arrangements were made for enlargement of agricultural quotas.

COMMON MARKET TIMETABLE

Underlined entries show measures taken under the decisions of May 12, 1960, and May 15, 1962, to speed up the Common Market timetable.

Date		Internal Tariff Cuts		Quota Enlargements (total)	Alignment of National Tariffs on Common External Tariff Reduction of difference (up or down)
		Total	Minimum for each product		
Stage II					
1962	July 1	By 10%	By 10%	—	—
1963	July 1	By 10%	By 5%	—	By 30%
1964	Dec. 31	By 10%	By 5%	—	—
1965	Dec. 31	By 10%	By 5%	—	—

By end of Stage II: Total internal tariff cuts on each product will be at least 65%. This Stage may only be prolonged by unanimous vote of the Council on a proposal by the Common Market Commission.

COMMON MARKET TIMETABLE

Date	Internal Tariff Cuts		Quota Enlargements (total)	Alignment of National Tariffs on Common External Tariff Reduction of difference (up or down)
	Total	Minimum for each product		
Stage III				
1966 Jan. 1	Acting on the Commission's proposal, the Council fixes the rate of remaining internal tariff cuts during Stage 3. TO ZERO	TO ZERO	—	—
1969 Dec. 31			—	FULL ADOPTION OF COMMON EXTERNAL TARIFF

By end of Stage III: All internal tariffs and quotas, and restrictions on the free movement of men, services and capital, to be removed. This Stage may only be prolonged by unanimous vote of the Council on a proposal by the Commission; the total transition period may not be prolonged by more than three years.

195

Trade Between Member Countries
(Indices of dollar value of imports)
1958 = 100

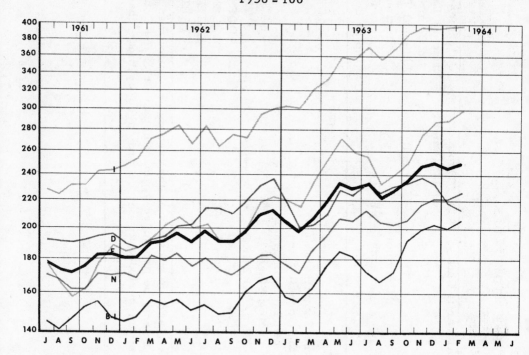

NOTES: C.i.f.; excluding gold for monetary purposes. Three -
month moving average. Conversion at official exchange rates.
- Belgium and Luxembourg: common curve.

INTRA-COMMUNITY TRADE (Imports)

(in million $)

1958	6,790.3
1959	8,091.0
1960	10,150.4
1961	11,718.4
1962	13,416.4
1963	15,705.6

Movement of trade among member countries by main classes of products (1)

Classes of products	(in millions of units of account)					Increase in 1963 over 1962 (in %) (2)
	1959	1960	1961	1962	1963	
Food, beverages and tobacco	753.6	942.4	1030.1	1194	1355	+ 14
Fuels	547.0	616.1	603.3	642	717	+ 12
Other raw materials	550.0	733.9	767.7	832	865	+ 4
Chemicals	417.4	548.5	622.2	697	824	+ 18
Machinery and transport equipment	——	1640	2181	2682	3185	+ 19
Miscellaneous manufactured articles	2110.3	2895.6	3283.9	3621	4191	+ 15

(1) On the basis of import statistics; classes of products are in accordance with SITC headings. Totals and growth rates refer to the first nine months of the year only.

(2) No correction has been made to take account of the changes in import statistics introduced in Germany and France at the beginning of 1962.

6.1 TARIFF REDUCTION AND ADJUSTMENT*

The first of July 1963 is an important date in the implementation of the Treaty of Rome. The measures taken at that date - a new 10% reduction of duties amongst the Member States and the second approximation to the common external tariff - represent a considerable step forward in the establishment of a customs union.

Under the provisions of the Treaty and by virtue of the acceleration decisions the reduction of internal duties already made amounted to:

i)   50% of the basic duty for manufactured goods and
ii)   35% of the basic duty for non-liberalized agricultural products.

On 1 July the duties were therefore reduced by a total of 60% on industrial goods and 45% on non-liberalized agricultural products. The target set in the Treaty, which was that duties must be reduced by 50% by the end of the second stage, was exceeded by 1 July this year so far as manufactured goods are concerned.

This internal dismantlement of duties is particularly welcome at this moment when there is full employment and a growing strain on prices. The Member States themselves felt the need for this step.

On 27 August 1962 Italy, for instance, had unilaterally applied an additional 10% reduction of the duties in force at the time (or a 5% reduction of the basic duties) for manufactured goods other than those in respect of which measures of safeguard were authorized under Article 226 of the Treaty (silk, lead and zinc products) and for agricultural products other than those falling under a Community market organization with a levy system. The new general reduction of 1 July absorbs this anticipatory reduction, so that Italy is now in the same position as the other Member States.

The second approximation of the national tariffs to the common external tariff also took place on 1 July 1963 - two and a half years earlier than was stipulated in the Treaty. It was effected in the same way as the first approximation of 1 January 1961.

At that time the Community was negotiating at GATT (General Agreement on Tariffs and Trade) for recognition of its common external tariff. To demonstrate the liberal nature of its commercial policy the Community has decided to offer the other members of GATT a 20% linear reduction of this tariff on a basis of reciprocity. The calculation of the first approximation was, therefore, made assuming a common external tariff reduced by 20%, provided however that the duties so arrived at should not be lower than those of the full tariff.

The Community did not obtain from the non-member countries the tariff concessions it expected. In certain cases the product-by-product negotiations in GATT led to a 20% reduction of the common external tariff, but in others the reduction was less or had to be withdrawn for lack of reciprocity.

Despite this experience and with an eye to the new tariff negotiations proposed by the United States, the representatives of the Governments of the Member States, meeting in the Council of Ministers, decided to repeat the liberal gesture they had made at the time of the first approximation. The second approximation will, therefore, also be effected on the basis of the initial duties reduced by 20%, even if that reduction has not been negotiated or bound at GATT. Nevertheless, by decision of the Member Governments of 23 May 1963(1) this basis of calculation will not apply after 31 December 1965 unless an adequate degree of reciprocity has been obtained from the non-Member States in the coming GATT negotiations.

As in the case of the first approximation, the method of calculation will not apply to certain sensitive products on List G (2) (paper pulp, ferro-alloys, aluminium, lead and zinc, etc.) (3). In the case of these products the second approximation will be made towards the non-reduced common external tariff.

----

(1) See official gazette of the European Communities, No. 83, 1 June 1963.

(2) Ibid., No. 37, 2 June 1961.

(3) The Commission has proposed to the Council that the 20% reduction should apply to cocoa paste in bulk, cocoa butter and cocoa powder; this proposal appears on the agenda for the Council session of 10 and 11 July 1963.

*Bulletin of the EEC, August 1963, pp. 9, 11.

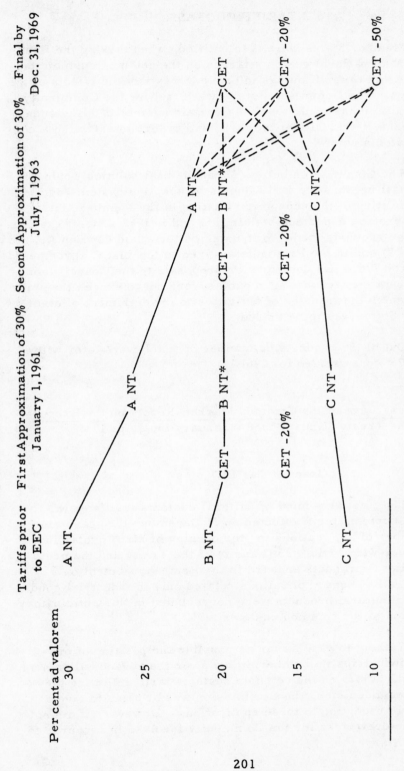

Application of the Common External Tariff

A, B, C -- EEC Countries;   NT -- National Tariff;   CET -- Common External Tariff;   CET -20% is
CET with current reductions in effect;   CET -50% is CET with proposed Kennedy Round reductions;
* -- NT cannot fall below non-reduced CET.

Source: EEC Commission Bulletin, August 1963.

6.2 TARIFF QUOTAS*

7.　　Member States were also entitled, when making the first alignment of national customs tariffs on the common customs tariff, to resort to tariff quotas in order to restrict the effects of the alignment. The Commission was aware that for the Community these tariff quotas could involve a certain number of risks such as a breach in the unity of the tariff and failure to establish a complete customs union.

8.　　The Commission believed that the best solution would be to forestall recourse to tariff quotas by adapting customs duties to the realities of the economic situation in the Member States, and it therefore undertook both in 1961 and in 1962 a strict examination of the requests made to it, using criteria laid down in Article 25 (1 and 2) and in the Protocols annexed to the List G agreement of 2 March 1960. Its decisions or proposals to the Council took into account the fact that such quotas were not to exceed the limits beyond which the transfer of activities to the detriment of other Member States was to be feared.

　　Out of 159 requests, a number of which were later withdrawn, 78 were granted for 1961.

---

*The First Stage of the Common Market: Report on the Execution of the Treaty (January 1958 - January 1962), p. 19.

Grant of Tariff Quotas*

12.　　The first alignment of national customs tariffs on the common customs tariff effected on 31 December 1960 gave rise to a number of applications for the opening of tariff quotas in accordance with Article 25 (1 and 2) of the Treaty and the protocols on list G products annexed to the Rome Agreement on 2 March 1960. These applications related only to industrial goods, since agricultural products were not included in this anticipatory application of the common customs tariff.

　　Wishing to ease as far as possible the position of processing industries in Member States after the advance alignment of national tariffs on the common customs tariff following the acceleration decision, the Commission was at pains to give a favourable reception to these applications. However, it did not forget the drawbacks for the Community involved in recourse to tariff quotas, the most serious of which is to slow or prevent the establishment of the customs union.

The tariff quotas opened by Member States have consequently been provisional and have related to tentative amounts. The establishment of tariff quotas for 1961 was effected after consultation with the Member States.

The Commission has tried to limit the number and volume of tariff quotas and encouraged Member States to withdraw applications. Wherever possible the Commission has tried to reach a Community solution - particularly the suspension of the duties in the common customs tariff.

In 1962 also an effort was made to reduce the number of applications as far as possible. In some cases Member States submitted their applications for tariff quotas as an alternative to applications to postpone the alignment of certain duties under their national customs tariffs or to suspend the duties under the common customs tariff.

---

*Fifth General Report on the Activities of the Community,pp. 37-39.

Tariff Quotas*

In its Action Programme the Commission says it aims to have national tariff quotas abolished by the end of the transition period at the latest. In pursuing this aim the Commission's rule is to take account of the degree of progress in establishing the common market (particularly the abolition of internal customs duties concurrently with the gradual introduction of the external tariff), and to see that the quotas granted to not exceed the limits beyong which transfers of activities to the detriment of other Member States might be feared.

---

*Sixth General Report on the Activities of the Community, pp. 33-34.

TABLE 1

Comparative table of applications for tariff quotas (1961, 1962 and 1963)

Provisions invoked

	1961 Article 25					1962 Article 25					1963 Article 25				
	par. 1	par. 2	par. 3	List G	Total	par. 1	par. 2	par. 3	List G	Total	par. 1	par. 2	par. 3	List G	Total
Applications made	55	58	-	46	159	58	92	85	43	278	29	27	43	36	135
Withdrawn a) by the applicant Member State	13	21	-	2	36	17	41	22	1	81	3	2	1	-	6
b) with a Community solution	12	19	-	9	40	13	32	5	5	55	-	6	-	-	6
Totals:	25	40	-	11	76	30	73	27	6	136	3	8	1	-	12
Applications not yet dealt with	30	18	-	35	83	28	19	58	37	142	26	19	42	36	123
Refused	4	7	-	1	12	-	9	28	1	38	-	-	-	-	-
Granted	26	11	-	34	71	28	10	30	36	104	21	3	23	36	83
Applications on which decision is pending											5	16	19	-	40

204

6.3 HARMONIZATION OF CUSTOMS REGULATIONS*

10.   The effectiveness of the steps to abolish internal frontiers
by eliminating tariffs and quotas will depend on the readiness of
the customs authorities of the six Member States to respect
common principles and to apply the same rules in taxing goods.
The incidence of a rate of duty depends on many factors (value
for customs purposes, effective date of the duty, payment credit,
clearance procedure). Common rules will have to be worked
out for exemption from duty, for suspending duties and for goods
in transit.

Acting under Article 27 of the Treaty and in close collaboration with the national authorities, the Commission has started
to put through a programme of harmonization based on a system
of priorities. Some recommendations have been submitted to all
the Member States.

---

*The First Stage of the Common Market: Report on the Execu-
tion of the Treaty (January 1958 - January 1962), p. 20.

Customs Rules Governing Trade and Harmonization
of Customs Legislation*

13.   The system of free circulation certificates (1) instituted
by the Commission's decisions of 4 December 1958 and 5 December 1960 operated in 1961 to the satisfaction of business and of
customs administrations. There were no difficulties in applying
tariff advantages (a 30% cut in duties for most goods) and quota
advantages in trade within EEC gave rise to no difficulties.

It should only be noted that this system of free circulation certificates is playing an increasing role of national customs
legislation since it grows in complexity with the development
of the Common Market, which is based on the free movement
of goods.

14.   The levy system for processing traffic (2) came into
force on 1 January 1961. Government and business adapted themselves without difficulty to this wholly original arrangement,
which provides a satisfactory solution to the problem of processed
products within the Community under systems of suspended payment of customs duties. In 1961 the levy was at the rate of 25%
of the duties of the common customs tariff laid down for "non-

Community" products. The rate was fixed at 35% from 1 January 1962 by a Commission decision of 2 December 1961.

15.   In 1961 the EEC began to achieve results in the harmonization of customs legislation.

In this field the Commission can do no more than make recommendations (Articles 27 and 155 of the Treaty) and makes every effort to obtain the agreement of the national administrations concerned.

---

(1) See Fourth General Report, sec. 19.

(2) The mechanism of this was analysed in the Fourth General Report, pp. 37-39, sec. 20.

*Fifth General Report on the Activities of the Community, pp. 40-41.

Approximation of Customs Legislation*

15.   If the customs union is to be established by the end of the transition period, much more vigorous action than is being taken at present will be needed in approximating national customs legislation.   The Commission therefore proposes in its Action Programme to submit to the Governments a harmonization plan which it considers should be carried out without fail in the next four years.   The execution of this plan would be supervised by the Customs Committee, which includes the directors of customs departments of the member Governments.

---

*Sixth General Report on the Activities of the Community, p. 36.

Definition of Origin of Imports*

21.   In order to establish an effective customs union a body of Community customs legislation is needed, and among the common rules to be adopted those on origin of imports are of special interest.

On this matter the laws and regulations of the Member States must be brought into alignment so as to apply in a uniform manner the measures to be taken to implement the common commercial policy vis-a-vis third countries, which will largely depend on the origin of the goods in question, and to give effect to the new Convention of Association.

In view of the tariff and quota advantages the Member States and the associated overseas States accord each other, the criteria to be adopted in defining origin for the purposes of the Convention may in general be stricter than those used in Community trade with non-member countries. For this reason the Member States and the Commission have examined separately the problems arising in these two cases.

Work was begun on defining the concept of origin for the purposes of the Convention of Association. This was more urgent because Protocol No. 3 to the Convention requires the Commission to submit a draft decision to the Association Council, within six months from the date of entry into force of the Convention, defining the concept of "goods originating...." to be adopted in giving effect to Title I of the Convention.

The Member States' experts, in conjunction with representatives of the Commission, are therefore working on the definition of this concept, which concerns all items liable to enter into trade between the Member States and the associated States except petroleum products. These were provisionally excluded from the discussion at the request of the Member States' representatives. Enough progress has been made to ensure that the time-limit laid down in Protocol No. 3 will be complied with.

The criteria adopted in defining the concept of "goods originating...." for the purposes of the Association Convention are broadly speaking as follows:

Goods will be regarded as originating in the Member States or in the associated States if:

a)   They have been obtained entirely in the said States (for example minerals extracted from their soil and products derived therefrom);

b)   They have been obtained either wholly or in part from products imported from countries not parties to the Association provided that these imported products are processed to an extent sufficient to place them in a new tariff heading in the Brussels Nomenclature (for example fabrics manufactured from yarns imported from countries not parties to the Association). Since the application of this straightforward rule may in certain cases have

economically undesirable consequences, the necessary adjustments have been made by drawing up:

i)   First, a "negative" list of operations which, although
their effect is to place the item under a different tariff heading,
will not be deemed to confer on them the origin of the Member
State or of the associated State in which the operations were
carried out;

ii)   Secondly, a "positive" list of operations which, although
they do not have the effect of placing the item under a different
tariff heading, will nevertheless be deemed to confer on it the
origin of the Member State or of the associated State in which
the operations were carried out.

        Attestation that items entering into trade between the
EEC Member States and the associated States fulfill the above
conditions and are entitled to benefit of the preferential system
laid down in the Association Convention will be furnished by
the presentation to the customs of the importing Member or
associated State of a special certificate issued by the appropriate authority of the exporting Member or associated State
on the basis of assurances given by the exporter.

        The establishment of a common definition of origin
applying to Community trade with non-member countries will
be undertaken in the near future, as soon as the work relating
to trade under the Association Convention has been completed.

_____

*Bulletin of the EEC, July 1963, pp. 30-31.

6.4 RULES FOR DEALING WITH PROCESSING TRAFFIC*

11.   On the other hand, the Commission laid down as early
as 1958 Community rules for dealing with processing traffic.
The system is intended to help those activities in the various
countries which are concerned with exports; various methods
are used to allow the duty-free import of foreign products, provided these are to be re-exported after processing. The advent
of the Common Market raises this problem in quite new terms,
as it is not possible to adapt the preferences between Member
States to the presence in the goods being traded of "non-member"
elements on which the appropriate duty has not been paid. To
solve this problem the Commission has instituted a customs levy

at a rate equal to a percentage of the national duty applicable
to products imported from non-member countries. This rate
goes up as the duties between Member States come down, till
it falls into line with the relevant rate in the common customs
tariff. For the period from 1 January to 31 December 1961 the
rate was 25%. The levy had not been collected before 1 January
1961 because of the low incidence of the first customs reductions
and their more or less general extension to non-member countries. After a transition period, "non-member" products will
be free to circulate throughout the Community once the duty
shown in the common customs tariff has been paid.

The formula for the levy caused no major difficulty
from the point of view of customs technicalities, nor did it place
any great burden on traders. A feature of the levy is that it
will lead to the collection of the common customs duty, of which
it is a percentage, well before the end of the transition period.

---

*The First Stage of the Common Market: Report on the Execu-
tion of the Treaty (January 1958 - January 1962), pp. 21-22.

Processing Traffic*

14.   On 25 June 1962(1) the Commission took a new decision
on processing traffic(2) raising the rate of the "customs" levy
to 45% of the common external tariff to allow for the new reduction of customs duties in intra-Community trade. Nevertheless it appears that where non-agricultural products have
been obtained by the conversion of products subject to agricultural levies, the application of the "customs" levy is in many
cases no longer sufficient to ensure the protection which farmers
are entitled to expect from the new system. The Commission
is studying whether the basis of the "customs" levy should be
changed in this sector.

---

(1) See official gazette of the European Communities, No. 59,
    13 July 1962.

(2) See Fourth General Report, sec. 20, and Fifth General
    Report, sec. 14.

*Sixth General Report on the Activities of the Community, p. 36.

6.5 ELIMINATION OF QUOTAS IN THE INDUSTRIAL SECTOR*

12.   As far as the elimination of quotas is concerned, suffice it to say that more has already been done than is required by the Treaty and that, as the result of the speed-up decision of 12 May 1960, the process of eliminating quotas on industrial products has at the end of the first stage almost ceased for lack of quotas to eliminate. The age of quantitative restrictions may be considered to be passed and in future trade will be carried on under the system of liberalization, except in agriculture and the sectors where the State intervenes directly in selling.

As early as 1958 a considerable part of trade between Member States was freed from all quantitative restrictions. Only France was an exception, but the policy of financial recovery instituted by the French Government at the end of 1958 has enabled the situation in France to be brought gradually into line with that in the other Member States.

Under Article 31 of the Treaty Member States have bound between themselves the level of liberalization and the lists of products liberalized by them within the framework of the OEEC on 14 January 1955. It is of course not possible to apply new restrictions on the imports liberalized and bound products unless one of the safeguard clauses of the Treaty has been invoked.

From 1959 onwards a multilateral system was substituted for the previous bilateral system, when global quotas were opened on a non-discriminatory basis to other Member States. Three successive increases in the global quotas were made in 1959, 1960 and 1961. The acceleration decision included an additional increase on quotas for certain agricultural products in 1961, and industrial quotas were abolished on 31 December 1961.

This increase had a remarkable effect on the opening of markets for products that had enjoyed strict protection when the Treaty came into force.

---

*The First Stage of the Common Market: Report on the Execution of the Treaty (January 1958 - January 1962), p.22.

Elimination of Quantitative Restrictions*

16. Further progress has been made since the beginning of 1962 in the suppression of quotas and the liberalization of trade within the Community.

The speed-up decision of 12 May 1960 stipulated that quantitative restrictions were to be totally abolished in the industrial sector on 31 December 1961. This obligation has on the whole been fulfilled by Member States, except in the case of some products of the food-processing industry. For these certain Member States have requested the prior application of compensatory charges in pursuance of the Council's decision, under Article 235 of the Treaty, on goods processed from agricultural products. On the basis of Article 226 of the Treaty the Commission has authorized the maintenance for a limited period of the quotas for citric acid and calcium citrate in Italy, and in Benelux for penicillin and medicaments based on penicillin and for semi-conductors in France(1). For this last product the French Government had applied the liberalization laid down in the speed-up decision of 1 October 1961 and invoked Article 226 on the grounds of temporary difficulties of adaptation confronting the national industry. Quotas for products not listed in Annex II to the Treaty will probably be completely removed very soon except for some goods covered by State monopolies of a commercial nature.

Under the provisions of Article 33(4), the European Commission must also render a decision on whether imports of a product in the cause of two successive years have been less than the quotas opened. In such case the Member State shall abolish the quota for the product concerned.

The Commission has adopted the principle of a series of decisions based on the results of the years 1959 and 1960 and these decisions must be communicated to the Member States. Their economic scope, however, is very limited because of the decisions providing for the general suppression of quotas, such as the decision to speed up the pace at which the aims of the Treaty are to be realized in the industrial sphere (where restrictions of this nature have practically disappeared). In the same way, the regulations under the common agricultural policy will lead to the suppression of quota systems in the Member States for a number of particularly important agricultural products as from 1 July 1962.

211

Lastly, quantitative restrictions on exports were
to be totally eliminated at the end of the first stage. This
requirement was complied with by Member States with
a slight delay due to the need to finalize Community
measures to alleviate certain difficulties and prevent disruption of trade in sensitive sectors such as leather and
skins, wood, non-ferrous waste and scrap and unworked
diamonds. Recommendations to this end have been sent
to Member States on the basis of Articles 155 and 115 of
the Treaty.

After these various measures of trade liberalization there are then only a limited number of agricultural
products still covered by the quota system laid down in
Article 33. The fourth increase of global quotas was
effected in 1962 in accordance with the Treaty. The infringements mentioned in the Fourth General Report
have been regularized, and at present only two new cases
are being investigated in connection with the requirements
of Articles 30 to 36.

In these circumstances more attention will henceforth have to be given to measures with equivalent effect
to quantitative restrictions that can be applied to either
imports or exports. Apart from the fact that the protectionist nature of these provisions is difficult to prove
it seems that the majority of such obstacles will disappear
with the harmonization of legislative and administrative
provisions, the disparity between which affects the operation of the Common Market. In any case the Commission
would issue directives under Article 33(7) if it should prove
that such provisions restricted trade and protected domestic production and that their alignment at Community
level could not be effected in the near future.

---

(1) These are pieces of radio-electric equipment covering
one heading and three sub-headings.

*Fifth General Report on the Activities of the Community,
pp. 43-44.

6.6 THE INTERPENETRATION OF
THE MARKETS*

General

65.   The considerable efforts made by business circles
as early as 1958 to adapt themselves to common market
conditions were intensified during 1960 and at the beginning of 1961.   They have been along two general lines:
first new trade associations have been set up at the level
of the Six, bringing together the individual national associations and accompanied by greater activity on the part
of those which had been pioneers in this field; secondly,
and particularly in industry trade and handicrafts, a great
many forms of co-operation have been applied.   They range
from technical agreements to the establishment of new
companies grouping different enterprises in a single country,
enterprises in several Member States, or enterprises in a
Member State and in one or several non-member countries -
all bent on fresh effort to penetrate the common market.

The main objective of the trade associations at
the level of the Six has been to arrive at a Community
position on matters of common concern and they have
multiplied their contacts with the European Commission.
The Commission, for its part, has always welcomed the
formation of trade associations at Community level and
the tendency for these groupings to keep it informed
of the views common to the mass of their members.

The development of the common market since
the speed-up decision of 12 May 1960 and the irrevocable
nature of its progress have induced enterprises to hasten
the measures they are taking to adapt themselves to
the new conditions which it has engendered.

They are concentrating on heavier investment to
increase capacity and bring their plant up to date.
Mergers and takeovers bear witness to a movement towards the larger unit; specialization is gaining ground
and firms manufacturing neighbouring ranges of products
are concluding specialization agreements and establishing networks of sales subsidiaries in the six countries.

The tendency to form new companies in which enterprises of two Member States or of one Member State and of one non-member country often have a holding has become stronger in the period under review.

Broadly speaking, these reactions among business circles are borne out in annual company reports. Many of these refer to the development of the Common Market as the reason for investments in hand or planned, or to explain the purpose of financial operations carried out as part of a policy of consolidation and progress within the Community.

66. The effects of the Common Market on supplies to the consumer are so varied that it would seem impossible to summarize them accurately.

What is certain is that prosperity would have grown less rapidly had it not been for the gradual implementation of the Treaty of Rome. One of the features of the adaptation of production and trade to a steadily expanding market is that thanks to the gradual integration of separate economies the consumer is offered a distinctly fuller and more attractive range of merchandise. The primary reason for this is that wholesalers, and even retailers, have sharply stepped up trade across frontiers by fresh contacts, business trips, visits to trade fairs and market research. But it has also been noted, particularly during the past year, that consumer goods manufacturers in the various countries have also shown great initiative in expanding their markets within the EEC.

Several signs confirm this impression:

a) External trade statistics in the Member States show that trade with other EEC countries has been making ever greater strides;

b) Industry is endeavouring to establish a "European style" in the widest sense of the term, this being essential if wide outlets for the production of the different countries is to be secured;

214

c) Although admittedly still far from complete price statistics show that producers are giving more and more attention to external markets and that with the aim of stepping up their exports, they have been exercising price restraint where these markets are concerned.

But the expansion of trade has also made it much more difficult for national industry, now that import barriers are lower, effectively to impose the price increases it wishes on the market. In this way increased trade has had a stabilizing effect on prices within the individual countries.

67.   A sample survey covering several department stores in the Member States bears out these generalizations.

In the opinion of the stores managers questioned, the main effect of the establishment of the common market has been to spur on manufacturers to conquer new markets and to improve production methods. In relation with the cuts in customs duties, these factors are exerting steady pressure on prices, curbing increases and setting in train, or reinforcing, reductions; the effects of the common market on "national" prices are clearly reflected, for example, in prices for the following articles: refrigerators, nylon raincoats, Italian wines, French brandy, woollen blankets from the Netherlands and Belgium, knitwear, etc. In an exhibition "France and the Common Market", one department store has already put on display the various lines it has been able to mark down thanks to the EEC.

---

*Fifth General Report on the Activities of the Community, pp. 92-94.

6.7 THE COMMON MARKET'S EFFECTS FOR THE CONSUMER*

69.   In order to ascertain what has been the initial impact of
the establishment of the Common Market on the consumer's standard of living and way of life, the Commission itself has made
arrangements to obtain the necessary information, particularly
statistical data, since it could not be immediately derived from
the usual sources.

The effects on prices are much more difficult to discern.
Several attempts have been made without any real success so far
because of the difficulty of following closely the import and consumer prices of certain products in intra-Community trade. A
new survey of consumer prices for some hundred products is to
begin in 1963 with the assistance of the distributors, but we shall
have to wait until 1964 to evaluate the price trends for these
articles.

The distributors have agreed to co-operate in an annual
survey of intra-Community trade in consumer goods and their
price trend.

70.   The gain brought to consumers by the Common Market
may be judged by the level of personal income and how it is
spent.

It is, of course, impossible to say exactly what effects
the Common Market is beginning to have on consumer income
levels; a study of this kind would require close analysis by
regions, occupational groups and sectors of the population.
However, to the extent that the Common Market has helped the
expansion of economic activity and industrial production in particular, its effects have spread to wages and personal incomes,
which have continued to grow in all Community countries since
1958. At constant prices, the increase in personal income by
1961 was nearly 25% in Germany and Italy, around 15% in the
Netherlands and France and 10% in Belgium.

71.   The ways in which the opening of frontiers has affected
the spending of consumer incomes are easier to ascertain.

Trade flows within the Community have multiplied not
only for supplies to industry and agriculture but also, and even
slightly more substantially, for household articles.

The following tables give the essential data on the trend of imports between 1958 and 1961:

TABLE 4

Imports of articles for domestic consumption in 1961 (1)

	Germany (F.R.)	France	Italy	BLEU	Nether-lands	EEC
	In million dollars					
Total imports	2 093	1 242	562	653	765	5 380
Imports from Community countries	1 100	376	192	454	505	2 625
Imports from other sources (2)	993	866	370	199	260	2 754
	Increase since 1958 in %					
Total imports	+60	+13	+40	+19	+70	+41
Imports from Community countries	+86	+132	+58	+26	+83	+73
Imports from other sources (2)	+36	−8	+32	+6	+51	+20

(1) The relevant statistical calculations are made only once a year, in or around July.

(2) Including associated overseas countries

The increase in four years in intra-Community imports of articles for domestic consumption was 130% in France, 80-90% in Germany and the Netherlands, 60% in Italy and 25% in Belgium. All these percentages are appreciably above the growth of income. It will also be noted that in three countries the increase in imports from non-member countries is also higher than that of family incomes. Thus consumers in each country are being offered a widening range of products from their partners in the Six, and this trend continued in 1962.

It should also be noted that trade does not entirely reflect the realities of the economic situation: when industries are transferred from one country to another, when a firm established in one member country opens a subsidiary in another, this has a similar effect to those of international trade but does not find its way into customs returns. And this kind of operation has taken place a number of times - both in food production and in manufactures - since the Common Market was set up.

72.   On a rough estimate the share of imported goods in current consumer purchases is between 10 and 20% in Benelux but much lower in the other Community countries - 3 to 4% in Italy, 8 to 9% in Germany. France occupies an intermediate position.

By the very reason of their size the Benelux countries have always been more dependent than the other Community countries on outside sources for their supplies of everyday consumer goods, and this tendency became more marked between 1958 and 1962, particularly in the Netherlands.

In the other countries, especially France and Italy, there is much less sale for imported products and the increase in imports of consumer goods, though quite considerable in absolute terms, still failed to effect any transformation of consumer habits in general.

73.   In some sectors the opening of frontiers and freer competition not only increased supplies to the consumer but also had definite effects on prices, though here the situation varies from country to country depending on how competitive industry is in each.

74.   It is particularly in consumer durables mainly household electrical appliances, radio and television, that consumers in the Community have been offered a wider range of products at lower prices, thanks to keener competition combined with improved productivity. French and Benelux consumers have been the chief gainers from the broader flow of trade between their countries on the one hand and Germany and Italy - particularly the latter - on the other.

75.   Italian and French consumers have benefited most from the relaxation or abolition of quotas in the motor vehicles sector. In Belgium, too, purchases of German and French makes have gone up at the expense of non-Community manufacturers. The effects of the Common Market in this field have been less perceptible for German and Dutch customers. More severe com-

petition seems also to have brought car prices down in Italy and Belgium, while elsewhere in the Community new models with the latest improvements have been on sale at last year's prices.

76.   The initial impact of the Common Market in other sectors has been more limited. Although trade in food products has grown steadily almost everywhere, there have been spectacular rises only for some products in certain countries - imports of Italian and Dutch vegetables into France (partly as a result of exceptional weather conditions) and of French and Italian fruit into Belgium and Germany. In Germany imports increased for the following products in particular - butter and cheese from Holland and France, bakery products and poultry from Holland, wine from Italy and France and fruit juice and chocolate from France. In some cases the intensification of trade in these products put considerable pressure on domestic prices for similar products.

There was some movement in other products too. France imported appreciably more carpets and furniture from Belgium and plastics from Germany. Germany bought more jewelery, clothing, footwear, knitwear and photo-film from Italy. The Netherlands imported more medical preparations and textiles from Belgium and clothing from Italy and Germany; B.L.E.U. increased its purchases of textiles (women's clothing) and footwear from Italy, the Netherlands and Germany. Lastly, Italy bought more household goods, particularly porcelain, from Germany.

77.   The most spectacular price cuts for imported products and indirectly domestic products were probably in the textiles, clothing and footwear sectors. Various Italian products (textiles, plastics, footwear) set prices falling and even drew positive reactions from competing producers in Germany and France in particular (improvement of production techniques and price cuts). Continuing customs disarmament will encourage this trend and probably extend it to other products.

78.   The development of trade among the Six raises, and will go on raising, the problem of informing the consumer about new products on the market. It may be noted that various national bodies issue certificates of quality. These bodies belong to a "Permanent International Quality Conference", in which experience is exchanged and services rendered on a reciprocal basis, and each guarantees consumers in its own country that products tested by its counterparts in the other Member States are of satisfactory quality. The European Office of Consumer Associations also has plans to make comparative tests of products already enjoying wide

distribution among Community consumers.

79.   Finally, consumers have felt the need to form an association at Community level even though their organizations have
generally not attained such unity at national level. In May 1962
the "Liaison Committee of EEC Consumers" was set up, consisting of representatives of trade unions, family organizations,
consumer associations and consumer co-operatives.

The Commission has invited this Committee to send
delegates to the advisory committees set up for farm products
in which the market is subject to a common organization. In
the five committees so far constituted, sixteen seats (full members and alternates) are offered to consumers' representatives.
The Committee meets regularly, and in March 1963 it organized
a study group on "organized consumer action in the Common
Market" at Brussels, when food additives and price policy in
particular were discussed.

---

*The Sixth General Report on the Activities of the Community, pp. 87-9

6.8 THE RIGHT OF ESTABLISHMENT AND SERVICES*

31.   The free movement of workers envisaged by Articles 48
and 51 does not cover the whole field of application of the Treaty's
provision on the free movement of persons. Great importance
also attaches to the freedom of self-employed persons to establish themselves, a freedom covered by the right of establishment,
and freedom to supply services throughout the whole Community.

Apart from physical persons, companies also benefit
from the commercial provisions connected with the right of
establishment. On 18 December 1961 the Council, after consulting the Economic and Social Committee and the European Parliament, adopted the general programme drawn up by the Commission to implement Articles 54(1) and 63(1). These general
programmes settle the order of priority to be accorded to the
various activities in eliminating restrictions on freedom of
establishment and freedom to supply services. Both lay down
the principle that in each Member State the national of another
Member State shall be assimilated to the nationals of the receiving
country.

The guiding line is supplied by Article 54(3a) of the Treaty, which accords priority treatment to "activities in regard to which freedom of establishment constitutes a specially valuable contribution to the development of production and trade".

Consequently, most industrial and commercial activities will be liberalized before the end of the second year of the second stage. Where these activities are exercised on a non-industrial scale, they will be liberalized at the same time under conditions laid down in the general programme and intended to allow both great flexibility as regards co-ordination and the safeguarding of the essential interests of the small craftsmen.

In addition to the economic criterion indicated by the Treaty, the time-table takes into account the more or less detailed regulations to be found in the different States, regulations which might need to be co-ordinated before, at the same time as, or after the lifting of restrictions.

In the agricultural sphere the Commission will submit two directives to the Council, one detailing the procedures for the introduction of freedom of establishment on farms abandoned or left uncultivated for more than two years, and the other to increase the rights of farm labourers who have worked in this capacity for at least two years in the receiving country.

In transport the right of establishment should, in principle, be realized in the same way as in the other sectors of the economy.

The Commission's proposals provide for the abolition of restrictions before the end of the second year of the third stage for carriers and at the end of the second year of the second stage for the ancillary trades.

The Commission has carried out preparatory work on the co-ordination of the legislative and administrative provisions for admission to the profession of carrier.

It has also, on 5 May 1961, submitted to the Consultative Committee on Transport a study on the introduction of freedom of establishment for transport enterprises and forwarding agents within the Community.

32.   The general programme on "Services" also lays down priorities for the liberalization of services. The definition given to services is negative in form and, one might say "residual".

By the terms of Article 61 (1), the free movement of
services connected with transport must form part of the common transport policy (Article 75 and the immediately following
Articles). Moreover, in view of the special provisions of
Article 75 (la), the supply of services in respect of transport
cannot be included in the draft general programme for the
suppression of restrictions on the free movement of services.

As part of the action to establish free movement of
services in connection with transport, the Commission has
sent the Council a draft directive on certain common rules for
the international transport of goods by road.

The Commission has also proposed that discrimination
against the access of non-resident carriers to national transport
services should be abolished before the end of the second year
of the third stage.

33.   The implementation of the general programme will have
to be done by means of directives. The Commission has already
begun preparatory work on certain general problems involved and
on particular activities or branches of activity.

It should be noted from the second stage onward the
directives laying down the methods for realizing the right of
establishment and services are to be adopted by the Council
acting on a qualified majority vote.

---

*The First Stage of the Common Market: Report on the Execu-
tion of the Treaty (January 1958 - January 1962) pp. 39-41.

The Freedom to Supply Services*

40.   The definition of services given in the General Programme is mainly negative; it means services "to the extent
that they are not covered by the provisions on the free movement of goods, capital and persons" or by those in the chapter
dealing with transport. This somewhat residual definition
explains the lack of uniformity in this concept and the difference
between it and the notion accepted by economists and statisticians.

The Treaty provides for the freedom to supply services
"within the Community", and the supplier of the service must
be "established in a State of the Community other than that of

the person to whom the services are supplied" (Article 59, first sub-paragraph). Service therefore represents a link across a frontier which can result from:

a) The supplier moving to the recipient of the services: services supplied by contractors, the liberal professions in the wide sense of the word (consultations, experts opinions, entertainments), by industrial technicians (assembling, repairing or maintenance of machinery) and by those in certain ancillary activities (travelling representatives, market research workers, maintenance services), or by certain craftsmen or agricultural workers who are relatively rare and almost always frontier workers. This type of service differs from establishment in the temporary character of the independent activity in the receiving country.

b) The recipient moving to the supplier of the service: services supplied on the arrival of the recipient for personal reasons (tourism, family visits, study) for business or for medical or paramedical care, etc. in the Community country where the service is supplied.

c) The service itself being moved (the supplier and the recipient remaining in their own country, it being immaterial whether the object into which the service is "incorporated" (processing, finishing, testing, analysis, and so on) is moved, or the object used in performing the service is moved (certain banking, insurance or publicity services or services provided by the liberal professions in the form of written papers, supply of information and so on).

The distinction between the concept of establishment and that of the supply of services raises no difficulties save in the borderline case where the supplier of the service travels to the country of the person receiving the service, resides there for some time or carries out several operations there. Some of the guiding ideas outlined in the General Programme will be given detailed form in concrete cases should these arise.

As in the case of the right of establishment, one form of restriction on the supply of services is represented by differential treatment based on nationality. Any such restriction hampers the professional activity of the supplier of the service when he goes to the recipient of the service. There are other restrictions that are absolute and to which it is impossible simply to apply the principle of no discrimination on grounds of nationality -

such as barriers to the movement of the object on which or with
the aid of which the service itself is performed, or of the material
required for performing the service, or prohibitions on payment
for the service. As has already been indicated, these all come
within the scope of the chapter on services in so far as they do not
fall under the provisions on the free movement of goods and
capital.

Article 63(3) of the Treaty provides a criterion for priorities in abolishing these restrictions; it is similar to that applicable
to the right of establishment, but the rhythm is faster. In certain
circumstances it may be possible to issue implementing instructions
dealing with a particular activity both from the point of view of
establishment and from that of the supply of services.

Time-table

41. The interdependence of establishment and the supply of
services - and the fact that the economy does not recognize the
distinction drawn between these two concepts in the Treaty - is
the reason why, with certain exceptions, a single time-table has
been drawn up for the removal of restrictions in these two spheres.

The essential provisions (1) of these time-tables are as
follows:

a) By the end of 1963, almost the whole of industry and wholesale trade and reinsurance will be free of restrictions on establishment.

The right of nationals and companies of Member States to
be awarded public works contracts(2) in other States will gradually
be opened up, according to widely varying arrangements, between
31 December 1963 and 31 December 1969.

b) By the end of 1965, the abolition of restrictions on establishment will be extended to the foodstuffs industries, to the manufacture and wholesale distribution of pharmaceutical products, to
retail trade, to certain types of insurance (other than life insurance)
and to certain liberal professions such as agronomy, architecture,
accountancy, surveying and engineering consultancy.

c) By the end of 1967, the removal of restrictions will be
applied to the retailing of pharmaceuticals and drugs, to medicine
and veterinary medicine and to certain types of insurance(life insurance). (Restrictions on transport will also be eliminated by this

224

time but only in the field of establishment.) (3)

d) By the end of 1969, only a few industries such as ship-building, the manufacture of railway equipment and forestry will still have to be liberalized.

42.   The time-table for services includes the following provisions:

a) The abolition of restrictions on moving the object on which or with the aid of which the service itself is performed, or of the material required for performing the service, and the abolition of restrictions on the transfer of funds and on payments this is envisaged before the expiry of the first stage and is now being effected.

b) Restrictions on services with respect to insurance are to be removed by the end of 1967, except in the case of life insurance, which will not be liberalized before the end of 1969.

c) As for the film industry, the complete liberalization of services will not be effected before the end of 1969, though some measures should be taken when the General Programme is adopted.

Agriculture will require some special arrangements, for its liberalization, particularly liberalization of establishment, is phased throughout the transition period. In fact, the link between establishment and the common agricultural policy justifies the liberalization of establishment in agriculture - which has a special structure - being effected piecemeal but rapid liberalization is envisaged for certain types of activity and certain persons. Freedom of establishment on farmlands that have been derelict or uncultivated for more than two years, then will be assured as soon as the General Programme is adopted. The establishment as agricultural workers of persons who have been gainfully employed as such in the host country for two years was granted before the end of 1961. For the following stages of the transition period, the rights and facilities enjoyed by nationals will gradually be granted to foreign workers; for instance, foreigners will be entitled to receive any type of credit and to join co-operatives from 1 January 1966. Under these conditions the elimination of all restrictions will not be effective before the end of the transition period.

As regards services, the main point was to enable farmers to profit from services that will improve productivity. The schedule here will therefore be generally tighter than for establishment:

technical assistance will be liberalized before the end of 1963, and harvesting and threshing before the end of 1965.

The General Programmes will have to be put into effect by means of implementing directives. The Commission has already begun preparatory work on general problems and on various sectors of activity. A systematic study of the material has been undertaken, and national experts are now meeting for discussions on various fields under the aegis of the Commission.

---

(1) For provisions on energy, see sec. 93.

(2) See sec. 56.

(3) See sec. 43.

*Fifth General Report on the Activities of the Community, pp. 64-68.

General Directives*

30.   On 29 June the Commission approved a draft directive to remove restrictions on travel and residence within the Community in so far as they affect freedom of establishment and freedom to supply services. Nationals of the Member States will not benefit from these provisions until the occupations they intend to pursue have themselves been liberalized.

After debating a report by M. Kreyssig on 8 February 1963, the European Parliament, which had been consulted by the Council, passed a resolution expressing a favourable opinion on the Commission's proposal, subject to minor amendments.

The Economic and Social Committee rendered a favourable opinion during its session of 28 and 29 November 1962, subject to certain amendments.

31.   In accordance with the Treaty, the Member States remain free in any case to maintain certain restrictions on travel and residence if they are justified on grounds of "ordre public", public safety or public health. But under Article 56(2) of the Treaty provisions containing such restrictions must be co-ordinated, hence a further draft directive of the Commission of 4-5 July 1962. This applies to all nationals of Member States, no matter what their occupation, wage-earning or not, and is under consideration of the

Council.

The Council consulted the European Parliament, which formulated an opinion on 22 November 1962. The Parliament held that a correct interpretation of the concepts of "ordre public" and public safety was essential and that for this it was necessary for an examination to be made of any criminal convictions against persons concerned, both in their country of origin and in the host country; such convictions should not automatically justify refusal of entry or residence. The desirability was stressed of giving better protection against any refusal of entry or residence permit, and as a step to meet this need a form of notification was proposed that would inform the party concerned of the measures taken against him.

Where there are no economic restrictions on the supply of a service, Article 106 (1) of the Treaty requires Member States to authorize any payments relating to such service. Where payment restrictions are the only limiting factor, Article 106 (2) requires them to be removed under the provisions of the Chapter on services.

This is the background to the draft directive adopted by the Commission on 25 July 1962.

On 8 February 1963, after hearing a report by M. G. Philipp, the European Parliament passed a resolution embodying a favourable opinion on the Commission's draft, subject to certain amendments which the Commission is proposing to the Council.

The Economic and Social Committee gave a favourable opinion on 28 November 1962.

_____

*Sixth General Report on the Activities of the Community, pp. 53-54.

Right of Establishment and Freedom to Supply Services*

19. On 30 May 1963 the Council adopted a third directive in pursuance of the General Programmes to liberalize establishment and services.

This is a directive removing all prohibitions on or obstacles to payment for services where payment restrictions are the only limiting factor on their supply. (1)

At the time the Treaty was signed, severe restrictions on payments for services performed by foreigners were in force in more than one Member State. Since then, considerable progress has been made in this field: except for a few isolated cases examined by the Commission's staff, liberalization may now be considered complete in all six Member States. The directive is thereby robbed of a good deal of its significance; nevertheless it is still of undeniable value. It has a twofold objective: to abolish any provisions or practices which may still hamper the supply of services, and above all to consolidate the liberalization already achieved in the six countries. The attainment of this twofold objective will make it irrelevant to consider the economic value of the service of the desirability of calling upon a foreign supplier, as certain public authorities were still doing before authorizing the transfer of payment. Furthermore in the absence of this directive the Member States could without legal objection have reverted to the restrictions obtaining on 1 January 1958.

Subject to certain emendations, the directive is as proposed by the Commission and referred to the European Parliament (whose minor amendments were not accepted) and to the Economic and Social Committee. It contains three essential provisions:

In Article 1, it secures to the persons referred to in Title I of the General Programme for services, who will finally benefit by the directive, the right to receive payment for services supplied within the Community. This means in effect that their right to supply services is safeguarded since it was impeded only by restrictions on the relevant payments.

As the State in which the person receiving the service resides is, in the nature of things, more tempted than the supplying State to place obstacles in the way of payment for the service, the supplier will have the necessary assurance in that there will be an obligation on the receiving State to issue a licence for payment, it being understood that this licence must be issued automatically and at once, and that the exchange rates applied must be those prevailing for other current transactions.

The effect of Article 2 is to prevent any checking of the nature or genuineness of the payments from forming a hindrance to or restriction on payment for the service. The right of Member States to make such checks is written into the General Programme for services in Title III, section D, last paragraph. A similar right was also recognized in respect of capital transfers in the directives issued in pursuance of Article 67 of the Treaty.

Article 3 excludes transport services and foreign exchange allowances for tourists. Liberalization of transport is not covered by the General Programme for services; by Article 61 (1) of the Treaty, it is placed within the purview of Article 74 to 84. The liberalization of foreign exchange allowances for tourists is subject to special arrangements in the same Programme (Title V, B, second paragraph). A separate directive will therefore be issued.

Apart from transport and allowances for tourists, the entire services sector as defined in Articles 59 and 60 is covered by the directive.

Definition of origin of imports

21. In order to establish an effective customs union a body of Community customs legislation is needed, and among the common rules to be adopted those on origin of imports are of special interest.

On this matter the laws and regulations of the Member States must be brought into alignment so as to apply in a uniform manner the measures to be taken to implement the common commercial policy vis-a-vis third countries, which will largely depend on the origin of the goods in question, and to give effect to the new Convention of Association.

In view of the tariff and quota advantages the Member States and the associated overseas States accord each other, the criteria to be adopted in defining origin for the purposes of the Convention may in general be stricter than those used in Community trade with non-member countries. For this reason the Member States and the Commission have examined separately the problems arising in these two cases.

Work was begun on defining the concept of origin for the purposes of the Convention of Association. This was more urgent because Protocol No. 3 to the Convention requires the Commission to submit a draft decision to the Association Council, within six months from the date of entry into force of the Convention, defining the concept of "goods originating...." to be adopted in giving effect to Title I of the Convention.

The Member States' experts, in conjunction with representatives of the Commission, are therefore working on the definition of this concept, which concerns all items liable to enter trade between the Member States and the associated States except petroleum products. These were provisionally excluded from the discussion at the request of the Member States' representatives. Enough progress has been made to ensure that the time-limit laid down in Protocol No. 3 will be complied with.

The criteria adopted in defining the concept of "goods originating...." for the purposes of the Association Convention are broadly speaking as follows:

Goods will be regarded as originating in the Member States or in the associated States if:

a)   They have been obtained entirely in the said States (for example minerals extracted from their soil and products derived therefrom);

b)   They have been obtained either wholly or in part from products imported from countries not parties to the Association provided that these imported products are processed to an extent sufficient to place them in a new tariff heading in the Brussels Nomenclature (for example fabrics manufactured from yarns imported from countries not parties to the Association). Since the application of this straightforward rule may in certain cases have economically undesirable consequences, the necessary adjustments have been made by drawing up:

i)   First, a "negative" list of operations which, although their effect is to place the item under a different tariff heading, will not be deemed to confer on them the origin of the Member State or of the associated State in which the operations were carried out;

ii)   Secondly, a "positive" list of operations which, although they do not have the effect of placing the item under a different tariff heading, will nevertheless be deemed to confer on it the origin of the Member State or of the associated State in which the operations were carried out.

Attestation that items entering into trade between the EEC Member States and the associated States fulfil the above conditions and are entitled to benefit of the preferential system laid down in the Association Convention will be furnished by the presentation to the customs of the importing Member or associated State of a special certificate issued by the appropriate authority of the exporting Member or associated State on the basis of assurances given by the exporter.

The establishment of a common definition of origin applying to Community trade with non-member countries will be undertaken in the near future, as soon as the work relating to trade under the Association Convention has been completed.

---

(1) See official gazette of the European Communities, No. 86, 10 June 1963.

*Bulletin of the EEC, July 1963, pp. 28-31.

6.9 THE FIRST DIRECTIVE ON THE FREE MOVEMENT OF CAPITAL*

34.   Article 67 of the Treaty provides that restrictions on the movement of capital shall be abolished during the transition period to the extent necessary for the proper functioning of the common market. After careful study the Commission has come to the conclusion that there would have to be the broadest and most rapid liberalization possible, linked with the progress made in liberalizing trade, services and manpower movements. This conclusion rests on arguments which spring from the mechanics of economic development in the Community: liberalization measures under the Treaty affecting the movement of persons, goods and services and the right of establishment cannot yield the desired results unless the capital that is available can be transferred and invested without let or hindrance and unless the factors of production can all be brought to bear with maximum effectiveness.

The first directive pursuant to Article 67 of the Treaty, prepared by the Commission in close co-operation with the Monetary Committee, was adopted by the Council on 11 May 1960. It provides for the unconditional freeing of a considerable range of capital movements, the conditional liberalization of others, and indicated a third category of capital movements in connection with which Member States have as yet given no undertaking that they will be liberalized.

Liberalization of the first category cannot be reserved unless the safeguard clauses have been invoked (Articles 73, 108 and 109); this category comprises direct investment, capital movements of a personal nature, credits for particular commercial operations and dealings in securities quoted on stock exchanges, i.e. the movement of capital connected with the free movement of goods, services and persons, and with the right of establishment.

The second category of capital movements, which are to be liberalized subject to certain conditions, consists mainly of loans raised by business houses on the capital market, loans and credits of a purely financial character, whether medium-term or long-term, and dealings in papers not quoted on the stock exchanges. These capital movements are not liberalized if this would be likely to hamper the achievement of the economic policy objectives of the State concerned.

The third category, covering capital movements that are not to be liberalized immediately comprises mainly the movement of short-term capital.

The practical scope of the directive lies primarily in the fact that businesses in the Member States will in future be more sure of the legal position, since the measures taken to liberalize the movement of capital can no longer be revoked unilaterally, but only after the Community procedure has been strictly observed.

35. In June 1961 the Monetary Committee, acting upon Article 4 of the directive, began a further examination of restrictions still in force. On the basis of the Monetary Committee's conclusion, the Commission suggested to the Governments of Member States that they adopt several measures to make their regulations more flexible. It also drew the attention of Member States to the advisability of adopting a liberal attitude towards foreign firms which wished to raise money on their capital markets; this liberal attitude should be possible in view of the favourable way their economic and financial situation was shaping in the member countries and the progress achieved in co-ordinating monetary policies within the Community.

_____

*The First Stage of the Common Market: Report on the Execution of the Treaty (January 1958 - January 1962), pp. 41-43.

The Free Movement of Capital*

45. On 11 May 1960, the Council adopted the first directive pursuant to Article 67 of the Treaty concerning the liberalization of capital movements within the Community (1).

The directive provides that the Monetary Committee will review each year the restrictions still existing on the movement of capital, with a view to their gradual elimination. The Monetary Committee's review has covered, among other things, the problem of free exchange markets, Government licensing procedure and the removal of restrictions on issues by firms in the Common Market on the financial markets of other Member States; these last operations will remain subject to conditional liberalization as laid down in Article 3 of the first directive.

In view of the favourable development of the economic and financial situation in Member States, of the advance made in co-ordinating economic and monetary policy in those States and of the conclusions reached by the Monetary Committee, the Commission has suggested that Member States adopt a liberal attitude in authorizing these issues. Such an attitude could in the first place be shown towards any loan issues by certain European institutions. The Netherlands Government informed the Commission that in 1961 it intended to re-open the Dutch capital market to foreign issues and that it would fix a new ceiling for any subsequent issues after the first quota (fixed at the beginning of 1961) was exhausted. The same policy was followed in 1962. The Italian Government has authorized the World Bank and the European Investment Bank to float loans on the Italian capital market.

To further the process of liberalizing capital begun by the first directive, the Commission, after consulting the Monetary Committee, has issued a draft second directive pursuant to Article 67 of the Treaty. This second directive envisages the complete liberalization of movements of capital belonging to residents who emigrate or to emigrants who return to their country of origin. These capital movements were already included in schedule A of Annex I to the first directive, but their liberalization was limited as far as the amounts that could be transferred were concerned.

The directive also provides for the liberalization of transfers relating to certain invisible transactions in Annex III to the Treaty, the liberalization of which was originally provided for under Article 106 (1, 2 and 3) and Article 63 (2). These are operations that should be considered as having the nature of capital transactions.

It also provides for the liberalization of transfers of funds needed for the supply of services and for access to various types

233

of credit coming under the supply of services.

In respect of the invisible transactions listed in Annex III to the Treaty, the Commission, after consulting the Monetary Committee, laid before the Council on 22 March 1962 a draft directive for the liberalization of transfers relating to invisible transactions not connected with the movement of goods, services capital or persons (Articles 63 and 106 (3)).

---

(1) See Fourth General Report, Chap. 1, sec. 56.

*Fifth General Report on the Activities of the Community, pp. 71-72.

Free Movement of Capital*

36.   On 18 December 1962 the Council issued a second directive in pursuance of Article 67 of the Treaty on the removal of restrictions on capital movements within the Community. This directive, which the Commission had submitted to the Council after consulting the Monetary Committee, supplements in a more liberal sense the first directive issued on 11 May 1960.

The new provisions have omitted paragraph 3 of Article 2 of the 1960 directive, which was intended to restrict transactions in stocks and shares by authorizing the Member States to confine acquisition of foreign securities by residents to finance houses and undertakings which acquire securities of foreign companies trading for a similar purpose. Now that the right to deal in securities has been extended to natural persons and undertakings other than those mentioned above, liberalization may be regarded as complete and unconditional in all the member countries. This new directive also completes the liberalization of transactions connected with the movement of persons and the supply of services. Lastly, there are further measures of liberalization to cover less important items such as the transfer of blocked funds or the cession of author's rights.

In pursuance of Article 4 of the first directive the Monetary Committee has made its second annual examination of restrictions still applied to capital movements. It has studied types of capital movement still subject to Article 3 of the above-mentioned directive, such as transactions in investment-trust shares, medium-term and long-term loans and credits not tied to commercial transactions and the issue and sale of stocks and shares of a national enterprise

on a foreign capital market or of a foreign enterprise on the
national capital market.

On this last point, further progress was made in 1962
when the Netherlands Government authorized more foreign issues
and three loans were floated on the Italian market by international
financial institutions.

The Monetary Committee has also studied legislative and
administrative obstacles to the placing of foreign securities with
savings institutions and the quotation of foreign securities on
domestic stock exchanges.

The elimination of these obstacles is essential for satisfactory operation of the system of liberalization of capital movements introduced by the first directive.

---

*Sixth General Report on the Activities of the Community, pp. 57-58.

CHAPTER 7

FAIR COMPETITION

Fair competition among the enterprises of the six European Community states is essential for the harmonious development of the common market, according to the Rome Treaty. Community institutions, principally the Commission, are empowered to supervise and administer the system governing competition, outlined in articles 85 and 86.

The Council and the Commission have developed rules to put the Treaty provisions into effect. The most important of these are Regulation 17 adopted by the Council and Regulation 27 adopted by the Commission. Subsequent rules have been issued concerning the scope of these regulations, dates for making submissions, registration forms, and hearings procedures.

The Commission has handed down several decisions under these regulations. The first dealt with an exclusive marketing agreement between a French manufacturer (Grosfillex) and a Swiss dealer (Fillistorf) forbidding re-exports into the Community. Such re-exports were, in fact, impossible, since they would have been subject to customs duties in both directions. The Commission granted the firms a "negative clearance", i.e. a ruling that they were not violating the Treaty.

The second decision under the competition regulations concerned an agreement between an American manufacturer (Bendix) and a Belgian dealer (Mertens and Straet). The agreement provided that the Belgian dealer would service the Bendix products sold, but did not state that Mertens and Straet were to be assured a share of the market or an exclusive dealership. A "negative clearance" was granted.

The Commission indicated in a third case that the agreement between the French company Nicholas Freres S.A. and the English company, Vitapro Ltd., was not in violation of the

Treaty. Nicholas had acquired the French firm Vitapointe and had sold Vitapointe's interests outside the EEC to Vitapro. The English firm was barred from selling Vitapointe products in the Community or selling other hair dressing there for a five-year period. The Commission found that the agreement did not provide for market-sharing within the Community and that the limits on Vitapro's sales in the Community would end in January 1966. A "negative clearance" was granted.

The Commission decided in 1963 that collective, exclusive marketing arrangements agreed upon mutually by manufacturers and purchasers, infringe the anti-cartel provisions of Article 85. Thus participants in the so-called "pottery convention" were asked to alter their agreements.

The Community program to insure fair competition has not been limited to the decisions discussed above. Other areas in which action has been proposed or begun are: anti-dumping, state aids, harmonization of taxes, transport, and the approximation of national laws.

The Commission is authorized to deal only with cases of dumping in intra-Community trade. Dumping exists if exports of a given product are made at prices below the normal value on the home market and cause material injury to the industry in the importing country. The Commission has received 23 dumping complaints. In only two cases thus far has the Commission issued recommendations to firms. Firms actually engaged in dumping prefer to end the practice rather than being officially requested to do so by the Commission.

The appraisal of the effect of state aids on competition is based on two principles: first, measures are to be judged in relation to all other measures and their joint effect and not in isolation, and second, any action concerning state aids must contribute to the creation of the common market. The Commission has studied the effect of existing state aids on competition and has ruled on their validity in about sixty cases. A regulation concerning state aids and the application of Article 93 has not been possible since no criteria have been established to determine which state aids are likely to have an effect on the Common Market and which would not. In the absence of this regulation, investigations have been made in such areas as export aids and aids in the shipbuilding, film, civil aircraft construction, mineral oil industries and in agriculture.

237

The most important activity in the harmonization of taxes relates to turnover taxes. The Commission has proposed that the tax be a general consumer tax proportional to the retail price of the goods or services regardless of the number of steps in the manufacturing process. It would be levied, however, at each step in production. Each producer would determine the value of an item and the tax on it would be determined. He would only pay the government an amount equal to the tax so computed less the amount of the tax on the value of the goods that he bought. Thus the added value tax would not be cumulative. The member states might choose to levy a separate tax on retail sales rather than the added value tax, but they would be required to levy it on wholesale sales and would have to pass on the tax to consumers.

Other indirect taxes have been studied, although the Commission has not yet put forward proposals for dealing with them. These taxes include excises, certain export refunds, taxes on capital movements, and taxes on insurance policies. Two groups have studied direct taxes: one investigated depreciation and taxes on asset appreciation and the other studied the relations between member states and certain non-members with favourable tax systems. No final action has yet been taken in either case.

The Council has decided that the transport sector is not to be included under the anti-cartel and competition provisions of the Rome Treaty. This decision creates a completely exempt sector, although special rules are being created for other sectors such as agriculture.

The Commission attempts to foster the harmonization of legislation as it affects competition. It studies existing legislation, proposes multilateral conventions, prepares directives, and stimulates inter-state cooperation. These procedures are being applied in the following areas:

-       patents and trade marks

-       unfair competition

-       public contracts

-       technical and administrative obstacles to trade

-       recognition and enforcement of foreign judgements; bankruptcy law

238

-     company law

-     penal provisions in commercial law

Cases Before the Court of the European Communities Relating to Fair Competition

Chapter 14, Document 14.1 case: 13/61.

7.1 COUNCIL REGULATION NO. 17

First implementing regulation pursuant to Articles 85 and 86
of the Treaty as amended by Council Regulation No. 59
of 3 July 1962 and Resolution 118/63 (1)

Article 1

Basic provision

The agreements, decisions and concerted practices
referred to in Article 85, paragraph 1, of the Treaty and any
abuse of a dominant position on the market within the meaning
of Article 86 of the Treaty shall be prohibited, no prior
decision to this effect being required; Articles 6, 7 and 23 of
the present Regulation shall not be affected by this provision.

Article 2

Negative clearance

At the request of the enterprises or associations of
enterprises concerned, the Commission may find that, according to the information it has obtained, there are, under Article
85, paragraph 1, or Article 86 of the Treaty, no grounds for it
to intervene with respect to an agreement, decision or practice.

Article 3

Ending of infringements

1.　　　If, acting on request or ex officio, the Commission
finds that an enterprise or association of enterprises is infringing Article 85 or Article 86 of the Treaty, it can by means of a
decision oblige the enterprises or associations of enterprises
concerned to put an end to such infringement.

2.　　　A request to this effect may be submitted by:

　　　a) Member States;
　　　b) Natural and legal persons and associations of persons,
　　　　who show a justified interest.

3.　　　Without prejudice to the other provisions of the present
Regulation, the Commission, before taking the decision mentioned in paragraph 1, may address to the enterprises or

associations of enterprises concerned recommendations designed to put an end to the infringement.

Article 4

Notification of new agreements, decisions and practices

1.   The Commission shall be notified of any agreements, decisions or concerted practices referred to in Article 85, paragraph 1, of the Treaty which have come into being after the entry into force of the present Regulation and for which those concerned wish to invoke Article 85, paragraph 3. As long as such notification has not taken place, no decision to issue a declaration under Article 85, paragraph 3, may be rendered.

2.   Paragraph 1 shall not be applicable to agreements, decisions and concerted practices where:

1) enterprises of only one Member State take part and where such agreements, decisions and practices involve neither imports nor exports between Member States;

2) Only two enterprises take part and the sole effect of these agreements is:

a) to restrict the freedom of one party to the contract to fix prices or conditions of trading in the resale of goods which have been acquired from the other party to the contract, or

b) to impose restraint on the exercise of the rights of any person acquiring or using industrial property rights - particularly patents, utility models, registered designs or trade marks - or on the exercise of the rights of any person entitled, under a contract, to acquire or use manufacturing processes or knowledge relating to the utilization or application of industrial techniques;

3) their sole object is:

a) the development or the uniform application of standards and types,

b) joint research to improve techniques, provided that the result is accessible to all parties and that each of them can exploit it.

The Commission may be notified of such agreements, decisions and practices.

Article 5

Notification of existing agreements, decisions and practices

1.   The Commission must be notified before November 1, 1962, of any agreements, decisions and concerted practices referred to in Article 85, paragraph 1, of the Treaty which are already in existence at the date of entry into force of the present Regulation and in respect of which those concerned wish to invoke Article 85, paragraph 3, of the Treaty. Provided always that not withstanding the foregoing provision, any agreements, decisions and concerted practices to which not more than two enterprises are parties must be notified before February 1, 1963.

2.   Paragraph 1 is not applicable where the said agreements, decisions and concerted practices fall within the categories referred to in paragraph 2 of Article 4; the Commission may be notified of these.

Article 6

Decisions to issue a declaration under Article 85, paragraph 3

1.   When the Commission decides to issue a declaration under Article 85, paragraph 3, it shall indicate the date from which the decision shall take effect. This date shall not be prior to the date of notification.

2.   The second sentence of paragraph 1 shall not be applicable to the agreements, decisions and concerted practices referred to in Article 4, paragraph 2, and Article 5, paragraph 2, nor to those which are referred to in Article 5, paragraph 1, and of which the Commission has been notified within the time-limit fixed therein.

Article 7

<u>Special provisions for existing agreements,
decisions and practices</u>

1.   Where agreements, decisions and concerted practices
already in existence at the date of the entry into force of the
present Regulation and of which the Commission has been
notified within the time-limits set out in Article 5, paragraph 1,
do not meet the requirements of Article 85, paragraph 3, of the
Treaty, and where the enterprises and associations of enterprises concerned put an end to them or modify them so that
they no longer fall under the prohibition laid down in Article 85,
paragraph 1, or so that they then meet the requirements of
Article 85, paragraph 3, the prohibition laid down in Article 85,
paragraph 1, shall be applicable only for a period fixed by the
Commission. A decision by the Commission pursuant to the
foregoing sentence cannot be invoked against enterprises or
associations of enterprises which have not given their express
assent to the notification.

2.   Paragraph 1 shall be applicable to agreements, decisions
and concerted practices which are already in existence at the
date of the entry into force of the present Regulation and which
fall within the categories referred to in Article 4, paragraph 2,
provided that notification shall have taken place before January 1,
1967.

Article 8

<u>Period of validity and revoking of decisions
to issue a declaration under Article 85,
paragraph 3</u>

1.   A decision to issue a declaration under Article 85, paragraph 3, of the Treaty shall be valid for a specified period and
may have certain conditions and stipulations attached.

2.   The decision may be renewed on request provided that
the conditions laid down in Article 85, paragraph 3, of the
Treaty continue to be fulfilled.

3.   The Commission may revoke or alter its decisions or
prohibit those concerned from taking certain courses of action:

a. where the de facto situation has changed with respect to a factor essential in the granting of the decision,

b. where those concerned infringe a stipulation attached to the decision,

c. where the decision is based on false information or has been obtained fraudulently, or

d. where those concerned abuse the exemption from the provisions of Article 85, paragraph 1, of the Treaty granted to them by the decision.

In the cases covered by sub-paragraphs b, c and d, the decision can also be revoked with retroactive effect.

Article 9

Competence

1.   Subject to review of its decision by the Court of Justice, the Commission shall have sole competence to declare Article 85, paragraph 1, inapplicable pursuant to Article 85, paragraph 3, of the Treaty.

2.   The Commission shall have competence to apply Article 85, paragraph 1, and Article 86 of the Treaty, even if the time-limit for notification laid down in Article 5, paragraph 1, and Article 7, paragraph 2, have not expired.

3.   As long as the Commission has not initiated any procedure pursuant to Articles 2, 3 or 6, the authorities of the Member States shall remain competent to apply Article 85, paragraph 1, and Article 86 in accordance with Article 88 of the Treaty, even if the time-limits for notification laid down in Article 5, paragraph 1, and Article 7 have not expired.

Article 10

Liaison with the authorities of the Member States

1.   The Commission shall transmit without delay to the competent authorities of the Member States copies of the requests, applications and notifications together with copies of the most important documents which have been sent to it with the purpose of establishing the existence of infringements of Article 85 or Article 86 of the Treaty, or with the purpose of

obtaining negative clearance or a decision to issue a declaration under Article 85, paragraph 3.

2.   It shall carry out the procedures mentioned in paragraph 1 in close and constant liaison with the competent authorities of the Member States; and these authorities may submit their views on the said procedures.

3.   A Consultative Committee on Cartels and Monopolies shall be consulted prior to any decision consequent upon a course of procedure referred to in paragraph 1 and prior to any decision concerning the renewal, the alteration or the revocation of a decision to issue a declaration under Article 85, paragraph 3, of the Treaty.

4.   The Consultative Committee shall be composed of officials competent in the field of cartels and monopolies. Each Member State shall appoint one official to represent it, who, if he is prevented from attending, may be replaced by another official.

5.   The consultation shall take place at a joint meeting called by the Commission; the session shall take place fourteen days at the earliest after dispatch of the convocation letter. This letter shall be accompanied by an exposition of the case to be considered, indicating the most important documents, and a preliminary draft of the decision shall be enclosed.

6.   The Consultative Committee may tender an opinion even if some members are absent and have not been replaced by another official. The result of the consultation shall be set out in a written statement which shall be attached to the draft of the decision. It shall not be made public.

Article 11

Requests for information

1.   In the execution of the duties assigned to it by Article 89 and by provisions pursuant to Article 87 of the Treaty, the Commission shall have power to seek all necessary information from the Governments and competent authorities of the Member States as well as from enterprises and associations of enterprises.

2.   When sending a request for information to an enterprise or association of enterprises, the Commission shall at the same

time address a copy of this request to the competent authority in the Member State in the territory of which the principal place of business of the enterprise or the association of enterprises is situated.

3.   In its request the Commission shall indicate the legal basis and the purpose of the same, and the penalties for supplying false information laid down in Article 15, paragraph 1, sub-paragraph b.

4.   Information must be supplied on request by the owners of the enterprises or by their representatives and in the case of legal persons, of companies or of associations without legal personality, by the persons responsible for representing them according to the law or the memorandum or articles of association.

5.   Where the enterprise or association of enterprises does not supply the information required within the time-limit set by the Commission, or supplies incomplete information the Commission's request for information shall be made by means of a decision. This decision shall specify the information requested, fix an appropriate time-limit within which it is to be supplied and specify the santions applicable under Article 15, paragraph 1, sub-paragraph b, and under Article 16, paragraph 1, sub-paragraph c, and shall indicate that there is a right to institute proceedings against the decision before the Court of Justice.

6.   The Commission shall at the same time send a copy of its decision to the competent authority of the Member State in the territory of which the principal place of business of the enterprise or association of enterprises is situated.

Article 12

Enquiries by economic sectors

1.   If in any sector of the economy the trend of trade between Member States, price movements, inflexibility of prices or other circumstances suggest that in the economic sector concerned competition is being restricted or distorted within the Common Market, the Commission may decide to conduct a general enquiry in the course of which it may request enterprises in the sector concerned to supply the information necessary for giving effect to the principles laid down in Articles 85 and 86 of the Treaty and for carrying out the tasks entrusted

to the Commission.

2.　　The Commission may in particular request any enterprise or group of enterprises in the sector concerned to communicate to it all agreements, decisions and concerted practices which are exempted from notification by virtue of Article 4, paragraph 2, and Article 5, paragraph 2.

3.　　When making enquiries as provided for in paragraph 2, the Commission shall also request enterprises or groups of enterprises whose size suggest that they occupy a dominant position within the Common Market or within a substantial part thereof to supply any particulars relating to the structure of the enterprises and to the conduct of their affairs necessary to appraise their situation in the light of Article 86 of the Treaty.

4.　　Article 10, paragraphs 3 to 6, and Articles 11, 13 and 14 shall be applied mutatis mutandis.

Article 13

Investigations by authorities of the Member States

1.　　At the request of the Commission, the competent authorities of the Member States shall carry out the investigations which the Commission considers necessary under Article 14, paragraph 1, or which it has ordered by a decision taken pursuant to Article 14, paragraph 3. The servants of the competent authorities of the Member States carrying out this investigation shall exercise their powers on production of a written warrant issued by the competent authority of the Member State in the territory of which the investigation is to be carried out. This warrant shall indicate the subject and the purpose of the enquiry.

2.　　The servants of the Commission may, at its request or at that of the competent authority of the Member State in the territory of which the investigation is to be made, assist the servants of this authority in the execution of their duties.

Article 14

Investigating powers of the Commission

1.　　In execution of the duties assigned to it by Article 89 and by provisions laid down pursuant to Article 87 of the Treaty, the Commission may conduct all necessary investigations into the affairs of enterprises and associations of enterprises.

To this end the servants authorized by the Commission shall be vested with the following powers:

a. to examine the books and other business documents,

b. to make copies of, or extracts from the same,

c. to ask for verbal explanations on the spot,

d. to have access to all premises, land and vehicles of enterprises.

2.   The servants authorized by the Commission for these investigations shall exercise their powers on production of a written warrant stating the nature and purpose of the enquiry and the fines provided for in Article 15, paragraph 1, sub-paragraph c, in the event of incomplete submission of the books or other business documents required. The Commission shall in good time advise the competent authority of the Member State in the territory of which the investigation is to take place, of this investigation, stating the name and office of the authorized servant.

3.   The enterprises and associations of enterprises must submit to the investigations ordered by a decision of the Commission. The decision shall state the subject and purpose of the enquiry, fix the date when it is to begin and call attention to the sanctions provided for under Article 15, paragraph 1, subparagraph c, and Article 16, paragraph 1, sub-paragraph d, and shall indicate that there is a right to institute proceedings against the decision before the Court of Justice.

4.   Before taking the decisions referred to in paragraph 3, the Commission shall consult the competent authority of the Member State in the territory of which the investigation is to be carried out.

5.   The servants of the competent authority of the Member State in the territory of which the investigation is to be carried out may, at the request of this authority or of the Commission, lend assistance to the Commission's servants in the execution of their duties.

6.   Where an enterprise resists an investigation ordered pursuant to the present Article, the Member State concerned shall lend the servants authorized by the Commission the assistance necessary to enable them to carry out their investigation. The Member State shall, after consulting the Commission, take the necessary measures for this purpose before October 1, 1962.

Article 15

Fines

1.   The Commission may by means of a decision impose on enterprises and associations of enterprises fines of from one hundred to five thousand units of account where, wilfully or through negligence:

a. they supply false or misleading information in an application submitted pursuant to Article 2 or in a notification made pursuant to Articles 4 and 5,

b. they supply false information in reply to a request made pursuant to Article 11, paragraph 3 or 5, or to Article 12, or do not supply information within a time-limit fixed by a decision taken under Article 11, paragraph 5, or

c. they submit in incomplete form, on the occasion of investigations carried out under Article 13 or Article 14, the books or other business documents required, or decline to submit to an investigation ordered by means of a decision taken pursuant to Article 14, paragraph 3.

2.   The Commission may by means of a decision impose on enterprises and associations of enterprises fines of from one thousand to one million units of account; this last figure may be increased to 10% of the turnover of the preceding business year of each of the enterprises having taken in the infringement, where these enterprises, willfully or through negligence:

a. have infringed the provisions of Article 85, paragraph 1, or of Article 86 of the Treaty, or

b. have infringed a stipulation made under Article 8, paragraph 1.

In determining the amount of the fine the duration of the

infringement shall be considered in addition to its gravity.

3.   Article 10, paragraphs 3 to 6, shall apply.

4.   The decisions taken under paragraphs 1 and 2 shall have no penal character.

5.   The fines provided for in paragraph 2, sub-paragraph a, may not be imposed for actions taking place:

a. after the notification to the Commission and prior to its decision regarding the application of Article 85, paragraph 3, of the Treaty, in so far as these actions do not go beyond the limits of the activity described in the notification,

b. prior to the notification of and within the framework of the of the agreements, decisions and concerted practices existing at the date of entry into force of the present Regulation, provided that this notification has been made within the time-limits laid down in Article 5, paragraph 1, and Article 7, paragraph 2.

6.   Paragraph 5 shall not apply once the Commission has informed the enterprises concerned that after a preliminary examination it considers that the conditions of Article 85, paragraph 1, of the Treaty have been fulfilled and that application of Article 85, paragraph 3, is not warranted.

Article 16

Penalties

1.   The Commission may by means of a decision impose on enterprises or associations of enterprises penalties of from fifty to one thousand units of account per day of delay, reckoned from the date fixed in its decision, in order to oblige them:

a. to put an end to an infringement of Article 85 or Article 86 of the Treaty in conformity with a decision taken pursuant to Article 3,

b. to discontinue any action prohibited under Article 8, paragraph 3,

c. to supply completely and truthfully any information which it has requested by a decision taken under Article 11, paragraph 5,

d. to submit to any investigation it has ordered by a decision taken pursuant to Article 14, paragraph 3.

2. When the enterprises or associations of enterprises have fulfilled the obligation which it was the object of the penalty to enforce, the Commission may fix the final amount of the penalty at a figure lower than that which would result from the initial decision.

3. Article 10, paragraphs 3 to 6, shall apply.

Article 17

Review by the Court of Justice

The Court of Justice shall have full jurisdiction within the meaning of Article 172 of the Treaty to adjudicate on proceedings instituted against the decisions by which the Commission has fixed a fine or a penalty; it may cancel, reduce or increase the fine or the penalty imposed.

Article 18

Unit of account

For the purposes of Articles 15 to 17 the unit of account shall be that adopted for drawing up the budget of the Community in accordance with Articles 207 and 209 of the Treaty.

Article 19

Hearing of the parties concerned and of third parties

1. Before taking decisions as provided for in Articles 2, 3, 6, 7, 8, 15 and 16, the Commission shall give the enterprises or associations of enterprises concerned an opportunity to express their views on the points objected to which have been taken into consideration by the Commission.

2. So far as the Commission or the competent authorities of the Member States consider it necessary, they may also hear other natural or legal persons or associations of persons. If natural or legal persons or associations of persons who show that they have a sufficient interest ask to be heard, their request shall be granted.

251

3.   When the Commission intends to give negative clearance
pursuant to Article 2 or to issue a declaration under Article 85,
paragraph 3, of the Treaty, it shall publish the essential content
of the application or notification, inviting all interested third
parties to submit their observations within a time-limit which
it shall fix and which shall not be less than one month. Publication shall respect the justified interest of enterprises that their
business secrets should not be divulged.

Article 20

Professional secrets

1.   Information gathered pursuant to Articles 11, 12, 13 and
14 may not be used for any purpose other than that for which it
was requested.

2.   Without prejudice to the provisions of Articles 19 and
21, the Commission and the competent authorities of the Member
States as well as their officials and other employees may not
disclose matters which have come to their knowledge through
the application of the present Regulation and which by their
nature are professional secrets.

3.   The provisions of paragraphs 1 and 2 shall not hinder the
publication of general surveys or reviews not containing information relating to particular enterprises or associations of enterprises.

Article 21

Publication of decisions

1.   The Commission shall publish the decisions which it
takes pursuant to Articles 2, 3, 6, 7 and 8.

2.   The publication shall name the parties concerned and
give the essential content of the decisions; the justified interest
of the enterprises that their business secrets should not be
divulged shall be respected.

Article 22

Special provisions

1.   The Commission shall submit to the Council proposals

for making certain categories of agreements, decisions and concerted practices such as are referred to in Article 4, paragraph 2, and Article 5, paragraph 2, subject to the notification provided for in Articles 4 and 5.

2.   Within one year from the entry into force of the present Regulation the Council shall examine, on a proposal of the Commission, any special provisions which could be made in derogation from the provisions contained in this Regulation with respect to the agreements, decisions and concerted practices referred to in Article 4, paragraph 2, and Article 5, paragraph 2.

Article 23

Transitional system applicable to decisions taken by authorities of Member States

1.   Agreements, decisions and concerted practices referred to in Article 85, paragraph 1, of the Treaty to which, before the entry into force of this Regulation, the competent authority of a Member State has declared Article 85, paragraph 1, to be inapplicable pursuant to Article 85, paragraph 3, shall not be subject to the notification provided for in Article 5. The decision of the competent authority of the Member State shall be considered a decision within the meaning of Article 6; its validity shall expire at the latest on the date which the said authority has fixed, but may not exceed a duration of three years reckoned from the entry into force of the present Regulation. Article 8, paragraph 3 shall apply.

2.   Applications for renewal of the decisions referred to in paragraph 1 shall be settled by the Commission in accordance with Article 8, paragraph 2.

Article 24

Implementing provisions

The Commission shall have authority to lay down implementing provisions concerning the form, content and other details of applications submitted pursuant to Articles 2 and 3 and of the notification provided for in Articles 4 and 5, and to lay down those concerning the hearings provided for in Article 19, paragraphs 1 and 2.

The present Regulation shall be binding in every respect and directly applicable in each Member State.

---

(1) The amendments introduced by Regulation No. 59 and 118/63 are underlined.

7.2 COMMISSION REGULATION NO. 27

First Implementing Regulation pursuant to Council Regulation
No. 17 of 6 February 1962

(Content and other details concerning applications and notifications)

Article 1

Persons authorized to file applications and notifications

1.   Any enterprise party to the agreements, decisions, or practices coming under Article 85 or Article 86 of the Treaty shall be entitled to file an application under Article 2 or a notification under Articles 4 and 5 of Regulation No. 17. Where the application or notification is filed by only certain of the enterprises participating, they shall so inform the other enterprises.

2.   Where representatives of enterprises, of associations of enterprises, or of natural or legal persons or of associations of persons sign the applications and notifications provided for in Article 2 and in Article 3, paragraph 1 and paragraph 2, sub-paragraph b) and in Articles 4 and 5 of Regulation No. 17, they must submit written evidence that they are authorized to act in this capacity.

3.   Where an application or notification is filed jointly, a joint representative should be appointed.

Article 2

Filing of applications and notifications

1.   Applications, notifications and relevant enclosures are to be filed with the Commission, in seven copies.

2.   For enclosed documents, either the original or copies

may be sent. Copies must be certified as being true copies of the original.

3.   Applications and notifications shall be filed in one of the official languages of the Community. The documents shall be lodged in their original languages. Where the original language is not one of the official languages, a translation into one of these languages shall be enclosed.

Article 3

Date from which applications and notifications take effect

An application or notification shall take effect from the time it is received by the Commission. However, where the application or notification is sent by registered post, it shall take effect from the date shown on the postmark of the place of posting.

Article 4

Content of applications and notifications

1.   The applications provided for in Article 2 of Regulation No. 17 which concern Article 85, paragraph 1 of the Treaty, must be filed on Form A annexed hereto.

2.   The notifications provided for in Article 4 or Article 5 of Regulation No. 17 must be filed on Form B annexed hereto.

3.   Applications and notifications must give the information requested in the forms.

4.   Several participating enterprises may submit an application or notification on a single form.

5.   The applications provided for in Article 2 of Regulation No. 17 which concern Article 86 of the Treaty shall include a complete statement of the facts; this must cover, in particular, the practice in question and the position occupied by the enterprise or enterprises in the Common Market or in a substantial part of it with respect to the product or service concerned.

Article 5

Transitional provisions

1.   Any applications and notifications filed without use of this Regulation shall be considered as complying with Article 4 of the present Regulation.

2.   The Commission may require that a form, duly filled in, be submitted within such time as it shall determine. In this event, applications and notifications shall not be considered as properly filed unless the forms are submitted within the period so determined and in accordance with the provisions of the present Regulation.

Article 6

The present Regulation shall enter into force the day after its publication in the official gazette of the European Communities.

The present Regulation shall be binding in every respect and directly applicable in each Member State.

CHAPTER 8

SOCIAL AFFAIRS

The European Economic Community's social policies are aimed at improving wages and working conditions and at maintaining a high level of employment. The Rome Treaty provides a basis for equal pay for men and women, overtime pay, paid vacations and social services. High employment is to be ensured through the free movement of labor, investment in retraining and relocation of workers, and aids to economic development.

"Member States hereby agree upon the necessity to promote improvement of the living and working conditions in an upward direction." Thus the Rome Treaty established the basis for the Community's social policy. Conditions in all member countries raising standards in more backward countries, without any of the others delaying further progress. Efforts to achieve this goal have been taking place in three areas: equal pay for men and women, overtime pay, and equalization of vacation time.

Marked differences in national social policies are evident in comparing amounts spent per capita, types of programs, and methods of financing them. Harmonization of the various plans, now under way, will be a lengthy process; earliest changes are expected in the methods of financing the programs.

Labor is to move in complete freedom in the Common Market no later than the end of the transitional period -- December 31, 1969. In January 1959, the Community established the first regulations, providing for the conditions under which social security benefits are provided to non-nationals and the kind of benefits given, have been continually reviewed, supplemented and improved. Documents in this chapter provide examples of recent measures affecting frontier and seasonal workers.

The first two measures to free the movement of labor were

The first two measures to free the movement of labor were instituted in 1961 and 1964. They facilitate the employment of nationals from other member countries and give foreign workers the right to be treated as nationals of the country in which they are working, after they have fulfilled certain minimum requirements. These regulations have helped the Community meet its labor shortages, by permitting over 700,000 Italian workers to find jobs in other Community countries and, more recently, by opening the way for increasingly large numbers of non-Community workers.

The EEC's Social Fund and Investment Bank are doing much to ease labor problems. The Social Fund was set up to deal with unemployment created by the establishment of the Common Market. Such unemployment results from the closing of inefficient plants in the face of Community-wide competition. The Social Fund participates in national programs to reduce unemployment and to encourage resettlement in areas where labor is needed. The European Investment Bank has stimulated the economic development of less developed areas within the Community, especially southern Italy. The Bank's programs have resulted in the creation of new jobs for trained labor.

Cases Before the Court of the European Communities Relating to Social Affairs

Chapter 14, Dcoument 14.2 cases: 75/63, 92/63.

8.1 REGULATION AND DIRECTIVES ON THE FREE MOVEMENT OF LABOUR IN THE COMMUNITY*

At its session of June 12, 1961, the Council of the European Economic Community, having taken note of the opinion given by the European Parliament and the Economic and Social Committee, issued Regulation No. 438 and 573/61 and the Directives containing the first measures to implement Articles 48 and 49 of the Treaty of Rome, which deal with the free movement of labour within the Community. Proposals for these measures had been made by the Commission in June 1960.

Legal Basis

Article 48 lays down that free movement must be ensured not later than the date of the expiry of the transition period, that it shall involve "the abolition of any discrimination based on nationality between workers of the Member States as regards employment, remuneration, and other working conditions," and that the individual rights which it includes shall be subject to limitations only where justified by reasons of public order, public safety, and public health. These rights include:

a) The right to accept offers of employment actually made and to move about freely for this purpose within the territory of the Member States;

b) The right to stay in any Member State in order to carry on an employment in conformity with the legislative and administrative provisions governing the employment of the workers of that State.

Article 49 shows what must be done to attain the objectives fixed in Article 48. It lays down:

a) Close collaboration between the national labour administrations;

b) The progressive abolition of administrative procedures and practices and time limits in respect of eligibility for available employment, the maintenance of which would be an obstacle to the freeing of the movement of labour;

259

c) Progressive abolition of all time limits and other restrictions which impose on workers of other Member States conditions different from those imposed on workers of the State concerned;

d) Establishment of appropriate machinery for connecting offers of and applications for employment, with a view to equilibrating them in such a way as to avoid serious threats to the standard of living and employment in the various regions and industries.

Three Stages

As Article 49 lays down that the right of free movement must be translated into practice gradually in accordance with a plan, the Regulation drawn up by the Commission provides detailed measures for a first stage only. Nevertheless, the "Considerations" which serve as a basis for the interpretation of the document, provide the board outline of the measures which will have to be taken at later stages. It is envisaged, for instance, that during the second stage limitations will be imposed on the priority accorded to the domestic labour market and the right to invoke this priority will be restricted to certain cases only. Moreover, the Regulation gives evidence of the Commission's intention to strengthen the contact between the various employment services so as to facilitate clearing offers of and applications for employment within the Community. The third and final stage will be devoted to the complete removal of the difficulties encountered and to the abolition of the last obstacles standing in the way of the free movement of workers so that, not later than at the end of the transition period, the workers of all Member States shall be assured of access to paid employment in each Member State on the terms that apply to nationals of that State.

First Stage Measures

Main Points. In view of the Council's declaration of intention relating to the speedier implementation of the Treaty, in which particular mention was made of the free movement of labour, the Regulation lays down that the duration of the first stage shall not exceed two years.

During this stage the taking on of nationals from the other Member States remains subject to the labour situation on the domestic market to which priority is still given; however, the procedure is rendered considerably more flexible and certain steps of immediate liberalization are laid down. For instance, the time limit given to the domestic administration to find available manpower on the normal labour market is fixed at three weeks; labour permits are to be given automatically in the case of occupations in which there is a labour shortage; for these, lists covering the various regions are to be drawn up periodically. Also, workers for whom an employer has called by name will in certain cases be granted a permit without reference to the domestic labour market; these cases must be based on reasons of personal relationship or on the exigences of the enterprise concerned.

Largely with a view to attaining the highest possible level of employment in the Community, it was felt that unemployed workers from Community countries should be preferred to workers from non-member countries.

To this end there is a provision in the Regulation that, when an employer does not specify a worker by name, Member States shall endeavour to fill vacancies by offering the posts to workers from the Community.

In addition, none of the restrictions on the number or percentage of foreign workers who may be employed by enterprises, sectors of activity, regions, or on the national level any longer holds good in the Member States so far as the employment of nationals of the Community countries is concerned. These nationals are also granted the right to renew their labour permits for the same occupation after one year of regular employment, for any other occupation for which they are qualified after three years, and for any kind of paid work after four years of regular employment.

The periods of regular employment served by workers in a Member State other than their own before the entry into force of the Regulation have been taken into consideration. Workers to whom this applies benefit from the rights conferred by the Regulation so far as extension of employment and free access to any paid employment is concerned. However, to avoid the considerable disturbance which such a measure would have in the host countries, it has been decided that only half of the periods of regular employment served before the entry into force of the Regulation shall be counted.

The Regulation also guarantees the same treatment and the same protection in respect of all working conditions, particularly in connection with the search for employment. The medical and occupational criteria on which recruitment is based must not be discriminatory as compared with those applied to workers who are nationals of the host country.

Further, special measures are provided to enable the spouse and minor children of workers to join them and to take up employment.

In order to ensure concerted action by the Member States and the Commission, the Regulation sets up:

- a tripartite Consultative Committee (with equal representation of Governments, workers and employers);

- a Technical Committee (composed of government representatives);

- a Co-ordinating Office at Community level to clear offers of and applications for employment.

The work done by the Commission on clearing offers of and applications for employment through this Co-ordinating Office will be supplemented by measures to promote rapid vocational training for unskilled or insufficiently skilled workers in order to fit them for employment available in a country other than their own. The purpose of this action is to bring the applications for employment into line with the offers.

Within six months from the entry into force of the Regulation and Directives the Commission will submit proposals concerning frontier and seasonal workers. The Commission feels, and the Council agrees with this view, that the problems connected with these two groups of workers are too special to be treated simultaneously with those relating to the permanent labour force.

The Form of the Regulation and the Directives. In addition

to the "Considerations," the Regulation has four parts.

Part I lays down the principles which will govern the admission and employment of workers of one Member State who wish to take up paid employment in another; it also sets out the exceptions to these principles.

It further defines the particulars of application of these principles and lays down the steps to be taken for the benefit of the workers' families.

Part II, which relates to clearing offers of and applications for employment, establishes the rules for common action and cooperation between the labour services of the Member States and between these services and the staff of the Commission. The arrangements proposed in this field amount to the outline of a system which should normally lead to a "decentralization" of the clearing arrangements; at the end of the transition period this decentralization is to be the basic principle which will govern clearing operations in the Community.

Part III deals with the organs which are to ensure close cooperation amongst the Member States themselves and between these States and the Commission. They are the Consultative Committee and the Technical Committee, to which reference has been made above.

Part IV contains the final provisions; these cover matters such as the maintenance of established rights, measures concerning the transfer of workers' salaries and savings, and provisions forbidding the introduction by Member States of any new restriction or discrimination in their municipal legislation which would prejudice workers who are nationals of other Member States.

The Directives contain a preamble in the form of "Considerations" and provisions for the procedural and administrative measures to be taken by the Member States.

The Commission felt that it should state in one of these "Considerations" that the restrictions justified by reasons of public health and public safety provided for in Article 48 of the Treaty are those which apply to foreigners in general, and that they must not be used for economic ends.

263

The Directives lay down the conditions which shall govern the issue and the validity of passports and national identity cards and of residential and labour permits, and they provide for the abolition of visas.

---

*EEC Document P-5410, June 12, 1961.

New Regulation and Directive*

25. On 7 February 1963 the Council approved a new regulation and directive to replace Regulation No. 15 and its accompanying directive. The new enactments contain more far-reaching liberalization measures concerning manpower mobility.

Their main points are as follows:

a) Priority treatment for Community labour has been strengthened. A procedure for closer cooperation on this matter between the Member States and the Commission has been introduced;

b) Workers from other Member States will now be eligible to factory committees as well as being entitled to vote in elections to these committees, a right established by Regulation No. 15. To be eligible, they must have been employed in the new country by the same firm for three years, this without prejudice to any more liberal arrangement in certain Member States;

c) The rule concerning members of the family who may stay with the worker in the country of employment has been widened: it will cover not only the spouse and children under age but also dependent forbears and descendants provided that the worker can offer them satisfactory accommodation;

d) To enable better and more efficient use to be made of existing labour resources in the Community, the Council has worked out, by agreement with the Commission, an overall solution:

i) There will henceforth be no discrimination against

264

the employment of workers who are nationals
of other Member States;

ii) The Commission will prepare a report on the
situation on labour markets in the Community.
This will be examined by the Member States
with the Commission and will enable the Member
States to take into consideration, in their employment policies, the labour market situations
in the other Member States, and as far as possible to give priority to Community nationals
when filling vacancies;

iii) Machinery will be set up for the satisfactory
clearance of applications and vacancies.

The above methods and procedures were adopted
unanimously in a spirit of understanding on all sides, and
offer a solution to what was considered the key problem:
priority for Community labour.

---

*Bulletin of the EEC, March 1964.

8.2 REGULATION No. 9
CONCERNING THE EUROPEAN SOCIAL FUND

PART ONE

CONDITIONS FOR THE GRANTING OF AID
BY THE FUND

Field of Application

Article 1

The Fund, whose function is to promote within the
Community employment facilities and the geographical and
occupational mobility of workers, shall reimburse, under
the conditions and within the limits laid down by the Treaty
and by this Regulation, 50% of the expenses incurred by the
Member States or by bodies under public law for:

- the occupational re-training of unemployed workers;

- the resettlement of unemployed workers;

265

- the maintenance of the same wage level for workers affected by conversion operations.

However, the Fund shall not reimburse expenses incurred by the Member States or by bodies under public law in respect of personnel participating in the exercise of public authority.

Similarly, the Fund shall not assist in covering the expenses referred to in paragraph 1 of this Article if the expenses incurred fulfil the conditions for the granting by the High Authority of non-reimbursable aid under the provisions of the Treaty establishing the European Coal and Steel Community or of its Convention containing the transitional provisions.

On a proposal of the Commission and in conformity with the Treaty, the Council shall have power to entrust the Fund with any task connected with action to improve opportunities of employment and the geographical and occupational mobility of workers or the implementation, in application of Article 128 of the Treaty, of a common occupational training policy.

Article 4

The assistance of the Fund for the occupational re-training of unemployed workers shall only be granted if the workers concerned fulfil the following conditions:

1. That they have been unable to obtain employment in an activity of a similar nature and equivalent level to those of the activity previously exercised, or corresponding to their normal qualifications for work if they have not already been in paid employment;

2. That after their re-training they take up a new paid productive employment within the Community, in the occupation, trade, or work position for which they have been re-trained, or in a similar activity;

3. That they have been in this productive employment for at least six months in the course of the twelve months following the end of the re-training period.

Resettlement

Article 6

Resettlement of an unemployed worker within the meaning
of Article 1 of this Regulation shall mean any change in the place
of residence within the Community required to occupy a new
paid productive employment of a non-seasonal nature offered
or approved by the competent employment service(s). The old
and the new place of residence shall be those recognized as such
by the Member State(s) submitting the application for the assistance of the Fund under Article 17 of this Regulation.

Article 11

Within the meaning of Article 1 of this Regulation, the
maintenance of the same wage level for workers affected by
conversion shall be the maintenance of up to 90% of the gross
salary and of the payments necessary to preserve the statu-
tory and fringe benefits attached thereto, to which these workers were entitled for a normal pay period.

PART TWO

PROCEDURE FOR THE GRANTING OF
ASSISTANCE BY THE FUND

General provisions

Article 20

Any application for the assistance of the Fund for a
programme of occupational re-training which has been completed must show that the expenses as submitted conform with
the provisions of this Regulation.

To this end, it must contain at least the following details:

- The origin, nature and purpose of the programme;

- All necessary information on the characteristics of
  the programme, in particular its scope and content,
  duration, time-table, degree of proficiency aimed at,
  examination papers, numbers of training staff and their
  conditions of employment;

- All information necessary to establish that the application concerns unemployed workers within the meaning
  of Article 2;

- The total number of workers concerned in the programme and the number of re-trained workers who
have actually been in paid productive employment for
at least six months under the conditions laid down in
Article 4;

- Detailed expenses in connection with:

  1. Residence, allowances, board and lodging, travel
  expenses, bonuses for work, expenditure in connection with the complete maintenance of rights
  to family and social security benefits and also
  unemployment benefits and any other benefit
  granted to the persons being re-trained during the
  period of such re-training and in the light of its
  requirements;

  2. The salaries and related social costs for the personnel referred to in Article 5;

  3. Expenses for equipment, materials, administrative
  costs, rent of premises, insurance, maintenance,
  heating and light as the case may be;

- The value of practical work involving direct participation in production in the course of occupational re-
training.

Article 21

Any application for the assistance of the Fund in respect
of compensation for resettlement must show that the expenses
as presented conform with the provisions of this Regulation.

To this end, it must contain at least the following details:

- All information necessary to establish that the application concerns unemployment workers within the meaning
of Article 2;

- All information to establish the fact of the movement
and the necessity for the resettlement of the worker,
in particular his old and new place of residence, the
date of his departure and that of his resettlement, the
new employment offered or approved by the employment service(s) concerned and the date on which the

work actually began;

- All information likely to show that the workers who have moved have been in paid productive employment for at least six months under the conditions in Article 7;

- Details of the expenses listed in Article 8.

Submission of Applications Concerning Conversion

Article 22

The Member States shall submit to the Commission an application for prior approval in respect of any conversion project for which the assistance of the Fund is envisaged. This application shall contain, in addition to the reasoned opinion of the Government concerned, any data to make possible an appraisal of the conversion plan envisaged, and at least the following information:

- Need, purpose, scope and financing of the conversion;

- Planned duration of the conversion operations and pace at which they are to be carried out;

- Number of workers whose employment will be temporarily reduced or suspended wholly or in part, and description of the new employment planned for them; staggering of cuts in staff and re-employment;

- Financial repercussions of the maintenance, according to the provisions of Article 11, of the same wage level for workers affected;

- Reasons why the programme of occupational re-training seems called for, and the number of workers concerned;

- Financial repercussions for carrying out this programme of occupational re-training.

Examination of Applications and Possible Enquiries

Article 24

The Member States shall give every aid to the Commission

to enable it to assemble all further information which it deems necessary to verify the details contained in the applications for assistance from the Fund. Where necessary, they shall facilitate contacts with the bodies or enterprises concerned.

Article 25

The Commission shall examine whether applications conform with the provisions of this Regulation. The Committee of the Fund shall be associated with it in this examination in the manner laid down in Articles 28 to 30.

PART THREE

COMMITTEE OF THE EUROPEAN SOCIAL FUND

Article 27

The Commission shall be assisted in its task by a Committee, consisting of representatives of the Governments and of trade union and employers' organizations, the statutes of which shall be decided upon by the Council.

Article 28

The Committee shall be consulted on all questions of general importance or of principle concerning the administration of the Fund. To this end it shall receive all necessary documents and information.

According to its statutes it is also empowered to express opinions to the Commission on its own initiative.

Furthermore, the Committee shall be regularly informed of the activities of the Fund and of the various aspects of the general policy of the Commission in economic and social matters relating to such activities.

Article 29

The prior opinion of the Committee must be obtained in the following matters:

1.   The advance draft of the annual budget of the Fund;

2.   The establishment and keeping up to date of the list of

270

bodies under public law;

3. Applications for the assistance of the Fund, or the prior approval by the Commission of a conversion project;

4. Problems arising from any action by the Fund intended to achieve a common policy on occupational training;

5. Any action required for applying this Regulation;

6. The advisability of a revision of this Regulation and any proposals for such revision;

7. Any changes in the tasks of the Fund after the end of the transition period.

Statutes
of the Committee of the European Social Fund

THE COUNCIL OF THE EUROPEAN ECONOMIC COMMUNITY

HAVING REGARD to the provisions of the Treaty establishing the European Economic Community, in particular Articles 124 and 153 thereof,

HAVING HEARD the opinion of the Commission,

DECIDES:

Article 1

The Committee of the European Social Fund shall assist the Commission in the administration of the Fund in the conditions laid down by these States and by the Regulation provided for under Article 127 of the Treaty.

Article 2

The Committee shall consist of 36 members, being two representatives of the Government, two representatives of the trade unions' and two representatives of the employers' organizations for each of the six Member States.

Balance-sheet of the Fund for 1963*

29.   On 18 December the Commission approved seven applications submitted by Germany (FR), France, Italy and the Netherlands for refunds totalling 5,717,477 units of account.

This brings the total aid from the Fund for 1963 to 7,561,477 units of account, allocated as follows:

Germany (FR): 1,733,265 u.a.

Belgium: 350,532 u.a.

France: 2,602,450 u.a.

Italy: 2,134,371 u.a.

Netherlands: 740,859 u.a.

Under the schemes for which refunds have been made in 1963, 80,511 workers have found new jobs after retraining or resettlement.

The breakdown by country is as follows:

Germany (FR): 18,528 plus 35,740 Italian workers resettled

Belgium: 994

France: 5,304

Italy: 18,929

Netherlands: 1,016

The total aid granted by the European Social Fund in three years of operation is 19,853,275 units of account; the schemes for which refunds have been granted have helped 263,497 workers.

---

*Bulletin of the EEC, February 1964, p. 34.

8.3 REGULATION ON SOCIAL SECURITY
FOR FRONTIER WORKERS*

By definition, frontier workers are employed in and therefore affiliated to the social security scheme of the neighbouring
country to that in which they live. Consequently, they are not
eligible for all the social benefits to which they would normally
be entitled: for administrative reasons the social security
legislation of a given country generally makes the grant of
maternity, industrial accident or unemployment benefit and
family allowances conditional upon a period of residence on
its territory.

To remedy this situation, a number of conventions for the
benefit of frontier workers had been concluded before the European Economic Community was set up. There remained, however, many gaps.

The purpose of the Council regulation is to guarantee
frontier workers and their families the right to all social security benefits in the country where they are employed and to
ensure that the benefits are provided in their country of residence - if need be through the appropriate offices in the latter
country. The regulation will apply to refugees and stateless
persons as well as to nationals of Member States.

As regards sickness or maternity insurance, the regulation specifies that cash benefits (daily invalidity allowances)
will be paid to the frontier worker by the institution to which
he is affiliated, either in his country of residence by international money order, or in the country of employment at the
appropriate office.

Benefits in kind (medical care) are to be provided for
the frontier worker and his family through the office in their
place of residence, which must place them on the same footing
as its own insured persons. This office will then be reimbursed
by the institution in the country of employment to which the
worker is affiliated. The latter institution may also provide the
frontier worker with benefits in kind when he needs them in the
country of employment, and this also applies to members of his
family in certain cases - particularly in an emergency.

Industrial-accident or occupational-disease benefits will
be provided on the same lines. Compensation for accidents
occuring on the way between the place of residence and the fron-

tier will be paid in the same way as those taking place in the country of employment. Ambulance costs may also be charged to the institution to which the victim is affiliated.

In the case of unemployment, a distinction is made between full unemployment and partial or casual unemployment. For full unemployment, benefits - including related benefits such as medical care or family allowances - are provided by the institution of the place of residence and the unemployed worker is obliged to comply with the regulations in force in that country (signing on at the labour exchange, administrative control, etc.) while in the case of partial or casual unemployment the worker receives benefit from the country in which he was employed as if he were residing there.

With regard to family allowances, the frontier worker receives his children's allowances from the country in which he is employed, and these are paid up to the level of the rates in force in his home country.

The provisions applying to invalidity, old-age, industrial-accident or occupational-disease pensions are those already laid down in Regulations Nos. 3 and 4, which stipulate that insurance periods completed in different countries are taken into consideration for entitlement to benefit and the calculation of benefit, and that the pensions are paid in any Member State.

The regulation will supersede the provisions of existing bilateral conventions, except those which are more advantageous to the workers concerned and which the Council may maintain in force by a later regulation adopted on a proposal of the Commission within six months. The two regulations will come into force at the same time.

The number of frontier workers who will benefit from this regulation was put at 115,000 a year ago. With members of their families, the total number of persons benefiting may be estimated at 300,000.

The biggest movements of frontier workers are from Belgium to France (chiefly workers in the iron and steel and textiles industries) and from the Netherlands to Germany (mainly building and construction workers).

---

*EEC Commission Document, P/7(63), February 25, 1963.

8.4 SEASONAL AND OTHER WORKERS*

The EEC Commission has submitted to the Council of Ministers a draft regulation on social security matters affecting seasonal workers and other workers(1) not residing in the country to whose social security schemes they are affiliated. The draft does not concern frontier workers, for whom a special regulation was adopted by the Council on February 21, 1963.

Regulations Nos. 3 and 4 (social security for migrant workers) do not provide all these workers with the protection to which they would be entitled if they were resident in the countries in which they are insured. The purpose of the present proposal is therefore to remove these restrictions and to adapt and amend Regulations Nos. 3 and 4 so as to ensure for all these workers and their families the right to family allowances and sickness, unemployment and industrial-accident benefits in the countries in which they are insured without any stipulation as to residence, and to ensure that the benefits are provided in their countries of residence, if necessary through the social security institutions of these countries.

As regards sickness or maternity insurance, the proposal specifies that cash benefits (daily invalidity allowances) will be paid to all workers in their countries of residence by the institution to which they are affiliated. Benefits in kind (medical care) will be supplied to them and their families by the insurance office in their place of residence, which will accord them the same benefits as to its own insured workers; this office will then apply for reimbursement to the office at which the worker is registered in the country of employment. The latter office may also provide the worker with benefits in kind if he needs them in the country of employment, and this also applies to the members of his family in certain cases, notably cases of emergency.

Industrial-accident and occupational-disease benefits will be provided on the same lines. Ambulance costs for a seasonal worker who meets with an industrial accident may be defrayed by the institution.

With regard to unemployment, workers will be entitled to ordinary benefits in the country in which they become unemployed. On returning to their country of residence, they will continue to receive these benefits for a certain period. In addition, a seasonal worker who is unemployed in his country of residence at the end of the season may, under certain conditions, claim unemployment benefits from this country.

Workers will claim family allowances from the country
in which they are employed and these will be paid at rates not
exceeding those in force in the country of residence.

The number of seasonal workers affected by these regulations is estimated at about 200,000.

The biggest movements of seasonal workers are from
Italy to France (farming and building) and from Italy to Germany
and Luxembourg (building and metal industries). There is
also a movement of frontier workers every year from Belgium
to France during the beet season.

---

(1) These other workers are:

(a) Workers in embassies and consulates insured in their
own countries (not enjoying diplomatic status);

(b) Workers in enterprises divided by a frontier common
to two member countries, who are insured in the
country in which the enterprise has its principal place
of business although they reside in the other Member
State;

(c) Temporary workers (workers employed for a limited
period in a non-seasonal activity);

(d) Workers residing in one country and employed and
insured in another, but not qualifying as frontier
workers (since they go home less than once a week,
or since their place of employment or their domicile
lies outside the border areas between France and ad-
jacent Member States).

*EEC Commission Document P 10(63)-E, March 26, 1963. The
proposed regulation was subsequently adopted in the form described.

8.5 REGULATIONS ON SOCIAL SECURITY FOR CERTAIN CATEGORIES OF MIGRANT WORKERS*

1. On December 2, 1963 the Council of Ministers adopted,

on a proposal of the Commission, two regulations on social
security for frontier and seasonal workers, supplementing
the regulations on the same subject adopted on April 2 and
July 11, 1963 (see Information Memos P/7 and P/10).

All four regulations are to come into force on February
1, 1964, making up a social security system that affords fuller
protection than that embodied in the bilateral conventions concluded between some of the Member States.

These new provisions guarantee to frontier and seasonal
workers and their families the right to all the social security
benefits of the country where they work and ensure that the benefits are provided in the country where they live.

For frontier workers and their families, the arrangements are as follows:

(a)   Benefits in kind (medical and other expenses) will be
        provided by the institution in the worker's place of re-
        sidence and charged by the institution to which the
        worker is affiliated in his country of employment. The
        latter institution may also provide the frontier worker
        and his family with benefits in kind when they need them
        in the country of employment. When they are tempor-
        arily in another Community country, they may also
        claim from the institution in that country any benefits
        required because of their state of health;

(b)   Daily invalidity allowances will be paid to the frontier
        worker direct by the institution to which he is affiliated,
        and compensation for accidents occuring between his
        place of residence and the frontier will be paid in the
        same way as those occuring in the country of employment;

(c)   Unemployment benefit will be paid by the country of em-
        ployment if the frontier worker is partially or accident-
        ally unemployed and by the country of residence if he is
        fully unemployed;

(d)   Family allowances will be paid direct by the country of
        employment; in some cases, they will not be allowed to
        exceed the rates in force in the home country.

When a seasonal worker falls sick or has an accident,
benefits will still be paid by his country of employment if he

277

returns to his home country for treatment; in the case of an accident at work, transport too will be paid to the place of origin. Benefits in kind for the families of seasonal workers will be provided through the institution in their place of residence, and family allowances will be paid by the country of employment up to the level of the rates obtaining in the country of residence.

As regards invalidity, old-age, life and industrial injury insurance, frontier and seasonal workers come under the provisions already laid down in Regulations Nos. 3 and 4 on social security for migrant workers: their pensions will be calculated on the basis of all contributions paid and will be payable in the country of residence.

Some 115,000 frontier workers and 100,000 seasonal workers will come under these new provisions. The biggest movements of frontier workers are from Belgium to France (45,000) and from the Netherlands to Germany (25,000) and Belgium (15,000). The biggest movements of seasonal workers are from Italy to Germany (55,000) and France (20,000) and from Belgium to France (15,000).

2.   The Council also adopted a regulation amending certain provisions of the Community regulations on social security for migrant workers dealing with allowances for children of pensioners and children who have lost one or both parents. The new provisions considerably simplify the method of calculating these allowances.

---

*EEC Commission Document, P/48/63, December 1963.

8.6 HARMONIZATION OF SOCIAL SYSTEMS*

147.   The Commission has continued its work on the harmonization of social systems (Articles 117 and 118). Progressive harmonization in this field constitutes an important factor in development designed to level living and working conditions in an upward direction. The Commission sees harmonization not as a standardization nor as the mere alignment of the various regulations and practices on those of the member country which would seem the most advanced in these matters, but rather as a progressive narrowing of differences between them in a common effort to make social progress within each country

first of all and then in an integrated Europe, through co-operation of all the social forces in the six countries.

---

*Fifth General Report on the Activities of the Community, pp. 179-180.

Wages and Working Conditions*

192. Working parties, drawn from employers' and workers' organizations, some of them assisted by government experts, met on several occasions during the past year.

The joint working party on labour relations made a comparative study of law and practice in collective bargaining and later took up other special aspects of labour relations. The Commission, desirous of providing Member States with a standing source of information on collective bargaining developments, considered early in 1963 in conjunction with government services and both sides of industry plans to study collective wage agreements by up-to-date methods. A three-party group has dealt with the protection of young people and women at work while joint groups have looked into working hours and wages.

A fuller knowledge of wage costs has been acquired during the past few years thanks to two surveys, one for 1959 concerning fourteen branches of industry, the second for 1960 concerning eight other branches. The results of the latter survey are about to be published. A third survey of thirteen other branches is in progress covering the year 1961. It will be followed, between 1963 and 1965 by a second review of the same branches of industry which will enable developments to be gauged with accuracy.

At the invitation and with the help of the Commission, employers'& workers' organizations are now studying certain findings of these surveys, in particular the discrepancies which occur in some branches as regards the structure and average level of labour costs.

193. The Commission pursued its work on the subject of working hours. Apart from the above-mentioned wage surveys with the pointers they afford to the annual total of hours worked, and a special survey of employment which provided data on the working week, the Commission has appointed two joint study groups to examine respectively the working day and week and

the working year. Its purpose in so doing is to arrive at common concepts that will enable developments in working hours to be followed more closely, with special reference to collective bargaining, and to lay the foundations for harmonization in this matter of topical interest to workers. These studies, in which the relevant government department will assist, will be followed by more detailed inquiries in certain branches.

---

*Sixth General Report on the Activities of the Community, pp. 183-184.

Equal Pay for Men and Women Workers*

57. The Council's wish to proceed more speedily with putting into practice the principle of equal remuneration for equal work as between men and women workers (Article 119) appears in the declaration of intention attached to the programme, approved by the representatives of the Member States in May 1960, for speeding up the implementation of the Treaty. In line with this programme the Commission on 20 July 1960 submitted to the Member States a recommendation summing up its interpretation of Article 119 and indicating the ways and means by which it should be applied from 1 July 1961 onward.

The Commission believes that the principle of equal pay rules out discrimination on the basis of sex in the determination of wages, whilst the other customary criteria such as ability, age, seniority on the job and family circumstances can continue to be taken into consideration.

Job classifications must apply to male and female workers without distinction, and it would be incompatible with the principle of equal pay to lay down lower rates or special categories for women workers.

As a result of this recommendation numerous studies have been made by the Commission and the Member States jointly to determine in common accord the procedures for the practical application of the principle of equality. As a result of this work and in fulfillment of the obligations arising out of Article 119 of the Treaty the representatives of the Governments of the Member States agreed at the 60th session of the Council (30 December 1961) to bring the pay of men and women workers progressively into line.

The following time-table has been adopted:

(a)   By 30 June 1962 any difference exceeding 15% to be re-
        duced to that amount;

(b)   By 30 June 1963 any difference exceeding 10% to be re-
        duced to that amount;

(c)   By 31 December 1964 all discrimination should be abolished.

Various supplementary measures have been adopted.

The Member States will apply, in accordance with their
national systems for the fixing of wages, the appropriate procedures to ensure that the principle of equal remuneration for
men and women workers can be enforced by the Courts.

The Member States have further undertaken to co-operate
in organizing a statistical enquiry into the wages structure of the
six countries.

*The First Stage of the Common Market: Report on the Execu-
tion of the Treaty (January 1958 - January 1962), pp. 75-76.

Industrial Health and Safety*

In the matter of industrial health, the Commission has
concerned itself from the outset mainly with prevention, and
after a favourable opinion from the European Parliament on
11 May 1962 and from the Economic and Social Committee, it
addressed two recommendations on the subject to the member
Governments in August 1962.

197.   The first concerns industrial medicine(1). It is based on
ILO Recommendation No. 12 but proposes higher and more
exacting standards. It aims in the first place to make the provision of industrial medical services compulsory in Member
States in all branches of industry beginning with those employing
a large labour force and those in which the frequency of risk is
highest. It advocates at the same time the early introduction of
industrial health services in other spheres of activity. The
recommendation also deals with the university training and
status of doctors in industrial medicine. The Commission
paid due regard to the concern of the European Parliament, as

expressed in its formal opinion, that the independence of doctors
in industrial medicine should be ensured with respect to both
employers and workers, and that medical services be set up
as soon as possible in all firms employing over fifty workers.

198.   The second recommendation concerns the adoption of a
European list of occupational diseases(1).

While this recommendation deals first and foremost with
compensation under social security arrangements (see sec. 202),
it is likewise of interest from the standpoint of prevention.
Legal recognition that a disease is due to an occupational risk
inevitably causes attention to be paid to that risk; it entails
compulsory preventive measures and gives rise to stricter
supervision than would be the case with dangers not specified
as jeopardizing the health of workers.

The first intimations of the effect that the governments
intend to give to these recommendations are now being received by the Commission.

---

(1) See official gazette of the European Communities, No. 80,
    31 August 1962.

*Sixth General Report on the Activities of the Community,
    pp. 186-187.

Housing Policy and Family Questions*

199.   Housing is among the problems to which the Commission
attaches special importance in its Action Programme and this
has led to its convening a seminar on housing requirements
for the end of 1963.

Pending this opportunity to compare notes and opinions,
experts from the government departments concerned and from
employers' and workers' associations have held further meetings, at the Commission's initiative, to exchange views on
housing policy in general and on rural dwellings in particular.
A comparative survey of the financing of housing schemes is
about to be addressed to Member States.

200.   The Commission proceeded with its study of developments in family welfare policy in each of the Member States,

notably at a meeting of representatives from the competent
ministries and family, employers' and workers' organizations.

---

*Sixth General Report on the Activities of the Community,
 p. 187.

Social Security*

201. The Commission has completed extensive basic documentation on the social security schemes of Member States.
A European Conference on Social Security, organized on its
initiative by the executives of the three Communities enabled
it in addition to inform itself of the main trends appearing
in circles concerned with the harmonizing of these schemes.

---

*Sixth General Report on the Activities of the Community,
 p. 188.

8.7 EMPLOYMENT AND VOCATIONAL TRAINING

Employment Policy*

188. The Commission noted the growing shortage of manpower
in a large area of the Community, especially in Federal Germany and the Netherlands, and the opposite trend in countries
where labour surpluses give rise to increasing difficulties
mainly because applicants for employment are all too often
unskilled. The Commission therefore recommended in its
report that efforts be made to further policies likely to ensure
a better balance between the national and Community labour
markets. It advocated closer collaboration between Member
States in the field of employment, and in particular a more
precise survey of the situation and prospects in each area
and in each branch of industry as regards the trades and de-
grees of skill required.

On 21 February 1963, the Council requested the Commission to put forward proposals to the Member States, in
accordance with the conclusions of the above-mentioned report,
with a view to such measures and programmes as were likely
to meet the situations described.

*Sixth General Report on the Activities of the Community, p. 180.

General Principles on Vocational Training*

On February 21, 1963 the Council of Ministers adopted certain general principles on vocational training proposed by the EEC Commission.

The first principle defines the field of application of the common vocational training policy. It concerns young people and adults employed in or intending to take up jobs up to the level of medium-grade supervisory staff.

The second principle defines the main objectives of the common policy, which are:

(i) To give everyone the right to receive adequate vocational training and to reach the higher grades in his career;

(ii) To organize in good time the training facilities needed to meet the requirements of the economy;

(iii) To broaden general basic training in order to develop the worker's personality and keep up with technical progress which, besides appropriate specialization, demands a solid foundation in general technical skills;

(iv) To enable the worker to improve his skill throughout his whole career and thus give real meaning to the term "social advancement";

(v) To ensure that "training" and "production" no longer form two separate worlds but that all circles concerned participate in solving the problems of modern and efficient vocational training.

The third principle lays down the prior conditions for the implementation of the common policy, i.e. forecasting of both quantitative and qualitative requirements and constant guidance of young people and adults in the light of their capabilities and of the openings existing in the various sectors of the economy.

The fourth principle empowers the European Commission to propose to the Council or the Member States, in the frame-

284

work of the Rome Treaty, all measures necessary to implement the common vocational policy. The special import of this principle is that it makes possible genuine Community action in the vocational training field.

The fifth principle provides for the permanent exchange of information and for studies on new teaching methods and the trend of national vocational training systems.

The sixth principle also provides for exchange of experiences on new departures in this field between the responsible specialized services.

The seventh principle concerns the particular measures required to ensure the technical training and further training of teachers and instructors, in particular those who are called upon to work in the less-favoured regions of the Community and in the developing States and territories.

The eighth principle provides for the progressive narrowing of differences in training levels with a view to the mutual recognition of certificates and diplomas, which is essential to the free movement of workers in the Community.

The ninth principle concerns arrangements for rapid training courses to ensure overall balance between labour demand and supply in the Community in the light of the forecasts which will be established to this end.

The tenth principle concerns training problems arising in certain sectors and for certain categories of workers. It also provides that measures to implement the common vocational training policy may be financed jointly.

---

*EEC Commission Document P/6(63), February 22, 1963.

CHAPTER **9**

AGRICULTURE

A common agricultural policy is being created by the EEC
to cover all of the principal commodities produced in the Community. The policy will encompass almost 90 per cent of the
total agricultural production of the Six.

The first regulations were approved in January 1962 and
came into effect on August 1, 1962. They cover grains, fruits
and vegetables, wine, pork, poultry and eggs. Additional regulations were agreed upon in December 1963 and entered into
effect on September 1 and November 1, 1964. They governed rice,
beef and veal and milk products. These regulations are described
in the accompanying documents. Additional products still to be
brought under the common policy are fats and sugar. The sugar
regulation will be modeled on the basic grain regulation.

The most important decision still needed to complete the
common farm policy is the setting of a common grain price for
the Six. This price would affect not only the grains, but also
the so-called conversion products which are based on grain. In
November 1963, the EEC Commission proposed a grain price
which has served as the basis of continuing discussions.

The Community's farm production is becoming more
efficient due to the application of the common policy and
the reduction of the farm population which is finding work
in expanding industries. Nonetheless, Community imports
of commodities under the common policy have increased.
Exports have also shown gains.

EEC TRADE IN COMMODITIES
UNDER COMMON AGRICULTURAL POLICY

(in billion dollars)

	1958	1959	1960	1961	1962	1963
Imports	2.06	2.03	2.15	2.24	2.56	2.51
Exports	.83	.81	.92	1.01	1.06	1.22
Imports from U.S.*	.25	.38	.35	.49	.55	.55
Exports to U.S.*	.08	.08	.08	.08	.09	.09

*Represents only trade in farm products under common policy.
Many U.S. exports not produced in EEC. Total farm exports
to EEC are approximately$1.4 billion annually.

The EEC has proposed that the Kennedy Round trade negotiations should deal with the amount or "margin" of support for
farm products in establishing balanced world agricultural trade.
(The margin of support for any commodity is defined by the
Community as the difference between the world market price
of the product and the payment actually received by the farmer).
Negotiations on the margin of support would aim at the binding
of a maximum support margin. Binding would no longer be restricted to tariffs; it would freeze the over-all effect of all
support measures for all farm products. The value of such
binding would depend on the level at which the maximum support
margin were bound. Ideally, the EEC says, it would represent
a fair compromise between domestic agricultural and political
realities and the world trade situation. Bound supports would
stabilize the conditions of access to import markets, since these
could not be upset by unforeseen changes in supports.

Machinery would be established for setting the reference
price used to determine the amount of support. The reference
price could be either a price calculated on the basis of world
market prices or prices at the frontier during a base period.
The GATT parties could negotiate a reference price when automatic methods were deemed unsuitable. The actual payment
received by the farmer on the home market would be the average
annual price at the farm, plus any direct subsidies.

The Community proposal deals with the amount of support

rather than the kinds of support given. It lays stress on the overall effect of all measures and leaves the ultimate control over the measures with the governments.

GATT parties would pledge not to exceed the support ceiling agreed upon in the Kennedy Round negotiations. The EEC proposes that such commitments be made for three years. During this period, the support margin could be altered if the exchange rates between two parties were changed. In addition, the bound support margin could be increased if prices on the world market or free-at-frontier offer prices fell below the reference price. The reference price could serve as a price stabilizer in international trade, since it would discourage offers at a lower price level.

A price bracket would be set rather than a single reference price so that changes would not be caused by minor price fluctuation. If a GATT party found it necessary to exceed the bound support level due to unusual circumstances, it could do so. The party would then be required to grant compensation to other parties, especially if the increase had led to a greater supply on the world market. The EEC has emphasized that all bindings should be made on a reciprocal basis. This rule would not necessarily be applied, however, to developing countries.

The Community has proposed that, in addition to bindings for support margins, the GATT parties should conclude world agreements for the most important farm products in international trade. The agreements would cover products for which a permanent imbalance between supply and demand exists. World commodity agreements might be concluded for wheat and feed grains, beef, butter, sugar, and oil-bearing fruits and seeds.

Each agreement would cover a certain percentage, fixed in advance, of world trade in a given commodity. All GATT parties participating significantly in this trade would be invited to take part in the agreement. The agreements would not, however, be tied to GATT, thus allowing the eventual accession of member countries of the U.N. and its specialized agencies who are not GATT parties. In the world agreements, the reference price would serve as a balancing price in international trade and a long-term guide price. Reference prices for commodities covered by world agreements would be negotiated rather than automatically set.

Other activities have been undertaken outside the framework of the common agricultural policy. The Community participated in the London fisheries conference in 1964 which resulted in the establishment of fishing zones to be observed by the United Kingdom and the Six. In another sector, the Commission has made a study of European woodlands and forestry problems as the first step in the development of a coordination program for the Six.

The Commission has proposed directives for the harmonization of national laws affecting agriculture. These dealt with food preservatives, food coloring, cocoa, jams, marmalades, conserves, animal feeds, sanitary problems of fresh meat, and trade in seeds and seedlings.

A social policy for agricultural workers is being developed in order to deal with the numerous workers leaving farms and with social problems which may hamper the application of the common agricultural policy.

Cases Before the Court of the European Communities Relating to Agriculture

Chapter 14, Document 14.2 cases: 103/63, 106-7/63.

9.1 COMMON AGRICULTURAL POLICY -
FIRST REGULATIONS*

On January 14, 1962 the Council of Ministers adopted the following regulations and decisions:

1. Regulation on grain - 2. Regulations on pigmeat - 3. Regulation on eggs - 4. Regulation on poultry - 5. Regulation on fruit and vegetables - 6. Regulation on wine-growing - 7. Decision on wine quotas - 8. Regulation under Article 42 (rules of competition) - 9. Decision under Article 235 (processed agricultural products) plus a list of products - 10. Decision under Article 44 (objective criteria for minimum prices) - 11. Resolution on dairy produce, beef and sugar - 12. Financial regulation.

(All these decisions, with the exception of No. 11, will be published in the Community official gazette).

Regulations are fully binding and directly applicable in all Member States. The levy system, for instance, will be introduced on 1 July 1962. Before that date all national governments must adjust their legislation and their administrative practice and the Community itself must take a number of implementing measures.

These measures will represent a considerable simplification as compared with the sum of the measures at present existing in each country. Although the overall impression may be very complicated, it is nevertheless a logical system. No country possesses such a complex of legislation devised at one stroke. So far national market organizations in the various countries have been set up and have evolved as dicated by necessity and in most cases in answer to crises.

The products so far covered account for more than half of the Community's agricultural production and for 47% of trade within the Community.

The substance of the relevant decisions is given below.

Levies

The system of levies adopted for the grain, pigmeat, eggs and poultry sectors, supersedes all national measures of protection at the frontier. The levies will be the dominant factor in trade policy vis-a-vis non member countries both during the transition period and after the single market stage has been reached. During the preparatory stage a system of intra-Community levies will also be in force. In order to maintain the preference resulting for the Member States from the application of the Treaty, the amount of the intra-Community levies will be lower. The system thus aims at the gradual development of a common market by providing adequate guarantees for the farming population and effective support for agricultural markets while making possible the development of free movement within the Community and giving a clear picture of the Community's trade policy vis-a-vis the non-member countries.

The amount of the levies on soft wheat and coarse grains from non-member countries is equal to the difference between the most favourable cif price for the product and the threshold price (see under price system) of the importing Member State.

For intra-Community trade the amount thus calculated is reduced by a lump sum. The Member States producing hard wheat fix the levies for this type of wheat in accordance with an analogous procedure, the threshold price being fixed at a level at least 5% higher than that for soft wheat. The amount of the intra-Community levy will be the same as that imposed upon imports from non-member countries in the case of imports from a Member State where no hard wheat is grown.

For a number of products of grain processing (malt, gluten, bran, feeding-stuffs, etc.) the levy will contain a first amount corresponding to the effect on the cost price of these products of the levies introduced for the basic products. A second amount will alow for the need to protect the processing industry. This last element will be progressively reduced in the case of the intra-Community levies.

For livestock products (by grain conversion) such as pigmeat, poultry and eggs, there is also a system of levies which is not uniform for the three products because the present level of protection also differs. Egg production is protected only be tariffs in all member countries, while pig raising is often protected under the national policies of the member countries by other commercial policy measures such as quotas, minimum prices, etc. The import of poultry is free except in France.

291

The levy will therefore include for the three products a first element corresponding to the difference between the cost of feeding-stuffs in the importing country and the corresponding cost in the exporting country. As the prices of grain in the six countries come closer together during the transition period, this element will disappear from the intra-Community levy.

A second fixed element is added to the first. For pigmeat, this second element is limited in that the two amounts taken together must not be greater than the difference between the average market prices recorded in the exporting country and the importing country during a given reference period. For eggs and poultry, the second fixed amount is calculated on the current customs duty actually applied to the various products. In the poultry sector it may nevertheless in certain cases be determined in the manner described above for pigmeat. The second element will be reduced to nil over a period of 7 1/2 years.

Levies applicable to imports from non-member countries are fixed in the same way. They also cover differences in the cost of feeding-stuffs and the second element referred to above, plus a third element which, beginning at 2%, will in the end amount to 7% of an average import price.

The Commission may also in certain circumstances authorize a Member State, on the latter's request, to reduce the amount of these levies to the level of the country applying the lowest levy to its trade with non-member countries.

In the single market stage receipts from levies on imports from non-member countries go to the Community (see financial regulation).

Price System

Grain

In order to maintain for Community producers the necessary guarantees, each Member State will fix basic target prices yearly for wheat and rye and also for maize and barley, when there is a substantial production of these products. This price is the one ruling in the marketing centre of the area with the largest deficit (in the transition period there will be a centre for each Member State, in the single market stage one area will be indicated for the whole Community). Adjusted target prices in the important marketing centres on the regional plane are determined in the light of price differences due to the natural conditions governing their formation.

In order to guarantee producers sales at a price as close as possible to the target prices, taking into account market fluctuations, the Member States also fix intervention prices. These are equal to the target prices reduced by a fixed percentage determined by each Member State between a minimum of 5% and a maximum of 10%. In order to compensate producers in remote areas, Member States may in certain circumstances during the transition period fix adjusted intervention prices at a level slightly higher than the natural conditions governing their formation would have justified. (See also the special arrangements for corn, barley and rye under "transitional measures".)

For hard wheat these Member States fix the target and intervention prices applying in the important marketing centres situated in these areas of production.

The threshold prices - on the basis of which the levies are fixed - are determined in such a way that the sale price of imported grains and flour shall make it possible to reach the target price fixed. The threshold price for hard wheat must be fixed at a level at least 5% above that for soft wheat.

Pigmeat, Eggs, Poultry

There are no target prices for intervention prices (and thus no guaranteed price) for grain conversion products. Nevertheless, a Member State may, during the preparatory period, request authorization to take measures on its pigmeat market to mitigate any considerable price fall.

For each of these three products the Council will fix a sluice-gate price in order to avoid disturbances caused by offers at abnormally low prices from non-member countries. This sluice-gate price is uniform throughout the Community and is fixed on the basis of the world market prices of feed grains and of a representative conversion rate. This sluice-gate price - like the threshold price itself - operates as a minimum import price. In other words, import below this price is not permitted: either the non-member country guarantees that the imports it provides shall be at the sluice-gate price, or the importing

Member State increases the amount of the levy correspondingly.

For the pigmeat sector an intra-Community sluice-gate price has also been instituted. This price is fixed for each Member State with due regard to the margin of Community preference. It will cease to apply as soon as the intra-Community levies disappear.

Approximation of Prices

The criteria for the upper and lower limits of target prices for the marketing of the harvest beginning on 1 July 1962 have been fixed for wheat, barley and rye. These limits apply to all the Member States. The upper limit will be based on the intervention prices guaranteed to the producer in that area of the principal cereal-importing Member State which had the greatest deficit in the 1961/62 season, and the lower limit on the intervention prices guaranteed to producers in the country where prices were lowest during the same period. For maize, only a lower limit has been set.

It should be noted that there is not exactly a price standstill since regional price differentials will affect the present situation.

For the marketing of the harvest beginning on 1 July 1963 prices will be fixed before 1 April 1963. For the crop year measures of price approximation are taken each year before 1 July and on the first occasion before 1 September 1963.

In this way there will be a trial year before beginning the approximation of prices, as was requested by the Federal Republic, but it will not be necessary to lose a whole year because the prices decided on in April 1963 will be valid for the harvests after the following 1 July.

In addition, the Council must fix before 1 September 1962 the criteria for the approximation of prices. These criteria must be designed to promote a degree of specialization consistent with the economic structures and natural conditions of the Community, without obstructing the aims of the common agricultural policy as laid down in Article 39 of the Treaty, and especially the assurance of a fair standard of living for the farming population.

This means that the future Community target prices

will be determined in relation to efficient and viable farming
and be such as to maintain a reasonable balance of prices
among the various products.

Export Refunds

These refunds are in general intended to enable countries
with a higher price level to export their produce to other
countries.

In order to permit exports to non-member countries at
the rates obtaining on the world market, the difference between
these rates and prices in the exporting Member State may be
covered by a refund. These refunds are sometimes called
negative levies and they are in fact calculated in a manner
roughly similar to that applied to levies.

The way in which the funds operate in the grain sector
will be decided by the Commission after hearing the Management Committee (see Institutional questions and rules of competition).

For pigmeat, eggs and poultry the refunds comprise two
amounts: the first corresponds to the effect on feeding costs
of differences in the prices of feed grains, and the second takes
into account the trend of prices in the sector concerned.

For these three products, intra-Community refunds can
be made in two ways.

The amount of refund may be equal to the difference in
the cost of feeding-stuffs resulting from price differences for
feed grain. Or the amount of refund may equal the levy applied
to trade with non-member countries, but in this case the
importing Member State may impose on the imported products
the levy it imposes on similar imports from non-member
countries. These refunds, however, do not include those
parts of the levies on trade element with non-member countries
which correspond to the preferential element ranging from 2
to 7%.

The amount of refunds for grains can be specifically
calculated for some cases of intra-Community trade. In these
cases the amount is equal to the difference between the price
of the product free frontier and the threshold price of the
importing Member State, such difference being increased by

295

the lump sum (see "Transitional measures" for some cases
in which this method of calculation is employed).

Refunds on exports to third countries will be increasingly
borne by the European Agricultural Guidance and Guarantee
Fund during the preparatory period. At the single market
stage the financial burden of these refunds will rest entirely
on the Community.

Rules of Competition

As from 1 July 1962 the chapter of the Treaty concerning
rules of competition will apply to agricultural products (listed
in Annex II).

The section dealing with aids granted by States (Articles
92 to 94 of the Treaty) applies to production of, and trade in,
products covered by the Regulations on the pigmeat, poultry
meat, eggs and fruit and vegetables sectors. For eggs, however, the Member States which at present grant deficiency payments to compensate for differences in grain prices may continue this practice but they must gradually abolish these payments during the transition period.

In the grain sector, Articles 92 to 94 will apply to aids
the effect of which is to bring prices below those on which the
levy was calculated, or which directly influence the relationship
between the price of processed products and the price of products used in their manufacture. In certain cases, however,
the Member States may grant aids to producers of hard wheat.
They may also refund the levy charged on imports if at any
given time consumers do not pay for imported grains the price
obtaining for homegrown grains.

Within certain limits and subject to certain conditions
export refunds remain permissible for all products subject to
the levy system (see above).

With effect from 1 February 1962 the procedure stipulated
in the Treaty for the listing and multilateral examination of aids
will be applied to the systems introduced to promote production
of, and trade in, all agricultural products.

The Treaty rules on dumping will also apply to all agricultural products, with the exception however of the so-called
"boomerang" practice (Article 91 (2)).

With effect from 1 July 1962 the rules applicable to
enterprises on the subject of understandings or the abuse of a
dominant position on the market will apply to the production of,
and trade in, agricultural produce (Articles 85 to 90 of the
Treaty and Regulation No. 17). Nevertheless, agreements
or practices which are an integral part of a national market
organization, or which are necessary to attain the objectives
of the common agricultural policy, will not be prohibited
(e.g. agricultural co-operatives provided their purpose is
the common use of installations or the production or sale of
farm produce without any obligation to charge a fixed price -
(see chapter on Institutional Questions).

Processed Products

Processed agricultural products fall into two categories.
The first comprises the products listed in Annex II of the
Treaty (products covered by the Title on agriculture); the
second comprises the processed products to which the
common agricultural policy does not apply.

For products which are subject to the levy system,
the practice in the processing trade, by which trade in processed
products incorporating imported produce is carried on between
the Member States on the basis of the world prices for these
basic products, is not compatible with the levy system.

These products are specified in each Regulation (cereal
flours, cereal groats, semolina, malt, potato starch, fodder
preparations, sausages and other preserves containing pigmeat
or poultry meat, dried eggs, etc.).

The processed products of the second category are
governed by a special Decision (under Article 235 of the
Treaty) covering a three-year period. (These are processed
cereal products, sugar, molasses, potato starch, chicory
and milk. The list of these products is drawn up by the
Council; it contains inter alia confectionery, chocolates,
macaroni, spaghetti and similar products, bread and bakery
products, beer and ice creams.

If the industries producing such products in a Member
State are endangered, the Commission may authorize an importing Member State to impose a fixed compensatory levy
on such products, unless the exporting Member State applies
such a levy on exports of these products. The levy, which is

fixed by the Commission, is computed according to the effect on the list of processed products of differing prices for the agricultural products used in their manufacture; an amount may be added to protect the processing industry. During the first year this amount must not exceed 5% of the price of the goods; this percentage is reduced by 1/5 each subsequent year. The total of these two elements is then reduced by the amount of the customs duty imposed on the goods.

However, the second amount is reduced in so far as the total protection exceeds that obtaining on 1 January 1958.

This levy is intended to maintain a Community preference. The Commission can therefore make the levy subject to the application of protection measures towards non-member countries.

Standardization and Quality Control

There will be no levy system for the fruit and vegetables and wine sectors, where the liberalization of trade within the Community will be governed by considerations of quality.

For the fruit and vegetables sector, common quality standards are laid down for each product or for categories of products. With effect from 1 July 1962 these standards will apply to 21 products to be consumed fresh which are listed in Annex I to the Regulation. In the case of nine of these products the standards have already been defined (by the United Nations Economic Commission for Europe and by the European Productivity Agency). For the remaining twelve they must still be laid down before that date. The Council may add other products to the list in Annex I. Standards have already been laid down for cauliflowers, lettuce, curled and plain endives, onions, tomatoes, apples, pears, apricots, peaches, plums. Standards are to defined before 1 July 1962 for spinach, witloof, chicory, peas, beans, carrots, artichokes, China oranges, mandarines, clementines, lemons, dessert grapes, cherries, strawberries. It also lays down common standards for products intended for industrial use.

The common quality standards will be progressively applied to fruit and vegetables marketed within the producing Member States. The exporting Member State will submit products for exports to another Member State to a quality control before they are exported. A quality and grading certificate will accompany the goods. The importing Member State can check whether the grading of the product is in conformity with the certificate. Quantitative import restrictions will be abolished for graded products in accordance with the following time-table:

"Special" Grade by 1 July 1962
"Grade I" by 1 January 1964
"Grade II" by 1 January 1966.

The Member States will adhere to the same time-table in abolishing minimum prices for these categories of produce (Article 44 of the Treaty).

In France and Italy the import of wine is also governed by quality. These countries will each offer to all the Member States an annual quota of 150,000 hectolitres of quality wines of specified origin. Before 1 January 1963 the Council will issue a Community Regulation on quality wines. Pending the entry into force of this Regulation the import of quality wines will be limited to the origins, and where appropriate the varieties, specified in the present Council decision. The wines must be accompanied by a certificate of origin or quality, or by the national stamp (in the case of Luxembourg wines) and must be supplied for consumption in receptacles containing not more than 3 litres (the label must show the name of the importer and the place where the wine was bottled).

Minimum Prices

The Council has decided the objective criteria for minimum price systems and for the fixing of these prices. This decision, which is based on Article 44 of the Treaty, is not part of the common agricultural policy. On the contrary, the five Regulations relating to the products for which a marketing system has been set up, declare Article 44 to be no longer applicable to these sectors. From 1 July 1962 the appropriate safeguard measures for grain, pigmeat, eggs, poultry, fruit and vegetables will be the safeguard clause provided.

The minimum price system can only be fixed by a Member State for the duration of one year, it applies only during the marketing period for the domestic production of the Member State concerned. At least 14 days notice must be given of any Member State's intention to introduce a minimum price system.

The level of the minimum price fixed must be notified at least three working days in advance of the entry into force of the system. The Commission can, if necessary, arrange for a multilateral discussion on this subject.

Where there is in operation a system of minimum prices below which imports can be temporarily suspended or reduced, such measures are subject to three successive quotations showing that the reference price has remained below the minimum price fixed for the product in question (i.e. minimum import prices). Imports must be re-admitted as soon as the reference price on three successive quotations is equal to or higher than the minimum price fixed for the product in question. Time allowed for transport must not be less than three days.

The importing Member State may also accept a guarantee from the exporting Member State that it will respect the minimum price above which imports will be admitted (i.e. minimum export prices). When making the initial notification the Member State must also indicate the price it would adopt if it applied the alternative system. However, the principle of non-discrimination among the Member States must be respected even if a Member State applied the two minimum price systems simultaneously.

The minimum price may not be fixed at more than 105% of the intervention price for a product governed by a national market organization. For the other products the level must not exceed 92% of the average reference price on the wholesale markets during the three preceding years. To calculate minimum prices, the Member State must adjust the figures for abnormal years or periods by reference to the average domestic cost price. The Commission may recommend such adjustments. The Member State may fix seasonal minimum prices.

A Member State applying the minimum price system must also apply it to imports from non-member countries. In order to ensure a Community preference the minimum prices for such imports must be fixed at a level higher than that applicable to the Member States.

The decision will come into force on 1 July 1962 and is to be reviewed at the latest three years after that date.

The fruit and vegetables Regulation also provides for the introduction of a minimum price system applicable to non-member countries. Where the Community markets suffer from, or are threatened by, serious dislocation due to imports from non-member countries, these imports may be suspended or subjected to a uniform compensatory levy charged on entry by all Member States.

The amount of this compensatory levy, which can be fixed on a flat rate basis, will be equal to the difference between the reference price and the import price of a product excluding customs duty. The reference price is calculated on the basis of the average prices recorded over a certain period on the producer markets with the lowest prices in the Community.

Safeguard Clause

A general formula has been adopted for all products for which the trading system has been liberalized (therefore not for wine, where only the quotas have been fixed). According to this general formula Member States may resort to safeguard measures should there be great disturbance or threat of such disturbance in their market. They are required to inform the Commission and the other Member States of these measures at the latest when they come into force. If the frontier is closed (goods in transit will not be affected) the time allowed for transport must not be less than three days. The Commission must then decide in the Management Committee, within a maximum of four working days, whether the measures are to be maintained, amended or abolished. Should the Member State be unable to conform with the Commission's decision, it may appeal to the Council, which will decide by qualified majority. Nevertheless, this appeal will not suspend the Commission's decision: the Member States therefore can only take autonomous measures for a period of four days.

The following two exceptions to this general clause were agreed:

- In the case of grain the appeal to the Council will suspend the Commission's decision for ten days.

- For top quality fruit and vegetables. Here there is no possibility of autonomous measures, but each member country may request of the Commission authorization to take safeguard measures. In this connection the only possibility of appeal is to the Court of Justice. The Commission has declared that in finding that a serious disturbance has been caused it will take as a determining factor any fall of prices below 82% of the average wholesale market prices of the three preceding years (compare this with the criterion of 92% fixed for the minimum price.

Furthermore, no steps can be taken with regard to a superior grade of fruit or vegetables unless at least equivalent steps have been taken with regard to poorer grades.

Any safeguard measure affecting trade between the Member States will be simultaneously applied to non-member countries, with due regard to the principle of Community preference.

The level of protection which would result from the application of this clause must be lower than, or at most equal to, the level of protection obtaining on 1 July 1962.

Measures Applicable to One Sector Only

Grains

The national market organizations may sell wheat and rye at a price lower than the target price, provided they are rendered unfit for human consumption. These organizations may also offer compensation for such treatment to holders of wheat and rye stocks.

All imports and exports will be subject to import certificates. These certificates, issued by the Member State concerned, will be valid for three months (from the first day of the month following that in which the certificate is issued). The certificate is issued on the deposit of a surety for the import; the surety will be forfeited if no import takes place.

Pigmeat

During the transition period each State may intervene on its own markets. A Community procedure for mutual information is planned and also progressive co-ordination of such intervention at the Community level. Four years

at the latest after the entry into force of the regulation the
Council, acting on a proposal of the Commission, will have
to decide as to its retention at the single market stage and
lay down procedures for applying it at that stage.

Fruits and Vegetables

Before 1 July 1964 the Council will draw up, on a proposal from the Commission, Community rules concerning
the functioning of the market and commercial dealings.

The market in this sector will be protected by the
gradual establishment of the common external tariff and the
elimination of customs duties amongst the Member States
under the general rules of the Treaty. The Council will
also decide as to the co-ordination and unification of the
import systems operated by each Member State with regard
to non-member countries (see also the chapter on minimum
prices).

Wines

The wine-growing policies of the various Member
States differ considerably. To stabilize markets and prices
it will be necessary to adapt resources to requirements and
to do so on the basis of quality (see chapter on quality control). To this end a register of vineyards is to be established before 30 June 1963; wine growers must declare
their harvests and stocks from 1962 onwards, and annual
forecasts are to be made. Also, the Council must, before
1 January 1963, issue Community regulations on quality
wines of specified origin.

Until the entry into force of this Regulation, wine imports into France and Italy are governed by a quota for
quality wines (150, 000 hectolitres in 1962). In the Federal
Republic of Germany, where there is no excess production
and where import requirements are not limited to quality wines,
which must nevertheless account for 1/4 of the table wines
quota, the import quota has been fixed at 800, 000 hectolitres
for 1962 (including a maximum of 210, 000 hl. of white wines).

A 400, 000 hectolitre quota has been opened by this coun-
try for wines serving as a basis for sparkling wines. The
Council, acting by a qualified majority on a proposal of the
Commission, will decide annually as to the expansion of

these quotas.

Transition Measures Applicable to Various Countries

In the Regulations as a whole account has been taken as far as possible of the difficulties Member States may encounter in bringing their laws and regulations into line before the appointed date of 1 July 1962. Nevertheless, exceptions or privileges must not create obstacles to the development of trade or be damaging to other member countries. Moreover, these arrangements are limited to specified time, or at the most to the duration of the transition period.

In the preceding pages several references have already been made to these special arrangements. Further examples follow below:

For France:
Guaranteed grain prices apply to a certain quantity only; intra-Community levies on poultry are calculated in the same way as those on pigmeat; refunds for maize may be calculated by special arrangement;

For Italy:
The maintenance of state trading in grain may be requested at least for one year on certain conditions; for a period of three years no intervention is necessary in the case of maize, barley or rye;

For Luxembourg:
Special arrangements are provided for refunds on grain and pigmeat. Under a special protocol to the Treaty of Rome this country is also authorized to maintain quantitative import restrictions on all agricultural produce.

For West Germany:
Intervention prices can be adjusted in the framework of the system of target prices organized on a regional basis in order to compensate grain producers in areas remote from the centres of greatest deficit; egg prices may be subsidized; traditional trade can be preserved (e.g. in rye) through specifically calculated refunds.

Financial Regulation

A European Agricultural Guidance and Guarantee
Fund is set up.

Expenditure:
a. Refunds on exports to non-member countries (calculated
    on the quantities of net exports and the rate of refund of
    the Member State with the lowest price level)

b. Interventions on the internal market in accordance with
    a decision by the Council;

c. Measures to achieve the aims of the common agricultural
    policy, including structural changes, taken in accordance
    with a decision by the Council.

Before 1 October 1962 the Commission will make proposals for Community financing from 1962/63 on.

Annual review by the Council (pattern of production,
development of markets, financial consequences of the common
agricultural policy). The situation as a whole will be reviewed
by the Council before the end of the third year.

The contribution of the Fund to the expenditure under a.
and b. will be roughly 1/6 for 1962/63, 2/6 for 1963/64 and 3/6
for 1964/65.

Contributions under c. will as far as possible be 1/3 of
the contributions to the other expenditure.

Contributions by the Fund to items under a., b. and c.
will increase regularly till at the end of the preparatory stage
all the appropriate expenditure is financed by the Fund.

Resources:
The amount of money available will be fixed annually by
the Council. The receipts of the Fund during the first three
years will consist of financial contributions from the Member
States, one part being calculated according to the scale for
the budget laid down in Article 200 (1) of the Treaty, and the
other proportionately to the net imports of each Member
State from non-member countries.

The two parts of the contributions from Member States will constitute the total receipts of the Fund in the following proportions:

(in %)

	1962/1963	1963/1964	1964/1965
According to the scale laid down in Article 200 (1)	100	90	80
Proportionate to net imports	-	10	20

The Council has also fixed a ceiling for the contributions of each Member State during the first three years: 10.5% for B.L.E.U., 31% for the Federal Republic, 28% for Italy and 13% for the Netherlands.

The Federal Republic and the Netherlands will therefore have to pay more than they would under the general budget scale in Article 200 (1). In other words, the countries with net imports (from non-member countries) must contribute to a part of the refunds on exports to non-member countries. (France for its grain and Holland for its dairy produce will benefit most from this arrangement).

Before the end of the third year the Council will lay down rules to ensure gradual progress towards a single market system.

In this single market phase receipts from levies charged on imports from non-member countries will go to the Community and be used to cover Community expenditure. The budgetary funds of the Community will then be derived from these receipts and any other revenue decided on under the rules of the Treaty plus the budget contributions made by the States under Article 200 of the Treaty.

The Fund will be a part of the budget of the Community.

The Regulation will apply to the grain, pigmeat, egg and poultry markets from 1 July 1962, to the dairy produce market from 1 November 1962, and where necessary to other markets on dates to be fixed by the Council.

Institutions

The regulations on the common agricultural policy

indicate in detail how the powers of decision are divided between the Council of Ministers and the Commission. The Council takes certain major decisions - on proposals from the Commission - by unanimous vote in the second stage, and by qualified majority vote in the third (see Article 43 of the Treaty). These decisions cover measures such as those relating to the approximation of grain prices and criteria for Community financing of refunds or Community rules concerning the operation of markets and commercial transactions in the fruit and vegetables sector. Other decisions will be taken by the Council by qualified majority once the regulations come into force. Instances are the arrangements for products processed from grain and the co-ordination and unification of import systems in trade with non-member countries in the fruit and vegetables sector.

In addition, five Management Committees are set up for grain, pigmeat, eggs and poultry, fruit and vegetables and wines. These Committees consist of representatives of the Member States presided over by a representative of the Commission, who has no vote. In appropriate cases the Commission seeks the opinion of the relevant Committee on the draft of a proposed measure. The Committee decides by qualified majority vote (procedure as under Article 148 (2) of the Treaty).

The Commission then decides on the measures to be taken, and these are immediately applicable. If these are at variance with the opinion given by the Committee, the Commission has power to postpone their application for a maximum period of one month. The Council, deciding by qualified majority vote, can then take a different decision within the time-limit set. This procedure has been laid down for fixing the lump sum figure which in effect determines the margin of Community preference and for the arrangements to avoid diversion of trade in the grain sector; it will be used to determine inter-Community sluice-gate prices for pigmeat, the levies on eggs and poultry and the common quality standards for about a dozen products in the fruit and vegetables sector (List B).

In a number of cases the Commission can, without consulting the Management Committee, make decisions which are not subject to revision by the Council. These include authorizing a Member State to reduce the amount of levies on pigmeat, noting of prices delivered free at frontier or prices

on world grain markets, authorizing safeguard measures for
"top quality" fruit and vegetables, and decisions as to whether
agreements between or practices followed by agricultural
producers are incompatible with the Common Market.

It should be pointed out that almost all the implementing
action is left to the authorities of the Member States; the
Commission is thus the co-ordinating body for the national
organizations and also watches over the implementation of
the regulations.

Length of the Preparatory Period

The Regulations are to come into force on 1 July 1962.
Seven and a half years have been allowed for the progressive
implementation of the agricultural common market, i. e. by
31 December 1969, unless there is meanwhile a decision
ensuring earlier implementation. The tranches referred to
in the financial regulation have already been fixed at one-
sixth instead of two-fifteenths for the first three years. All
the other adjustments will be made on the two-fifteenths
basis.

Time-Table for 1962 Agreed by the Council

	Proposals by Commission before:	Decision by Council before:	Entry into force
Rice	30.4.1962	1.7.1962	
Dairy produce	1.5.1962	31.7.1962	1.11.1962
Beef and veal	1.5.1962	31.7.1962	1.11.1962
Veterinary system	1.7.1962		1.1.1962
Sugar	15.7.1962	1.11.1962	

For the dairy produce sector the Council has already
agreed in principle to a levy system and Community financial
support for the common agriculture policy.

Now that the major decisions of principle have been
taken it will obviously be easier to make the appropriate
regulations under the above programme.

Statistics of Production and Intra-Community Trade

Production (base year 1958)
Percentage ratio of production (in terms of value) to the total
agricultural production of the Six (*).

Grain	12%
Fruits and vegetables	12%
Eggs	6%
Pigmeat	13%
Poultry (dead)	3%
Wine	7%
	53%

Rice	0.4%
Beef and veal	14%
Milk	19%
Sugar (sugar beet)	3%
	36.4%

Total   89.4%

Trade (base year 1960)
Percentage ratio of trade (in terms of value) to total intra-
Community trade in agricultural products (*).

Grain	8.2%
Pigmeat	4.7%
Eggs	.7.7%
Fresh fruit and vegetables	19.8%
Poultry (dead)	2.7%
Wine	3.8%
	46.9%

Rice	0.3%
Beef and veal	6.9%
Dairy produce	7.6%
Sugar	1.7%
	16.5%

Total   63.4%

(*) Agricultural products as defined in Annex II of the Treaty.

*EEC Official Spokesman, A Farm Policy for Europe,
Publication 8040/5/III/1962/5.

9.2 NEW COMMON ORGANIZATIONS OF AGRICULTURAL MARKETS*

Just before Christmas, on December 23, 1963, the
Council agreed to Commission proposals for the establishment of three new market organizations - dairy produce,
beef and rice - and a resolution on the broad lines of a
common policy on fats and oils.

This means that the major political choices have been
made and that the basic regulations for the three products
mentioned above are now adopted, save, however, for a few
secondary matters which were not settled last year for lack
of time. This outstanding business was dispatched at the
Council's session early in February and the various regulations
and decisions were adopted officially - in the four Community
languages - on February 5.

The entry into force of the common agricultural policy
has for the moment been fixed at July 1, 1964 for dairy produce, beef and rice, and November 1, 1964 for fats and oils.
For this last sector, the regulation has yet to be drafted
(no opinion has yet been rendered by the European Parliament).
About 70 implementing regulations are to be adopted either by
the Council of Ministers or by the Commission for the three
new market organizations and for the Agricultural Fund
(FEOGA). This means a heavy programme in coming months;
it is however planned that all the necessary implementing
regulations will be adopted by May 1. Government departments
will then have two months in hand to make preparations for the
entry into force of the new arrangements on July 1, 1964.

The Member States have pledged themselves to take the
necessary steps to adjust their laws and regulations so that
the three new regulations can take effect on the appointed
date. They are, for example, required to organize a system
of official and publicized price quotations for all dairy produce
having a determining influence as regards levies.

The regulation altering refunds on exports to non-member
countries of pigmeat, eggs and poultry will also enter into force
on July 1. This regulation abolishes the original refunds and

stipulates that refunds henceforth must be calculated only on the basis of the incidence of differences in costs of raw materials.

It should be added that the Council has noted the Commission's undertaking to submit a proposal to amplify the regulations in force (cereals, pigmeat, eggs, poultry, fruit and vegetables) or in course of adoption so that in their implementation due regard will be had at the same time to the interests of the common agricultural policy (see Article 39 of the Treaty) and of those of the Community's commercial policy (Article 110 of the Treaty).

The three new common organizations of markets will fit into the general framework of the agricultural policy and will be largely based on the regulations already in force. For example, the regulation on the financing of the common agricultural policy applies to the three new sectors. The safeguard clauses for which provision is made in the new regulation are similar to the clauses of those two years ago. The machinery will be similar: Management Committees will be set up for milk and milk products and for beef, and the Cereals Management Committee will henceforth be competent for rice as well. Many other arrangements already written into the cereals or pigmeat common organization recur in the new organization of internal markets or among the measures to be taken when produce is imported from non-member countries.

Milk and Milk Products

Milk accounts for about 20% of the total value of agricultural production. One third of farm incomes in the Community is derived from dairy products and beef and veal, against only 12% from cereals. Dairy products account for some 7.5% of the value of intra-Community trade in farm products. In 1962 the Member States spent more than DM 1 500 million in aids (Italy is the only country that does not support dairy farming from public funds).

Products:

The following products come under the common organization of the markets in milk and milk products: milk and cream, fresh, preserved, concentrated or sweetened; butter, cheese and curds; lactose and lactose syrup, and fodder containing certain other products of which a list is given, excluding products falling within the scope of the cereals regulation.

However, the regulation will not yet cover the dairy milk market. Only the provisions concerning prices and aids will affect milk and fresh cream. The Council will make a special regulation for these products before July 1, 1965.

For non-agricultural derived products (therefore not included in Annex II of the Treaty) a decision will be taken as soon as possible (procedure of Article 235 of the Treaty), just as was done for second-processed cereal products.

The milk year runs from April 1 to March 31.

Import and Export Arrangements

The levies on imports are to be equal to the difference between the threshold price in the importing Member State and the price free at frontier. The levy is to be reduced by a sum representing the incidence of internal imposts on imports from Member States. The levy is also to be reduced by a fixed amount designed to secure intra-Community preference and to encourage the development of Community trade. The intra-Community levies will be eliminated gradually during the transition period in step with the alignment of prices for dairy products.

In fixing the prices to serve as a basis for calculating the levies, any difference in the composition or in the quality grade of the products will be taken into consideration if it materially affects marketing.

In view of the great variety of milk products, some of them - cheeses, for instance - are to be grouped (the same kind of simplification was adopted for cuts of pork. For the "pilot" products in these groups the levies will be calculated as indicated above; for the other products in each group the levies will be the same, unless it is decided to apply derived levies. The amounts of the levies will be fixed by the Member States. The levies will be collected by the importing Member States and will accrue to that State. During the transitional period, the Commission may authorize a Member State, under certain conditions and at its request, to reduce the levies on one or more milk products for reasons connected with the current trade situation.

312

A Member State giving aid to production may in the case of exportation make a charge not greater than the incidence of this aid on the price of the products exported, on condition however that this Member State shall grant for products imported from the other Member States a subsidy having the same effect on the price.

Special Arrangements

The levies on fodder will be made up of three components: a variable component corresponding to the levies on milk products, an additional component corresponding to the levies for cereal products and a fixed component constituting protection for the processing industry. This last component will be equal, for intra-Community levies, to nine fifteenths of the levy on trade with non-member countries, and it will be tapered down from the 1965/66 season onwards by two fifteenths each year.

For Emmental, Gruyere, Sbrinz, Cheddar and Glaris cheeses imported from non-member countries, the levies cannot exceed the customs duties laid down in the common external tariff and bound in GATT as long as the conditions specified in the customs tariff of the European Communities are complied with.

Price System

The free-at-frontier prices are to be determined on the basis of the prices ex works plus a fixed amount representing costs of transport to the frontier of the importing country. The free-at-frontier prices thus fixed will be reduced by a sum worked out on a standard rate basis corresponding to the incidence of internal taxes refunded on exports. For imports from non-member countries the free-at-frontier prices will be determined on the basis of the most favourable prices in international trade. For the importation of butter from non-member countries a differing cif price will be fixed according to whether the product is fresh cream butter or sour cream butter.

The threshold prices will be fixed annually by the Member States. For the milk year 1964/65, threshold prices have been fixed on the basis of reference prices reflecting average market prices. To the reference prices must be added the fixed amounts. The threshold price of best butter may however be increased by an amount corresponding to the

313

difference between the intervention price and the reference price. Where this difference is less than 0.05 u.a., an increase of 0.05 u.a. can nevertheless be made. But the difference may not exceed 0.075 u.a. per kg. The differences and the intervention price will gradually be harmonized. For other products the Council may authorize a Member State at its request to increase its reference price by not more than 2%, when the threshold price is fixed for the first time. The reference prices are to be calculated for each Member State on the basis of the arithmetical average of the prices at which the producers delivered to wholesalers during 1963. The reference prices may be adjusted in relation with changes in the milk target prices and with the reduction of aids (see domestic market). If it is impossible to establish the reference price for a product in this way, the prices will be calculated on the basis of similar products, or else the price at which the product in question was imported during 1963 will be taken as a basis. The reference prices will be fixed by the Council acting unanimously on proposals from the Commission.

All imports of butter, milk and cream (concentrated or sweetened) from outside the Community and, during the transition period, from other Member States as well, will be subject to the import licence (excepting whole powdered milk in airtight containers of a net weight of not more than 1 kg). A surety must also be deposited.

Until March 31, 1966 any Member State may prohibit the importation of butter with a fat content lower than 82%, a water content of more than 16% and a non-fat content of more than 2% if such butter does not fulfill the requirements of the importing Member State, when the relevant regulation comes into force, concerning best butter of domestic origin. However, such prohibition will only be allowed until the date on which laws in this field are harmonized, which is to be done by March 31, 1966.

In order to allow of exports to non-member countries at prices prevailing in international trade, the difference between these prices and prices in the exporting Member State may be covered by a refund. In intra-Community trade the Member States will be authorized to refund an amount corresponding to the difference between the free-at-frontier price and the threshold price of the importing Member State plus a fixed amount corresponding to the incidence of internal taxes on imports.

Incompatibilities

Subject to any provisions to the contrary, the proposed arrangement will replace national restrictive measures such as quota restrictions, minimum prices, special charges and customs duty (except in the case of Luxembourg in respect of the maintenance of quantitative restrictions).

Safeguard Clauses

During the transition period, a safeguard clause is provided for, both in intra-Community trade and trade with non-member countries, where there is serious disturbance or a threat of serious disturbance of the market in one or more Member States. This clause is exactly the same as the normal safeguard clause in force for other products already subject to a common organization of markets. However, for butter and milk the major suspension clause has been adopted which is also written into the cereals regulation: for these products there will therefore be suspension of the Commission's decision for ten days where reference is made to the Council.

After the expiry of the transition period, the issuing of import licences for produce from non-member countries may be suspended if there is a serious disturbance of the market (particularly if intervention agencies are obliged to make substantial purchases on the domestic market). This provision therefore constitutes a safeguard clause vis-a-vis non-member countries.

The Domestic Market

The national target price will be the price which it is sought to ensure for all farmers for all milk sold during the milk year. During the transition period each Member State will fix annually before February 15 a target price ex farm for milk containing 3.7% fat, valid for the subsequent milk year. These prices will be fixed for the first time before March 15, 1964. For the year 1964/65, the Council will establish the upper and lower limits of the national milk target prices. They will be fixed on the basis of the average price for milk ex farm which all the farmers of each Member State have received for the whole of their milk production marketed, with due regard to any changes in producers' prices in relation with the reference period caused by changes in price objectives or by the normal development of the markets and of prices. The Member States may attempt to attain the national target price solely by receipts from the sales of dairy products, but they will also retain during the transition period the option of granting national aids.

A common target price for milk ex farm will be fixed by the Council each year from 1965/66 onwards. During the transition period the Council will decide each year on the measures the Member States must apply with a view to approximation of prices. The national target prices are to be approximated on the basis of common target prices. In the final, single-market stage, the national target price will be the same as the common target price. The approximation of threshold prices will also be carried out on the basis of common target prices. Uniform costs and yields will be taken as a basis in calculations for each product.

The Council is also to decide the criteria for fixing the amount intended to protect the processing industry and the valorization ratio of the milk used in the various processed products.

Those Member States which subsidize production must increase their market prices in the transition period so that in the final, single-market stage they will be at the same level as the common target prices. The target price for milk will then be the price which market policy aims at ensuring for Community producers as a whole for all the milk marketed.

During the transition direct aids may be granted at national level, i.e. aids for specific milk products and aids in respect of the milk sold by farmers. The Member States will inform the Commission of the details of their national aids. National aids will be tapered down each year by one seventh if they bring the market prices for the products in question below the prices corresponding to the lower limit of the bracket laid down by the Council for the target price of milk for the 1964/65 marketing year. Assistance from public equalization funds for milk for manufacture (supported in fact by the dairy milk market) will be authorized until a regulation for dairy milk comes into operation (at latest December 1, 1965); the new regulation will decide what should then become of this assistance. If, however, payments are linked with specific

316

products, they must be reduced as indicated above.

For the rest, the Council, on proposals from the Commission, will fix by what amount aids are to be cut in relation with the alignment of national target prices and the raising of threshold prices: the general principle under the common agricultural policy is that the farmer's income should be derived solely from sales.

If, as a consequence of the harmonization of national target prices, the target price in a given Member State falls below the price per kilogramme of milk paid to producers during 1963 for all milk sold, the Member State in question may compensate for this difference. Such compensation may be granted per kilogramme of milk, and not later than the end of the transition period it will assume a form independent of milk production. The aid arrangements will have to be gradually adapted so that the transition to arrangements for the definitive stage is made smoothly. To this purpose, the Commission will address to the Member States concerned, and in particular to the Federal Republic of Germany and to Luxembourg, a recommendation that they begin adjusting these aids during 1966/67.

Account will be taken under the FEOGA (the European Agricultural Guidance and Guarantee Fund) of the incidence of national aids on the amount of refunds made on exports of dairy produce to non-member countries.

Subject to provisions to the contrary in the milk regulation, Article 92 to 94 of the Treaty (arrangements governing state aids) will apply to production of and trade in dairy produce.

Community aids are obviously not prohibited. For instance, provision is made for intervention, notably in the butter market. The Member States will fix an intervention price for fresh best butter. Throughout the dairy year the intervention agencies will have to purchase any best home-produced fresh butter offered to them. When first fixed, the intervention price will be equal to the reference price, though this figure may be reduced by a maximum of 0.075 units of account. Butter from stock must be sold in such a way as not to disturb sales of fresh butter. The Member States may also grant aids in respect of private stocks of butter and frozen cream.

During the transition period a Member State may also

purchase products other than best butter in order to prevent any imbalance on its market. A procedure for Community consultation is laid down for such cases. The intervention must be co-ordinated during the transition period, and within two years the Council will determine what other products will be subject to Community intervention measures and how the measures shall be applied.

Fats and Oils

Before November 1, 1964 the Council will adopt, on a proposal from the Commission a regulation applying a Community fats and oils policy. This will be done on the basis of principles laid down in a resolution of the Council containing the following main points:

(a) Free importation of oil-seeds and of fats and oils of vegetable origin or extracted from marine mammals, and application to these products (except olive oil) of the duties in the common external tariff. It should be noted that oil-seeds and oleaginous fruit are exempt from duty;

(b) Granting of direct aids to producers of oil-seeds and oleaginous fruit in order to maintain the necessary volume of production in the Community. (Community output of seed oils accounts for only about 6% of Community needs with a total of about 150,000 metric tons per year);

(c) Annual establishment of a target price for olive oil enabling the necessary volume of production in the Community to be maintained at fair prices for the producers (the quantity of olive oil produced in the Community is estimated at an average of 350,000 metric tons per year);

(d) Annual establishment of an intervention price for olive oil so as to guarantee for producers sales at a price as near the target price as possible;

(e) Constitution of buffer stocks so as to stabilize consumer prices;

(f) Fixing of a threshold price for olive oil and institution of levies on imports;

318

(g)　Should it prove necessary to fix the target price at a
　　level below that indicated above in order to combat
　　an appreciable fall in olive-oil consumption resulting
　　from low prices for competing products on the world
　　market, granting of direct Community aids to producers;

(h)　Establishment by the Italian Government in co-oper-
　　ation with the Commission of a programme to improve
　　conditions under which olives and olive oil are produced
　　and marketed and to help olive-growing areas; for the
　　implementation of this programme, intervention of the
　　European Agricultural Guidance and Guarantee Fund
　　within its terms of reference without prejudice to any
　　intervention by other Community institutions;

(i)　As regards oleaginous products from the associated
　　African States or Madagascar imported into the Com-
　　munity: for oils, elimination of the customs duties in
　　the national tariffs in the same way as the Member
　　States are eliminating duties as between themselves;
　　for seed, in case of need, special measures to ensure
　　a certain privileged position;

(j)　As regards oleaginous products from the associated
　　African States or Madagascar imported into the
　　Community, granting of aid to mitigate the effects of
　　a fall in world prices below an average price to be
　　fixed as a reference.

　　The Community financing of this policy will be ensured by
a contribution on edible fats and oils of vegetable or marine
origin imported into or produced in the Community. This
contribution will be limited to a total of DM 350 million
(estimated at DM 0.14 per kg). The European Agricultural
Guidance and Guarantee Fund will provide the rest. However,
for a year from the entry into force of the relevant regulation,
and possible for a further year, certain Member States may
dispense with the contribution and provide the necessary funds,
for example, by budget appropriations.

　　If the common policy on dairy produce or that on vegetable
fats and oils leads to substantial changes in the markets for these
two groups of products in the various Member States, the Commission will make appropriate proposals to the Council.

Beef and Veal

Production of beef and veal accounts for 14% of the total earnings of agriculture in the Six. The value of intra-Community trade in this sector represents almost 7% of the total. The organization of a common market in the beef sector is relatively simple, firstly because the Community is a net importer (243, 000 metric tons imported in 1960/61), and secondly because there are no great divergences of price from one member country to another.

The sector obviously has close links with the milk sector, and the regulation lays down that one of the points to be taken into account in fixing the guide prices of beef and veal is the development of the market in milk and milk products.

The products covered are live cattle (other than for blood-stock breeding), beef and offal (fresh and other), sausages, other prepared or preserved meats and unrendered fats and tallow.

Customs duties will be the principal means of normalizing competition from non-member countries. In the common external tariff the duty on live animals is 16% and on meat 20%. The time-table for reducing internal duties and putting the common external tariff into effect is as follows:

Reduction of duties in intra-Community trade		Alignment on the CET
60%	1. 4. 64	
	31. 3. 65	(as in Article 23 of the Treaty)
50%	1. 4. 65	50%
40%	1. 4. 66	65%
30%	1. 4. 67	
20%	1. 4. 68	85%
10%	1. 4. 69	
All duties abolished	1. 1. 70	CET in force.

For certain products, however, account will have to be taken of the maximum rate of duty bound in GATT. For frozen meat, see below. In addition, the Federal Republic of Germany will apply a duty reduced in proportion with the incidence of the

Umsatzausgleichsteuer.

Price and Levy System

In each Member State, annual guide prices will be determined for calves and for grown animals. For the 1964/65 and 1965/66 marketing years these prices will be fixed by the State concerned within a price bracket determined by the Council. For the first year the upper and lower limits of the bracket will be determined in relation to the weighted average of prices in each State from November 1, 1962 to October 31, 1963 and to the direction in which beef production is to be guided. From the marketing year beginning on April 1, 1966 the Council will fix the guide price on a proposal from the Commission. During the first two seasons Belgium may request authorization for a seasonal adjustment of prices.

The width of the bracket will be reduced and the guide prices aligned by annual stages. By December 31, 1969 at latest there is to be a single guide price for the whole Community.

At regular intervals the Commission will fix import prices for calves and grown animals on the basis of the prices quoted on the most typical markets in non-member countries. If for either group the import price (including customs duty) is lower than the guide price of the importing Member State, the difference between the two will be made up by a "non-member country" levy. No levy will be charged, however, if the market price in the importing Member State is more than 5% higher than the guide price. Until March 31, 1966 the importing Member State's market price will be equal to the weighted average of the prices charged in this Member State at a given stage of wholesale distribution. The Commission may on certain conditions authorize a Member State, at its request and for reasons connected with the current business situation, to reduce the customs duties and the levies. When a levy is imposed on live cattle, a corresponding levy will also be charged on fresh, chilled or frozen meat and cuts. The levies for these products will be derived from the levies on the live animals by applying a table of equivalence.

The Member States may on certain conditions intervene on their markets in order to mitigate a substantial fall in prices. These intervention measures may come into operation at a level - to be decided by the Member States - somewhere between 96% and 93% of the guide price. Any Member State that has to intervene must inform the Commission in advance. The measures may only be taken if the price for the commodity is at or below its intervention price. The Council must co-ordinate intervention measures and then specify, not later than three years after the entry into force of the regulation, the way in which, in case of necessity, Community intervention measures will be applied in the final, single-market stage.

During the transition period the Member States may apply intra-Community levies for as long as a Member State intervenes on its market even if intervention affects only one of the commodities covered by a market organization. The levy must be equal to the difference between the offer price plus the customs duty and 95% of the guide price. However, if a Member State intervenes at the level of 96% of the guide price, the levy may not exceed the difference between the offer price and 96% of the guide price. Where a Member State does not intervene on its market, it may impose a levy on imports from other Member States in order to bring back prices to a maximum level of 90% of the guide price.

Special Arrangements

For offals, salted, dried or smoked meats, sausages, and other prepared or preserved meats, there will be neither guide price nor levy. Each Member State is free to establish import licence and surety systems for these products.

For imports of frozen meat from other Member States and from outside the Community, import licences will be compulsory. Those Member States whose frozen meat customs duty is below the common external duty will apply on April 1, 1964 a duty of 17.5% and on April 1, 1965 the CET. In addition to the tariff quota of 22,000 metric tons, bound under GATT, an additional tonnage of frozen meat for the processing indus-tries, to be determined by the Council, may be imported at a customs duty of not more than 20%.

During the period for which a supplementary quota has been arranged, customs duties and levies on intra-Community trade in frozen meat will be suspended.

Until 1965, by way of exception, it has been provided that the Federal Republic of Germany may import 16,000 head of cattle from Denmark during the period when cattle are being brought in from pasture (from September 1 to November 30). However, these animals cannot enter at a price below the German guide price.

Refunds

On exports to non-member countries a Member State may refund a sum calculated according to price trends in the exporting Member State and on the world markets.

Frozen meats made available as the result of intervention measures cannot be traded between member countries at prices below those of the world market. The Council is to lay down implementing details, particularly those concerning intra-Community refunds. In addition, for one year after the entry into force of the regulation, an exporting Member State may still refund the difference between costs resulting from health protection measures required by the importing Member State and similar charges imposed by the exporting Member State.

Incompatibilities

Unless otherwise provided, national restrictive measures such as quotas, minimum prices, and special taxes other than the customs duties provided for in the regulation shall be considered incompatible with the arrangement now adopted.

In addition, Articles 92 to 94 of the Treaty (state aids) will be applicable to production of and trade in beef and veal products. Some exceptions have, however, been provided for in the case of Luxembourg.

Safeguard Clauses

The safeguard clause in the regulation is the normal clause applicable to other sectors already covered by a common organization of the market.

Rice

The Community produces about 750,000 metric tons of rice a year, equivalent to some 600,000 tons of husked rice. The quantities of rice imported and exported are in balance, but net imports of broken rice are about 100,000 tons a year. The value of rice grown in the Community, and also of intra-Community trade in this commodity, is less then 0.5% of the total value of agricultural production.

The rice regulation is based largely on that adopted for other cereals, but some adaptation proved necessary to take account of the special features of the sector. This was because rice is grown in only two of the Member States and the other Member States place virtually no obstacles in the way of trade in rice.

Products: The regulation applies to rice in all its forms, to broken rice and to rice flour, rice groats, ground rice and rice starch.

Arrangements for non-producing Member States

A single market for rice and broken rice will be set up on July 1, 1964 in the four non-producing Member States. This makes possible a single threshold price, a single cif price and a single levy on imports from non-member countries.

The common threshold price will be fixed by the Council. For the first year it will be equal to the most typical price on world markets plus 5%, but may not be lower than 12.5 units of account per 100 kg.

The Levy System

During a transition period the two producing countries will fix the threshold price each year with respect to a husked short grain rice of a standard of quality identical for all Member States. The threshold price will be fixed so that the selling price of the imported product, including the fixed amount, will, in the area of largest deficit, be at the level of the basic target price. The threshold price for broken rice will be equal to the threshold price for husked rice less a percentage fixed by reference to a specified period.

The import levy will be equal to the difference between the threshold price and the cif price (where the product is imported from non-member countries) or the free-at-frontier price (if the import comes from a producing Member State). In the latter case, the difference will be reduced by a fixed amount to ensure intra-Community preference. For imports of paddy, the levy on husked rice will be adjusted in accordance with a table of equivalence. Where the selling price does not correspond to the free quotations on world markets on which the cif price is based, the cif price will be replaced by a price determined in relation to the selling price.

The levy system for processed rice and for rice flour, rice groats, ground rice and rice starch will be similar to that for processed products based on cereals. These levies therefore have two components: a variable component corresponding to the levy on the basic product and a fixed component representing protection for the processing industry.

If the price free-at-frontier of rice from a producing Member State is higher than the threshold price in an importing Member State, the producing State may grant a refund. To facilitate exports to non-member countries, the Member States may cover the difference between their prices and world market prices by a refund. A refund system will also be introduced for broken rice, rice flour, ground rice and rice starch.

If a Member State grants refunds on exports of processed rice, it will also grant refunds on exports of husked rice and paddy; if it grants a refund on exports of husked rice, it will also grant a refund on exports of paddy.

Import Licences

All imports and exports of rice are subject to the presentation of an import or export licence. Licences will only be issued on deposit of a surety. The import licence will be valid until the end of the third month following that in which it was issued, and its validity may be extended by another month when certain conditions are fulfilled.

Price System

Each year the producing Member State will fix for husked rice a basic target price, at the wholesale buying stage, for an identical standard of quality, together with derived target prices and a monthly graduated scale over a period of eight consecutive months. An intervention price for paddy will be fixed each year by the producing Member States; in the transition period, this price must be 7% below the derived target price adjusted in relation to the quality standard for which the intervention price is fixed, and 4% below at the final, single-market stage.

The Member States will be obliged to buy up all paddy offered to them at the intervention price throughout the marketing year. They will not be allowed to resell the product on terms that will prevent prices in the producing areas from reaching the target price obtaining in the marketing centres of these areas. By April 1, 1964 the Council must fix a maximum and a minimum for the basic target price. These limits will correspond to the minimum prices guaranteed to growers during the previous year plus 7%.

At the end of the transition period a single threshold price and a single (basic) target price for the whole Community will be fixed by the Council. In the final, single-market stage the various derived target prices will be established in relation to the basic target price valid throughout the Community with due regard to the natural conditions of price formation.

Other Provisions

The provisions stating how the levy is to be fixed in advance, and those concerning correcting factors, determination of the fixed amount, the safeguard clause, incompatibilities and the possible abolition of national aids will be the same as those in Regulation No. 19 (cereals). The Cereals Management Committee will also be responsible for this sector.

In addition, before February 1, 1964 the Commission will make proposals concerning imports of rice from the associated States of Africa and Madagascar and from Surinam, so that arrangements for these imports can be brought into force on the same date as the rice regulation.

———————

*EEC Document P-3/64 final.

9.3 FINANCING OF THE COMMON AGRICULTURAL POLICY: THE AGRICULTURAL FUND

The regulation on the financing of the common agricultural policy was adopted early in 1962. It provides for the establishment of a European Agricultural Guidance and Guarantee Fund (FEOGA) and sets out general rules concerning its receipts and expenditure, for both the transition period and the definitive single market stage.

326

During the second agricultural "marathon" in December
1963 the Council of Ministers adopted two supplementary
regulations on this matter. One of these sets out the conditions
for the grant of aid from the Fund and the other is the financial
regulation governing the Fund. A third regulation is concerned
with implementation of the cereals regulation and lays down
rules for financing action in that sector.

These regulations provide the Community with a third
executive body through which it can directly and indirectly
influence activities in the economic and social fields. The
Commission ensures that the Agricultural Fund's activities
are in harmony with those of the other two bodies, the
European Investment Bank and the European Social Fund. The
Agricultural Fund is the third fund, coming after the Social
Fund and the European Fund for Overseas Development (FEDOM),
administered by the European Economic Community.

The Agricultural Fund has two sections: the Guarantee
Section operates as an equalization fund for products coming
under the levy system, while the Guidance Section grants
capital subsidies to farming in general or for individual products.
About 3/4 of the Fund will be used for "non-member country"
refunds and action on the internal market, and 1/4 to finance
structural changes.

Guarantee Section

The Guarantee Section is concerned with expenditure
in respect of export refunds in trade with non-member countries
and of interventions on the home market. For 1962/1963 the
contribution of the Fund for such refunds and intervention has
been fixed at one-sixth, for 1963/1964 at one-third, and for
1964/1965 at one-half (3/6).

These contributions will then increase regularly until
at the single-market stage the Community will be bearing 100%
of the expenditure. With the exception of the percentage Community contribution from 1 July 1965 to 31 December 1969, the
rules for partial or total repayment for refunds are laid down
in detail. Some general rules have been fixed for the repayment of expenditure on intervention. The conditions and details
of eligibility for aid will be specified in regulations on individual
sectors.

The "non-member country" refunds are calculated on

the basis of net exports and of the refund rate of the Member State with the lowest average refund. The net quantities are calculated by the so-called basic products method, derived products being expressed as basic product equivalents. This is normally done by applying the conversion factors laid down under the common organization of markets.

Each Member State must compute once a year the average refund for each basic product. This is done by dividing the total amount of the refunds by the gross quantities exported to non-member countries. Adjustments are made to the average refunds when these are influenced by certain special measures taken under the common organization of markets. The amounts "additional" to the refunds must be included because they are also financed by the Community. Average refunds which concern quantities of less than 5% of the total exported by the Community are considered as non-representative and therefore ignored in arriving at the lowest rate.

The "third-country" refunds for the cereals, pigmeat, eggs and poultry sectors will be repaid from 30 July 1962. For rice, dairy products and beef and veal the effective date will be 1 July 1964.

Two types of intervention on the internal market are eligible under the Fund: (a) measures to withdraw from the markets quantities of products which it cannot absorb on condition that action is taken to find an alternative outlet for these on the home market; (b) other interventions under Community rules when it is a question of compulsory action or of measures taken to avoid such action.

For the cereals sector these these eligible interventions have been defined as follows:

(i)   The denaturing bonuses granted by the Member States in respect of wheat other than durum and of barley and the losses resulting from the sale of these two cereals at a price below the target prices provided they have been made unfit for human consumption. In fact the aim and function of these denaturing operations are the same as those of refunds.

(ii)   Expenditure borne or losses incurred in the transition from one marketing year to the next on stocks of home-grown cereals which have been purchased by government agencies.

For the dairy produce and rice sectors, the eligible interventions have still to be defined for the period beginning in July this year. For the pigmeat sector the Council must decide before April 1966 on the advisability of Community intervention measures, and for the beef sector before March 1967. The common organization of the market in fats as laid down by Council decision and similar agreements for the market in sugar proposed by the Commission also provide for Community intervention.

Guidance Section

The Guidance Section is concerned with expenditure financed by the Fund in respect of common action to increase the productivity of agriculture by promoting technical progress, rational development of output and optimum use of the factors of production, in particular manpower. It includes structural changes made necessary by the development of the Common Market or essential to its proper functioning. Intervention by the Fund must not disturb the conditions of competition to an extent incompatible with the principles of the Treaty.

This section takes within its purview action:

1. To adapt and improve production conditions in agriculture and adapt and guide agricultural output;

2. To adapt and improve marketing and develop outlets for agricultural products subject to a common organization of markets.

The first type of action means the effective marshalling of the factors of production in agriculture for their optimum employment in the setting of the general economy and the adjustment of the volume of production to outlets. This may include the conversion of certain types of production, including reafforestation, and the improvement of the quality of products.

The second type of action means Community measures to increase the consumption of certain products and improve distribution channels and, finally, to provide better knowledge of data concerning price formation.

Aid from the Fund consists of capital subsidies paid as a lump sum or in installments. The subsidies may not exceed 25% for any given project and the recipient must him-

329

self put up at least 30%. The Member State on whose territory the project is carried out must share in the financing (this condition may be waived during the first two years if it is incompatible with the laws in force in that State).

The Council did not agree to other forms of aid proposed by the Commission, in particular interest rate subsidies. However, before 30 June 1967, the Commission is to submit a report to the Council on the lessons drawn from experience, and it can then propose diversification of the forms of aid.

Public, semi-public or private projects may be helped by the Fund if their purpose is to improve agricultural structures.

They must then conform to all the following general criteria:

(i)   Be part of a Community programme;

(ii)   Offer adequate assurances as to their lasting economic effects;

(iii)   Aim at an adaptation or guidance of agriculture necessitated by the implementation of the common agricultural policy or designed to meet its requirements;

The first type of project must also:

(a)   Aim at making or keeping farms economically viable and enhancing their competitive capacity;

(b)   Attach sufficient importance to advisory services and occupational training;

(c)   Contribute to improving the social and economic situation of workers in agriculture.

Each project must have been approved by the Member State in whose territory it is to be carried out.

Priority is given to projects which fit into the general development plan for a region. But if necessary finance exceeds the Fund's liquid resources the projects will be selected in such a way that aid from the Fund will be equally and harmoniously distributed throughout the Community territory.

The Community programmes are drawn up by the
Council on proposals from the Commission. They must take
into account the co-ordination of agricultural structure policy
and state, among other things, the areas in which the main
effort is to be concentrated, the total expenditure and the
duration of the work involved. The programme will be
published in the official gazette. For two years at the most
the Fund may grant aid even if there is no programme.

Aid from the Fund is accorded to natural or legal
persons or associations of such persons bearing the ultimate
financial responsibility for the projects. This aid is granted
through the body or bodies designated by the Member State
concerned.

Applications for aid must be submitted to the Commission through the Member States concerned before 1 October
each year. The Commission must make a decision on the
substance within 15 months. For 1964, however, applications
may be submitted only up to 1 July.

Resources

The Fund forms part of the Community's budget and
the appropriations are approved by the Council with the annual
estimates. The percentage contributions of the Member States
vary from year to year. Receipts during the first three years
are made up of financial contributions from these States. One
part of these contributions is computed according to the
budget scale shown in Article 200 (1) and the second proportion-
ally to the value of each Member State's net imports from
non-member countries. The value of these imports is computed for each common organization of markets.

The two components of Member States' contributions
make up the total income of the Fund in the following proportions:

	1962/1963 %	1963/1964 %	1964/1965 %
According to the scale in Article 200 (1)	100	90	80
Proportionally to net imports	-	10	20

The Council has also fixed a ceiling for the contribution from each Member State during the first three years. This is 10.5% for B.L.E.U., 31% for the Federal Republic, 28% for Italy and France and 13% for the Netherlands. The Federal Republic and the Netherlands will therefore have to pay more than would be required by the general budget scale in Article 200 (1), because they have relatively the highest net imports from non-member countries.

Before the end of the third year the Council will draw up rules for the gradual advance towards the single-market system. In this phase the proceeds of levies on imports from non-member countries accrue to the Community and are used to meet Community expenditure in such a way that the Community's budget resources shall consist of (a) this income from levies, (b) all other income decided on under the rules of the EEC Treaty and (c) budget contributions from the States as laid down in Article 200. In order that the Community may obtain these "independent resources", it will be necessary at the appropriate time to apply the special procedure provided for in Article 201 of the Treaty.

A special financial regulation governs budget matters and the annual repayment to Member States of expenditure under the Guarantee Section. The accounting period runs from 1 July to 30 June. Appropriations under the "Guidance Section" are automatically carried forward during the first 5 years if they are still due after the financial year in respect of which the commitment was made. The Council has also adopted a resolution inviting the Commission to present detailed estimates of total Community expenditure in respect of the common agricultural policy at the same time as it introduces its annual proposals for fixing the prices of cereals, milk and, possibly, other farm products (for instance, sugar and olive oil once these come under a common organization of markets). The Council will discuss these proposals as a whole and as far as possible fix these prices simultaneously.

Moreover the Council decided in 1962 to examine each year the consequences of Community financing of refunds on the pattern of production and the development of markets. Before the end of the third year the Council will make a general review.

The Machinery

In general the Commission administers the budget within the limits of the allocations made by the Council. This therefore also applies to the financial management of the Agricultural Fund. The Fund will not require a large staff since, as with the common agricultural policy in general, most of the executive action is left to authorities in the member countries: the Commission mainly co-ordinates and supervises. Thus, applications for aid from the Guidance Section of the Fund can be submitted only through the Member State concerned. The authority or the body designated by that State transmits to the Commission all relevant material to substantiate that the necessary conditions for each project are fulfilled. If need be the Commission can check on the spot. The Member States are also required to send the Commission information each quarter on the growth of exports and imports, "non-member country" refunds, and interventions.

Certain major decisions are reserved for the Council of Ministers. These include details and conditions for eligibility of expenditure in respect of intervention, the percentage contribution of the Fund to eligible expenditure, the amount of the Fund's resources and Community programmes to improve agricultural structures.

The Commission will be assisted by various Committees of representatives of the Member States under the chairmanship of a Commission representative having no voting rights. The function of the Committees is advisory. In several specific cases the Commission must refer to them a draft of the proposed measures for comment. The Committee deciees by qualified majority (procedure under Article 148 (2) of the Treaty).

Finally the Commission decides on measures which are immediately applicable. If these conflict with the opinion rendered by the Committee the Commission may postpone their application for a maximum of one month. The Council may then take a different decision by qualified majority within the same time-limit.

The Committees in question are:

(a)   The Committee of the Fund, recently set up to deal with the financial aspects and particularly the Guarantee

333

Section (determination of the lowest average refund or calculation of the net quantities exported).

(b)   The Management Committee for technical questions relating to the operation of the common organizations of markets (conversion factor for derived products).

(c)   The Standing Committee on agricultural structure to deal with matters affecting the Guidance Section (decisions concerning aid from the Guidance Section and suspension or withdrawal of such aid if the required conditions are not complied with).

Because of the large sums needed to finance the common agricultural policy and the Commission's specific responsibility in this matter, the question of democratic control has been raised. Under the Treaty of Rome the European Parliament has no power to decide on the budget. The Council of Ministers has stressed the importance it attaches to strengthening the Parliament's budgetary powers. It will deal with this question when it studies the Permanent Representatives' report on the merger of the Executives and the general broadening of the Parliament's functions.

_____

*EEC Document P-12/64, February 1964.

9.4 COMMON GRAIN PRICE*

Common grain price at middle level from July 1, 1964
Compensatory measures for farms in Germany, Italy and
Luxembourg from 1966 on Community plans to improve the
Standard of living of farmers in the EEC.

An analysis of the situation in the EEC shows that a resolute settlement of the grain price problem will be an effective instrument for internal development of the EEC and for the development of its relations with non-member countries.

Internal aspects

The establishment of a common grain price level "in one operation" would not only be a decisive step forward in strengthening the Community internally but would also help to iron out political difficulties in individual member countries;

the recurrence each year of negotiations on the gradual adjustment of grain prices are a factor making for internal disquiet.

Farm policy aspects

Only when the price level of grain in the Community has been finally settled will economic conditions become so clear that a definite line can be worked out for the adjustments and conversions which are in any case needed in the agriculture of all Member States. The long uncertainty about the level of farm prices, especially grain prices, in the Common Market is making medium term planning difficult for farmers and may lead to misinvestments which will cause additional difficulty in the necessary process of adjustment.

Commercial policy aspects

When finally fixing the level of its grain prices the EEC can give concrete and visible proof that in its common agricultural policy it does not intend to pursue a policy of high prices which could lead to self-sufficiency, but that it is rather endeavouring to maintain adequate facilities for imports from non-member countries.

The fate of the approaching GATT negotiations clearly depends on whether agreement can be reached on the treatment of farm produce. A lasting solution of the agricultural problem, and one which will satisfy the importing as well as the exporting countries, can be found only if a long-term balance can be established between demand and supply for the most important commodities throughout the world. This means that the production policy - and therefore the price policy - of the Contracting Parties will be the focal point of the negotiations. If a common grain price is fixed the Community will be in a position to take an active part in these negotiations and to make a positive contribution to them.

These considerations have led the Commission to submit to the Council of Ministers today a number of proposals which can be summarized in the following six points:

1. Common market for grain with a common price level from 1964/65

For the year 1964/65, which begins on 1 July 1964, one

335

basic target price would for the first time be fixed for each of the various types of grain throughout the Community. These basic target prices would then be reviewed each year, beginning with the year 1965/66. In doing so, special account would be taken of agricultural incomes, prices for the means of production, wages, consumer prices and the supply and market situation.

The basic target prices would apply in the areas of largest deficit in the EEC; these are the regions encompassing the marketing centres of Rotterdam, Amsterdam, Veghel, Terneuzen, Duisburg, Cologne, Brussels, Liege, Ghent and Antwerp, as well as southern Italy and the Italian islands, with the commercial centres of Reggio di Calabria, Messina, Catania, Palermo, Cagliari, and Olbia.

The common target prices will serve as a basis for calculating the threshold prices applicable to imports from non-member countries at the common external frontier, for working out the regional target prices applicable in the various areas of cultivation - due account being taken of transport costs - and for determining the intervention prices which protect producers by preventing local market prices dropping below a certain level.

In practice, this would mean that from 1 July 1964 onwards there would be a common market for grain which would have all the characteristics of a domestic market, and a uniform system with uniform threshold prices at the external frontier. This would free intra-Community trade from a number of administrative procedures and eliminate many difficulties which can arise in trade amongst Member States, especially in trade with conversion products. Not only would collection of the levy on grain traded between Member States disappear but also, in the case of all livestock products or products processed from grain, that part of the levy would be eliminated which so far has reflected the differences between grain prices in the Member States; the remaining "levy elements" in intra-Community trade for these products would then in practice be no more than specific duties, automatically eliminated over the transitional period. In the same way refunds in intra-Community trade would disappear; for exports to non-member countries they could be unified.

2. Common grain price at middle level

The basic target prices for the year 1964/65 would be fixed between the highest and the lowest target price laid down by the Member States in 1963/64. The basic target price for 1964/65 for wheat would be DM 425 per ton and for barley DM 370 per ton (for other currencies see table 1).

The level of the 1964/65 target prices would be mainly determined by the consideration that adjustment of prices must not lead to any undue expansion of grain cultivation in the EEC. Forecasts concerning grain production and consumption in the EEC show that the present total import requirements of approximately 10 million tons of grain could be the same in ten or twelve years from now, provided the acreage under grain in the EEC remains more or less the same. As considerable reserves of arable land are still available in France, special attention must be given to the possible reactions of grain producers in that country. Several inquiries have shown that the proposed raising of target prices in France, which would be less than 10%, is not likely to lead to an expansion of French grain cultivation which would be serious for the Community.

The proposed 1964/65 prices for the other types of grain have been related to the price for wheat in a way which takes account of the EEC's supply situation and import requirements. Whereas there is a tendency to produce more wheat and rye than can be marketed in the Community and outside, the demand for coarse grain (barley and maize) is constantly increasing. If some sensible economic guidance is to be given to the production and utilization of the various types of grain, the difference between bread grain and coarse grain prices must not be too great; especially in France and Italy, therefore, coarse grain prices must be brought closer to wheat prices.

The 1964/65 common grain price level of DM 425 for wheat and DM 370 for barley takes into account not only the EEC's supply situation for the various types of grain, and in particular the EEC's future import requirements, but also represents a balanced compromise between consumers' and farmers' interests in the Community.

The establishment of this common grain price (see table 2) would mean:

i) A reduction of grain prices in Germany - and in Italy and Luxembourg, a reduction for wheat and rye - and thus a loss of farm income in these countries;

ii) A rise of prices in France, Italy and the Netherlands, which - especially where price increases for coarse grain are concerned - would affect consumer prices for eggs, poultry and pigmeat.

The increase of barley prices in Belgium and Luxembourg would hardly affect consumer prices.

In judging the effects of falling or rising prices for farmers on the one hand and consumers on the other, it must be remembered that price changes for grain are fully reflected in producer prices and producer incomes, whilst their incidence is only one quarter or one third in the case of consumer prices because these contain processing and distribution costs, which are not affected by changes in the grain price.

The grain prices proposed by the Commission for 1964/65 would probably be reflected as follows in the various Member States' producer and consumer prices.

In the Federal Republic of Germany, prices for all types of grain (wheat, rye, barley, oats and maize) would fall; the drop would be between 11 and 15%.

In Luxembourg, the price of wheat would drop by 16% that of rye by 8% and barley would rise by 7%.

In Italy, wheat prices (durum and other) would decline by about 11%, but maize and barley prices would rise. In Italy's area of largest surplus (Reggio Emilia) the rise in the inter-vention price would amount to 23% for maize and 15%, for barley. In assessing the effects of higher coarse grain prices on the prices for eggs, poultry and pigmeat it must however be remembered that in Italy market prices for maize and barley will rise by about 18% only, because in 1963/64 they were excessively high for a number of special reasons.

In France and the Netherlands, all grain prices would rise. In France, prices for wheat other than durum would be 8% higher than in the previous year, for barley they would rise by 16% and for maize by 1%. In the Netherlands, the price increase for wheat would be 6% and for barley 15%.

338

In Belgium, wheat prices would rise by a mere 2%, and barley prices by about 7%.

Looking at agriculture as a whole, the changes in Germany would be marked. The overall drop in prices for the various types of grain, for pigs, eggs and poultry would be about 7%.

For France, on the other hand, it can be estimated that in 1964/65 consumer prices for bread, pastes, pigmeat, eggs and poultry as a whole might be as much as 3% higher than they would otherwise have been, 5% higher in the Netherlands and 1 to 2% higher in Italy. In Italy, the higher prices for livestock products would be partly offset by the fall in the price of bread and pastes, of which consumption is heavy. However, there is no reason why all this should lead to any absolute rise in prices in these countries. The adjustment of prices would coincide with one of the cyclical falls in prices characteristic of livestock products. In other words, the price adjustment would mean that the drop in prices for pigmeat and eggs from the high level which they reached in 1963 would be less marked. In some countries there are, furthermore, ways and means of reducing the difference between producer prices and consumer prices, including the public charges which help to widen the gap.

3.   Compensatory measures for farmers in Germany, Italy and Luxembourg during the transition period

In view of these probable effects of a price adjustment it is clear that for the sake of balanced development in all economic sectors in the Community immediate action must be taken to compensate farmers in Germany, Italy and Luxembourg for the consequences of a "price adjustment in one operation". However, special measures to compensate loss in farm incomes in some Member States resulting from the establishment of a common grain price level throughout the EEC in 1964/65 would be limited to the transitional period. At the latest in 1970 they would be replaced by measures in the form of "Community plans" for the benefit of farmers in all Member States.

The amounts which would be given by way of compensation to farmers in these countries during the transitional period would correspond to the loss of income resulting from the establishment of a common level of grain prices in

1964/65. This loss would amount to:

In Germany (FR)   140 million units of account

In Italy   65 million units of account

In Luxembourg   0.9 million units of account

  This calculation takes into account the fact that changes in prices for coarse grain affect producer prices and therefore the yield which farmers receive from pigs, eggs and poultry.

  Such compensatory measures are justified not only because it would be incompatible with the spirit of the Treaty of Rome or the objectives of the common agricultural policy if the establishment of a common agricultural market were to be accompanied by a noticeable decline of farm incomes in certain parts of the Community. They are justified by economic considerations too. For instance, the medium- and long-term investments made by farmers in the past years - largely with borrowed capital - rested upon calculations of interest and amortization based on the present price level. In the over-all economic context this level also corresponded with the costs situation and with the structure and organization of farming in the countries concerned. These, as well as the still existing differences in competitive positions - for instance as a result of tax policy or social policy in the various countries - will be only gradually aligned as the Common Market develops.

  Compensatory measures could take the following forms.

a) Direct payments to farmers whose incomes are reduced by the reduction of grain prices;

b) Contributions to improved social benefits made specifically available to farmers and their families;

c) Aids granted to improve productivity and to rationalize farms;

d) Aids granted to producers of durum wheat under terms and conditions to be laid down by the Council.

  The Member States would be free to allocate to any of these four forms whatever part of the overall compensation amount they chose. It goes without saying that these measures are not intended to take the place of anything already done in the Member States to improve agricultural incomes, but would be additional to it. On the other hand, the proposal that compensatory measures could also take the form of contribution to improve social services or to increase productivity does not in any way restrict the Member States' freedom of action in these fields.

However, if the Member States decided to make direct payments, they would have to adhere to certain principles. Direct payments must not be tied to the price of certain agricultural products or means of production. Furthermore, provision must be made for the capitalization of direct payments, for instance to enable a farmer to rationalize his farm, to turn marginal land into woodland or to take up a new, non-agricultural, activity if he decides to quit the land. This would give direct payments a dynamic character. Above all, however, direct payments under the annual compensation plan could only be paid up to a maximum total amount. For 1964, 1965 and 1966 this maximum amount would be the same as the calculated loss of income, that is to say, the Member States could pay the total amount of compensation in the form of direct payments. In subsequent years the maximum amount of direct payments would be gradually reduced, so that in 1969 a maximum of two-thirds of the calculated loss of income could be compensated through direct payments and at least one third would have to be made available in one or more of the other forms mentioned above.

4. Financing of compensatory measures from the EEC Budget

Since the "adjustment of grain prices in one operation" is a measure intended to strengthen the Community internally and to reinforce its position in the coming international negotiations, the compensatory measures would be financed from the EEC Budget.

For the first three years (1964 to 1966) this would be done in the form of payments from the Community Budget amounting to the full amount spent by the Member States on compensatory measures. From 1967 onwards these payments would be gradually reduced in such a way that in 1969 they would still amount to two thirds of the original amount, because the first "Community plan", proposed for 1966, provides for financial contributions by the Community to measures which

341

are similar to the compensatory measures. This is true in particular of steps taken to increase farm productivity and to improve social benefits for the farming population. The financial contributions to be made available from Community funds to Germany, Italy and Luxembourg under the first Community plan must be at least equal to the amount by which the financial contributions to the compensatory measures would be reduced.

5. Complete financing of refunds and of intervention on the domestic market by the Guidance and Guarantee Fund from 1964/65 onwards

If, as a result of the establishment of a common level of grain prices, the Community accepts responsibility for the injurious effects on farm incomes in some Member States, it is fair that the Community should also take upon itself all other financial burdens arising under the common market regulations for grain and the livestock products based thereon, particularly in view of the fact that the fixing of uniform basic target prices and threshold prices for grain and the regionalization of the target and intervention prices at Community level would in practice establish a common market for grain. The Commission therefore proposes that from 1964/65 onwards the Member States' expenditure on refunds for grain, flour, pig-meat, egg, and poultry exports to non-member countries and on domestic interventions relating to grain should, in derogation from Article 5 (1) of Council Regulation No. 25 on the Financing of the Common Agricultural Policy, be fully borne by the Guidance and Guarantee Fund.

6. From 1966 on: Community plans to improve the standard of living of farmers in the EEC

While political and economic considerations demand that in connection with the establishment of the common grain market certain immediate measures be taken to prevent a slump of farm incomes in certain Member States, it must just at this important stage of the EEC's development also be recalled that the objectives of the Treaty and of the common agricultural policy are not limited to establishing common market organizations for agricultural products. One of the main aims is to ensure an adequate standard of living for the farming population. At present, however, the standard of living and incomes is unsatisfactory in many agricultural areas of the EEC when compared with the standard of living and in-

comes in other economic sectors. At the same time, therefore, as the Commission submits proposals which it is convinced will prove of relations with non-member countries, it
is also proposing "Community plans to improve the standard
of living of farmers in the EEC". These plans are to be drawn
up on a proposal by the Commission and put into operation
from 1966 onwards by Member States, with financial support
from the Community.

These Community plans would comprise the following
categories of measures:

a)   Steps to improve farm incomes in economically under-
        developed areas. This would in particular involve co-
        ordinated financial assistance for structural changes
        both in agriculture and in other sectors (regional
        economic policy);

b)   Special programmes to benefit certain farms whose
        economic and social situation is particularly unsatis-
        factory, for instance farms in high and medium altitudes,
        on sandy soils, of inadequate size, or far removed from
        markets, and farms in areas affected by the division of
        Germany;

c)   Improvements to social policy systems in agriculture,
        in line with the principles established in the Commis-
        sion's Action Programme.

Such measures could be temporarily supplemented by
aids to income paid to certain farmers in accordance with
common criteria but independently of what they produced.
This facility should be used where the measures listed above
are not sufficient to provide, in good time, a lasting improvement in the standard of living of the farming population in
certain areas.

The Community would contribute financially to the implementation of the Community plans. Where the provisions governing these Funds permit, the necessary means would be provided
by the Agricultural Guidance and Guarantee Fund and by the Social
Fund. Any further means required to operate the Community plans
drawn up by the Council would be provided from the Community
budget.

343

*EEC Commission, Common Grain Price, Publication 8107/
1-5/XII/1963/5.

Table 1: Basic target prices, basic intervention prices and
threshold prices at the beginning of the 1964/65 year

National currency/ton

	DM	FF	Lit.	Bfrs. Lfrs	Fl.
Wheat other than durum					
Basic target price	425	524.56	66 406	5 312.5	384.63
Basic intervention price	395	487.54	61 719	4 937.5	357.48
Threshold price	420	518.39	65 625	5 250.0	380.10
Rye					
Basic target price	375	462.85	58 594	4 687.5	339.38
Basic intervention price	350	432.00	54 688	4 375.0	316.75
Threshold price	370	456.68	57 813	4 625.0	334.85
Barley					
Basic target price	370	456.68	57 813	4 625.0	334.85
Basic intervention price	345	425.82	53 906	4 312.5	312.23
Threshold price	365	450.51	57 031	4 562.5	330.33
Maize					
Basic target price	375	462.85	58 594	4 687.5	339.38
Basic intervention price	350	432.00	54 688	4 375.0	316.75
Threshold price	370	456.68	57 813	4 625.0	334.85
Durum wheat					
Basic target price	500	617.14	78 125	6 250.0	452.50
Basic intervention price	470	580.11	73 438	5 875.0	425.35
Threshold price	495	610.96	77 344	6 187.5	447.98

TABLE 2: Intervention prices in DM/ton at the beginning of the 1963/64 and 1965 marketing years

		Wheat other than durum		Rye		Barley	
		1963/64	1964/65	1963/64(1)	1964/65	1963/64(1)	1964/65
Germany	Duisburg	442.50	395.00	402.50	350.00	383.50	345.00
	Passau	427.50	368.99	387.50	323.99	368.50	318.99
Luxembourg	(1964/65 Mersch)	444.00	382.68	401.76(2)	337.68	323.20	332.68
Belgium	(1964/65 Brussels)	388.80	395.00	300.80	350.00	323.20	345.00
Netherlands	(1964/65 Rotterdam)	372.37	395.00	269.75(3)	350.00	300.06(3)	345.00
France	Lille	346.68	389.33	265.58	344.33	282.92	339.33
	Chartres	346.68	374.74	265.58	329.74	279.68	324.74
	Toulouse	346.68	362.23	265.58	314.59	286.16	309.59
Italy	Reggio di Calabria	419.20	395.00	382.47(4)	350.00	263.79	345.00
	Reggio Emilia	400.00	357.92	382.47(4)	298.11	263.79	293.11
	Rome	409.60	368.32	382.47(4)	314.63	263.79	309.63

1) For the Netherlands, Luxembourg and Italy, the 1963/64 intervention price assumed at 93% of target price.
2) Applicable only to milling quota.
3) Excl. area subsidy for sandy soils (DM 193/ha), which is equivalent to –
    DM 55.00/ton for barley (3 500 kg/ha)
    DM 64.30/ton for rye (3 000 kg/ha).

4) Target price and intervention price calculated on threshold price.

TABLE 2: Intervention prices in DM/ton at the beginning of the 1963/64 and 1964/65 marketing years

		Maize		Durum Wheat	
		1963/64(1)	1964/65	1963/64	1964/65
Germany	Duisburg	–	350.00	–	–
	Passau	–	323.99	–	–
Luxembourg	(1964/65 Mersch)	–	337.68	–	–
Belgium	(1964/65 Brussels)	–	350.00	–	–
Netherlands	(1964/65 Rotterdam)	–	350.00	–	470.00
France	Lille	323.75	344.33	–	–
	Chartres	306.25	329.74	–	–
	Toulouse	305.04	314.59	423.98	452.69
Italy	Reggio di Calabria	254.51	350.00	547.20(5)	433.52
	Reggio Emilia	254.51	312.92	531.20	–
	Rome	254.51	323.32	531.20	451.13

1) For the Netherlands, Luxembourg and Italy, the 1963/64 intervention price assumed at 93% of target price.

5) Intervention price incl. producers' bonus which, in Calabria and Sicily, amounts to DM 25.60/ton and to DM 41.60 in Sardinia.

*EEC Commission, Common Grain Price, Publication 8107/1-5/XII/1963/5.

CHAPTER **10**

TRANSPORT

The EEC Commission has proposed a common transport policy which will govern intra-Community transport by the end of the transitional period. The policy must eliminate national discrimination in the use of transport facilities and provide for a free choice of transport facilities at the most economical rates.

Rules to end discrimination came into force on July 1, 1961. They require transport rates and conditions to be notified to the Commission, which is empowered to inspect books and impose heavy fines on offenders.

Additional proposals have been made to apply the action program in the field of transport. They provide the use of a rate scale with upper and lower limits for all means of internal transport, a Community quota system for merchandise deliveries by motor vehicle between member states, the harmonization of rules affecting transport competition, a study of infra-structure costs of all modes of transport, and the fixing of uniform procedures for issuing transport authorizations between members.

The Commission is responsible for examining legislative or administrative provisions affecting transport before they are adopted by the member states. It issues opinions on the suitability of proposed rules.

Technical harmonization of the policies and practices of the member states affects many sectors: weight and dimensions of motor vehicles, naval construction, infra-structure, transport costs and rate and fiscal policy, discrimination and supports for prices and other rates, improvement of frontier crossings, and the application of fair competition rules to transport.

The Commission assists the national administration in studying the economic aspect of certain projects and in seeking additional sources of finance. The European Investment Bank, after consulting the Commission has granted substantial loans to the Italian, French and German railroads for the improvement and electrification of several important lines.

The Standard Goods Nomenclature for Transport Statistics (NST) came into effect on January 1, 1962. On the basis of the NST, the member states transmit regularly comparable statistics on national and international transport by rail and inland waterways and on international transport by road.

10.1 EEC COMMISSION PROPOSALS FOR COMMON TRANSPORT POLICY*

The Commission has laid before the Council proposals outlining a common transport policy. These proposals embody the ideas expressed in the Memorandum on a Common Transport Policy of 10 April 1961 and in the transport section of the Commission's Action Programme of 23 May 1962. The Commission has also taken into account the discussions on the Action Programme which took place in the Council of Ministers, the Economic and Social Committee and the European Parliament.

Of the five proposals submitted the three most important are:

To establish a system of rate brackets applicable to road, rail and inland waterway transport;

To introduce a Community quota for goods transport by road between Member States;

To harmonize certain provisions affecting competition in the transport sector.

These proposals are designed to meet what the Commission feels should be the Community's three main preoccupations in transport matters: integration, organization and harmonization. They also reflect the need for gradual and co-ordinated action, to which the Commission had drawn attention in its Action Programme.

On 14 June 1963 these proposals, of which details are appended will go before the Council for initial discussion; thence they will be immediately referred to the Economic and Social Committee and the European Parliament. It may therefore be expected that the Council will be able to adopt them before the end of this year.

The Commission believes that these proposals represent a first step towards the implementation of a common transport policy, the purpose of which is to create by the end of the transition period a jointly regulated transport market which will meet the increased transport requirements of the Community and eliminate all discrimination on grounds of nationality.

Proposal for a Council Regulation
introducing a bracket rate system for the transport
of goods by rail, road and inland waterway.

In all countries the system of transport rates and conditions is an important element of transport policy. The
Commission considers that at Community level this system
should allow of the widest possible competition compatible
with the special features of transport. With this object in
view the Commission proposes the gradual introduction of a
system of rate brackets within which carriers will be free to
choose the rates they apply.

The novelty of this system is that the brackets leave
sufficient latitude for free and fair competition between types
of transport and between firms, the abuse of dominant positions
being prevented by the upper limits and cut-throat competition
by the lower.

However, the aims of the bracket system will not be
fully attained unless the rates are based on costs and there
is adequate transparency of the market. Only then can users
choose advisedly the means of transport to supply the service
they require on the best terms. Hence the regulation lays
down common rules for determining the transport costs to
be taken into consideration in the tariffs, and introduces
appropriate arrangements for publishing tariffs.

In an initial stage, and pending the adoption of uniform
criteria, the proposed regulation provides that the brackets
shall have a range equal to at least 10% and at most 30% of the
upper limit, the level of the tariffs being fixed in accordance
with certain principles of an economic nature.

The bracket rates, which it will be possible to differen-
tiate according to types of transport and nature of the services
supplied, will have to be approved by the public authorities in
the Member States on a proposal from the carriers and after
consulting users.

The proposed regulation also allows carriers in exceptional circumstances to conclude special contracts at prices
outside the brackets and, as a general rule, subject to official
authorization. Furthermore, Member States will be empowered,
in the public interest and under certain conditions, to take

special measures regarding transport tariffs.

The above-mentioned tariffs and special tariff measures will have to be published officially in the Member States concerned. Special contracts will be published after the event, only the essential facts about the transport operations being given in order to respect the confidential nature of this type of contract.

The tariff system proposed is to come into force on 1 January 1965 and will apply throughout the territory of the Community to all national and international transport with the exception of short-distance transport, small consignments and transport effected by firms for their own requirements, i.e. transport "on own account". It will also apply to transport usually described as transport coming under the ECSC Treaty so far as is compatible with this Treaty and the arrangements pursuant to it.

The proposed regulation lays down procedure for establishing the tariffs, fixing the respective powers of carriers, users and public authorities, but it makes no detailed stipulation as to implementation. In national transport it leaves to the Member States the task of deciding on the implementing measures while at the same time advocating the progressive unification of these measures. As regards transport between the Member States, Community machinery is still needed for standing co-operation between all the competent authorities with regard to the establishment and approval of tariffs and oversight of their application.

Finally the regulation provides for the possibility of adjusting the bracket rate system in the light of experience and of the development of the common transport policy, and also of setting up a special Community body to ensure the proper functioning of the system.

Proposal for a Council Regulation
on the establishment and operation of a Community
quota for goods transport by road with the Community

One of the most difficult problems to solve in any transport policy is that of adjusting capacity to requirements. The reason for this lies in the special aspects of transport, and particularly in the mobility of enterprises and the insufficient elasticity of supply in relation to prices.

Whilst this problem also arises in inland waterway transport and in road haulage in the member countries, the Commission nevertheless feels that there is a specially urgent need to solve it as regards road haulage between the member countries. It is here that the present situation is least in line with the spirit and objectives of the Treaty; it is the outcome of bilateral or multilateral regulations and a great variety of bilateral agreements. The regulation proposed by the Commission aims at liberalizing transport on own account and setting a Community quota amongst the Member States in respect to transport for hire or reward, which will ensure smooth and constant adjustment of supply to demand. It meets five desiderata, since it opens the way to:

(i)   permanent control of transport capacity;
(ii)   sharing by carriers of all Member States on equal terms in international transport within the Community;
(iii) division of labour at Community level in relation to the productivity of carriers in the six countries;
(iv)   development of road haulage commensurate with the needs of the Common Market and the potentialities of this mode of transport;
(v)   more efficient use of vehicles.

Clearly, an innovation such as the Community quota can only be introduced gradually. Therefore, under the terms of the proposal, it will not be until the end of the transition period that all transport operations between Member States will be effected under Community licences issued within the limits of the quota. During the transition period this objective will be gradually approached by building up the Community quota and dismantling the bilateral system; the bilateral quotas will be gradually brought down and the Community quota gradually built up.

Whilst the bilateral quotas can be automatically whittled down, the Commission believes - after careful study - that no automatic mechanism is possible to introduce and gradually to develop the Community quota. For this reason it is proposed to set up a committee which will ensure permanent and well-balanced co-operation between the Commission and the Member

352

States in fixing the volume of the Community quota and distributing it amongst the Member States. The rules of procedure for the committee are so devised as to prevent any
blockage of the system and to avoid unduly frequent intervention by the Council.

Despite every care in fixing and distributing the Community quota, it may still be necessary to deal with unforeseen
developments or temporary imbalances. The need may also
arise of coping with exceptional and transient requirements.
The regulation provides the means for handling such situations.
These means, which the Commission will apply, may be comprehensive or selective - the issue of Community licences or
licences valid only for transport between two Member States.

Provision is made for adjustments, adopted on a proposal of the Commission, to the Community quota system in
the light of the results attained and the general development
of the common transport policy.

Finally, road haulage by firms for their own account,
either with their own vehicles or with vehicles used solely
by them for at least one year, will not be affected by the Community quota system or by any other system of quotas or
licensing.

Proposal for a Council Decision
on the harmonization of certain provisions affecting
competition in rail, road and inland waterway transport

In the "Memorandum on the general lines of a common
transport policy" the Commission held that equality of treatment between modes of transport and between transport firms
was a prerequisite for the creation of healthy competitive
conditions in transport.

It has been found that certain regulations governing
transport now in force in the Member States of the European
Economic Community are having a marked impact on competition between the different modes of transport and between
transport firms, and are therefore causing disparities.

The elimination of the disparities arising from these
regulations, which are distorting the play of competition both
at Community and at national level, is one of the vital tasks

to be undertaken under the common transport policy: it will enable business to be distributed between firms and modes of transport in relation to their natural advantages and respective levels of productivity. It is also particularly important in the context of Article 75 (1 b), which deals with the admission of non-resident carriers to domestic transport services in a Member State.

Unquestionably the organization and integration of the transport market, which the proposed regulations given in Annexes I and II are designed to promote, will be all the more easily effected the more closely they are linked with harmonization measures.

The Commission's proposals for the introduction of a bracket rate system and of a Community quota for road haulage between the Member States cover the entire transition period and involve commitments even after this period. Harmonization must therefore be phased over the same period. For this reason the present proposal attempts to establish a comprehensive schedule for the operation planned, defining the fields it must cover, the measures to be adopted in each of these fields and the time-table for their implementation.

The choice of harmonization measures has been made in the light of the scope and range of intervention by public authorities and of the effect of such intervention on competition in transport.

The fields in which harmonization is required are taxation, insurance and social legislation. The need to settle problems arising from certain forms of government intervention, notably with regard to public service obligations, and the need to normalize financial relationships between Governments and railways have also been taken into account.

In the field of taxation, harmonization includes the abolition, by 1 January 1965, of double taxation, which affects international traffic through taxation of vehicles. By the same date, it is also planned to standardize provisions concerning the free admission of fuel contained in vehicles' tanks. Present disparities between these provisions affect competition since fuel taxes vary considerably in the six countries. The tax assessment of vehicles is also to be standardized - by 1 January 1966 - and this will make it less difficult to adjust tax systems applying to transport for hire or reward and tran-

sport on own account so that they become equivalent
in effect.

From 1 January 1967 onwards, transport will be subject in each Member State to the general turnover tax system.

When taxation on transport has been adjusted in this
way, it will be possible, from 1 January 1969 onwards, to
carry harmonization further; infrastructure costs will be
broken down and charged on an appropriate scale to users.
The harmonization of fuel taxes will be carried out with due
regard to the objectives of the common energy policy.

In the field of insurance, regulations will be issued,
with effect from 1 January 1965, concerning compulsory third-
party cover for road and inland waterway transport.

Regulations concerning insurance of the carrier against
damage to freight will be harmonized for these two types of
transport by 1 January 1966.

Certain forms of government intervention must be kept
to a minimum, particularly those imposing on transport firms
- notably the railways - obligations inherent in the public
service nature of certain tranport operations. This is left
in the hands of the Member States, which will work on the
basis of common principles to be agreed on before 1 January
1965. Compulsory compensation has been provided for to
offset costs arising from the maintenance of public service
obligations considered indispensable.

Before 1 January 1966 the accounts of railway firms
will be normalized on the basis of common rules and from
1 January 1965 onwards the rules governing financial relationships between railways and Governments will be gradually
harmonized.

The harmonization provisions in the social field are
designed to align in an upward direction from 1 January 1965
onwards - but before the end of the transition period - the
rules and regulations governing working conditions within each
mode of transport and to co-ordinate regulations on the composition of crews in each mode of transport on the basis of Community standards. This co-ordination is to be completed by
the end of 1966. The harmonizing of regulations concerning
working hours and time off in each mode of transport will

take place from 1 January 1965 onwards concurrently with measures to harmonize overtime arrangements. This also is to be done by 1966. A log-book for each worker, ensuring compliance with regulations on working conditions, will be required from 1 January 1965 onwards, and in the field of social security a decision will be taken before 1 January 1966 as to the application of special arrangements to the transport sector.

The decision on harmonization also instructs the Commission to follow closely the progress made, so that any adaptations and additions which may prove necessary as the Common Market goes ahead and the common transport policy develops may be introduced in good time.

Proposed Council Decision
on the organization of an inquiry into infrastructure
costs in transport by rail, road and inland waterway.

It is extremely important for the development of the Common transport policy that types of transport and transport firms should be put on an equal footing as regards the burden of infrastructure costs they bear.

There can be no doubt that the present differences in this sphere between Member States and between types of transport and categories of users are likely to distort competition in the transport sector within the Community and impede the rational sharing of traffic according to the natural advantages of each type of transport.

As far back as December 1960, a committee of Government experts was therefore convened to help the Commission in its studies of transport costs, and the question of how infrastructure costs are determined and apportioned was placed high up on its agenda.

The committee of experts recognized from the outset that it was not possible to limit the study of infrastructure costs to an examination of methods but that it was indispensable to furnish the Community authorities responsible for devising measures in this field with comprehensive figures to enable them to take well-informed decisions.

The aim of the proposal now submitted to the Council is

to establish the necessary legal basis for obtaining this information by organizing a general inquiry throughout the Community into the cost of the infrastructure of transport by rail, road and inland waterway.

The inquiry will cover the year 1965 and it is expected that the Commission will submit to the Council an overall report on the results before 1 July 1967.

The Commission feels that this inquiry will be a decisive step towards obtaining a precise knowledge of transport costs, which is rightly considered essential in order to establish the common transport policy on an economically sound footing.

Proposal for a Council Directive
on unifying procedures for issuing licences for goods
transport by road between the Member States.

The aim of the directive unifying procedures for the issue of licences for goods transport by road is to rationalize, at Community level, the various practices at present in force in Member States regarding bilateral quotas. It will be an effective help in the transition from the system of bilateral quotas - where it will make the issue procedure uniform and standardize the form of documents, thus facilitating the necessary controls - to the Community quota system.

---

*EEC Document P-12/63, May 1963.

CHAPTER **11**

ENERGY

The common energy policy will be established through the joint efforts of the EEC, the European Coal and Steel Community and the European Atomic Energy Community. The various sources of energy, including coal, oil, and atomic energy will be developed in accordance with Community needs over the next 20 years.

The three Community executives proposed a common energy policy in 1962. The plan included a timetable to be completed by 1970 and suggested an open market for oil and assistance, preferably as subsidies, for coal. This memorandum has been supplemented by a protocol adopted in 1964. The common policy will probably not be placed in effect until after the fusion of the executives of the three Communities, which is scheduled for 1965.

The EEC is responsible for the progressive establishment of a common market for oil, gas and electricity. Oil tariffs have been set, thus completing the common external tariff schedule. The Commission has examined the oil supply situation and concluded that about 90 per cent of Community oil must be imported. The Commission and the member states have discussed means of assuring supplies and reasonable prices and of establishing stocks. Measures have been taken to insure the free circulation of oil throughout the Community. Commission experts have also studied fair competition policies for oil and energy investment policies.

Large gas discoveries in the Netherlands and imports from North Africa have prompted the Commission to ask member states to study the effects of gas production on the overall energy supply. Electricity costs and their effect on economic development will be investigated by a group of independent experts.

11.1 TOWARDS A CO-ORDINATED ENERGY POLICY*

A decision on the draft agreement for co-ordination of energy policies drawn up by the representatives of the European Executives and the administrations of national governments, will be the major question before the ECSC Council of Minister's meeting to be held on 21st April 1964 at Luxembourg.

This draft agreement proposes replacing the existing national regulations, often differing in many important respects, by uniform Community rules in the three following fields:

1. Foreign trade policy,

2. State subsidies or other interventions,

3. Rules of competition.

These Community regulations would apply to all the different sources of energy and should be drawn up within the framework of the preparatory study for the merger of the three European Communities.

While these rules are being examined, the High Authority will be called on to give priority to the preparation of proposals for the procedure to be followed in establishing a Community regime for state subsidies.

Although not meeting all the requirements for an overall policy for energy, the draft agreement, which is based partly on the draft resolution discussed by the Council on 2nd December 1963, partly on ideas subsequently put forward by Mr. Dino Del Bo, President of the High Authority, thus holds out hopes of achieving some real progress.

The different proposals of the draft apply to fields where the existing interests of member states are noticeably different. Thus, for coal, the governments of producer countries have carried out a number of interventions of an increasingly national character which are, as a result, ever further removed from the spirit of the Treaty. Considerable disparities exist between customs duties, import policies and contributions by the different states to the coalmining industry with the consequence that the differences in coal prices in the chief regions of the Community are very much greater than would be justified by transport costs or mining conditions taken on their own. These national interventions not only endanger the prospects for drawing up a common energy policy but also involve the risk of a slow but certain disintegration of what was put in common ten years ago.

It is for this reason that it is essential that these national actions should be replaced within a Community framework, and that an outline of some concrete plan for a common energy policy be agreed to in the very near future. The implementation of this policy should logically be harmonized with the successive stages of the Community's progress over the next few years such as they can now be seen: the merger of the Executives and then of the Communities, and the completion of the transitional period of the general Common Market.

The European Parliament showed itself greatly concerned with the deadlock caused by the series of disagreements between the governments on this subject. In its Resolution of 22nd January 1964, the Parliament called on the three European Executives to surrender their responsibilities for drawing up proposals to the Council of Ministers if no positive decision had been taken before 5th April 1964.

Background to the Present Situation

The preparatory studies for a co-ordination of energy policies were begun in 1957 and have since continued without major interruption until the present time. The following are the most important stages which have marked the intermediate period:

8th October 1957, the Council of Ministers of the ECSC and the High Authority signed a "Protocol on the means of ensuring a co-ordinated energy policy". By virtue of this protocol, the High Authority, and from the moment they took up their responsibilities the Commissions of the EEC and Euratom, were called on to submit to the Council of Ministers general proposals for energy policy, for the conditions in which such a policy could be implemented, and for an outline of the necessary specific measures to be taken.

On the basis of this protocol, the following documents were drawn up and transmitted to the Council of Ministers:

- Report of the Joint Committee for co-ordinated energy policy, April 1959;

- Interim Note on the co-ordination of energy policies with appendices, 19th March 1960;

- Note setting out proposals for initial measures for the co-ordination of energy policies, 10th January 1961;

- Note on the proposals for initial measures for coal imports from non-member countries, 26th October 1961.

The last three documents were drawn up by the Inter-executive Working Group on Energy Policy (co-ordination between the three European Executives, presided by the High Authority).

When the Ministers of the six member states met at Rome on 5th April 1962 to discuss these documents, they showed, in their request to the three Executives to draw up proposals for the creation of a common market for energy, that they were prepared to go beyond the 1957 Protocol. According to the mandate which was then given to the three Executives, the new proposals should not be limited to the strict legal position offered by the existing treaties.

On the basis of this new mandate, the three Executives submitted to the ECSC Council of Ministers, on 25th June 1962, a "Memorandum on Energy Policy". This was followed, on 21st December 1962, by the "Study on the long-term energy prospects for the Community".

After examining the Memorandum the Council of Ministers asked the Executives to study its legal implications.

This was done by the three Executives and the High Authority set out in detail the modifications which would be necessary to the Paris Treaty if the Memorandum were to be applied in practice. As a result of these studies the High Authority sent to the Council of Ministers on 10th April 1963 a "Draft Agreement for the creation, as regards the treaty establishing the European Coal and Steel Community, of conditions for the implementation of a common market for energy".

On 21st March 1963 the Council discussed the study on

the long-term energy prospects. After an exchange of views the Council decided, at the suggestion of the Interexecutive Committee, to institute a working group with the task of studying the basic elements of this document.

On 2nd May 1963, the Council took note of the High Authority's "Draft Agreement". At the same meeting the Council decided to charge a special committee of national energy experts, under the chairmanship of the High Authority, with a study of the Memorandum. The working group would continue its studies parallel to those of the Special Committee and would submit the results to this latter.

The Special Committee of national energy experts was required to submit its report to the Council of Ministers by the 31st October. In the event its studies were completed in time for its report to be able to be examined as part of the agenda of the Council meeting of 2nd December 1963.

Following the completion of the Special Committee's work, the representatives of the member governments drew up a draft resolution which was sent to the Council of Ministers on 22nd November 1963.

No unanimous decision was possible at the Council meeting of 2nd December 1963 on the draft resolution which, in the opinion of governmental experts, represented the minimum agreement which the six governments would have been able to reach in the immediate future on a common energy policy. For their part, the three European Executives considered the draft to be insufficient for the implementation of a common energy policy. The High Authority declared that the following five conditions would have to be fulfilled before it could agree to the draft:

- The common energy policy would have to be applied from 1st January 1970, at the latest;

- The draft resolution should represent a first step towards the application of the principles laid down in the Memorandum of the Interexecutive Committee;

- The High Authority's conception of the common energy policy is set out in the above mentioned Memorandum and confirmed in the draft agreement;

- The giving of subsidies must be subject to the prior authorization of the High Authority;

- Special measures should be established for coke.

Unable to reach immediate agreement, the Council called on the Special Committee of national energy officials to re-examine the documents already before it, viz. the Memorandum and complementary papers, and to study the draft resolution presented by the government representatives at the same time.

Faced with this new delay, the High Authority invest-igated the ways and means of escaping from a deadlock which concerned not only the future prospects of a common energy policy but also risked to prevent the elaboration of Community solutions for the difficult problems in coal policy requiring immediate action.

It was these considerations which led the President of the High Authority, Mr. Dino Del Bo, accompanied by the Chairman of the Interexecutive Committee, Mr. P.-O. Lapie, to make bilateral contacts with the member governments in an attempt to draw up an outline of concrete plans for a common energy policy. The draft agreement which is now submitted to the Council of Ministers can be considered as the indirect result of this "tour of the capitals" which took place in February and March of this year.

----

*European Coal and Steel Community Spokesman, Document 2571/64e, April 20, 1964.

11.2 INTER-EXECUTIVE ENERGY COMMITTEE'S MEMORANDUM ON ENERGY POLICY PUBLISHED BY THE HIGH AUTHORITY OF THE EUROPEAN COAL AND STEEL COMMUNITY

Introduction

The development of the Common Market necessitates the gradual harmonization of member countries' economic policies in various fields. Energy policy is of particular importance because:

- energy plays a part in practically all economic activities, and any failure of supply to keep up with demand would have very serious consequences;

- the cost of energy is one of the major factors determining a country's international competitive position and the location of its industries; (1)

- the coal industry employs more workers than most other Community industries, and a number of densely-populated industrial areas are dependent on it for their wellbeing.

The Community countries have adopted different and often conflicting positions on energy problems: the task is therefore to define the principles of a common energy policy that will best meet the needs of the European economy. The Community's recent success in reaching agreement on a common agricultural policy showed that accord is possible between member countries on the aims and methods of common action, even in the most difficult fields. What has been done for agriculture should also be possible in the realm of energy policy.

The purpose of the Energy Committee's memorandum was to outline the general principles on which an energy policy might be based. It follows two earlier reports submitted to member Governments by the Committee: the first, in March 1960, suggested a method for coordinating national policies, and the second, in January 1961, proposed a number of preparatory steps to be taken immediately. The memorandum defines the objectives of a comprehensive common policy and the ways in which it might be implemented. This entails laying down both long-term aims and transitional rules to facilitate the gradual harmonization of national policies.

The principles which should underline a common energy policy have been subject of much debate. The European Parliament in its resolution of February 20, 1962, listed them as follows:

1. reduction of costs;
2. security of supply;
3. gradual application to avoid sudden disturbance of national economies;
4. long-term stability of supply;
5. freedom of choice for the consumer;

6. a single market;

With the same objectives, and seeking to achieve a balance between these principles, the Council of Ministers, meeting in Rome on April 5, 1962, instructed the Executives to submit proposals for a common energy policy within two months.

The Council specified that the proposals should take account of:

- the increasing demand for energy;
- the increasing proportion of imported energy;
- the fact that imported energy prices are in some cases lower than those of the Community's own energy sources.

The Council also stated that the proposals should lead to a common policy covering all fields of economic activity in the Community and all sources of energy. The aim of this policy would be the progressive establishment of a common market for energy based on fair competition, the free movement of energy products and the supply of energy at the lowest possible price. As well as framing the general policy, the Executives were also asked to propose measures to put it into effect.

The Present Position and the Outlook for Energy

The Community's energy requirements are increasing rapidly: they rose from 290 million metric tons, hard-coal equivalent, in 1950, to 470 million in 1960. If economic expansion continues at the rate expected, they will be in the region of 700 million tons by 1970 and 800 million tons by 1975. One of the common policy's main objectives will therefore be to ensure that supplies are available in these quantities.

Recent trends in comparative prices for different types of energy, particularly the relative fall in the price of oil compared with coal, make it unrealistic to envisage any increase in coal production. On the contrary, output of coal is likely to be scaled down progressively by the closure of uneconomic pits.

The other traditional sources of energy in the Community (with the possible exception of natural gas) cannot be expanded sufficiently to meet the rapid increase in energy requirements.

This gap will therefore be filled largely by oil and, possibly, American coal pending the advent of nuclear energy at competitive prices by about 1970.

While coal met 70 per cent of energy requirements in countries now forming the European Community in 1950, by 1960 its share had fallen to 52 per cent. By 1970 it will probably not exceed 35 per cent. Oil's share on the other hand, rose from 10 per cent of total energy consumption in 1950 to 30 per cent in 1960, and is expected to reach about 50 per cent by 1970. Substitution has been most rapid in industry: in 1950 only 12 per cent of the energy consumed by industry came from oil, in 1960 the figure was close on 40 per cent. The proportion seems certain to continue rising rapidly in the years ahead as a result of that sector's search for cheap energy supplies.

The implications of this trend are two-fold. Firstly, the price of imported energy will be the most important element in determining the cost of energy in the Community. Secondly, increasing use of oil raises the problem of security of supply. A variation of a few million tons, or even of tens of millions of tons, in the output of steam-raising coal would not appreciably affect the degree of security. There is therefore no justification in aligning the prices of petroleum products with those of coal, or restricting the expansion of oil consumption by artifically raising its price.

Intensive prospecting in Europe will probably lead to the discovery of fairly substantial oil and natural gas reserves, but these will cover only a limited proportion of requirements. A larger and increasing share of the demand will have to be met by supplies from other parts of the world. Since the end of the Second World War, the Middle East, with its huge reserves and low production costs, has become the Community's main source of imports. It will remain so for a long time to come, although the resources recently discovered in North Africa and the continuation of prospecting there are of greatest importance to the European market. Nevertheless, the problems of price and security connected with Middle East imports need special attention.

Prices of crude oil and refined products

Proved Middle East reserves are calculated at 26, 000 million recoverable tons, representing two-thirds of present world reserves and a hundred years' production at the present rate.

There is every indication that by 1975 they will still represent fifty years' production at the then current rate of output if proved and probable reserves are included, and if it is
assumed that further large deposits will have been discovered
by then. Subject to price, therefore, the Middle East contains
sufficient reserves to cover a considerable proportion of the
growing world demand for oil for a long time to come.

The actual prices charged for Europe-bound oil are at
present well below the posted prices and it is quite common for
producing companies to allow independent operators 15-20 per
cent rebates. Sales by integrated companies to their subsidiaries are often made at the posted price, but the reductions
which the latter are obliged to offer on products in the countries where they operate are about the same as those allowed
to independents on purchases of crude. The present level of
oil prices enables demand to be met in full and enables the
petroleum companies to cover the whole of their costs, including prospecting and other investment.

Extraction costs will tend to rise in the future as deposits
are worked out, but on the other hand, technical progress and
increased production may result in substantial savings. The
use of larger tankers will also procuce considerable savings on
transport. The two opposing trends will thus tend to cancel
each other out and oil imports may therefore continue for many
years at about current price levels.

Crude prices include royalties paid to the Government of
the producing country. In the Middle East, these work out at
about $5.00 a ton on posted prices of about $12.50 a ton. The
Governments concerned have in the past always opposed reduction in posted prices as these would have resulted in a drop
in their revenues. There is a definite risk that in the future
political pressure may be brought to bear by these countries to
secure a larger share of the proceeds of their subsoil, although
their revenues from this source have already increased considerably in recent years and will continue to rise steeply as a
result of expanding production alone. Royalties paid annually
to the four main Middle East producing countries rose from
$136 million to $1,355 million between 1949 and 1960.

Oil price policy may assume an important role in the
course of the next few years. The Community will increase its

purchases considerably and its negotiating position vis-a-vis the producing countries will thus be strengthened. Therefore the Community would be well advised not to turn down any prospective supplier and to do business with all comers. The Community's bargaining position would be even stronger if energy prices were brought closer to the real level of production costs by the removal of part at any rate of the taxes payable on energy in the consumer countries. If, on the other hand, the Community were to align the price of imported energy with that of Community coal - with the object of protecting the latter - the oil-producing countries would have an excellent reason for demanding a still larger increase in royalties.

Consumer Prices

If this analysis is applied to consumer prices, the margin of uncertainty becomes greater. It is conceivable that the price of fuel oil - to take the only petroleum product in direct competition with coal - will fall below real long-term production costs for varying periods owing to surpluses on the world market, or to particularly keen competition in individual markets. This would seem to be the case at present in several European markets.

In the long term, on the other hand, it seems likely that demand will focus more on fuel oil (this tendency is apparent even now in certain markets, where fuel oil already accounts for a high proportion of total consumption) and prices may therefore rise slightly until they cover actual production costs.. But if the price of crude oil does not rise, it is unlikely that there will be any major movement in fuel-oil prices in the foreseeable future. This point is of importance in determining the competitiveness of Community coal compared with fuel-oil.

The prices of refined products are related to crude oil prices, and also, up to a point, inter-related. If their relations to one another and to the cost of crude are to be satisfactory, they will need to be harmonized throughout the Community, though with due regard to the product pattern of markets in different areas. This will entail, firstly, the introduction of free movement for all products within the Community, and secondly, thoroughgoing harmonization of the rules of competition and of legislation relating to conditions of competition. Moreover, to avoid distortion of competition among the oil consuming industries, taxes on fuel-oil will have to be

harmonized.　This in turn will entail the harmonization of
taxes on motor fuels.

Security of Supply

　　　Security of supply is a concept which is found in a variety
of forms and has been interpreted in a variety of ways.　It is
difficult to make plans for action in the event of a general out-
break of hostilities, since presumably neither the Community
coal industry nor the flow of supplies from outside would remain unaffected.　For practical purposes, the only security
problems are, firstly, the risk of political disturbances in oil-
producing areas - which might result in the partial interruption
of supplies for some time - and secondly, the risk of an artifi-
cial increase in prices.

　　　The report of the European Parliament's Energy Committee states, that in the interests of greater security of supply
it would be desirable to:

- decentralize and diversify supply zones as far a geographically
　possible;

- accept certain price margins from which to finance reason-
　able stocks and to ensure access to sources which, though not
　always the most economic, would serve to increase the sources
　of supply and thus reduce the political risks;

- avoid complete dependence on outside supplies and ensure
　that energy requirements are at least partly covered by
　internal Community resources.

　　　The Community's coal production, particularly coking
coal, is an important element in ensuring security of supply.
Even though output is certain to contract to some extent in the
next few years, care must be taken to ensure that the contraction is not so great as to prejudice security (bearing in mind
that additional coal can be imported in the event of a shortage).
For oil, the security position is improving with the discovery
of new reserves in various parts of the world, aided by a surplus of both productive and transport capacity.　Finally, long-
term security will be further reinforced by the exploitation of
natural-gas reserves recently discovered in Europe and the
Sahara, and by the development of nuclear energy.

　　　Generally speaking, diversification of supply is aided by

the structure of the oil industry, whose investments are
widely dispersed in the fields of both prospecting and
production. Thus, high-cost production is offset by the
exploitation of low-cost reserves, and the necessity of
diversification is taken into account in fixing the market
price of oil.

This compensation may not operate in every case,
however. The Community's oil resources are meagre in
comparison with its requirements, and production costs are
often higher than those of imported oil. Output has only been
maintained by means of national protection, which must be
progressively reduced as the Common Market develops.
There are also outside sources which, though their production costs are higher than those of the Middle East,
might, owing to their geographical position, be worth consideration from the security standpoint. It may be that the
relatively high production costs of the oil concerned serve
to restrict their sales outlets, or that the oil is produced by
non-integrated companies with no distribution network of
their own. It might therefore be to the advantage of the
Community to maintain, and even to develop, these sources
in order to ensure effective diversification of supply. Various steps might be taken to stimulate production and encourage further prospecting in these areas.

At the same time stocks of imported oil should be built
up. These would be used to tide the Community over any
temporary interruption of supplies or until such time as
alternative sources could be tapped.

The problem of security is not only one of tonnages,
but perhaps even more one of price - as the European
Parliament's Energy Committee emphasized. 'Bottlenecks
due to temporary circumstances or to the state of the market
may, of course, occur,' the Committee's report states, 'but
these would certainly not persist for long provided there was
willingness to pay high enough for alternative supplies. There
is every prospect that Europe will not lack for energy in the
future - but at what price?'

An adequate level of stocks coupled with effective diversification of supply should enable the Community to cover its
needs over a fairly long period. But this period would have to
be long enough for the producer countries to realize the
implications for their national economies of any interruption

370

in shipments, and to learn to forego this method of exerting
pressure on prices.

The question of imports from the Eastern bloc is
closely bound up with security. The Community cannot
afford to ignore the danger which a suspension of these imports would represent. The world is at present in a period
of energy surplus, and the current level of imports from the
Soviet countries is not sufficient to render the Community
dangerously dependent. But this position might change if
certain common rules are not put into practice. Member
countries already consult each other regularly on the amount
of oil included in their trade agreements with the Eastern
European countries. Further steps should be taken under
the Common Market Treaty provisions for a common commercial policy to fix an overall Community quota.

Coal

Dependence on coal in the Community countries fell
from 70 per cent of total energy requirements in 1950 to 57
per cent in 1960.

In absolute terms, coal has stood its ground better than
the relative figures would suggest, since the tonnages actually produced in the Community countries in 1950 and 1960
were practically the same: about 230 million metric tons.
In 1956, however, the total rose to 249 million tons.

The relative contraction is the result of the strong
pressure to which coal is subject in competition with the
other sources of energy. Only action on a broad front by the
coalmining industry, the Governments and the High Authority
has prevented the effects from being greater than they have
in fact been.

Coal's decline has been caused partly by technological
factors and partly by the difficulty of competing with the
lower prices of other forms of energy. Nevertheless, great
efforts have been made to meet this competition.

The following figures give some idea of the scale on
which rationalization is being conducted, either by closing
uneconomic mines and abandoning uneconomic districts and
seams, or by technical improvements such as mechanization,
concentration, or reorganization.

1. Between 1957 and 1961, Community coal production was reduced from 249 million to 230 million metric tons, and the labour force producing it from 1,076,000 to 830,000.

2. In the same period, 104 pits in the Community were either closed altogether or absorbed in concentration schemes. This represents a reduction of 25 per cent in the number of pits.

3. Average saleable output per day per Community pit rose as follows:
   1953: 2,000 metric tons   1958: 2,300 metric tons
   1961: 2,850 metric tons
   In 1961 the extraction rate was 24 per cent higher than in 1958, and 42 per cent higher than in 1953.

4. The proportion of Community coal won by fully-mechanical equipment increased as follows:
   1952: 9.6 per cent   1956: 19.8 per cent   1959: 21.7 per cent   1961: 40.0 per cent

5. The average output of coalface workers per shift rose from 1.5 tons in 1956 to 2.1 tons at the beginning of 1962 - an increase of 38 per cent.

Coal is therefore faced with two great questions:

- Will the pressure of competition continue as powerfully during the next ten years?

- Can the industry continue to adjust itself as fast as it has done in the past few years? And even if this is possible will it be enough to ensure a ready sale for the present volume of coal production in an open energy market?

Since no long-term answer can be given to these questions, the prospects of maintaining an economically sound coalmining industry (characterized by stable employment and regional prosperity) are attended by two risks:

- That the labour force and managerial personnel will drift away from the mines through doubts of the future - a trend which is already making itself felt. This factor is hampering full exploitation of the best pits, and its continuation or acceleration would jeopardize the success of rationalization by driving up costs.

- That doubts about the future will also hinder the progress of rationalization schemes by affecting the supply of new capital.

In areas whose whole economic activity centres on coal-mining, adjustment is beginning, and will continue to demand industrial redevelopment. For obvious social and economic reasons, contraction of the coalmining industry must be accompanied by the establishment of new industries. The initiative in this field rests, of course, with the Governments, but the Community has various means at its disposal for assisting the process. To be deployed effectively, these would need to be co-ordinated by an overall long-term policy.

In view of the risks and uncertainties, it appears - short of an unforeseen technological revolution - that nothing but assistance for European coal can prevent a drastic decline in production. Such a decline would cause intolerable social and economic tensions at both the regional and national levels.

As stated above, even the most pessimistic view of future trends in oil prices gives no prospect of a fundamental change in the competitive pressure on coal.

Foreseeable trends in production and transport costs and transatlantic freight rates also make it unlikely that American coal prices will rise much above their present level: Competitive pressure on European coal is therefore not expected to slacken in this quarter either.

The future cost position for European coal may be summed up as follows:

- Miners' wages cannot be allowed to fall in relation to wages in other sectors;

- Productivity in the coalmining industry is unlikely to remain above the average level of productivity in the other industries indefinitely.

Aid for Coal

Taking the most likely hypotheses on oil prices, Ameri-can coal prices and the cost trend for European coal, it is un-

373

likely that more than about 50 per cent of present total production will still be competitive by the 1970's.

Hence to opt for an open energy market necessitates the acceptance of assistance for Community coal to enable larger tonnages to be sold than would be possible on the basis of competitive capacity alone.

We must therefore now examine the factors involved in choosing the appropriate system of assistance.

The choice must serve to reduce changes in the pattern of demand to a minimum, and cause the least possible disturbance in the relations of one type of energy to another in the relation of the energy sector as a whole to the rest of the economy.

Three systems are possible - protection, subsidies, or a combination of the two.

To continue to produce coal above the level at which it ceases to be truly competive places a burden on the whole economy. The burden itself is the same whatever the system of assistance adopted: it is the result of producing coal at, say, $15 a ton when it could be imported and paid for by the export of other goods to the value of, say $13. Protection and subsidies are two ways of spreading the burden.

Protection consists of imposing an additional charge on cheaper fuels. It may be carried out at the frontier, by means of a duty, or in the market, by means of consumption taxes. Its effect is to increase the price payable by the consumer.

Subsidies entail lowering the price of dearer fuels. They can be either direct or indirect subsidies. Indirect subsidies may be applied at any point in the production or marketing process, by reducing fiscal or social charges, wage or transport costs, the terms on which consumers can raise loans for equipment, and so on.

At the same time, owing to their particular characteristics, both systems - protection and subsidies - are liable to produce side-effects beyond the original aim of spreading the burden caused by the maintenance of uncompetitive production. Moreover, the practicability of the two systems varies.

Tariff protection, by pushing up prices for all internally produced energy, gives not only assistance to uncompetitive coal but a guaranteed extra profit to all other energy produced internally. In theory, this drawback can be reduced, if not eliminated altogether, by applying protection in the form of consumption taxes on fuels of outside origin only.

Subsidies do not involve making a present of extra profits to producers of other forms of energy. Where the subsidy is payable at a flat rate per ton produced, however, it has to be so fixed at a level which ensures the sale of the highest-cost ton produced and therefore affords a guaranteed profit to other coal producers in a better competitive position. Where it is selective, that is, designed purely to make up the difference between each producer's actual competitive position and what his position would need to be to enable him to market his output in competition with the other sources of energy - guaranteed extra profits for competitive producers are eliminated. Thus selective subsidies, while spreading the burden of maintaining production above the competitive level, reduce the risk of unwanted side-effects.

Tariff protection has the advantage of simplicity in practice. Furthermore, if properly co-ordinated, it need not interfere with competition among the Community collieries themselves. Protection by means of consumption taxes is rather more complicated since it presupposes that products of outside origin should be readily identifiable. Accordingly, while feasible for oil products, it would be more difficult to apply for coal.

Flat-rate subsidies are also fairly simple to operate, and not likely to cause any serious distortion in competition between Community collieries. This is not necessarily so in the case of selective subsidies, however. If they are not to impair competition, and more particularly to hamper rationalization and reorganization, either intricate financial arrangements have to be instituted, or the market organization must be such as to enable control to be exerted over the relationship between subsidies and the implementation of reorganization programs. In more concrete terms, if subsidies are to stand in the correct relationship to a reorganization program, administrative arrangements must be centralized to some extent by such means as nationalization, co-operative rationalization schemes or selling agencies.

From this it can be seen that subsidies, direct or indirect, are the most appropriate system for an open market aimed at ensuring cheap energy. These might be accompanied by moderate consumption taxes on fuel oil, as suggested later.

Nuclear Energy

Nuclear energy as a source of electric power has now advanced beyond the experimental stage. Industrial power-stations of various types with installed capacities of 150 MW or more are in service or being built in a number of countries.

As the result of unceasing research, nuclear power will become competitive with other forms of energy in a few years' time. Moreover, its cost per kWh will continue to fall thereafter further and further below that of electricity generated by conventional means.

Nuclear energy, as it becomes available more and more cheaply, will be a major factor - though perhaps not the complete answer - in the question of security of supply. Fissionable materials not normally found in the Community may of course be stockpiled. Nuclear energy's role in lowering prices and ensuring security of supply will be all the more important in view of the fact that it will be used to produce electricity - consumption of which will continue to soar for a long time to come.

The Euratom Commission, in accordance with the Euratom Treaty, has already established a common market for nuclear products and equipment, and removed restrictions on the free movement of nuclear technicians within the Community. In addition, it is encouraging the development of nuclear energy by a variety of means, with the object of making it competitive with conventional energy. Research and technical development are being integrated with policies designed to encourage the development of nuclear industries in the Community, and the training of sufficient nuclear technicians.

A Common Energy Policy

In the light of the preceding analysis, the following suggestions are put forward as the basis for a common energy policy to be established progressively during the Common Market's transition period.

The Long-Term Aims

The long-term objective is to make energy as cheap as possible and to safeguard supplies. This calls for different methods for oil and for coal.

For oil, the following measures have already been introduced, or are in the process of being introduced, in accordance with the Rome Treaty:

1. free movement of crude oil products within the Community;

2. unrestricted import of crude oil and oil products from non-member countries (except the Eastern bloc - see below);

3. Community quotas for imports from the Eastern bloc;

4. nil external tariffs on crude oil;

5. low external tariffs on oil products;

6. uniform consumption taxes on fuel oil throughout the Community, fixed at the lowest level compatible with budgetary consideration (probably about $2 per metric ton);

7. harmonization of consumption taxes on motor spirits to avoid distortion of the refining pattern in the Community;

8. possible preferential treatment for crude oil of Community origin and from other specified areas to promote diversification of supply;

9. a Community stockpiling policy, and harmonization of national regulations in this field;

10. price publicity for oil products, and application of the Rome Treaty's rules of competition to the oil-product market;

11. regular consultation between member Governments and the Common Market Commission on trends in the oil market;

12. regular consultation between Governments and the Commission on oil industry investment to ensure balanced development in the refining, transport and distribution sectors.

Where practicable, similar arrangements should be made for natural gas.

Coal policy in the final Community energy market should be based on the following factors:

- the ultimate advantage to all of an open energy market, resulting from the increasing importance of imported energy;

- assistance for the Community coal industry.

Prior agreement by Governments on the eventual upper and lower limits of assistance for the coal industry does not commit them to guaranteeing markets for coal. All they will be doing is to define the market conditions under which producers will have to operate and attempt to sell their coal.

On the other hand, prior agreement on the upper and lower limits of assistance will provide:

- a basis for producers' investment and personal policies;

- an indication of the extent to which member countries, particularly those without coal industries of their own, are committing themselves by agreeing in advance to a policy of assistance for Community collieries;

- a basis for area redevelopment plans in producing countries;

- a firm set of objectives for rationalization and adjustment to help member countries and the Coal-Steel Community High Authority in framing an overall policy for coal.

By prior agreement on the main outlines of the coal policy, the Governments and the High Authority would be providing themselves with common criteria on which to harmonize the previous national regulations in this field.

These are the suggested final arrangements for the Community coal market:

378

1. a system of Community assistance for internal production - based on direct or indirect subsidies to preserve an open market for energy generally;

2. free movement for coal within the Community;

3. imports of coal from non-member countries to be free
   of tariff or quota restrictions (except from the Eastern
   bloc);

4. a Community quota system for coal from the Eastern
   bloc;

5. relaxation of the methods of application of article 60
   of the ECSC Treaty concerning price publicity and
   conditions of sale, to ensure fair competition with oil;

6. regular consultation between the Governments and the
   High Authority on trends in the coal market;

7. the establishment of General Objectives for coal to
   provide a guide for investment - as required under
   articles 46 and 54 of the Paris Treaty.

The Transition Period

Having defined the ultimate aims, we must now describe
the measures which will be needed in the transition period -
during which national policies will be either harmonized or
superseded by Community arrangements. Care will be necessary to ensure a smooth transition from one system to the
other, and to avoid side-effects which might be prejudicial to
the industries concerned, the labour force or the regional
economies of Community countries.

Oil

In the first place, member countries should refrain
from taking new measures, or strengthening existing measures, which run counter to the proposed common policy or
its implementing regulations. No action should be taken in
this field without prior consultation with the other Governments and the Commission.

The following stages are envisaged for the realization
of the objectives listed above:

1.   Free movement of crude oil and oil products within
      the Community

      Restrictions on the free movement of oil within the
Community are already being removed according to the
precise timetable laid down in the Rome Treaty for the
elimination of customs duties. By the end of the Common
Market's transition period, member countries must have
abolished all discriminatory trade practices based on
nationality.

2.   Elimination of restrictions on imports from non-member
      countries

      Most imports of crude oil and oil products from non-
member countries (except the Eastern bloc) are already free
of restrictions. Remaining restrictions on crude oil should
be abolished by the end of the Common Market's second stage
at the latest, and by the end of the transition period for oil
products.

3.   Community quotas for Communist oil

      A Council of Ministers decision of July 1961, already
provides for prior consultation between Community countries
on trade agreements. What is now required is an annual
Community quota - fixed by the Council on a proposal by the
Common Market Commission - for oil products from the
Eastern bloc. This would be determined in accordance with
current needs. The machinery for deciding the size of the
quota should be set up during 1963, to enable the Council to
fix the first quota for 1964.

4.   A common external tariff for oil products

      The common external tariff for refined products should
be set up as soon as possible, and certainly not later than
January 1, 1964, when the Protocol on mineral oils expires.
The Commission has already submitted proposals in this
field to the member Governments.

5.   Consumption taxes

      Consumption taxes on fuel oil should be reduced by
stages down to the level fixed for the end of the transition
period. If that level were $2 per metric ton, the upper limit

380

at the end of the second stage should not be more than $4 per metric ton. Taxes on motor spirits should also be progressively harmonized.

6.   Diversification of supply

Products derived from crude oil of Community origin should receive preferential treatment.   This system might also be applied, in full or in part, to products from other areas whose oil production the Community might wish to encourage.

7.   Oil stocks

The Commission is to submit proposals for a common policy on crude oil and product stocks to the Council of Ministers before the end of the second stage.   These would include proposals for the minimum level of stocks to be held (4-6 months' current consumption, for example) and for methods by which the Community would finance them.

8.   Competition

The Commission is required under articles 85 and 86 of the Rome Treaty to examine all "practices.... which have as their object or result, the prevention, restriction or distortion of competition within the Common Market." These articles already apply in their entirety to oil firms. A system of ex post facto price publicity for the oil market would be an effective check of whether the rules were being observed.

9.   Regular consultation on investment

A standing committee of Government and Commission representatives should be appointed to follow developments in the oil market, with particular reference to prices and security of supply.

10.   Regular consultation on investment

A Community system of consultation on refinery, transport and distribution investment in the oil industry is already in operation. Under this system, the Commission would submit recommendations to the Governments if it found that investment was likely to be duplicated.

Coal

The more quickly the main features of the proposed energy market (particularly those relating to the removal of restrictions, oil supplies and coal subsidies) can be agreed and defined, the greater will be each individual country's freedom of action in adapting its own national system to the agreed common policy during the preparation period. Unless the basic principles are agreed, the co-ordination of national policies needed to set up a common market for energy cannot be planned, either in terms of its general outline, the speed with which it is to take place, or the practical steps by which it is to be achieved.

In addition, the more clearly the practical details of the coal policy to be pursued in each member country can be defined, the greater will be the degree of coordination possible between oil and coal. The following suggestions are made in relation to those listed above for oil during the transition period:

1. Subsidies for Community production

The existing systems of assistance for coal production in Community countries are protective (comprising duties, quotas, taxes on competing fuels, etc.). The aim should be to replace these highly divergent systems by a more homogeneous system based on subsidies.

During the transition period, therefore, the systems might be combined to offer both protection and subsidies in various forms. The timetable for oil products stipulates that consumption taxes on fuel oil from non-member countries must be reduced to a maximum of $4 per metric ton by 1966. This might therefore be a suitable date on which to take stock of the energy market as a whole, and to make a thorough and comprehensive examination of progress to date, the effectiveness of measures then in force, the outlook for the energy market, and the possible means of attaining the objectives of the common energy policy.

It will be necessary to decide, before the start of the transition period, whether the coal subsidies should be direct or indirect, and whether they should be payable on every ton produced or on a differential basis to avoid guaranteed extra profits for competitive producers. (The relative costs of the

two systems would also need to be considered.) It will also
be necessary to ensure that the subsidies operate effectively
in relation to the various marketing organizations already in
existence or those which may have to be established during
the transition period.

The Inter-Executive Energy Committee recommends
that:

- present readaptation and redevelopment assistance should
  be supplemented by direct grants for pit closures, payable
  in a single lump sum;

- during the transition period the Community should progressively assume responsibility for the payment of sales subsidies. The fact that the Community would be providing this
  additional aid would enable its institutions to ensure that it
  was being properly and usefully employed. This Community
  supervision, which should be systematic and thorough,
  would be adapted to the regional structure of the coal industry
  before the beginning of the transition period. The amount
  of the subsidies and the tonnages to which they would apply
  should be fixed annually by the Council of Ministers.

- funds for closure grants should be provided in equal proportions by the Government concerned and by the Community.
  (This is already the practice for readaptation and redevelopment aid.)

- a European Energy Support and Redevelopment Fund should
  be set up to be responsible, inter alia, for Community
  financing of coal sales subsidies and pit closure grants,
  and for promoting oil exploration to increase security of
  supply. The Fund's operations should begin during the
  transition period and continue after it;

- at the earliest practicable date each Government should submit details of the measures it thinks appropriate for dealing
  with its energy problems to the Community Executives and
  the Council of Ministers.

- measures and implementing methods proposed by Governments should be coordinated by the Executives and the
  Council prior to the beginning of the transition period.
  This would enable the Community to organize such matters
  as additional subsidies, supervision, etc.

2.   Free movement

Free movement for coal throughout the Community should be established during the transition period; the greater the harmonization between individual countries' aid systems for production and between their coal import arrangements, the easier this will be.

3.   Imports from non-member countries in the free world

If an open energy market is to be established, coal imports, like oil imports, should be freed from quantitative restrictions. The latter will be progressively liberalized until, in 1966, all such restrictions have been removed.

4.   Imports from the Eastern bloc

From the beginning of the transition period, oil imports from the Communist countries should be subject to an overall quota, fixed each year by the Council of Ministers.

5.   Harmonizing the rules of competition

Rules of competition should be so harmonized as to permit equitable competition between individual firms and between the various forms of energy from the start of the transition period.

Nuclear Energy

In the field of nuclear energy, member Governments should:

- support the Euratom Commission in stepping up its research activities and its drive to promote the industrial development of nuclear energy in the Community. The latter can be achieved by improving existing industrial techniques and by developing more advanced techniques for the economic exploitation of nuclear energy. The second five-year research program recently approved by the Council of Ministers (see Community Topics 7) is a major step towards equipping the nuclear industries of the Community for the vital part they will be called upon to assume when nuclear energy becomes competitive with other conventional forms of energy;

- facilitate the free movement of nuclear products and per-

sonnel employed in nuclear industries or research within
the Community, and ensure that the freedom of nuclear
industries to set up anywhere in the Community is not
unnecessarily hampered;

- maintain the Euratom Commission's liberal import policies
for nuclear plant and products, particularly special fissionable materials coming from non-member countries. Nil-
tariffs for reactors and nuclear fuels should be reintroduced,
firstly to ensure that Community industries enjoy the greatest
possible freedom of supply, and secondly, to ensure the widest
possible choice among the various types of installation under
development;

- refrain from introducing administrative or fiscal measures
designed to prevent or delay the fall in energy prices which
will certainly occur as nuclear energy becomes increasingly
competitive;

- play a positive role in the development of nuclear energy.

The Preparatory Period

To sum up, the Council of Ministers is being asked to
agree to the progressive establishment of a common market
for energy, accompanied by assistance for internal production.
The establishment of this open market would have to be carried
out in three stages:

- a preparatory period to end on January 1, 1964.

- a transition period from January 1, 1964 to January 1, 1970.

- a final period to begin on January 1, 1970.

The main objectives of the transition and final periods
have been outlined above. The preparatory period would be
devoted to hammering out the instruments and procedures
needed to implement the proposals.

A start should therefore be made on seeking agreement
between member Governments and the Community Executives
on:

1.   the principles on which the common market for energy
       are to be based;

2.   the principles on which assistance for internal production are to be based, and the maximum levels of such assistance;

3.   supply policy;

4.   special measures which may be necessary during the transition period (possibly on a country-by-country basis);

5.   a timetable for the stages by which the common policies for oil and coal will be introduced, dovetailed with other aspects of the Community's development. (Voting procedures should be based on those laid down in the Rome Treaty.)

The preparatory period should end not later than January 1, 1964. By that date, the principal arrangements for the transition period (the support fund, special measures, and a detailed timetable) would have to be complete.

---

(1) For example, energy costs account for over 25 per cent of total costs in the iron and steel industry, 20 per cent in non-ferrous metals, 10-15 per cent in chemicals, and up to 8 per cent in a manufacturing industry.

11.3 PROTOCOL OF AGREEMENT ON ENERGY*

On 21st April 1964 the representatives of member governments of the ECSC, at a meeting of the Council of Ministers, adopted a Protocol of Agreement (the text of which is given overleaf) on energy policy which had been drawn up by the Special Committee for energy policy meeting under the Chairmanship of Mr. P.-O. Lapie.

The High Authority was represented at the Council meeting by the President, Mr. Dino Del Bo, and by the Chairman of the Inter-Executive Working Party on Energy, Mr. P.-O. Lapie. The EEC Commission was represented by Messrs. Marjolin and Van Der Groeben.

The Protocol was described as a starting point for the difficult task of drawing up a common energy policy by the Chairman in office of the Council of Ministers, Mr. Paul Elvinger, Luxembourg Economic Minister. He expressed gratitude for the efforts of all those who had worked to reach this agreement and in particular the Chairman of the Inter-Executive Group on Energy, (which co-ordinates the efforts of the three European Communities in this field) Mr. P. -O. Lapie.

He also expressed great appreciation for the contribution made by President Del Bo in taking the initiative in February/March of this year for a "tour of the capitals" to help the governments reach agreement on the future outline of a common energy policy.

The Chairman of the Council also praised the spirit of solidarity shown by the member states and the three European Executive bodies of the Community and declared himself convinced that the same spirit of solidarity would not be lacking when it came to examining the proposals which the High Authority was to draw up for the application of a Community regime for state-aids to the coal industry.

Protocol

The Governments of the Member States of the European Communities, represented at a Session of the Special Council of Ministers of E. C. S. C. ,

1)   Convinced of the need to establish within the General Common Market a Common Market for energy based on due recognition of

(a) the following facts:

the growing proportion of imported hydrocarbons, which the Inter-Executive Working Party considers will in a few more years cover over one-half of the Community's total energy requirements,

the presence of indigenous energy resources in the Community,

the prospects opened up by the development of nuclear energy,

the importance of social considerations;

(b) the following objectives:

cheapness of supply,

security of supply,

phasing of substitution processes,

stability of supply as regards both cost and quantities available,

freedom of choice for the consumer,

fair competition among the different energy sources within the Common Market,

general economic policy;

2) Having regard to the time which must still elapse before the formulation of a common energy policy;

3) Being of the opinion that the present coal situation calls for immediate action;

4) Having regard to the decision taken by the six Governments on February 24, 1964, to merge the Communities;

I.

5) Are resolved to pursue their endeavours to frame and carry into effect a common policy for energy, in the context of the above decision, more especially with regard to

policy on foreign trade and imports from non-member countries,

the system of state-aids,

rules and conditions of competition for the different energy sources;

II.

6) Are prepared, having regard to the foregoing,

(a) to establish conditions of a nature to ensure the economically rational exploitation of the energy sources available, while avoiding distortions among Community producers liable to disturb the proper functioning of the Common Market,

(b) to promote the development of energy production in the Community in the manner indicated below.

III.

Coal

With regard to coal, the Governments

7) take due account of the need, in accordance with appropriate legal arrangements, to further by means of State aid the measures, and in particular the rationalization measures, adopted by the collieries for the purpose of adjusting their operations to the state of the market, and as complement to this to afford the collieries assistance, in general to be gradually phased out, in the form of protective or supporting measures;

8) Will arrange for appropriate action to be taken to ensure that cyclical factors do not interfere with the establishment of their energy policy and the smooth operation of the Common Market;

9) Consider it desirable that the energy policy measures should enable the countries concerned to draw up medium-term quantitative forecasts of production by coalfields;

10) Undertake to direct the measures envisaged under this Section, and those already adopted, towards the objectives set forth in subsection 1) above;

Resolve to begin, in the Special Council of Ministers with the High Authority, consultations on the measures envisaged under this Section before they are put into effect, except, where necessary, in cases of special urgency;

Will do their utmost to co-ordinate these various measures;

11) Request the High Authority to submit to them, where necessary in accordance with the Treaty of Paris and where-

ever necessary, procedural proposals for the institution of a Community system of State aids;

12) Consider that the Council should devote special attention to the question of the Community's long-term supply
position for coking coal.

IV.

Hydrocarbons (Oil and Natural Gas)

With regard to the hydrocarbon sector, the Governments, in the context of the Treaty of Rome,

13) Declare their willingness to introduce a common policy
ensuring widely diversified supplies at prices as low and
as stable as possible, in accordance with arrangements
which can be adapted to prevailing circumstances;

14) Are prepared to promote the economically rational
development of the production of hydrocarbons in the
Community;

15) Will endeavour to agree a common policy on hydrocarbon stocks;

16) Reaffirm that they are resolved progressively to eliminate from their municipal laws and regulations and the
application thereof all discrimination between their own
nationals and those of the other member States.

17) Will endeavour to work out for fuel oils a fiscal system
appropriate to the objectives of the energy policy set
forth above;

18) Trust that the question of harmonizing taxes on the other
petroleum products will be duly examined;

19) Resolve to institute standing arrangements for consultation with the E. E. C. Commission with a view to
attaining the above objectives and to co-ordinating the
measures taken in the hydrocarbon sector.

V.

Nuclear Energy

With regard to nuclear energy, the Governments, in accordance with the provisions of the Treaty establishing the European Atomic Energy Community,

20) are prepared to promote and intensify research and experimental work and assistance for the industrial development of nuclear energy in the Community, in order that this new energy source may come at the earliest possible date to make its full contribution, at economic costs, to the coverage of Community energy requirements.

---

*European Coal and Steel Community Spokesman, Document 2777/64e, April 24, 1964.

CHAPTER **12**

OVERSEAS DEVELOPMENT AND ASSOCIATION AGREEMENTS

An association between the EEC and eighteen dependent African territories formed an integral part of the Rome Treaty. This agreement was concluded for a five year period. Before its expiration, however, the dependent areas had become independent and sovereign states. Substantial aid was channelled through this association in addition to the bilateral programs of the member countries. The success and utility of the first agreement led to the conclusion of a second agreement for the period 1963-1967 at the request of the associated states.

Certain overseas territories and the French overseas departments participated in the first program and became eligible for continued participation under arrangements similar to those for the independent states. The main difference between the association agreement and the program for dependent areas is that the latter is not provided with a full institutional framework. Separate but similar agreements have been reached with Surinam (entered into force September 1, 1962) and the Netherlands Antilles (not yet fully ratified).

The association agreement provides three major means for stimulating the economic development of the associates: grants and loans, technical assistance, and trade expansion through non-reciprocal liberalization. Aid, to be channelled through the European Development Fund and the European Investment Bank, will be used to finance a wide range of programs: economic and social investment (basic development, production projects), technical cooperation (assessments of economic potential), price stabilization, aiding and diversifying production, and emergency measures in the event of natural disaster.

Technical assistance, not a part of the first agreement, has been made an important part of the second one. Financing by the Development Fund will underwrite the costs of regional surveys, technical and economic surveys, provision of expert personnel, supply of materials for information, reference and experimental purposes, provision for trainee scholarships, and organization of training courses.

The provisions of the first agreement concerning trade were extended under the newer arrangements. Community tariffs on many tropical products have been abolished completely, (in addition to the zero tariff applied to all industrial raw materials), while remaining exports to the Community from the associates benefits from the reductions of the Community's internal tariffs.

Associated states are committed in principle to reduce tariffs on Community imports by 15 per cent annually and to remove quota restrictions within the first four years of the new agreement. The agreement provides, however, that old tariffs may be retained and new ones created when they are needed to protect infant industries.

The member states issued a declaration of intention when the second agreement was signed indicating that they were willing to consider agreements with other states having economies similar to the associated states. These agreements could take one of three forms: accession to the association agreement, other association agreements including reciprocal rights and obligations, and commercial agreements aimed at increasing trade between the Community and these states. Nigeria, after discussions with the EEC Commission, indicated its interest in reaching an agreement of the second kind and further talks are leading toward negotiation of such a sui generis accord. Tanganyika, Uganda, and Kenya have also asked for talks with the Community based on the declaration of intention.

The Community plays an active and important role in the development programs for countries not associated with it as well as for the associates. Principal activity has taken place in the framework of the General Agreement on Tariffs and Trade, the Organization for Economic Cooperation and Development and the United Nations World Conference for Trade and Development.

The Community participates in the work of the Development Assistance Group of the OECD. It maintains a permanent office at OECD headquarters. Through this participation the Community is able to coordinate its aid programs with those of the other OECD members in order to encourage the most efficient use of aid resources. In GATT, the Community, together with the contracting parties, seeks to establish rules lowering trade barriers to the export of the developing countries on a non-reciprocal basis. The Community also favors the creation of organized markets for the exports of the developing countries in order to allow these countries to adapt to the free market system. The Kennedy Round of trade negotiations allows for the Community and other states to take such steps to increase the exports of the developing countries. During the U.N. Conference, the Community went on record in favor of several policies designed to aid the development of the newer countries:

1. price stabilization for basic products;

2. preferences (relaxation of most-favored-nation rule) for semi-finished and manufactured products of developing countries;

3. regional cooperation among developing countries;

4. world commodity agreements (also supported in GATT);

5. increased aid.

12.1 CONVENTION OF ASSOCIATION BETWEEN THE EUROPEAN ECONOMIC COMMUNITY AND THE AFRICAN AND MALAGASY STATES ASSOCIATED WITH THAT COMMUNITY AND ANNEXED DOCUMENTS

Title I - Trade

Article 1

With a view to promoting an increase of trade between the Associated States and the Member States, strengthening their economic relations and the economic independence of the Associated States and thereby contributing to the development of international trade, the High Contracting Parties have agreed upon the following provisions which shall regulate their mutual trade relations.

Chapter I

Customs duties and quantitative restrictions

Article 2

1. Goods originating in Associated States shall, when imported into Member States, benefit from the progressive abolition of customs duties and charges having an effect equivalent to such duties, resulting between Member States under the provisions of Articles 12, 13, 14, 15 and 17 of the Treaty and the decisions which have been or may be adopted to accelerate the rate of achieving the aims of the Treaty.

2. Nevertheless, upon the entry into force of the Convention, Member States shall abolish the customs duties and charges having an effect equivalent to such duties which they apply to the goods originating in Associated States which are listed in the Annex to this convention.

At the same time Member States shall apply the common customs tariff duties of the Community to imports of these goods from third countries.

3. Imports from third countries of unroasted coffee into the Benelux countries on the one hand, and of bananas into the Federal Republic of Germany on the other hand, shall be subject to the terms set out respectively, as to unroasted coffee, in the Protocol this day concluded between the Member States

and, as to bananas, in the Protocol concluded on 25 March 1957 between the Member States and in the Declaration annexed to this Convention.

4.   Application of the provisions of this Article shall not predetermine the treatment to be applied to certain agricultural products under the provisions of Article 11 of this Convention.

5.   At the request of an Associated State, there shall be consultations within the Association Council regarding the conditions of application of this Article.

Article 3

1.   Each Associated State shall accord identical tariff treatment to goods originating in any of the Member States; Associated States not applying this rule on the entry into force of this Convention shall do so within the following six months.

2.   In each Associated State goods originating in Member States shall benefit, under the terms set out in Protocol No. 1 annexed to this Convention, from the progressive abolition of customs duties and charges having an effect equivalent to such duties which that Associated State applies to imports of these goods into its territory.

Provided always that each Associated State may retain or introduce customs duties and charges having an effect equivalent to such duties which correspond to its development needs or its industrialization requirements or which are intended to contribute to its budget.

The customs duties and charges having an effect equivalent to such duties levied by Associated States in accordance with the foregoing sub-paragraph, as also any alteration which they may make in these duties and charges under the provisions of Protocol No. 1, may not either de jure or de facto give rise to any direct or indirect discrimination between Member States.

3.   At the request of the Community and in accordance with the procedures laid down in Protocol No. 1, there shall be consultations within the Association Council regarding the conditions of application of this Article.

Article 4

1.   Insofar as an Associated State levies export duties on exports of its products to Member States, these duties may not give rise, de jure or de facto, to any direct or indirect discrimination between Member States and may not be greater than those applied to products exported to the most favoured third country.

2.   Without prejudice to the application of Article 13, paragraph 2 of this Convention, the Association Council shall take suitable measures if application of such duties leads to serious disturbances in the conditions of competition.

Article 5

1.   With regard to the abolition of quantitative restrictions, Member States shall apply to imports of goods originating in the Associated States the relevant provisions of the Treaty, and of the decisions which have been or may be adopted to accelerate the rate of achieving the aims of the Treaty, which they apply in their relations with each other.

2.   At the request of an Associated State, there shall be consultations within the Association Council regarding the conditions of application of this Article.

Article 6

1.   Associated States shall, not later than four years after the entry into force of the Convention, abolish all quantitative restrictions on imports of goods originating in Member States and all measures having equivalent effect.   This abolition shall be carried out progressively under the conditions set out in Protocol No. 2 annexed to this Convention.

2.   Associated States shall refrain from introducing any new quantitative restrictions or measures having equivalent effect on imports of goods originating in Member States.

3.   Should the measures provided for in Article 3 prove insufficient to meet their development needs and their industrialization requirements, or in the event of difficulties in their balance of payments, or, where agricultural products are concerned, in connection with the requirements arising from existing regional market organizations, Associated States may,

notwithstanding the provisions of the two foregoing paragraphs and subject to the terms of Protocol No. 2, retain or introduce quantitative restrictions on imports of goods originating in Member States.

4.   Associated States in which imports come within the province of a State trading monopoly or of any body which, de jure or de facto, either directly or indirectly limits, controls, directs or influences them, shall take any steps necessary to attain the objectives defined in this Title and to abolish progressively any discrimination in conditions of supply and marketing of goods.

Without prejudice to the application of Article 7 below, foreign trade plans drawn up by the Associated States shall not contain or bring about, de jure or de facto, any direct or indirect discrimination between Member States.

The Associated States concerned shall inform the Associated Council of the steps taken to implement the provisions of this paragraph.

5.   At the request of the Community, there shall be consultations within the Association Council regarding the conditions of application of this Article.

Article 7

Without prejudice to the special provisions for border trade, the treatment that the Associated States apply by virtue of this Title to goods originating in Member States shall in no case be less favourable than that applied to goods originating in the most favoured third country.

Article 8

This Convention shall not preclude the maintenance or establishment of customs unions or free-trade areas among Associated States.

Article 9

This Convention shall not preclude the maintenance or establishment of customs union or free-trade areas between one or more Associated States and one or more third countries insofar as they neither are nor prove to be incompatible with the principles and provisions of the said Convention.

Article 10

The provisions of the foregoing Articles 3, 4 and 6 shall not preclude prohibitions or restrictions on imports, exports or goods in transit justified on grounds of public morality, public policy, public security, the protection of human, animal or plant life or health, the protection of national treasures possessing artistic, historic or archaelogical value, or the protection of industrial and commercial property. Provided always that such prohibitions or restrictions shall not be used as a means of arbitrary discrimination nor as a disguised restriction on trade.

Chapter 2

Provisions concerning certain agricultural products

Article 11

When drawing up its common agricultural policy, the Community shall take the interests of the Associated States into consideration as regards products similar to and competitive with European products. The Community and the Associated States concerned shall consult together for this purpose.

The treatment applicable to imports into the Community of these products, if they have originated in the Associated States, shall be determined by the Community in the course of defining its common agricultural policy, after consultation within the Association Council.

Chapter 3

Provisions concerning commercial policy

Article 12

1.   On matters of commercial policy, the Contracting Parties agree to keep each other informed and, should one of them so request, to consult together for the purpose of giving good effect to this Convention.

2.   Such consultation shall bear on measures concerning trade with third countries if these measures are likely to harm the interests of one or more Contracting Parties, with particular reference to:

a) the suspension, alteration or abolition of customs
    duties,

b) the granting of tariff quotas at reduced or zero duties,
    other than the quotas referred to in Article 2, para-
    graph 3, above,

c) the introduction, reduction or abolition of quantitative
    restrictions, without prejudice to the obligations in-
    cumbent upon certain Contracting Parties by reason
    of their membership of G. A. T. T.

3.   Upon the entry into force of this Convention, the Association Council shall define the procedure for consultation and exchange of information in respect of the implementation of this
Article.

Chapter 4

Safeguard Clauses

Article 13

1.   If serious disturbances occur in one sector of the economy
of an Associated State or jeopardize its external financial stability,
that State may take the necessary protective measures, notwithstanding the provisions of Article 3, paragraph 2, sub-paragraph
1 and Article 6, paragraphs 1, 2 and 4.

        The measures and the methods of applying them shall be
notified immediately to the Association Council.

2.   If serious disturbances occur in one sector of the economy
of the Community or of one or more Member States, or jeopardize
their external financial stability, and if difficulties arise which
may result in a region suffering grave economic hardship, the
Community may take, or may authorize the Member State or
States concerned to take such measures as may prove necessary
in their relations with the Associated States, notwithstanding the
provisions of Articles 2 and 5.

        These measures and the methods of applying them shall
be notified immediately to the Association Council.

3.   For the purpose of implementing paragraphs 1 and 2 of
this Article, priority shall be given to such measures as will

least disturb the functioning of the Association. These measures shall not exceed the limits strictly necessary to remedy the difficulties that have arisen.

4.   There shall be consultations within the Association Council regarding the measures taken under paragraphs 1 and 2 of this Article.

Such consultations shall be held at the request of the Community in respect of measures under paragraph 1 and at the request of one or more Associated States in respect of those under paragraph 2.

Chapter 5

General Provisions

Article 14

Without prejudice to the special provisions laid down in this Convention, and particularly those of Article 3 above, each Contracting Party shall refrain from any measure or practice of an internal fiscal nature that directly or indirectly sets up any discrimination between its own products and similar products originating in the territories of the other Contracting Parties.

Title II - Financial and technical co-operation

Article 15

Under the conditions determined below the Community shall participate in measures calculated to promote the economic and social development of the Associated States, by supplementing the efforts achieved by those States.

Article 16

For the purposes set out in Article 15, and for the duration of this Convention, an aggregate amount of 730 million units of account shall be provided as follows:

a)   666 million units of account by the Member States; this amount to be paid into the European Development Fund, hereinafter referred to as "the Fund", shall be employed up to 620 million units of account in the form of grants and the balance in the form of loans on special terms;

b)   up to 64 million units of account by the European Investment Bank hereinafter referred to as "the Bank", in the
form of loans granted by it under the terms set out in
Protocol No. 5 concerning the administration of the
financial aids, annexed to this Convention.

Article 17

Under the terms laid down by this Convention and by
Protocol No. 5, the amount fixed in Article 16 above shall be
employed as follows:

1. in the field of economic and social investments,
   - for basic economic and social schemes,
   - for production schemes of general interest,
   - for production schemes providing normal financial returns,
   - for relevant technical assistance before, during and after
     such investments;

2. in the field of general technical co-operation,
   - for surveying the development prospects of the economies
     of the Associated States,
   - for staff training and vocational training programmes;

3. in the field of aids for diversification and production,
   - for measures essentially intended to make marketing
     possible at competitive prices on the Community's markets
     as a whole, by encouraging, in particular, rationalization
     of cropping and sales methods, and by aiding producers
     to make the necessary adaptations;

4. in the field of price stabilization,
   - for advances for the purpose of helping to alleviate the
     effects of temporary fluctuations in world prices.

Article 18

Grants and loans shall be assigned as follows:

a)   up to 500 million units of account for financing the measures
referred to in Article 17, paragraphs 1 and 2,

b)   up to 230 million units of account for financing the measures
referred to in Article 17, paragraph 3.

Article 19

The Bank loans referred to in Article 16 b) may carry a rebate on the interest. The rate of such rebates may be up to 3% on loans of a maximum duration of 25 years.

The amounts required to pay such rebates shall, so long as the Fund exists, be charged to the amount of the grants provided for in Article 16 a).

Article 20

1. The Community may grant advances from the liquid assets of the Fund up to a ceiling of 50 million units of account for the operations provided for in Article 17, paragraph 4.

2. Such advances shall be granted according to the terms set out in Protocol No. 5.

Article 21

In order to finance the measures referred to in Article 17, the Associated State or group of Associated States concerned shall, as prescribed in Protocol No. 5, open a file for each scheme or programme for which it is requesting financial assistance. It shall send this file to the Community, addressed to the Commission.

Article 22

The Community shall examine the requests for financing that are brought before it by virtue of the provisions of the foregoing Article. It shall maintain such contacts with the Associated States concerned as it may require in order that its decisions on the schemes or programmes submitted to it may be formulated in full knowledge of the facts. The Associated State or group of Associated States concerned shall be informed of the decision taken regarding its request.

Article 23

Aid contributed by the Community for the purpose of carrying out certain schemes or programmes may take the form of participation in financing in which, in particular, third countries, international finance organizations, or credit and development institutions and authorities, whether of the Associated States or the Member States, may take part.

Article 24

1.   The following shall be entitled to benefit from aids from the Fund:

a) as regards grants:
   - for economic and social investment schemes: either the Associated States, or legal persons who are non-profit-making in their main capacity, who have a status of general or social interest, and who are subject in those States to government inspection;

   - for staff training and vocational training programmes and for economic surveys: the Governments of the Associated States specialized bodies and institutions; or on exceptional grounds, scholars and trainees;

   - for aid towards production: producers;

   - for aid towards diversification: the Associated States, producer groups or similar bodies approved by the Community; or, failing these, producers themselves;

b) as regards loans on special terms and rebates on interest:
   - for economic and social investment schemes: either the Associated States, or legal persons who are non-profit-making in their main capacity, who have a status of general or social interest, and who are subject in those States to government inspection, or, possibly, private enterprises by special decision of the Community;

   - for aid towards diversification: the Associated States, producer groups or similar bodies approved by the Community, or, failing these, producers themselves and, possibly, private enterprises by special decision of the Community.

2.   Financial aids may not be used to cover current administrative, maintenance and operating expenses.

Article 25

As regards operations financed by the Fund or by the Bank, participation in the letting out of contracts, invitations for tenders, purchasing and other contracts shall be open, on equal terms, to all natural and legal persons who are nationals of the Member States or the Associated States.

Article 26

The amounts allocated for financing schemes or programmes, under the provisions of this Title, shall be utilized in accordance with the purposes decided upon and shall be expended to the best economic advantage.

Article 27

The Association Council shall lay down the general pattern for financial and technical co-operation within the framework of association, more particularly in the light of an annual report to be submitted to it by the organ responsible for administering the Community's financial and technical aid.

Article 28

If any Associated State should fail to ratify the Convention, under the terms set out in Article 57, or denounce the Convention in accordance with Article 60, it shall then be obligatory upon the Contracting Parties to adjust the amount of financial aid fixed in Article 16 and 18.

Title III - Right of establishment, services, payments and capital

Article 29

Without prejudice to measures adopted in implementation of the Treaty, in each Associated State nationals and companies of every Member State shall be placed on equal footing as regards the right of establishment and provision of services, progressively and not later than three years after the entry into force of this Convention.

The Association Council may authorize an Associated State, at its request, to suspend implementation of the provisions of the foregoing sub-paragraph over a given period and for a given activity.

Nevertheless, in an Associated State nationals and companies of a Member State may benefit from the provisions of the first sub-paragraph, in respect of a given activity, only in so far as the State to which they belong grants similar advantages for the same activity to the nationals and companies of the Associated State in question.

Article 30

Should an Associated State grant nationals or companies of a State which is neither a Member State of the Community nor an Associated State within the meaning of this Convention, more favourable treatment than that which implementation of the provisions of this Title afford to nationals, such treatment shall be extended to nationals or companies of the Member States, excepting where it arises out of regional agreements.

Article 31

Subject to the provisions relating to movements of capital, the right of establishment within the meaning of this Convention shall include the right to engage in and carry on non-wage-earning activities, to set up and manage undertakings and in particular companies, and to set up agencies, branches or subsidiaries.

Article 32

Services within the meaning of this Convention shall be deemed to be services normally provided against remuneration, insofar as they are not governed by the provisions relating to trade, the right of establishment and movements of capital. Services shall include in particular activities of an industrial character, activities of a commercial character, artisan activities and activities of the liberal professions, excluding wage-earning activities.

Article 33

Companies within the meaning of this Convention shall be deemed to be companies under civil or commercial law, including co-operative societies and other legal persons under public or private law, but not including non-profit-making companies.

Companies of a Member State or an Associated State shall be companies constituted in accordance with the law of a Member State or an Associated State, and having their registered office, central administration, or main establishment in a

Member State or an Associated State; nevertheless, should they have only their registered office in a Member State or an Associated State, their business must be actively and continuously linked with the economy of that Member State or Associated State.

Article 34

The Association Council shall take any decisions required to further the implementation of Articles 29 to 33 above.

Article 35

Each Signatory State undertakes, to the full extent of its powers, to authorize payments relating to trade in goods, services and capital and to wages, as also the transfer of such payments to the Member State or Associated State in which the creditor or the beneficiary is resident, in so far as the movement of such goods, services, capital or persons has been liberalized in implementation of this Convention.

Article 36

Throughout the whole duration of the loans and advances referred to in Chapters III, IV and V of Protocol No. 5, the Associated States undertake to make available to debtors the foreign currency necessary for the repayment of capital and interest on loans granted for schemes to be carried out in their territory and for repayment of advances granted to the stabilization funds.

Article 37

1.   Associated States shall make every endeavour not to introduce any new exchange restriction that would affect the treatment applied to investments and to current payments connected with the movements of capital resulting therefrom, where these are effected by persons residing in the Member States, and not to make the existing controls more restrictive.

2.   To the extent necessary for achieving the objectives of this Convention, the Associated States undertake to treat nationals and companies of Member States on an equal footing, not later than 1 January 1965, in respect of investments made by them as from the date of the entry into force of the Convention, as also of movements of capital resulting therefrom.

407

Article 38

The Association Council shall formulate any appropriate recommendations to the Contracting Parties concerning the implementation of Articles 35, 36 and 37 above.

Title IV - Institutions of the Association

Article 39

The Institutions of the Association shall be:
- the Association Council assisted by the Association Committee,
- the Parliamentary Conference of the Association,
- the Court of Arbitration of the Association.

Article 40

The Association Council shall be composed, on the one hand, of the members of the Council of the European Economic Community and members of the Commission of the European Economic Community and, on the other hand, of one member of the Government of each Associated State.

Any member of the Association Council prevented from attending may be represented. The representative shall exercise all the rights of the accredited member.

Proceedings of the Association Council shall only be valid if half the members of the Council of the Community, one member of the Commission and half the accredited members representing the Governments of the Associated States are present.

Article 41

The office of the President of the Association Council shall be exercised alternately by a member of the Council of the European Economic Community and a member of the Government of an Associated State.

Article 42

Meetings of the Association Council shall be called once a year by the President.

Furthermore it shall meet whenever necessary, in accordance with the conditions laid down in its rules of procedure.

Article 43

The Association Council shall express itself by mutual agreement between the Community on the one hand and the Associated States on the other.

The Community on the one hand and the Associated States on the other shall each by means of an internal Protocol determine their procedure for arriving at their respective positions.

Article 44

In cases covered by this Convention, the Association Council shall dispose of the power of decision; such decisions shall be binding upon the Contracting Parties, who shall be under the obligation to take all necessary measures to carry them out.

The Association Council may likewise formulate such resolutions, recommendations or opinions as it may deem necessary to achieve the common objectives and to ensure that the Association system works efficiently.

The Association Council shall periodically study the results of the Association system in the light of that system's objectives.

The Association Council shall lay down its rules of procedure.

Article 45

The Association Council shall be assisted in the performance of its task by an Association Committee composed on the one hand of one representative of each Member State and one representative of the Commission and, on the other, of one representative of each Associated State.

Article 46

The Office of the Chairman of the Association Committee

shall be filled by the State which is presiding over the Association Council.

The Association Committee shall lay down its rules of procedure, which shall be submitted to the Association Council for approval.

Article 47

1.   In its rules of procedure the Association Council shall define the duties and powers of the Association Committee, with the object, in particular, of ensuring the continuity of co-operation essential to the satisfactory operation of the Association.

2.   The Association Council may when necessary delegate to the Association Committee the exercise of the powers entrusted to it by this Convention, under the terms and within the limits laid down by the Council.

In that event, the Committee shall give its decisions in accordance with the terms of Article 43.

Article 48

The Association Committee shall account for its actions to the Association Council, particularly in matters which have been the subject of a delegation of powers.

It shall also submit any useful proposal to the Association Council.

Article 49

The duties of the Secretariat of the Association Council and the Association Committee shall be carried out on a basis of parity and in accordance with the rules of procedure of the Association Council.

Article 50

The Parliamentary Conference of the Association shall meet once a year. It shall be composed, on a basis of parity, of members of the Assembly and members of the Parliaments of the Associated States.

Each year the Association Council shall submit a report

on its activities to the Parliamentary Conference.

The Parliamentary Conference may vote resolutions on matters concerning the Association. It shall appoint its President and its officers and shall adopt its own rules of procedure.

The Parliamentary Conference shall be prepared by a Joint Committee set up on a basis of parity.

Article 51

1.   Disputes concerning the interpretation or the application of the present Convention which might arise between one Member State, several Member States or the Community on the one hand, and one or more Associated States on the other, shall be submitted by one of the parties to the dispute to the Association Council which shall seek an amicable settlement at its next meeting. If this cannot be achieved and if the parties to the dispute fail to agree upon an appropriate solution, the dispute shall, at the request of the earliest petitioner, be submitted to the Court of Arbitration of the Association.

2.   The Court of Arbitration shall be composed of five members: a President who shall be appointed by the Association Council and four judges from among persons whose independence and competence can be fully guaranteed. The judges shall be appointed by the Association Council within three months after the entry into force of the Convention and for duration therof. Two of the judges shall be appointed by the Council of the European Economic Community and the other two by the Associated States. For each judge, following the same procedure, the Association Council shall appoint a deputy who shall sit in the event of the accredited judge being unable to do so.

3.   The Court of Arbitration shall act by majority vote.

4.   The decisions of the Court of Arbitration shall be binding on the parties to the dispute who shall be under the obligation to take all necessary measures to carry them out.

5.   Within three months after the judges are appointed, the Association Council shall lay down the Statute of the Court of Arbitration, on a proposal of that Court.

6.   The Court of Arbitration shall adopt its rules of procedure within the same period.

Article 52

The Association Council may make any useful recommendation for the purpose of facilitating contacts between the Community and the representatives of the various trades and professions of the Associated States.

Article 53

The administrative expenses of the Institutions of the Association shall be defrayed in accordance with the terms set out in Protocol No. 6 annexed to this Convention.

Title V - General and final provisions

Article 54

No treaties, conventions, agreements or arrangements of whatever form or nature between one or more Member States and one or more Associated States shall preclude the implementation of the provisions of this Convention.

Article 55

This Convention shall apply to the European territory of the Member States of the Community on the one hand, and to the territory of the Associated States on the other.

The First Title of this Convention shall also apply to the relations between the French Overseas Territories and the Associated States.

Article 56

As far as the Community is concerned, this Convention shall be validly concluded by a decision of the Council of the Community taken in conformity with the provisions of the Treaty and notified to the Parties. It shall be ratified by the Signatory States in conformity with their respective constitutional requirements.

The instruments of ratification and the act of notification of the conclusion of the Convention shall be deposited with the

Secretariat of the Councils of the European Communities, who shall give notice thereof to the Signatory States.

Article 57

1.   This Convention shall enter into force on the first day of the month following the date on which the instruments of ratification of the Member States and of at least fifteen of the Associated States and the instrument notifying the conclusion of the Convention by the Community have been deposited.

2.   Any Associated State which has not ratified the Convention by the date of its entry into force as provided for in the previous paragraph, shall be able to proceed with this ratification only during the twelve months following such entry into force, unless before the expiry of this period it gives notice to the Association Council of its intention to ratify the Convention not later than six months after this period, and on condition that it deposits its instruments of ratification within the same time limit.

3.   As regards those States which have not ratified the Convention by the date of its entry into force as laid down in paragraph 1, the provisions of the Convention shall become applicable on the first day of the month following the deposit of their respective instruments of ratification.

      Signatory States who ratify the Convention in accordance with the terms of paragraph 2 shall recognize the validity of all measures taken in implementation of the said Convention between the date of its entry into force and the date when its provisions become applicable to them. Without prejudice to any delay which might be granted to them by the Association Council, they shall, not later than six months after depositing their instruments of ratification, carry out all the obligations which devolve upon them under the terms of this Convention or of implementing decisions adopted by the Association Council.

4.   The rules of procedure of the organs of the Association shall lay down if and under what conditions the representatives of Signatory States which, on the date of entry into force of the Convention, have not yet ratified it, shall sit in the organs of the Association as observers. The arrangements thus adopted shall only be effective until the date on which the Convention becomes applicable to these States; in any case, they shall cease to apply on the date on which, according to the terms of para-

graph 2 above, the State concerned shall no longer be able to proceed with the ratification of the Convention.

Article 58

1.   The Association Council shall be informed of any request made by a State for accession to or association with the Community.

2.   There shall be consultations within the Association Council on any request for association with the Community made by a State which has an economic structure and production comparable to those of the Associated States if the Community, after examining the said request, has laid it before the Association Council.

3.   The agreement of association between the Community and any State covered by the previous paragraph may provide for the accession of that State to the present Convention. That State shall then enjoy the same rights and be subject to the same obligations as the Associated States. Provided always that the agreement which associates it with the Community may determine the date on which certain of these rights and obligations shall become applicable to it.

Such accession shall not adversely affect the advantages accruing to the Associated States which are signatories to this Convention from the provisions relating to financial and technical co-operation.

Article 59

This Convention shall be concluded for a period of five years from the date of its entry into force.

Article 60

One year before the expiry of this Convention, the Contracting Parties shall examine the provisions which might be made for a further period.

The Association Council shall if necessary take any transitional measures required until the new Convention enters into force.

414

Article 61

The Community and the Member States shall undertake the obligations set out in Articles 2, 5 and 11 of the Convention with respect to Associated States which, on the grounds of international obligations applying at the time of the entry into force of the Treaty establishing the European Economic Community and subjecting them to a particular customs treatment, may consider themselves not yet able to offer the Community the reciprocity provided for by Article 3, paragraph 2 of the Convention.

The Contracting Parties concerned shall re-examine the situation not later than three years after the entry into force of the Convention.

Article 62

This Convention may be denounced by the Community in respect of any Associated State and by any Associated State in respect of the Community by means of six months' notice.

Article 63

The Protocols annexed to this Convention shall form an integral part thereof.

Article 64

The present Convention, drawn up in a single original in the German, French, Italian and Dutch languages, each of these texts being equally authentic, shall be deposited in the archives of the Secretariat of the Councils of the European Communities which shall transmit a certified copy to the Government of each of the Signatory States.

Protocols

PROTOCOL No. 1

concerning the implementation of Article 3
of the Convention of Association

THE HIGH CONTRACTING PARTIES HAVE AGREED upon the following provisions which shall be annexed to the Convention:

Article 1

1.   For the purpose of implementing Article 3 of the Convention, each Associated State shall, within a period of two months from the entry into force of this Convention, communicate to the Association Council its customs tariff or the complete list of customs duties and charges having an effect equivalent to such duties imposed on 31 December 1962 on all imported goods, indicating the duties and charges that apply to goods originating in Member States and other Associated States, those that apply to goods originating in third countries, and the export duties.

In this communication, each Associated State shall specify those of the duties or charges referred to in the foregoing paragraph which, in its opinion, correspond to its development needs or its industrialization requirements or are intended to contribute to its budget. It shall give the reasons for their retention or introduction.

2.   At the request of the Community, there shall be consultations within the Association Council on the customs tariffs or lists referred to in paragraph 1 above. If no request for consultation has been made within a time-limit of three months, the Association Council shall be deemed to have noted these tariffs or lists.

Article 2

On the basis of the tariffs or lists which the Association Council has noted, and without prejudice to the provisions of Article 3, paragraph 1, of the Convention, each Associated State shall make an annual reduction of 15%, as from the first day of the seventh month after the entry into force of the Convention, in the customs duties and charges having an effect equivalent to such duties applicable to imports of goods originating in the Member States, other than those which are recognized as being necessary to the development and industrialization of the Associated State concerned or which are intended to contribute to its budget.

Article 3

Each Associated State hereby declares its readiness to reduce customs duties and charges having an effect equivalent to such duties, in respect of Member States, more rapidly than is provided for under the foregoing article if its economic situation so permits.

Article 4

Any increase in customs duties and charges having an effect equivalent to such duties which are recognized as necessary to the development and industrialization of an Associated State, or which are intended to contribute to its budget, shall be communicated by that State to the Association Council before entering into force and shall be a matter for consultation should the Community so request.

PROTOCOL No. 2

concerning the implementation of Article 6 of the Convention of Association

THE HIGH CONTRACTING PARTIES HAVE AGREED upon the following provisions which shall be annexed to the Convention:

Article 1

For any product originating in Member States, imports of which into the territory of an Associated State are subject to quantitative restrictions or measures having an effect equivalent to such restriction, that Associated State shall establish a global quota which it shall open without discrimination to Member States other than that State, imports from which are already unrestricted.

Where the Association Council finds that imports of a given product have, for two consecutive years, been less than the quotas opened under Article 2 below, the Associated State shall abolish all quotas on this product.

Article 2

The global quota referred to in the first sub-paragraph of Article 1 above shall be established and increased in accordance with the following provisions:

a)   In each Associated State where imports are limited by quantitative restrictions, the amount of the basic quota shall be equal to the amount of the quota for the year 1959, calculated in accordance with Article 11 of the Implementing Convention

concerning the Association with the Community of the Overseas
Countries and Territories signed on 25 March 1957 and annexed
to the Treaty, and increased by 75%. This basic quota shall
amount to at least 15% of the total imports of the said product
into the Associated State during the last year for which statistical data are available.

Where, in respect of a non-liberalized product, no
quota has been opened for imports into an Associated State,
that State shall establish a quota equal to at least 15% of the
total imports of the said product into that Associated State during
the last year for which statistical data are available.

In respect of products which have never been imported
by an Associated State, that State shall establish an appropriate
quota.

The basic quota thus established shall be increased by
20% for the first year and then annually, in relation to the
previous year, by 20% for the second year, by 30% for the
third year, and by 40% for the fourth year.

b)   Each Associated State into which imports are limited
other than by quantitative restriction shall establish a global
quota for each non-liberalized product from the date of the
entry into force of the Convention; the quota shall be open to
the Member States without discrimination and equal to the
amount of the product imported from Member States by that
Associated State during the last year for which statistics are
available. This quota shall not be less than 15% of the total
imports of the same product into that Associated State during
the reference year.

The basic quota thus established shall be increased in
accordance with the terms set out in sub-paragraph 4 of paragraph a) above.

Article 3

Each Associated State shall, not later than 1 February
of each year, open the quotas established in conformity with
Article 2 of this Protocol for imports of goods originating in
Member States. These measures, as also those referred to in
Article 5 below, shall be published in the official Gazette of
the State concerned and shall furthermore be the subject of a
communication to the Association Council.

Article 4

Each Associated State hereby declares its readiness
to abolish quantitative restrictions on imports and measures
having equivalent effect more rapidly than is provided for in
this Protocol, if its economic situation so permits.

Article 5

1.   Under the conditions set out in Article 6, paragraph 3
of the Convention, an Associated State may retain or introduce
quantitative restrictions on imports of goods originating in
Member States, subject to prior consultation within the Association Council and to the establishment of global quotas open without discrimination to goods originating in Member States.

2.   The Association Council shall hold the consultation
referred to in the foregoing paragraph not later than two months
after the date on which the Associated State requests authority
to adopt the measures referred to in the said paragraph.

If there has been no consultation within this time-limit,
the Associated State may adopt the measures which it has
requested.

PROTOCOL No. 5
concerning the administration
of the financial aids

THE HIGH CONTRACTING PARTIES HAVE AGREED upon the
following provisions which shall be annexed to the Convention:

Chapter I

Economic and social investments and technical assistance
connected with investments

Article 1

1.   For the financing of the measures referred to in Article
17, paragraph 1 of the Convention, the Governments of the Associated States shall establish, as far as possible within the framework of a development plan, basic economic and social schemes,
production schemes providing normal financial returns, and shall
prepare requests for technical assistance connected with investments.

2.   Nevertheless, the Community may, where necessary, set up technical assistance schemes connected with investments, with the consent and for the benefit of an Associated State.

Article 2

Schemes shall be financed by grants, by loans on special terms, by loans granted by the Bank possibly carrying rebates of interest, or by the simultaneous use of several of the above means.

Article 3

Schemes shall be submitted to the Community, addressed to the Commission. However, those schemes for which a loan is requested from the Bank shall be addressed to the Bank, either directly by the parties concerned, or through the Commission, or through the Associated State on whose territory the scheme is to be carried out.

Article 4

1.   Technical assistance connected with investments shall be financed by grants.

2.   Such assistance shall cover the following measures in particular:

- planning,
- special and regional development surveys,
- technical and economic surveys needed for the preparation of investment schemes,
- help in preparing files,
- help with the technical execution and supervision of work,
- temporary help in setting up, starting, and running a particular investment or plant,
- temporary responsibility for expenses in respect of the technicians and supplies needed to carry out an investment scheme efficiently.

Article 5

The competent authorities of the Associated States shall be responsible for carrying out the schemes submitted by their respective governments and financed by the Community.

Chapter II

Technical co-operation

Article 6

The financing of the measures referred to in Article 17, paragraph 2 of the Convention shall be effected either at the request of the Governments of Associated States, to be presented preferably within the context of programmes covering one or more years, or on a proposal of the Community.

Article 7

Measures taken by the Community in the field of technical co-operation shall be financed by grants.

Article 8

Requests from Associated States shall be submitted to the Community, addressed to the Commission.

Article 9

The Community's financial measures in the field of technical co-operation shall in particular include:

a) sending experts, advisers, technicians and instructors to Associated States, at the request of such States, for a definite task and a limited period;

b) supplying materials for experiments and demonstrations;

c) preparing surveys of the development and diversification prospects of the economies of Associated States, surveys of problems of interest to the associated countries as a whole, such as the preparation and distribution of standard plans for certain buildings or market surveys;

d) granting scholarships for the purpose of training staff, in the universities and specialized institutions of Associated States or, where this is not possible, of Member States;

e) vocational training by means of grants or training schemes in Associated States or, where this is not possible, in

Member States;

f)   organizing short training courses for nationals of Associated States;

g)   general information and documentation for the purpose of encouraging the economic and social development of the Associated States, the development of trade between these States and the Community, and the efficient attainment of the Fund's objectives.

Article 10

The Governments of the Associated States and, where appropriate, specialized institutions or other specialized bodies of Member States or Associated States, shall be responsible for carrying out the technical co-operation programmes submitted by the Governments.

Chapter III

Loans on special terms

Article 11

The loans on special terms referred to in Article 16 of the Convention shall be used for financing investment schemes of general interest to the recipient State insofar as the capacity of these schemes to show direct profits, as also the capacity of the State concerned to bear the debt at the time when the loan is granted, permit of such financing.

Article 12

Such loans may be granted for a maximum period of 40 years and may be exempted from amortization for a period of up to 10 years. They shall enjoy favourable terms of interest.

Article 13

The Community shall lay down the terms under which loans are to be granted and the procedures for effecting and recovering them.

Chapter IV

Loans by the European Investment Bank

Article 14

The examination by the Bank of the eligibility of schemes and the granting of loans to Associated States or to enterprises under their jurisdiction shall be carried out in accordance with the terms, conditions and procedures laid down by the Statutes of the Bank and shall take into consideration the capacity of the State concerned to bear the debt. The Bank shall finance only those schemes upon which the Associated State or States concerned have expressed a favourable opinion.

Article 15

The length of the amortization period for each loan shall be determined on the basis of the economic characteristics of the scheme to be financed; this period may not exceed 25 years.

Article 16

Loans may be used to meet import expenditure and local expenditure needed for carrying out approved investment schemes.

Article 17

Loans shall carry the same rate of interest as that employed by the Bank at the time when the loan is signed. At the request of the recipients loans may carry a rebate on interest under the terms of Article 19 of the Convention.

Article 18

The decision to grant rebates on interest shall be taken by the Community. The amount of the rebates shall be paid directly to the Bank.

Chapter V

Advances to stabilization funds

Article 19

423

For the purpose of financing the measures referred to in Article 17, paragraph 4 of the Convention, advances may be granted to stabilization funds existing or to be set up in the Associated States.

Article 20

Requests for advances shall be submitted to the Community, addressed to the Commission, by the Governments of the Associated States concerned. They shall be accompanied by a report prepared by the Board of Directors of the stabilization fund concerned.

Article 21

The Community shall determine the amount and the duration of advances. These advances shall be guaranteed by the Associated State concerned. Their normal term shall be that of the Convention.

Chapter VI

Aids for diversification and production

Article 22

The aids for production and diversification referred to in Article 17, paragraph 3 and Article 18, b) of the Convention shall be apportioned and used in accordance with the terms set out below.

Article 23

The purpose of aids for production shall be to assist producers of the Associated States in progressively adapting their production to the requirements of marketing at world prices.

The purpose of aids for diversification shall be to enable the Associated States to reform their structure and to achieve appropriate diversification in the fields of agriculture, industry and commerce.

Article 24

Aids for production and diversification shall be apportioned as follows:

1)   183 million units of account to aids for production and
        diversification to the following eleven Associated States:
        Cameroon, the Central African Republic, Chad, Congo
        (Brazzaville), Dahomey, the Ivory Coast, Madagascar,
        Mali, Niger, Senegal and Togo;

2)   32 million units of account to aids for diversification
        to the following four Associated States: Burundi, Congo
        (Leopoldville), Rwanda and Somalia;

3)   15 million units of account to aids for diversification
        to the following three Associated States: Gabon,
        Mauritania and Upper Volta.

Article 25

For the purpose of financing the measures set out in
Article 23 above, and within the limit of the amount allocated
to it under that Article, each Associated State shall within
three months after the Convention enters into force submit a
programme covering a period not longer than the duration of
the Convention, which shall provide either for aids for production and for diversification simultaneously, or for aids for
diversification only.

A. - States benefiting simultaneously from aids for diversification and production

Article 26

1.   For each of the eleven Associated States benefiting
simultaneously from aids for diversification and production,
the five-year share of the sum of 183 million units of account
to be used for establishing its programme shall be calculated
in relation to its exports of the following products: coffee,
groundnuts, groundnut oil, palm oil, dessicated coconut, cotton,
pepper, rice, sugar, gum arabic.

2.   On the basis of the provisions in the foregoing paragraph, the five-year share of each of these Associated States
shall be fixed as follows (in millions of units of account):

Cameroon   15. 8
Central African Republic   6. 8

425

Chad	5.7
Congo (Brazzaville)	6.4
Dahomey	5.5
Ivory Coast	46.7
Madagascar	31.6
Mali	5.6
Niger	6.5
Senegal	46.7
Togo	5.7

Article 27

Each Associated State receiving aids for production and aids for diversification simultaneously shall take the following principles into account when drawing up its five-year programme:

1. aids to production may not exceed three-quarters of the five-yearly amount granted by the Community to that Associated State under the combined heading of aids for production and diversification;

2. aids for production may be allocated by the Community to each Associated State from the first year of the Convention. They shall be on a decreasing scale from the date when the procedure begins, in respect of each product, which is to lead to marketing at world prices, so that the complete abolition of such aids may be reached not later than the end of the duration of the Convention;

3. each Associated State shall see to it that, out of the amount allocated under the heading of aids to production, the producers devote a suitable proportion to the structural improvement of cropping plans.

Article 28

The Community shall examine, together with each Associated State, whether that State's programme conforms to the principles laid down in Article 27 above. After this scrutiny and, where appropriate, after the programme has been adjusted, the Community shall note it and decide upon the amount of the first yearly instalment of its contribution.

Article 29

1.　　Immediately after the end of each year as from the date of entry into force of the Convention, the Community shall examine whether the aids for diversification and for production have been used during the past year in accordance with the purposes assigned for these aids, as laid down in the provisions of the Convention and of this Protocol.

2.　　This scrutiny shall bear particularly upon:

- the analysis, product by product, of the movement of world prices in relation to the prices used as a basis for calculating the share of each Associated State mentioned in Article 26;

- the comparison, product by product, of the levels of tonnage actually exported in relation to the levels used as a basis for determining the said share;

- the amount of aids allocated by other sources for the purpose of achieving the objectives set out in Article 23.

3.　　Following this scrutiny, and after making any necessary adjustment to the next yearly instalment of the programme laid down in Article 25, the Community shall give its final decision on the amount of the said instalment.

4.　　If, at the end of this scrutiny, the Community observes that the aid for production allocated to the Associated State concerned in respect of the past year has not been fully utilized, the Community shall, after consulting with that State, decide how the balance should be appropriated.

Article 30

1.　　The amount of the aid allocated to producers, as determined under the provisions of Articles 28 and 29 above, shall be paid in the form of grants to bodies approved by the Community and by the Associated States.

2.　　The yearly amount and the procedures for utilizing the aid allocated to each State for each branch of production shall be published by appropriate means within that Associated State.

Article 31

The amounts allocated under the heading of aids to production shall be utilized in accordance with the appropriations and procedures laid down by the Community after consultation with the Associated State concerned.

Such action as needs to be taken for the purpose of implementing the provisions of this Chapter shall be the responsibility of each Associated State to the extent that it is concerned therein.

The Community shall see to it that the prescription in the first sub-paragraph of this Article is observed and shall take any appropriate measures where necessary.

Article 32

For the purpose of implementing Articles 28 to 30 above, each Associated State shall annually submit a detailed report on the use of the sums received under the heading of aids to production. It shall attach all relevant documents and in particular reports from the approved bodies.

The Associated State shall co-operate in any inspection considered desirable by the Community, especially with regard to the said bodies.

Article 33

Sums which are assigned to aid for diversification by Associated States benefiting simultaneously from aids to production and aids to diversification, shall be used in accordance with the provisions of Articles 36 to 38.

B. - States benefiting from aids for diversification

Article 34

1.   The sums provided for under Article 24, paragraph 2, shall be apportioned as follows (in millions of units of account):

- Burundi   5.25
- Congo (Leopoldville)   15
- Rwanda   5.25
- Somalia   6.50

2.   The sums provided for under Article 24, paragraph 3, shall be apportioned as follows (in millions of units of account):

- Gabon   4
- Mauritania   5
- Upper Volta   6

Article 35

On the basis of the programme provided for in Article 25 above, the Community, together with each of the seven Associated States referred to in the foregoing Article, shall consider whether their respective proposals concerning the use of aids for diversification takes the objectives assigned to these aids into account.

Article 36

Schemes under aids for diversification shall be financed by grants, by loans on special terms, by loans granted by the Bank possibly with rebates of interest, or by the simultaneous use of several of the above means.

Article 37

Within the context of its programme, each Associated State shall submit requests to the Community for aids for diversification on the basis of definite schemes.

Article 38

The provisions of Chapters I, II, III and IV of this Protocol shall apply, as necessary, to the financing of schemes to aid diversification.

Chapter VII

Miscellaneous provisions

Article 39

With a view to permitting of swift intervention to provide emergency help from Fund resources to any Associated State stricken by natural disaster, a Reserve Fund shall be created, to be financed by a levy of 1% on that part of the grants which is included in the amount referred to in Article 18, a) of the Convention.

Article 40

Financing and administrative expenses arising out of the administration of the Fund shall be charged to the resources set aside for grants.

Article 41

Goods which have been imported into an Associated State under a supply contract financed by the Community shall not be counted in the quotas open to Member States.

Article 42

The Community and the Associated States shall collaborate in all measures necessary to ensure that the amounts assigned by the Community are utilized in accordance with the provisions of Article 26 of the Convention.

12.2 EUROPEAN DEVELOPMENT FUND

Financing Approved at 31 December 1963

Country or territory		Number of projects	Amount
		(in thousand units of account)	
Congo (Leopoldville)		14	14 631
Rwanda		10	4 844
Burundi		11	3 133
	Total	35	22 608
Algeria (incl. Sahara)		9	20 427
Cameroon		26	44 406
Central African Republic		24	14 225
Comoro Islands		6	2 636
Congo (Brazzaville)		16	15 785
Ivory Coast		18	33 387
French Somaliland		2	1 367
Dahomey		18	18 658
Gabon		14	13 336
Guadeloupe		4	4 399
French Guiana		1	2 005
Upper Volta		11	25 948
Madagascar		39	50 773
Mali		24	32 644
Martinique		3	4 622
Mauritania		10	12 336
Niger		6	24 731
New Caledonia		5	1 560
Polynesia		1	2 474
Reunion		4	5 328
Saint-Pierre-et-Miquelon		1	3 545
Senegal		19	34 606
Chad		17	24 956
Togo		17	13 408
Group of States (Joint projects)		2	5 132
	Total	297	412 694
Somalia		4	5 060
New Guinea		4	7 458
Surinam		4	11 194
	Grand Total	344	459 014

431

Actual Allocation or Commitment of Funds
as of December 31, 1963 by Sectors
(in millions of dollars)

Social Sectors	No. of Projects	Allocation
1) Education and Vocational Training	69	75.678
2) Health	48	39.230
3) Water Development	18	14.959
4) Urban Development	14	11.847
5) Studies and Research	26	13.730
6) Others, Miscellaneous	9	7.417
Total	184	162.861

Economic Sectors	No. of Projects	Allocation
1) Transportation and Communications	110	210.760
2) Agriculture and Animal Breeding	45	82.693
3) Studies and Research	5	2.700
Total	160	296.153
Grand Total	344	459.014

European Development Fund Contributions
Under Convention of Association
(in millions of dollars)

Country	Contribution	Percentage
Belgium	69.0	9.45
France	246.5	33.75
F.R. of Germany	246.5	33.75
Italy	100.0	13.7
Luxembourg	2.0	0.3
Netherlands	66.0	9.05
Total	730.0	100

Planned Allocation of European Development Fund
(in millions of dollars)

	Grants	Special Loans	Total
1. African Associated States	620	46	666
2. Dependent Countries and Territories	60	4	64
Total	680	50	730

Planned Allocation of European Investment Bank Loans
(in millions of dollars)

1. African Associated States	64
2. Dependent Countries and Territories	6
Total	70

1. Total Allocation to African Associated States	730
2. Total Allocation to Dependent Countries and Territories	70
Grand Total of Assistance	800

CHAPTER **13**

ADMINISTRATION

The EEC staff is drawn almost entirely from the member countries. Together with their colleagues in other European organizations they form the European civil service. The operation of the EEC and the conditions of work for its staff are governed by rules adopted by the member states.

The allocation of posts among the different nationalities is regulated by an informal gentleman's agreement, which in effect apportions jobs roughly in relation to the contributions made by the individual member states to EEC operating expenses. In Article 200, the EEC's Rome Treaty provides that France, Germany and Italy will each contribute 28% of the total, Belgium and the Netherlands 7.9% each, and Luxembourg 0.2%. Belgium provides the exception to the rule: As host country, it has supplied a large number of personnel for those posts customarily held by local citizens, such as secretarial and maintenance jobs. Thus of the 2453 EEC employees at the end of April 1963 there were: 586 Germans, 567 Belgians, 471 Italians, 485 French, 229 Dutch, 78 Luxembourgeois and 37 "others." (Less than 2% of EEC employees are from non-member countries. Frequently these persons are employed for special skills.)

The European civil servants are exempted from national taxes on their salaries and instead pay a European income tax direct to the Community itself. This tax ranges from 8 per cent on that portion of earnings between $16 and $238 per month to a top of 45 per cent on any portion over $1,014 per month. The tax rate and other rules governing the conditions of employment are established in the statute of service of the Community.

Commissioners of the European Economic Community enjoy diplomatic immunity, and under a protocol annexed to the Rome Treaty, other employees are immune from legal process for acts

434

performed by them in their official capacity. They are also exempt from provisions limiting immigration and from formalities for the registration of foreign persons.

The EEC budget (see documents) is voted by the Council each year. All resources are based on contributions by member states, but the Community is eventually to have independent sources of income.

Several European schools have been established for the children of Community employees. These multi-lingual schools provide a high quality education and have already graduated their first classes.

Cases Before the Court of the European Communities on Administration Matters

Chapter 14, Documents 14.3 and 14.4;
              Documents 14.2 case: 101/63.

13.1 PROTOCOL ON THE PRIVILEGES AND IMMUNITIES OF THE EUROPEAN ECONOMIC COMMUNITY

CHAPTER 1

PROPERTY, FUNDS, ASSETS AND TRANSACTIONS OF THE COMMUNITY

ARTICLE 1

The premises and buildings of the Community shall be inviolable. They shall be exempt from search, requisition, confiscation or expropriation. The property and assets of the Community may not be the subject of any administrative or legal measure of constraint without the authorisation of the Court of Justice.

ARTICLE 2

The archives of the Community shall be inviolable.

ARTICLE 3

The Community, its assets, income and other property shall be exempt from all direct taxes.

CHAPTER 2

COMMUNICATIONS AND TRAVEL DOCUMENTS

ARTICLE 5

For their official communications and the transfer of all their documents the institutions of the Community shall enjoy in the territory of each Member State the treatment granted by that State to diplomatic missions.

Official correspondence and other official communications of the institutions of the Community shall not be subject to censorship.

CHAPTER 3

MEMBERS OF THE ASSEMBLY

ARTICLE 7

No restrictions of an administrative or other nature shall be imposed on the free movement of members of the Assembly proceeding to or coming from the place of meeting of the Assembly.

ARTICLE 9

During the sessions of the Assembly, its members shall enjoy:

(a) in their national territory, the immunities accorded in their country to members of Parliament; and

(b) in the territory of all other Member States, exemption from any measure of detention and from any legal prosecution.

This immunity shall also apply when they are proceeding to and from the place of meeting of the Assembly.

Such immunity shall not, however, apply when members are found committing, attempting to commit or just having committed an offence, and shall not prevent the Assembly from exercising its right to waive the immunity of any of its members.

CHAPTER 4

REPRESENTATIVES OF MEMBER STATES TAKING PART IN THE WORK OF THE INSTITUTIONS OF THE COMMUNITY

ARTICLE 10

Representatives of Member States taking part in the work of the institutions of the Community, as well as their advisers and technical experts shall, during the exercise of their functions and during their travel to and from the place of meeting, be accorded the customary privileges, immunities and facilities.

This Article shall also apply to members of the consultative organs of the Community.

CHAPTER 5

OFFICIALS AND OTHER EMPLOYEES
OF THE COMMUNITY

ARTICLE 11

In the territory of each Member State and whatsoever their nationality, the officials and other employees of the Community as mentioned to in Article 212 of this Treaty:

(a) shall, subject to the provisions of Articles 179 and 215 of this Treaty, be immune from legal process for acts performed by them in their official capacity, including their words spoken or written; they shall continue to benefit from such immunity after their functions have ceased;

ARTICLE 12

Subject to the conditions and in accordance with the procedure laid down by the Council acting on proposals submitted by the Commission within a period of one year after the date of the entry into force of this Treaty, the officials and other employees of the Community shall be liable, for the benefit of the latter, to a tax on the salaries, wages and emoluments paid to them by it.

They shall be exempt from national taxes on salaries, wages or emoluments paid by the Community.

CHAPTER 6

PRIVILEGES AND IMMUNITIES
OF MISSIONS TO THE COMMUNITY

ARTICLE 16

The Member State in whose territory the Community has its seat shall grant the customary diplomatic immunities to the missions of third countries accredited to the Community.

13.2 BUDGET*

Draft budget for 1964

65.   At its session of 14 and 15 October 1963 the Council

approved the draft operational budget of the European Economic Community for 1964. In accordance with Article 203 of the Treaty, this draft has been referred to the European Parliament.

The draft budget provides for total expenditure of 61 441 993 units of account (1) broken down as follows:

Part I :	Parliament	2 211 797 u.a.
Part II :	Council	2 325 823 u.a.
Part III:	Commission	56 470 780 u.a.
Part IV:	Court of Justice	433 593 u.a.

As regards Part III: Commission, the amount of 56 470 780 u.a. includes:

a) Remuneration of members of the Commission and staff — 10 365 980 u.a.

b) Building, supplies and miscellaneous — 8 794 300 u.a.

c) Joint Services and European School in Brussels — 5 112 640 u.a.

d) European Social Fund (retraining and resettlement) — 23 197 860 u.a.

---

(1) One unit of account is equivalent to $1 US.

*Bulletin of the EEC, December 1963, pp. 46, 47.

CHAPTER **14**

JUDICIAL DECISIONS

The Court of Justice of the European Communities is
empowered to hear cases involving the following matters:

- failure of a member state to fulfill its obligations
- lawfulness of acts of the Council and Commission
- the interpretation of the Treaty
- the interpretation of acts of Community institutions and
  of subsidiary institutions established by the Council
- granting of compensation for damages resulting from
  an action by the Community
- disputes between the Community and its employees
- activities of the European Investment Bank
- arbitration involving the Community
- settlement of disputes between member states over
  the object of the Treaty

Under varying circumstances the following are authorized
to bring cases before the Court:

- member states
- Community institutions
- "any natural or legal person"
- courts or tribunals of member states (for interlocutory
  decisions)

Most of the early decisions by the Court in matters concerning the EEC dealt with disputes arising under Community policies
being placed in effect, e.g. the elimination of tariffs. The Court,
which also is competent under the Coal and Steel Community and
Euratom Treaties, is the most active of the standing international
Courts. Since its decisions are binding and the judges are independent, it is an important supranational element in the Community
system.

Cases Before the Court of the European Communities Relating to
Powers of the Court

Document 14.1 cases 16-17/62, 19-22/62, 31/62, 33/62.

List of Cases

14.1 Cases Decided
(Arranged in chronological order)   Refers to subject of Chapter

7/61	6
10/61	6
13/61	7
2/62, 3/62	6
16-17/62, 19-22/62	14
31/62, 33/62	14
26/62	6
28-30/62	6
24/62	6
25/62	6
34/62	6
13/63	6
27/62	6
73-74/63	6

14.2 Cases Pending
(In order submitted to Court)

22/63	6
90-91/63	6
75/63	8
92/63	8
101/63	13
103/63	9
106-7/63	9
1/64	6

14.3-14.4 Cases on Personnel Matters refer to subject of Chapter 13.

Case 7-61: Action against Italy concerning the suspension of imports of pigmeat (Article 31 (2))

With effect from 18 June 1960 the Italian Government suspended imports of certain pigmeat products, the liberalization of which had been bound vis-a-vis EEC Member States in conformity with Article 31 (2) of the Treaty. On 21 December the Commission, acting in pursuance of Article 169, sent the Italian Government a considered opinion calling attention to an infringement of the standstill provided for by Article 31 (1) of the Treaty and requesting that the situation be remedied. By letter of 5 January 1961 the Italian Government informed the Commission that it was obliged to continue the suspension of the imports in question and requested the Commission to authorize this action by virtue of the provision for safeguard measures in Article 226.

On 20 March 1961 the Commission referred the matter to the Court of Justice.

In its judgement of 19 December 1961 the Court rules that by temporarily suspending imports of the products in question from the Member States the Italian Government had defaulted upon its obligation under Article 31 (1) of the Treaty. In the grounds of the judgement it was stated that:

a) The standstill obligation in Article 31 is absolute and allows of no exception even of a temporary nature;

b) The very fact that an emergency procedure is provided for in Article 226 precludes any unilateral action on the part of the Member States, which therefore may not invoke the urgency or seriousness of the situation to circumvent the procedure laid down in Article 226;

c) That Article 36 has reference to circumstances of a non-economic nature unlikely to impair the principles laid down in Article 30 to 34 and that it does not establish a general safeguard clause additional to that of Article 226 and enabling the Member States unilaterally to waive the procedure and guarantees provided for in that Article;

d) That the Commission need give no ruling as to the application of Article 226 until expressly requested to do so by the Member State concerned.

This is the first judgement delivered by the Court of Justice in a case brought by the Commission against a Member State in pursuance of Article 169 of the Treaty.

Case 10-61: Customs duties imposed by Italy on radio tubes, valves and lamps from other Member States (Articles 12 and 14)

On 27 February 1962 the Court of Justice gave judgement in case 10-61, the Commission v. the Italian Government. The Court found that the Italian Government had defaulted upon its obligations under Article 12 and Article 14 (1) of the Treaty in applying, after the entry into force of the Treaty, the minimum specific duty of 150 lire on lamps, tubes and valves for radio sets, with a customs value of less than 428 lire, imported from other member countries, and by making this the basic duty for the calculation of the successive reductions vis-a-vis the other Member States.

The Court held in favour of the European Commission. In the grounds of the judgement the Court confirmed the following principles which are of general application:

a) The customs duties of which Article 12 of the Treaty forbids any increase and those which are to be taken as a basis for the successive reductions of duties between the Member States are those actually applied on 1 January 1958 and 1 January 1957 respectively. This being so, it is irrelevant whether an administrative act on which their application is based has been properly decided or not.

b) The rights and obligations flowing from conventions concluded prior to the entry into force of the Treaty between a Member State and a non-member country and which, in conformity with Article 234 (1) of the Treaty are not affected by the provisions of the Treaty, are the rights of non-member countries and the obligations of the Member State. On the other hand, the principle of international law according to which a State which undertakes a new obligation incompatible with the exercise of its rights under earlier treaties thereby renounces the exercise of these rights in so far as may be necessary to fulfill its new obligations, applies to the rights which Member States enjoy under such conventions.

Cases 13-61: Interpretation of Article 85 of the Treaty

On 30 June 1961, the Court of Appeal at The Hague referred to the Court of Justice of the Communities a point of interpretation of the Treaty (case 13-61). This was the first time that the procedure under Article 177 had been applied. The question was whether an agreement between firms was null and void under Article 85 (2) of the Treaty. This raises the point whether Article 85 (1) is directly applicable to firms immediately upon the entry into force of the Treaty.

In a judgement of 6 April 1962 (1) in the case 13/61 (2) the Court of Justice, accepting in part the conclusions of the Advocate General and of the Commission, gave the preliminary ruling requested by the Hague Court of Appeal on 30 June 1961.

The most important principles laid down in the grounds and in the operative clauses of the judgement are as follows:

i)   Article 85 of the Treaty has in principle been applicable since the entry into force of the Treaty;

ii)   However, since the transitional arrangements instituted by Articles 88 and 89 are not such as to ensure full implementation of Article 85, this Article did not become fully operative on the entry into force of the Treaty and did not, in particular, render all prohibited agreements null and void;

iii)   Consequently, during the period preceding the entry into force of Regulation No. 17 (3) only those agreements were automatically null and void which the Member States' authorities had expressly held, on the basis of Article 85 (1), not to qualify for the declaration mentioned in Article 85 (3), or which the Commission had ruled by decision taken under Article 89 (2) to be contrary to Article 85;

iv)   After the entry into force of Regulation No. 17, "old" agreements banned under Article 85 (1) but notified to the Commission by the appointed date in accordance with Article 5 of the Regulation are provisionally valid;

v)   A refusal by the Commission to issue a declaration under Article 85 (3) signifies that the agreements in question are null and void from the entry into force of the Regulation, unless the Commission decides, under Article 7 of the Regulation, to lift the prohibition, wholly or in part, following the adjustment or termination of the agreement within the proper time-limit;

vi)   "Old" agreements which are banned under Article 85 (1)
and which are notifiable before 1 August 1962 if it is desired to
obtain a declaration under Article 85 (3) are automatically null
and void from the entry into force of the Regulation unless notified
within the time-limit set.

Cases Nos. 2 and 3-62: Increased duties imposed by
Belgium and Luxembourg on honeybread ("pain d'epice")

On 24 February 1962 the European Commission referred
to the Court of Justice its dispute with the Governments of Belgium
and Luxembourg concerning a special import duty on honeybread
("pain d'epice") and similar products to the Court of Justice of
the Communities.

The Commission seeks a finding that by increasing, after
the Treaty came into force, the special duty charged when import
licences are issued for "pain d'epice" and by extending this duty
to products similar to "pain d'epice" (heading 19.08 of the common
external tariff) the two countries in question have failed in their
obligations under the Treaty.

The Commission is of the opinion that the special duty
in question constitutes a charge with effect equivalent to a
customs duty, and that the States concerned have therefore infringed Article 12 of the Treaty, which forbids Member States
to introduce between themselves any new customs duties on
importation or charges with equivalent effect or to increase such
duties or charges as they apply in their commercial relations
with each other.

After inviting the comments of the Belgian and Luxembourg
Governments the Commission on 2 October 1961 rendered a considered opinion that an infringement had been committed. The Belgian
and Luxembourg Governments asked the Commission to approve
the measure taken, invoking Article 226 of the Treaty, but they
did not conform with the opinion within the time-limit fixed by
the Commission. The Commission therefore referred the matter
to the Court of Justice as provided by Article 169 of the Treaty.

In a judgement delivered on 14 December 1962 (1) the
Court, accepting the submissions of the Commission and of the
Advocate General, held that increases subsequent to 1 January
1958 in the special duty charged on the issue of import licences
for "pain d'epice", and the extension of this duty to similar products listed under heading 19.08 of the common external tariff,

were contrary to the Treaty. These measures had been adopted by Belgium and Luxembourg after the Treaty came into force.

In the grounds of the judgement, the Court of Justice laid down the following principles:

a)   An application for derogation from the rules of the Treaty cannot retrospectively render the original infringement lawful;

b)   The procedure for derogation cannot inhibit the com-minatory procedure open to the Commission under Article 169 of the Treaty;

c)   Under the terms of Articles 9 and 12 of the Treaty, a charge having an effect equivalent to that of a customs duty, how-soever called and howsoever applied, may be considered a duty imposed unilaterally, either at the time of importation or sub-sequently, and being imposed specifically on a product imported from a Member State but not on a similar national product, it consequently has, by altering the price, the same effect upon the free circulation of goods as a customs duty.

Consolidated actions 16/62 and 17/62

Confederation nationale des producteurs de fruits et legumes, Federation nationale des producteurs de fruits, Federa-tion nationale des producteurs de legumes (registered trade asso-ciations, headquarters in Paris) and - Federation nationale des producteurs de raisins de table, Luxembourg, plaintiffs: Assemblee permanente des presidents de chambres d'agriculture, a public board with headquarters in Paris, intervenor, v. the Council.

Consolidated actions 19/62, 20/62, 21/62, 22/62

Federation nationale de la boucherie en gros et du commerce de gros des viandes, headquarters in Paris; Stichting voor Nederlandse Zelstandige Handel en Industrie headquarters in the Hague; Syndicat de la boucherie en gros de Paris, with headquarters in Paris; Zentralverband des Deutschen Getreide-, Futter und Dungemittelhandels o. V., headquarters in Bonn v. the Council.

In the first of these two consolidated actions, the plain-tiffs sued for annulment of Council Regulations No. 23, which established a common organization of the fruit and vegetable market(1), and particularly Article 9 thereof.

In the second consolidated action, the Court was asked to annul Article 2(1), second sentence, of Council Regulation No. 26, which made certain rules of competition applicable to production of and trade in farm products(1).

In a judgement delivered on 14 December 1962(2), the Court dismissed all the suits as inadmissible, since private individuals or corporations cannot, under the terms of Article 173 of the Treaty, sue for annulment of general regulations.

Consolidated actions 31/62 and 33/62

Milchwerke Heinz Wohrmann & Sohn KG, Wesel/Rhein, and Firm Alfons Lutticke GmbH, Germinghausen/Westphalia v. the Commission.

On 4 October and 9 October 1962 respectively the two plaintiffs filed pleas invoking Article 184 or alternatively Article 173. They asked the Court to quash or to declare inapplicable Article 3 of the Commission's 15 March 1961 decision fixing a countervailing charge on imports of whole milk powder into the Federal Republic of Germany pursuant to Article 46 of the Treaty(1) and to quash or declare non-applicable the Commission's 13 December 1961 decision extending the original decision(2).

On 14 December 1962(3), the Court, accepting the submissions of the Commission and of the Advocate General, dismissed the applications as inadmissible.

On the grounds of this decision, the Court laid down the following principles:

i)　　　Under Article 184 of the Treaty, a party may invoke the non-applicability of a Council or Commission regulation only incidentally in a dispute pending before the Court of Justice based on another clause of the Treaty.

ii)　　In a dispute pending before a court of a Member State, it is for that court alone, in accordance with Article 177 of the Treaty, to suspend proceedings and refer a question to the Court of Justice for a preliminary ruling.

Case 26/62

On 5 February 1963 the Court of Justice gave judgement

in the following case(1):

Request for interlocutory rulings submitted to the Court under paragraphs 1 (a) and 3 of Article 177 of the EEC Treaty by the "Tariefcommissie", a Netherlands administrative court.

In 1960 the Benelux countries brought their old customs tariff into line with the new "Brussels" customs nomenclature. The new duties resulting from this operation were brought into force in the Netherlands from 1 March 1960 in a law ratifying a Benelux customs agreement.

Re-classification in the new nomenclature led, for certain products, to duties higher than those in force on 1 January 1958 under the old tariff. Dutch importers raised with the revenue departments the question whether these duties could be applied to products imported from the Member States, arguing that this would constitute a violation of the customs standstill between Community Member States introduced by Article 12 of the EEC Treaty. The revenue department maintained that the duties in question were payable. The importers then took the case to the Tariefcommissie, a Netherlands administrative tribunal which is the final authority in these matters.

The revenue department contended before this tribunal that the importers could not rest their case in Article 12 of the EEC Treaty and that in any case the duty increases at issue did not in the circumstances constitute an infringement of the Article. Taking the view that this raised a problem of Treaty interpretation, the Tariefcommissie asked the Court of Justice under Article 177 to give an interlocutory ruling on the following points:

a)   Whether Member States' nationals, relying on Article 12 of the EEC Treaty, could claim individual rights which municipal courts must uphold, and, if this were so;

b)   Whether any increase in the customs duties applied prior to 1 January 1958 which resulted from the introduction of the Brussels customs nomenclature in 1960 constituted an infringement of the standstill.

In accordance with its Statute, the Court of Justice transmitted the files of the case to the Commission and to the Member States' Government for their comments.

On various grounds, the Belgian, Dutch and German Governments and the Advocate-General, M. Roemer, maintained either that the Court was not competent to rule on a matter governed entirely by the municipal law of the Member States, or that Article 12 of the Treaty was without effect in municipal law. The other Governments made no comment.

On 31 October 1962 the Commission, in written and verbal submissions, argued, firstly, that the Court of Justice was competent to rule on the effect of Article 12 in municipal law, which effect could only be inferred from an interpretation of the EEC Treaty, and, secondly, that Article 12 conferred individual rights, which could therefore be vindicated in domestic courts.

In its judgment, the Court broadly accepted the Commission's submissions and gave the following ruling:

a)   "Article 12 of the Treaty establishing the European Economic Community has direct effects and creates individual rights for those affected that must be upheld by the domestic courts;

b)   In deciding whether customs duties or charges with equivalent effect have been increased contrary to Article 12 of the Treaty, the factor to be considered is the duties and charges actually applied by the Member State concerned at the date of entry into force of the Treaty.

Such an increase may equally well arise from a new arrangement of the customs tariff placing a product under a heading subject to a higher duty as it may from an actual increase in the rate of duty applied."

This ruling and the grounds stated are of considerable importance in defining the essence and effect of Community law.

Consolidated cases 28, 29 and 30/62 (Netherlands firms v. the Netherlands Revenue Department)

On 27 March 1963 the Court of Justice gave judgment in consolidated cases 28, 29 and 30/62, in which the Tariefcommissie, the Netherlands Supreme Administrative Tribunal, had applied to the Court for interlocutory rulings in its dispute with certain Netherlands firms(1).

The applicants had asked the Court whether Article 12 of the Treaty, introducing a customs standstill between the Member States, was directly effective in member countries and, if so, whether the Netherlands Revenue Department had not unlawfully increased the import duties on products purchased by the applicants. On 5 February last the Court had ruled on identical questions raised in a similar case (Case 26/62) (2).

The Commission contended that by virtue of the judgement cited the applications in these three cases had become nugatory. This argument was not entirely accepted. The Court agreed that, although national courts from whose decisions no appeal lay in domestic law - and therefore the Tariefcommissie - were obliged by the second paragraph of Article 177 to refer to it any question of interpretation raised before them, the authority of a previous interpretation by the Court could remove the ground for such obligation. This was true in particular, when the question raised was substantially identical with one on which an interlocutory ruling had already been given in an analogous case. But it was equally true that by the second paragraph of Article 177 national courts could always refer points of interpretation to the Court at their discretion. The Court was therefore obliged to give a ruling on the present applications.

On the substance the Court found that the questions of interpretation arising in these cases were identical to those already settled by judgement 26/62 and that no new factor had emerged. As was to be expected, the Court simply referred the Tariefcommissie to the judgement cited, stating that there were no grounds for any new interpretation of Article 12.

Case 24/62 - Federal Republic of Germany v. the Commission

Invoking Article 25(3) of the Treaty and a Commission declaration included in the Final Act of the agreement of 2 March 1962 establishing a part of the common external tariff covering products in List G of Annex I of the Treaty, the Federal Republic of Germany had applied to the Commission for a 1962 tariff quota of 450 000 hl. of distilling wines. By a decision of 11 May 1962 (1) the Commission granted a quota of 100 000 hl. only. In this appeal the Federal Republic of Germany asked the Court to quash the decision in so far as the Commission refused the application.

At a public hearing on 22 March 1963, the Advocate
General moved for the annulment of the decision.

On 4 July 1963 the Court of Justice quashed the EEC
Commission's decision of 11 May 1962, published in the official
gazette of the European Communities of 9 June 1962, granting
to the Federal Republic of Germany a tariff quota for distilling
wines. According to the Court's findings, the grounds for this
decision were insufficient, imprecise and contradictory and,
consequently, contrary to Article 190 which lays down that the
Commission's decisions shall be supported by reasons.

Nevertheless the Court did not find that the Commission
had violated the principles which govern the application of
Article 25(3). On the contrary, in its judgement, the Court of
Justice confirmed several principles on which the Commission
had based itself until now in applying Article 25, but which had
not yet been recognized by all the Member States.

Case 25/62 - Firma Plaumann & Co., Hamburg v. the
Commission

Invoking Article 25(3) of the Treaty, the Federal Republic
of Germany had applied for permission to suspend in part customs
duties on clementines during 1962 or alternatively to open a tariff
quota for this item. The Commission dismissed this application
in a decision of 22 May 1962.

In an appeal dated 27 July 1962, Plaumann & Co. asked
the Court to quash this decision and to declare that the Commission must either authorize the Federal Republic of Germany
to suspend the duties or open the quota applied for, or that it
must take a new decision on the German application. The applicant also asked the Court to rule that the Commission must
compensate Firma Plaumann & Co. for losses it would incur
through the Commission's refusal to grant the application.

On 27 August 1962 the Commission requested the Court
to give a preliminary ruling on the admissibility of this appeal
and to rule it inadmissible. On 24 October 1962 the Court
decided to combine the question of admissibility with the merits
of the case.

The applicant twice asked the Court to issue a summary
injunction to the Commission to authorize the Federal Republic
of Germany to suspend provisionally, against the deposit of a

surety, the additional part of the customs duty on clementines resulting from the Commission's negative decision of 22 May 1962.

By decisions of 31 August and 21 December 1962, the President of the Court dismissed the applications(1).

On 15 July 1963 the Court rejected as inadmissible this suit for annulment of the Commission's decision, S III 03079 of 22 May 1962, withholding authorization for the Federal Republic of Germany temporarily to reduce the customs duties on fresh tangerines and clementines imported from outside the Community.

Further, by this judgement the Court rejected the applicant's claim for damages as unfounded.

The Commission dismissed this application in a decision dated 3 May 1962. The plaintiff appealed to the Court on 10 September 1962 to quash the Commission's decision.

The Commission asked the Court on 2 October 1962 to give a preliminary ruling on the admissibility of this appeal and to rule it inadmissible.

On 16 December 1962 the Court decided to combine the question of admissibility with the merits of the case.

By decision of 9 October 1963, the Court of Justice of the European Communities struck out Case 27/62(1). "Warenwein der Hamburger Borse e.V." and "Firma Heinrich Bruening" v. the Commission of the European Economic Community.

Cases 73/63 and 74/63

In the cases "N.V. Internationale Crediet- en Handelsvereniging 'Rotterdam' " (registered office at Rotterdam) and "Cooperatieve Suikerfabriek en Raffinaderij G.A. 'Puttershoek'" (registered office at Puttershoek) v. the Netherlands Minister of Agriculture and Fisheries at The Hague, the College van Beroep voor het Bedrijfsleven(a tribunal of economic administration), by decisions of 10 July 1963 entered in the records on 11 July 1963, referred the following questions to the Court of Justice of the European Communities for interlocutory rulings:

1.   Does the decision of the Commission of the European

Economic Community of 27 July 1960, extended 21 December 1960, renewed 28 June 1961 and amended 27 February 1962, authorizing the Federal Republic of Germany to take safeguard measures with respect to imports from the other Member States of bread and fondant paste into the Federal Republic of Germany, empower the Netherlands Government to impose a tax on the export of fondant paste to the Federal Republic of Germany?

2.   If the reply to question 1 above is in the afirmative:

a)   Was the Commission competent, under Article 226 of the Treaty establishing the EEC, to give the Netherlands Government authority to take such action without being requested to do so by that Government?

     If the reply to this question is in the negative:

b)   Is the decision null and void in so far as it relates to such authorization?

3.   If the replies to question 2 a) and b) do not establish the nullity of the decision:

a)   Do the difficulties referred to in Article 226 (1) of the Treaty include difficulties caused solely by the application of mandatory provisions of the Treaty, and in particular by the provisions concerning abolition of internal tariffs?

     and, if so,

b)   Does that imply that the decision is null and void in so far as it confers upon the Netherlands Government the authority mentioned above? It is necessary to adduce further grounds for nullity of the decision, arising from an infringement of European Community law, and in particular from the fact, alleged by the plaintiffs, that the Commission had recourse to the procedure of Article 226 of the Treaty in order to avoid following the procedure provided for in Article 235?

     Case 34/62 - Federal Republic of Germany v. the Commission

     Invoking Article 25(3) of the Treaty, the Federal Republic of Germany had applied to the Commission for permission to suspend duties on oranges during 1962 at the level of 10% or alternatively to open a tariff quota at 10% for this item.

By a decision of 30 July 1962 the Commission rejected this application.

In an appeal dated 19 October 1962, the Federal Republic of Germany sued for the annulment of the Commission's decision.

On 15 July 1963 the Court rejected as unfounded this suit for annulment of the Commission's decision, III/COM (62) 219 final, of 30 July 1962, withholding authorization for the Federal Republic of Germany temporarily to reduce the customs duties on fresh sweet oranges imported from outside the Community.

Case 13/63 - Italian Republic v. the Commission

On 19 December 1962, the French Republic applied to the Commission for authorization to take safeguard measures under Article 226 of the Treaty to protect its refrigerator production. By a decision of 17 January 1962 (2) the Commission authorized the French Republic to impose a special degressive charge until 31 July 1963 on imports of household refrigerators and components thereof from Italy, unless Italy applied this charge on exports. The Italian Republic appealed against this decision on 18 February 1963.

On 17 July 1963 the Court rejected as unfounded the appeal by the Government of the Italian Republic against the Commission's decision of 17 January 1963 (official gazette of the European Communities, No. 23, 13 February 1963) authorizing the French Republic to levy a special charge on electric domestic refrigerators from Italy, as well as on sealed motor compressor units for electric domestic refrigerators and other components, unless the Italian Republic applied this charge on exportation. The charge was to be tapered down over a period and cease on 31 July 1963.

On 18 February 1964 the Court gave judgement in consolidated actions 73/63 and 74/63. The Court had been asked for preliminary rulings by the College van Beroep voor Bedrijfsleven (the Dutch appeal tribunal for trade and in industry), under Article 177 of the Treaty, on the interpretation of Article 226.

The Court's judgement was as follows:

1.   The Commission decisions at issue, laying down safeguard measures for imports into the Federal Republic of Germany of bread and fondant paste from other Member States, confer upon

the Government of the Kingdom of the Netherlands the power
to levy a charge of the same amount on exports of these
products to the Federal Republic of Germany.

2.   An examination of the issues presented to the Court has
revealed nothing that could affect the validity of the said decisions.

In the grounds for its judgement the Court stated that
although the decisions contained no explicit authorization they
nevertheless implied that the Dutch Government might levy the
charge in question.   In applying Article 226 the Commission
should employ such means as would have the least possible
impact on the State in which a given sector of the economy was
affected by the measures authorized.   The Court added that
Article 226 made no distinction between difficulties resulting or
not resulting from the application of the Treaty.

14.2 CASES PENDING (IN ORDER SUBMITTED TO COURT)

Case 22/63

On 29 April 1963 the EEC Commission brought before
the Court of Justice an action against the Government of the
Italian Republic.   The dispute concerns an increase in the levy
on imports into Italy of cotton and cotton waste, whether originating in a Member State or a non-member country, and had been in
free circulation in one of the Member States. By a ministerial
decree of 3 April 1958, which came into force on 27 November
1958, the charge on cotton was increased from Lit. 0.50/kg to
Lit 1.30/kg.

In the Commission's opinion this is a charge with effect
equivalent to a customs duty within the meaning of Article 12 of
the EEC Treaty, which forbids any increase in customs duties
or charges with equivalent effect in intra-Community trade.

The Italian Government has stated that it is unable to
consider the impost in question as a charge with effect equivalent to a customs duty because, in view of the very modest national
production, it has no protective effect, because all the proceeds
go to the Italian Cotton Institute, and it is therefore not of a fiscal
nature, and also because it represents the counterpart of a service.

The Italian Government has furthermore asked that this

charge should be counted as being among aids to promote the economic development of certain regions for which special provision is made (Article 92, 3 a).

The Commission does not feel that these arguments justify any change in the standpoint it adopted in the considered opinion addressed to the Italian Government. It feels that the objections raised by the Italian Government in no way modify either the fiscal nature of the charge in question - since it is imposed by the public authorities - or the fact that it is equivalent in effect to a customs duty since it applies to cotton imported into Italy from member countries but not to home-grown cotton and since the amount is added to the cost of imported cotton.

As for the application of Article 92, the granting of aid by introducing or increasing a customs duty or a charge with equivalent effect is not considered permissible.

As the Italian Government has declared itself unable to accept the Commission's opinion, the Commission has applied to the Court of Justice in order to obtain a definition of the scope of the obligations which the Treaty imposes on the Italian Republic in this matter.

Cases 90/63 and 91/63

The Commission of the EEC has referred to the Court of Justice its dispute with the Kingdom of Belgium and the Grand Duchy of Luxembourg regarding the introduction, after 1 January 1958, of a special charge on the issue of licences to import certain dairy produce, viz. milk powder, sweetened condensed milk in tins, hard and medium-hard cheeses, processed cheeses, blue-veined cheeses and soft cheeses.

The special charge in respect of some of these products was instituted in Belgium by Royal Decree dated 3 November 1958, and in Luxembourg by Grand-ducal Decree dated 17 November 1958. Subsequently, it was extended to certain other kinds of cheese, and various changes took place in the rates actually imposed; at the moment they are Bfrs. 10 per kiliogramme for cheeses of the Emmentaler type and for hard or medium-hard cheeses, Bfrs. 7.25 for processed cheeses and nil for Sapsago cheese. For milk in solid form, the rate is based on the lactose content, and is reckoned at Bfrs. 16 per kilogramme of lactose in 100 kg. of whole milk solid and unsweetened.

The Commission considers that this is a case of introduction of charges equivalent in effect to customs duties contrary
to Article 12 of the Treaty.

The respondents deny that the special charges are of
this nature. Further, they submit that Article 12 of the Treaty
does not prohibit the imposition of a charge with an effect equivalent to a customs duty if this charge replaces an obstacle to
the free circulation of goods, that is to say a quota, which has
been removed before the appointed date. Finally, they contend
that Article 12 of the Treaty can be waived when, as in the present case, it is a matter of protecting a national market organization which, but for this special charge, would be dismantled
during the period of transition before it could be replaced by a
common organization of the market as provided for by the agricultural policy of the Community.

In judging the nature of the special charges in dispute,
the Commission relies on the definition of a charge with an
effect equivalent to a customs duty given in the Decision of
the Court of 14 December 1962. The Commission considers
the other arguments of the respondents groundless in fact,
inasmuch as, at the time the Treaty came into force, all the
products concerned were liberalized and bound, and were not
subject to a national market organization.

In law the Commission holds that Article 12 of the Treaty
prescribes an unqualified standstill; in other words, this Article
would continue to be applicable even in a case where charges
with an effect equivalent to a customs duty were introduced in
order to replace a quota.

Finally, the Commission is of the opinion that even if it
were established that a national market organization existed on
1 January 1958, this in no way detracts from the obligation imposed by Article 12 of the Treaty.

Case 75/63
_____

By letter dated 12 July 1963, filed with the Clerk of the
Court on 15 July 1963, the Deputy President of the Centrale Raad
van Beroep at Utrecht (final court of appeal in matters of social
insurance in the Netherlands), in the appeal lodged by Mme K. H.
Hoekstra (nee Unger) of Amsterdam against the management of
the Bedrijfsvereniging voor Detailhandel en Ambachten at Utrecht,
requested the Court of Justice of the European Communities to

give an interlocutory interpretation of EEC Council Regulation
No. 3 (official gazette of the European Communities, 16 Dec-
ember 1958, page 581/58), made pursuant to Article 51 of the
Treaty establishing the EEC.

The question submitted by the Netherlands Tribunal
is as follows: "How should the Treaty, the enactments made
thereunder, and especially the regulation mentioned above, be
interpreted? In particular, is the concept 'employed person or
person treated as such' taken to be authoritatively defined by
the municipal law of the Member States, or is it defined by a
supranational provision? If the latter is the case, what is this
definition, in so far as knowledge thereof is necessary to judge
whether the first paragraph of Article 19 of the above mentioned
Council Regulation prohibits withholding payment of medical
expenses to a person in the situation in which the Tribunal has
classified the appellant?"

Case 92/63

The Court has received another request for a preliminary ruling submitted in pursuance of Article 177 of the Treaty.
This is case 92/63 and has reference to the action brought by
Mme M. Th. Nonnenmacher against Bestuur van de Sociale-
verzekeringsbank on 17 October 1963. As in case 75/63 (1), the
request is for interpretation of a clause in Council Regulation
No. 3 of 25 September 1958 concerning the social security of
migrant workers(2).

Case 101/63

By registered letter of 25 November 1963 the Court of
Justice notified the EEC Commission of an application for an
interlocutory ruling submitted to it on 29 May 1963 by the
Tribunal d'arrondissement of Luxembourg in pursuance of
Article 177 of the EEC Treaty and Article 150 of the Euratom
Treaty.

In this case (No. 101/63 - M. A. Wagner-Jung v. M. J.
Fohrmann and M. R. Krier), the question submitted to the court
concerns the interpretation of Articles 8 and 9 of the Protocol on the
Privileges and Immunities of EEC, ECSC and Euratom. The object
is to determine the extent of the Parliamentary immunity of the two
last-named persons(1).

Case 103/63

On 29 November 1963 three German internal waterway transport firms filed a complaint against the Commission under Article 175 of the Treaty, alleging failure of the Commission to take proceedings under Article 169 against the Federal Republic of Germany infringing Article 7 (2) of Regulation No. 19 in fixing the derived intervention prices for cereals too low in certain marketing centres(1).

Cases 106/63 and 107/63 (1)

On 18 December 1963 two German firms (Alfred C. Toepfer, Hamburg, and Getreide- Import GmbH, Duisburg) filed appeals seeking the nullification of the EEC Commission's decision of 3 October 1963 authorizing the Federal Republic of Germany to maintain safeguard measures for imports of maize, millet and sorghum(2). The Commission's decision was based on Article 22 of Council Regulation No. 19 establishing a common organization of the market in cereals. This lays down that the Commission shall decide whether safeguard measures taken by a Member State whose market is suffering from or threatened by serious disturbance should be maintained, amended or abolished.

Case 1/64(3)

On 13 January 1964 Glucoseries reunies SA, a Belgian firm producing glucose and dextrose, filed an appeal seeking the nullification of the EEC Commission's decision of 28 November 1963 authorizing France to impose countervailing charges on imports of glucose (dextrose from certain Member States(4). The Commission decision attacked was taken pursuant to the Council decision of 4 April 1962 (itself based on Article 235 of the Treaty) authorizing Member States, with the approval of the Commission, to impose a countervailing charge - under certain conditions and provided the exporting State makes no charge - on imports of certain processed agricultural products.

14.3 CASES DECIDED - PERSONNEL MATTERS (ARRANGED IN CHRONOLOGICAL ORDER)

Cases 43/59, 44/59, 45/59

On 15 July 1960 the Court of Justice pronounced its first

judgement on decisions of the Commission of the European Economic Community. The judgement concerned three joint complaints brought against the Commission by employees appealing for the annulment of a decision to terminate their services and for an award of damages. In its judgement the Court established principles applicable to the nature of the recruitment of staff by the Institutions of the Community before the entry into force of the Statute of service for officials of the Community provided for in Article 212 of the Treaty.

In application of these principles, the Court rejected the claims that the dismissal decision should be declared null and void. But it noted that no proper statement of the reasons for dismissal had been made, and awarded each plaintiff Bfrs. 60 000 as damages.

Case 48/59

In a fourth case the Court delivered a judgement on 16 December 1960 confirming the law which is derived from the previous judgement. In this case it also rejected a complaint of abuse of power put forward by the plaintiff against the dismissal decision.

Taking into account the plaintiff's age and family responsibilities the Court fixed compensation at Bfrs. 100 000.

Cases 12-61 and 15-61: Complaints of the staff of the Communities against the administration

On 14 December 1961 the Court of Justice dismissed a suit for damages brought by an official of the Secretariat of the Councils, who had been compelled to resign, so he claimed, by "moral pressure".

In another case brought by a staff member against the Secretariat of the European Parliament, the Court gave judgement on 1 March 1962 holding that the dismissal at the end of the probationary period was wrongful and awarding damages to the plaintiff.

14.4 CASES PENDING - PERSONNEL MATTERS

331.   Case 32/62: M. Maurice Alvis v. the Council

On 27 September 1962, M. Alvis, who had been employed

under contract as an auxiliary by the Secretary-General of the Councils, appealed to the Court of Justice under Article 179 of the Treaty inter alia to quash the Council's decision of 8 August 1962 terminating M. Alvis's contract by dismissal.

In his submissions at the hearing of 26 March 1963, the Advocate General moved the Court to dismiss the appeal.

Case 15/63: M. Claude Lassalle v. the European Parliament

On 28 February 1963, M. Lassalle, an official of the European Parliament, appealed to the Court of Justice to cancel Vacancy Notice No. 44, dated 1 February 1963, issued by the Secretariat of the European Parliament, and to award damages against the Parliament.

In an injunction of 13 March 1963(1), the President of the Court ordered that the European Parliament take no steps to fill the vacancy in question until the main issue had been decided.

Expeditiekantoor v/h Jacob Meyer; 30/62 - Hoechst-Holland N. V. v. Netherlands revenue department.

In the first case and in the consolidated actions the Tariefcommissie, a Netherlands administrative tribunal of final appeal referred to the Court of Justice two interlocutory questions on the interpretation of Article 12 of the Treaty.

In a judgement delivered on 27 March 1963, the Court of Justice, accepting in the main the submissions of the Advocate General agreed that the two questions of interpretation raised by the Tariefcommissie in consolidated actions 28/62, 29/62 and 30/62 were identical with these previously settled. Consequently it declared that there was no reason for a fresh interpretation of Article 12, although Article 177 of the Treaty did in fact empower a national tribunal to refer to the Court questions the latter had already answered.

With regard to the Statute of the Service of Community staff, twelve disputes were before the Court of Justice on 30 October 1963. Two cases (Case 27/63 Raponi v. EEC Commission, filed 15 May 1963 - Case 71/63 Mastropasqua v. EEC Commission, filed 1 July 1963) are suits by officials of the Community for cancellation of decisions promoting other candidates to the posts in question. Three cases (Cases 20 and 21/63, K. Maudet v. EEC Commission, filed 2 April 1963 - Case 79/63, J. Reynier

v. EEC Commission, and case 82/63 P. Erba v. EEC Commission, both filed 29 July 1963) are suits for cancellation of decisions regarding establishment of the applicants. Finally, seven cases (Case 18/63 Mme Schmity v. EEC Commission, filed 20 March 1963 - Case 26/63 P. Pistoj v. EEC Commission, filed 13 May 1963 - Case 72/63 F. E. Bering v. EEC Commission, filed 1 July 1963 - Case 77/63 Mme Heiers v. EEC Commission, 29 July 1963 - Case 78/63 Hubert v. EEC Commission, 29 July 1963 - Case 80/63 R. Degreef v. EEC Commission, 29 July 1963 - Case 81/63 J. Barnhorn v. EEC Commission, 29 July 1963), are complaints against the establishment procedure followed with regard to the applicants or decisions to terminate their appointments.

In (Cases 94 - 96/63 P. Bernusset, 95/63 P. Pistoj, 97/63 L. De Pascale), filed on 28 October 1963, the applicants are suing for annulment of Commission decisions appointing to vacant posts persons other than themselves.

Case 109 (63(1)

On 16 December 1963 another suit was filed against the EEC Commission by one of its officials, M. Charles Muller, who contests the Commission's refusal to establish him in the grade to which he considers he is entitled.

Footnotes for Chapter 14
Document 14. 1
   Case 13-61

(1) See official gazette of the European Communities, No. 33,
   4 May 1962.

(2) See Fifth General Report, sec. 255.

(3) See official gazette of the European Communities, No. 13,
   21 February 1962.

(1) See official gazette of the European Communities, No. 8,
   21 January 1963.

   Consolidated actions 19/62, 20/62, 21/62, 22/62

(1) See official gazette of the European Communities, No. 30,
   20 April 1962.

(2) See official gazette of the European Communities, No. 8,
   21 January 1963.

   Consolidated actions 31/62 and 32/62

(1) See official gazette of the European Communities, No. 26,
   13 April 1961.

(2) See official gazette of the European Communities, No. 7,
   27 January 1962.

(3) See official gazette of the European Communities, No. 8,
   21 January 1963.

   Case 26/62

(1) See official gazette of the European Communities, No. 32,
   4 March 1963.

   Consolidated cases 28, 29 and 30/62

(1) See official gazette of the European Communities, No. 63,
   20 April 1963.

(2) See Bulletin No. 4-62, Chap. IV and official gazette of
   4 March 1963.

Case 27/62

(1) See Bulletin No. 12-62, Chap. VI, C.

Document 14.2
Case 92/63

(1) See Bulletin No. 12-63, Chap. IV, C.

(2) See official gazette of the European Communities, No. 30, 16 December 1958.

Case 101/63

(1) See official gazette of the European Communities, No. 3, 13 January 1964.

Cases 106/63 and 107/63

(1) See official gazette of the European Communities, No. 16, 30 January 1964.

(2) Decision published in the official gazette of the European Communities, No. 146, 11 November 1963.

Case 1/64

(3) See official gazette of the European Communities, No. 21, 5 February 1964.

(4) Decision published in the official gazette of the European Communities, No. 183, 13 December 1963.

Document 14.4
Case 15/63

(1) See official gazette of the European Communities, No. 49, 27 March 1963.

CHAPTER 15

BIBLIOGRAPHY

     This bibliography includes a complete listing of official documents of the EEC which are available to the public. They may be purchased from the European Community Information Service. Mimeographed documents, not listed here, are occasionally made available to the public in limited quantities.

     Publications are listed here by institution and, within such categories, by groups of documents or by major subjects. The Journal Officiel(Official Gazette)is listed separately since it covers the activities of all institutions in all three European Communities.

     The abbreviations after each title indicate the languages in which the documents have been published, viz. d-German, f-French, i-Italian, n-Dutch, e-English, s-Spanish, e. g. (d-f-i-n) indicates that there are separate editions available in German, French, Italian and Dutch. The same abbreviations, but separated by oblique strokes instead of dashes, are used for bilingual and multilingual publications, e. g. (d/f), (i/n) indicates that two bilingual editions are available one in German and French and the other in Italian and Dutch;d/f/i/n indicates a single volume containing the text in all four official languages.

     Official Gazette of the European Communities

Official Gazette of the European Communities publishes inter alia

     (d-f-i-n)

-      the timetable of the sessions and meeting of the E. E. C. and the Euratom Commissions;

- the minutes of the sittings of the European Parliament, written questions and replies;

- the decisions and agreements of the Council of Ministers;

- the appeals brought before the Court of Justice and subsequent proceedings and judgements;

- the regulations, decisions, agreements, opinions and other official acts, and the budget estimates and accounts, of the three Communities;

- miscellaneous other information and announcements of competitive examinations for appointments.

With special reference to E.C.S.C.:

- the General Objectives of the High Authority, its quarterly programmes based on forecasts and lists of opinions on investment projects; details of financial grants;

With special reference to E.E.C.:

- Quarterly Reports on the economic situation in the Community; financial agreements; tenders invited and contracts awarded; projects for economic and social investments by the Development Fund for the overseas countries and territories; decisions of the Administrative Committee for the Social Security of Migrant Workers and of the Committee of European Social Fund.

With special reference to Euratom:

- Tenders invited and contracts awarded; research programmes; agreements.

The Supplement agricole (Agricultural Supplement) to the Journal officiel publishes the tables annexed to the E.E.C. Commission's decisions fixing the c.i.f. prices, the premiums added to the levies, the c.i.f. prices for forward purchases and the free-to-frontier prices for cereals.

466

General Publications

Treaties of Rome
Edition containing the text of the Treaties of Rome in
four languages in parallel columns
472 pp. (d/f/i/n)

Rules of Procedure of the European Parliament
64 pp. (d-f-i-n)

Official Documents

(d-f-i-n)

- a) Debates

  This series includes:
  Verbatim record and Index of contributions to proceedings, classified by names of Members, and an
  annual Index of contributions to proceedings, classified by subjects

- b) Committee Reports - Working Papers

  This series includes:
  Reports by Parliamentary Committees,
  proposals for resolutions,
  consultations

- c) Minutes of sittings

  (published in Official Gazette
  (of the European Communities
- d) Written questions and replies

Periodical Publications and Bibliographical Bulletins

- a) Yearbooks of the European Parliament

  Yearbook 1959-1960, 1960-1961, 1961-1962, 1962-1963
  528 pp. (d-f-i-n)

- b) Monthly bulletins on European documentation
  (d-f-i-n-e)

-   c) Quarterly bibliographical notes

-   d) Catalogue "The Common Market"
    1961-1962 Edition (5 volumes)
    List of all publications dealing with the Common
    Market available for consultation in the library of the
    European Parliament.

Miscellaneous Publications

-   a) Joint Sessions of the Members of the Consultative
    Assembly of the Council of Europe and the Members
    of the European Parliament (annual sessions)

    Verbatim record of debates
    (d-f-i-n-e)

    Last joint session:
    September 17-18, 1963

-   b) Conference of the European Parliament with the
    Parliaments of African States and Madagascar

    Verbatim record of sittings
    June 19-24, 1961

-   c) Election of the European Parliament by direct uni-
    versal suffrage

    Report by Messrs. Battista, Dehousse, Faure, Schuijt
    and Metzger
    October 1960, 80 pp. (d-f-i-n)

    Court of Justice of the European Communities

-   Compendia of Community Case Law
    Vols I-X, 1954-1964

    Compendium of texts on the organization, competencies
    and procedure of the Court, with analytical index

    Approx. 330 pp. (d-f-i-n)

    Legal commentary on European integration - legal
    bibliography (1 volume (f))
    offset

October 1962, 444 pp.

Supplements for 1963, 1964

European Economic Community

Basic Documents, Progress Reports, General Publications

Basic Documents

Treaty establishing the European Economic Community and Connected Documents
1962, 354 pp. (Unofficial English version)

Traite instituant la Communaute economique europeenne et documents annexes
Fevrier 1957, 354 pp. (d-f-i-n)

Progress Reports

First General Report on the Activities of the Community
(1 January 1958 to 17 September 1958)
September 1958, 143 p. (d-i-n; f-e: out of print)

Second General Report on the Activities of the Community (18 September 1958 to 20 March 1959)
March 1959, 149 pp. (d-f-i-n;e: out of print)

Third General Report on the Activities of the Community (21 March 1959 to 15 May 1960)
May 1960, 255 pp. (d-i-n;f-e: out of print)

Fourth General Report on the Activities of the Community (16 May 1960 to 30 April 1961)
May 1961, 269 pp. (f-d-i;n-e: out of print)

Fifth General Report on the Activities of the Community (1 May 1961 to 30 April 1962)
June 1962, 307 pp. (d-f-i-n-e)

Sixth General Report on the Activities of the Community (1 May 1962 to 31 March 1963)
June 1963, 318 pp. (d-f-i-n-e)

Report on the Development of the Social Situation in the Community in 1962 - appended to the "Sixth General

Report on the Activities of the Community" in pursuance
of Article 122 of the Treaty, also Reports 1-5.
July 1963, 360 pp. (d-f-i-n)

General Publications

The First Stage of the Common Market - Report on
the Execution of the Treaty (January 1958-January 1962)
July 1962, 121 pp. (d-f-i-e;n: out of print)

Memorandum of the Commission on the Action Programme of the Community for the Second Stage
October 24, 1962, 89 pp. (d-f-i-n-e)

Yearbook of the E.E.C. Commission
Brussels, August 1, 1963, 36 pp. (d-f-i-n)

Periodicals

Bulletin of the European Economic Community
Monthly (d-f-i-n-e-s)

External Relations

Agreement Setting up an Association Between the
European Economic Community and Greece and Re-
lated Documents
February 1962, 150 pp. (f-i-n;d: out of print)

Report to the European Parliament on the State of the
Negotiations with the United Kingdom.
March 1963, 112 pp. (d-f-i-n-e)

Diplomatic Corps accredited to the European Economic Community
1964, 80 pp. (f)

Economic and Financial Affairs

Report on the Economic Situation in the Countries of
the Community
September 1958, 608 pp.
(f-d-i-n: fully cloth-bound)
(e: paper-backed)

Recent developments in the economic situation
15 September 1958, 67 pp. (d-f-i-n)

Economic Development prospects in E.E.C. from
1960 to 1970
1962, 90 pp. (d-f-i-n;e: in preparation)

The instruments of monetary policy in the countries
of the European Economic Community
1962, 279 pp. (d-f-i-n-e)

Documents of the Conference on Regional Economies
Brussels, December 6-8, 1961
February 1963, Vol. I, 458 pp., Vol. II, 242 pp.

Monographs - Economic and Financial Series

No. 1/1962
Electricity prices in the Countries of the European
Economic Community
1962, 106 pp. (d-f-i-n)

Periodicals

Notes and Graphs on the Economic Situation in the
Community
Monthly (d/n-f/i-e/f)

The Economic Situation in the Community
Quarterly (d-f-i-n-e)

The Community business survey
3 issues per year (d/n-f/i-e/f)

Industry-Commerce-Handicrafts-Customs

List of joint bodies set up in the framework of E.E.C.
by the industrial, craft and commercial associations of
the six countries
1960, 513 pp. (d/f/i/n)

E.C.S.C.-E.E.C.-E.A.E.C. (Euratom)
Customs Tariff of the European Communities
July 1963, 332 pp. (d-f-i-n)
Loose-leaf binder

Competition

Articles 85 and 86 of the E.E.C. Treaty and the Relevant
Regulations: A Manual for Firms (Published by the Joint
Information Service)
1962, 23 plus 17 pp. (d-f-i-n-e)

General Report of Study Groups A, B and C on the
Harmonization of turnover taxes
January 1962 166 pp. (d-f-i-n)

Report of the Fiscal and Financial Committee
1962, 150 pp. (d-f-i-n)

Preliminary draft convention on a European system
of patent law drawn up by the Working Party on Patents
(edited by the "Co-ordinating Committee on Industrial
Property Rights set up by the Member States and the
Commission of the European Economic Community")
1962, 108 pp. (d/f, i/n)

Social Affairs

- Report on the Development of the Social Situation in
the Community (Annex to the General Reports on the
Activities of the Community)

Employment in the Member States (1954-1958)
March 1961, 280 pp. (d-f-i-n)

Comparative dictionary of trades in which migration
is most frequent in the E.E.C. Countries
March 1962 (Loose-leaf edition d/f/i/n)

E.E.C. - E.C.S.C. - EURATOM
European Conference on "Technical Progress and the
Common Market" - Economic and social consequences
of the use of new techniques
Brussels, Palais des Congres, December 5 to 10, 1960
1962, Volume I: 354 pp., Volume II: 736 pp. (d-f-i-n)

- E.E.C. - E.C.S.C
Comparative tables of social security systems in the
Member States of the European Communities

- General System 66 pp. (d-f-i-n)

472

Position as at January 1, 1962

- General System
  Position as at January 1, 1964

- Agricultural System (d-f-i-n)

- E.E.C.-E.C.S.C.
  Social security systems in the European Community -
  Systems other than those applicable to miners and
  steel workers
  October 1962, Loose-leaf edition (d-f-i-n)

Monographs - Social policy series

No. 1/1963
Vocational training of juveniles in industry, small
industry and commerce in the E.E.C. countries
1963, 126 pp. (d-f-i-n)

No. 2/1962
Legislation on holidays with pay in the six Community
Countries
1962, 121 pp. (d-i-n; f: out of print)

No. 3/1962
Monograph on the current situation in social security
in the E.E.C. countries
1962, 130 pp. (d-f-i-n)

No. 4/1962
Comparative study of social benefits in the E.E.C.
countries
1962, 145 pp. (d-f-i-n)

No. 5/1962
The financing of social security in the E.E.C. countries
1962, 164 pp. (d-f-i-n)

No. 6/1963
Law and practice of collective bargaining in the
E.E.C. countries
1963, 63 pp. (d-f-i-n)

473

Administrative Committee of the European Economic
Community for the Social Security of Migrant Workers

First Annual Report on the implementation of Regulations
No. 3 and No. 4 of the E. E. C. Council concerning the
social security of migrant workers (19 December 1958
to 31 December 1959)
March 1961, 109 pp. (d-f-i-n)

Second Annual Report on the implementation of Regulations No. 3 and No. 4 of the E. E. C. Council concerning
the social security of migrant workers
(January 1 - December 31, 1960)
February 1963, 164 pp. (d-f-i-n)

Agriculture

- Agricultural supplement to the Official Gazette of the
European Communities

Working document on the agricultural situation in the
Community drawn up for the Members of the European
Parliament
15 September 1958, 50 pp. (d-f-i-n)

List of non-governmental agricultural organizations
associated at Community level
1960, (Loose-leaf edition d/f/i/n)

Regulations and Decisions in the Field of Agriculture
Adopted by the Council on 14 January 1962 (translation
of text published in the Official Gazette of the European
Communities, No. 30 of 20 April 1962)
1962, 80pp. (e)

Monographs - Agricultural Series

No. 1/1960
The main agricultural areas in the E. E. C. (Joint study
by E. E. C. and O. E. E. C.)
1960, 60 pp. plus 5 maps. (d-f)

No. 2/1960
Trends in food production and consumption in E. E. C.
(1956-1965)
1960, 120 pp. (report) plus 145 pp. (annexes) (d-f-i-n)

No. 3/1961
G. Schmitt: Methods of drawing up long-term projections
for agricultural production
1961, 80 pp. (d-f)

No. 4/1961
Prof. Dr. Priebe-Prof. Dr. Moller: Regional economic
policy - a prerequisite for a successful agricultural
policy
1961, 20 pp. (d-f-i-n)

No. 5/1961
Raising production of beef and veal in the E.E.C.
countries
1961, 216 pp. (d-f)

No. 6/1961
Study of comparative law on relations between the
lessor and lessee of farmland in the E.E.C. countries
1961, 48 pp. (d-f-i-n)

No. 7/1962
M. Soenen-P.F. Pelshenke: The quality of wheat, flour
and bread in the E.E.C. countries
1962, 35 pp. (f-d-i; n: in preparation)

No. 8/1962
Consumption of mineral fertilizers in the E.E.C.
1962, 82 pp. (report) plus 32 pp. (annexes) plus 3 maps
(d-f)

No. 9/1963
Agricultural research arrangements in the E.E.C.
countries
1963, 128 pp. (d-f-i-n)

No. 10/1963
The Common Market for agricultural products:
outlook for 1970
1963, 198 pp. (d-f-i-n)

No. 11/1962
Effects of lower farm prices within the framework of
a common agricultural policy in E.E.C. on farm incomes
in Federal Germany
1962, 86 pp. (d-f-i-n-e)

475

Transport

Legal system governing transport by road, rail and inland waterway in the Member States of the European Economic Community. Situation on 1 July 1962
1962, Loose-leaf publication (d-f-i-n-e)

Map of trade flows in crude oil and oil products in Europe (Pipe-lines). Situation on 31 December 1961
December 1962, Map plus 12 pp. explanatory note (d-f-i-n)

Overseas Development

Report on the social situation in the overseas countries associated with the European Economic Community
September 1960, 254 pp. (d-f-i-n)

List of organizations active in Africa and Madagascar with headquarters in an E.E.C. Member State
1963, 144 pp. (d/f/i/n)

Studies - Overseas development series

No. 1/1963
The Coffee, Cocoa and Banana Markets in the E.E.C. countries
1963, 226 pp. (d-f-i-n)

Terminology Bureau at the Commission of the European Economic Community

EUROTERM Dictionary/Phraseological concordances
It is a loose-leaf publication, 8 1/4 X 11 1/2 (oblong format), supplied in clip binders
Subscription:
which includes the cost of the dictionary as it now stands plus additional sheets as publised, up to a total of 10,000 pages (including those replaced), together with the binders
The Indexes will be brought up to date regularly, and each successive issue will replace the previous one
(d-f-i-n-e)

Statistical Office of the European Communities

<u>Periodical Publications</u>

- General Statistical Bulletin (purple series)
  11 issues per year (d/f/i/n/e)

- Statistical Information (orange series)
  quarterly (d/f/i/n)

- Foreign Trade: Monthly Statistics
  red series (d/f) 11 issues yearly

- Foreign Trade:Analytical Tables
  red series (d/f)

  E.E.C. countries' trade figures, broken
  down by products and countries
  From 1961, quarterly publication in two
  volumes (imports/exports)

- Foreign Trade: Trade of the Overseas
  Associated Areas red series (d/f)
  Figures for all products imported and
  exported by 25 overseas countries
  From 1963, quarterly publication in two
  volumes (imports/exports)

- Coal and Other Sources of Energy
  blue series (d/f/i/n) two-monthly

- Industrial Statistics blue series bimonthly (d/f/i/n)

- Iron and Steel blue series quarterly (d/f/i/n)

- Social Statistics yellow series
  published at irregular intervals (d/f/i/n)
  From issue no. 2/1962,
  bilingual editions (d/f-i/n)

  No. 1/1960:
     Family budgets of E.C.S.C.
     workers, 1956-1957

No. 2/1960:
        E.C.S.C. real incomes,
        1954-1958

No. 3/1960:
        Wage statistics, 1959
        E.C.S.C. wage costs and
        real incomes, 1954-59

No. 1/1961:
        E.E.C. male and female
        workers' wages

No. 2/1961:
        E.C.S.C. workers' housing
        situation

No. 3/1961:
        E.E.C. labour costs, 1959

No. 1/1962:
        Wage statistics, 1960
        E.C.S.C. wage costs and
        real incomes, 1954-1959

No. 2/1962:
        Occupational accidents in
        the iron and steel industry,
        1960

No. 3/1962:
        Incomes of workers in
        E.E.C. industries in 1959,
        E.E.C. 1962

No. 4/1962:
        Social security statistics,
        1955-1960

No. 1/1963:
        Wages E.E.C. 1960

No. 2/1963:
        Wages E.C.S.C. 1961

No. 3/1963:
 Occupational accidents in
 the iron and steel industry
 1960-1961

No. 4/1963:
 Employment Statistics
 1958-1962
 (d/f; i/n: in preparation)

Supplement 1963
 E. E. C. labour costs, 1961
 E. C. S. C. labour costs, 1962

- Agricultural Statistics (green series)
 6-8 issues a year (d/f)

Non-Periodical Publications

- Basic Statistics 1963 (d-f-i-n-e)
 yearly

- Statistical and Tariff Classification for International
 Trade (C. S. T.) (d/f/i/n)

- Nomenclature of the Industries in the European
 Communities, N. I. C. E. (d/f/i/n)

- Foreign Trade: Geographical Code
 (d/f/i/n)

- Standard Goods Nomenclature for Transport statistics,
 N. S. T. (d/f)